The Essential Guide to HTML5 and CSS3 Web Design

Craig Grannell

Victor Sumner

Dionysios Synodinos

friendsof

DESIGNER TO DESIGNER™

an Apress® company

The Essential Guide to HTML5 and CSS3 Web Design

ISBN-13 (pbk): 978-1-4302-3786-0

ISBN-13 (electronic): 978-1-4302-3787-7

Distributed to the book trade worldwide by Springer Science+Business Media New York, 233 Spring Street, 6th Floor, New York, NY 10013. Phone 1-800-SPRINGER, fax (201) 348-4505, e-mail orders-ny@springer-sbm.com, or visit www.springeronline.com.

For information on translations, please e-mail rights@apress.com or visit www.apress.com.

Apress and friends of ED books may be purchased in bulk for academic, corporate, or promotional use. eBook versions and licenses are also available for most titles. For more information, reference our Special Bulk Sales–eBook Licensing web page at www.apress.com/bulk-sales.

Any source code or other supplementary materials referenced by the author in this text is available to readers at www.apress.com. For detailed information about how to locate your book's source code, go to www.apress.com/source-code.

Credits

President and Publisher: Paul Manning	**Copy Editor:** Kim Wimpsett
Lead Editor: Tom Welsh	**Compositor:** Bytheway Publishing Services
Technical Reviewer: Jeffrey Sambells	**Indexer:** SPi Global
Editorial Board: Steve Anglin, Ewan Buckingham, Gary Cornell, Louise Corrigan, Morgan Ertel, Jonathan Gennick, Jonathan Hassell, Robert Hutchinson, Michelle Lowman, James Markham, Matthew Moodie, Jeff Olson, Jeffrey Pepper, Douglas Pundick, Ben Renow-Clarke, Dominic Shakeshaft, Gwenan Spearing, Matt Wade, Tom Welsh	**Artist:** SPi Global
	Cover Image Artist: Corné van Dooren
	Cover Designer: Anna Ishchenko
Coordinating Editors: Jessica Belanger, Anamika Panchoo	

Dedicated to my grandmother, Ellen, whose passion for life has always inspired me to take on any challenge.

—Victor Sumner

I dedicate this book to my wonderful family.

To my loving mother, Aggeliki.

To my beautiful wife, Elisa.

To my beloved daughter, Aggeliki.

To my precious newborn son.

You make me feel like the luckiest person alive.

—Dionysios Synodinos

Contents at a Glance

Contents

About the Authors

Craig Grannell is a writer and designer. Originally trained in the fine arts, the mid-1990s saw Craig immersed in the world of digital media, his creative projects encompassing video, installation-based audio work, and strange live performances-sometimes with the aid of a computer, televisions, videos, and a PA system, and sometimes with a small bag of water above his head. His creative, playful art, which contained a dark, satirical edge, struck a chord with those who saw it, leading to successful appearances at a number of leading European media arts festivals.

Craig soon realized he'd actually have to make a proper living, however. Luckily, the Web caught his attention, initially as a means to promote his art via an online portfolio but then as a creative medium in itself, and he's been working with it ever since. He founded tiny studio Snub Communications (www.snubcommunications.com) and has subsequently worked on design and writing projects for a diverse range of clients.

Along with writing the original version of the book you're holding right now (this version ably updated by Victor Sumner and Dionysios Synodinos), Craig has authored *Web Designer's Reference* (friends of ED, 2005) and various books on Dreamweaver. Elsewhere, he's penned numerous articles for Computer Arts, MacFormat, .net, Digital Arts, TechRadar, Tap!, and many other publications besides.

When not designing websites, Craig can usually be found hard at work in his quest for global superstardom by way of his eclectic audio project, the delights of which you can sample at www.projectnoise.co.uk.

Victor Sumner is a senior software engineer at LookSmart, LTD, helping to build and maintain an online advertising platform. As a self-taught developer, he is always interested in emerging technologies and enjoys working on and solving problems that are outside his comfort zone.

When not at the office, Victor has a number of hobbies, including photography, horseback riding, and gaming. He lives in Ontario, Canada, with his wife, Alicia.

Dionysios Synodinos is the research platform team lead at C4Media and a freelance consultant, focusing on rich Internet applications, web application security, mobile web, and web services. He's the lead editor for HTML5 and JavaScript for InfoQ, where he regularly writes about the JVM platform. He's also the author of *Pro HTML5 and CSS3 Design Patterns*, published by Apress. Going back and forth between server-side programming and UI design for more than a decade, he has been involved in diverse software projects and has contributed to different technical publications.

About the Technical Reviewer

"I've seen the future. It's in my browser!"

Jeffrey Sambells does what he loves. He is a father, designer, developer, author, and entrepreneur, among many other things. He started dabbling in the Web more than a decade ago and has turned it into a passion, pushing the limits of what's possible. With an expertise in creating slick end-to-end user experiences, Jeffrey is always on top of the latest technologies, especially when it comes to mobile devices.

You can probably find him writing something interesting at http://jeffreysambells.com or possibly catch him working on a stealth project via Twitter's @iamamused.

About the Cover Image Artist

Corné van Dooren designed the front cover image for this book. After taking a break from friends of ED to create a new design for the Foundation series, he worked at combining technological and organic forms, with the results now appearing on the cover of this and other books.

Corné spent his childhood drawing on everything at hand and then began exploring the infinite world of multimedia—and his journey of discovery hasn't stopped since. His mantra has always been "the only limit to multimedia is the imagination," a saying that keeps him moving forward constantly.

Corné works for many international clients, writes features for multimedia magazines, reviews and tests software, authors multimedia studies, and works on many other friends of ED books. If you like Corné's work, be sure to check out his chapter in *New Masters of Photoshop: Volume 2* (friends of ED, 2004). You can see more of his work (and contact him) at his website, www.cornevandooren.com.

Acknowledgments

I would like to thank the Apress team for providing invaluable support putting this book together. Also, thanks to my wife and soul mate, Alicia, who continues to be supportive of everything I do and who inspires me to always do better.

—Victor Sumner

I'd like to thank Petros Efstathopoulos for motivating me to buy my first HTML book back in 1996 and for doing our first web programming together.

—Dionysios Synodinos

Introduction

The Web is an ever-changing, evolving entity, and it's easy to get left behind. As designers and writers, we see a lot of books on web design, and although many are well written, few are truly integrated, modular resources that anyone can find useful in their day-to-day work. Most web design books concentrate on a single technology (or, commonly, a piece of software), leaving you to figure out how to put the pieces together.

This book is different

The Essential Guide to HTML5 and CSS3 Web Design provides a modern, integrated approach to web design. Each of the chapters looks at a specific aspect of creating a web page, such as formatting type, working with images, creating navigation, and creating layout blocks. In each case, relevant technologies are explored in context and at the appropriate times, just like in real-world projects; for example, markup is explored along with associated CSS and JavaScript, rather than each technology being placed in separate chapters, and visual design ideas are discussed so you can get a feel for how code affects page layouts. Dozens of practical examples are provided, which you can use to further your understanding of each subject. This highly modular and integrated approach means you can dip in and out of the book as you need, crafting along the way a number of web page elements that you can use on countless sites in the future.

Because the entire skills gamut is covered—from foundation to advanced—this book is ideal for beginners and longtime professionals alike. If you're making your first move into standards-based web design, the "ground floor" is covered, rather than an assumption being made regarding your knowledge. However, contemporary ideas, techniques, and thinking are explored throughout, ensuring that the book is just as essential for the experienced designer wanting to work on CSS layouts or for the graphic designer who wants to discover how to create cutting-edge websites.

This book's advocacy of web standards, usability, and accessibility with a strong eye toward visual design makes it of use to technologists and designers alike, enabling everyone to build better websites. For those moments when a particular tag or property value slips your mind, this book provides a comprehensive reference guide that includes important and relevant HTML5 elements and attributes, HTML5 entities, web colors, and CSS 3 properties and values.

Code Examples

Remember that you can also download files associated with this book from www.apress.com—just find the book and follow its instructions to access downloads and other associated resources.

To make it easier to work through the exercises, each one has an introductory box that lists where you can find any required files and the completed files within the downloadable file archive. A short overview of what you'll learn is also included.

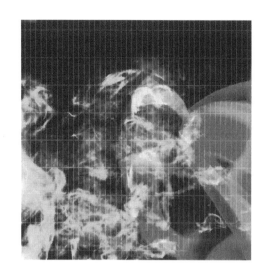

Chapter 1

An Introduction to Web Design

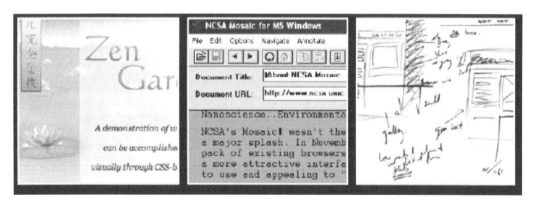

In this chapter:

- Introducing the Internet and web design
- Working with web standards
- Working with HTML
- Understanding and creating CSS rules
- Creating web page boilerplates

- Organizing web page content

A brief history of the Internet

Even in the wildest dreams of science-fiction and fantasy writers, few envisioned anything that offers the level of potential that the Internet now provides for sharing information on a worldwide basis. For both businesses and individuals, the Internet is now the medium of choice, largely because it enables you to present your wares to the entire world on a 24/7 basis. But the technology's origins were more ominous than and very different from the ever-growing, sprawling free-for-all that exists today.

In the 1960s, the American military was experimenting with methods by which the U.S. authorities might be able to communicate in the aftermath of a nuclear attack. The suggested solution was to replace point-to-point communication networks with one that was more akin to a net. This meant information could find its way from place to place even if certain sections of the network were destroyed. Despite the project eventually being shelved by the Pentagon, the concept itself lived on, eventually influencing a network that connected several American universities.

During the following decade, this fledgling network went international and began opening itself up to the general public. The term Internet was coined in the 1980s, which also heralded the invention of Transmission Control Protocol/Internet Protocol (TCP/IP), the networking software that makes possible communication between computers running on different systems. During the 1980s, Tim Berners-Lee was also busy working on HTML, his effort to weld hypertext to a markup language in an attempt to make communication of research between himself and his colleagues simpler.

Despite the technology's healthy level of expansion, the general public remained largely unaware of the Internet until well into the 1990s. By this time, HTML had evolved from a fairly loose set of rules—browsers having to make assumptions regarding coder intent and rendering output—to a somewhat stricter set of specifications and recommendations. This, along with a combination of inexpensive hardware, the advent of highly usable web browsers such as Mosaic (see the following image), and improved communications technology, saw an explosion of growth that continues to this day.

Initially, only the largest brands dipped their toes into these new waters, but soon thousands of companies were on the Web, enabling customers all over the globe to access information and, later, to shop online. Home users soon got in on the act, once it became clear that the basics of web design weren't rocket science and that, in a sense, everyone could do it—all you needed was a text editor, an FTP client, and some web space. Designers soon got in on the act, increasingly catered for by new elements within HTML; Cascading Style Sheets (CSS), which took a while to be adopted by browsers but eventually provided a means of creating highly advanced layouts for the Web; and faster web connections, which made media-rich sites accessible to the general public without forcing them to wait ages for content to download.

Therefore, unlike most media, the Web is truly a tool for everyone, and in many countries, the Internet has become ubiquitous. For those working in a related industry, it's hard to conceive that as recently as the mid-1990s relatively few people were even aware of the Internet's existence!

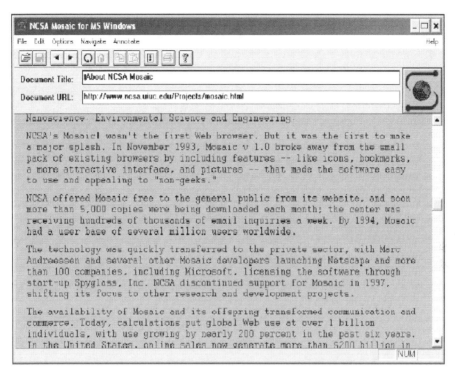

So, from obscure roots as a concept for military communications, the Internet has evolved into an essential tool for millions of people, enabling them to communicate with each other, research and gather information, telecommute, shop, play games, and become involved in countless other activities on a worldwide basis.

Why create a website?

Before putting pen to paper (and mouse to keyboard), it's important to think about the reason behind putting a site online. Millions already exist, so why do you need to create one yourself? Also, if you're working for a company, perhaps you already have plenty of marketing material, so why do you need a website as well?

I should mention here that I'm certainly not trying to put you off—far from it. Instead, I'm trying to reinforce the point that planning is key in any web design project, and although some people swear that "winging it" is the best way to go, most such projects end up gathering virtual dust online. Therefore, before doing anything else, think through why you should build a website and what you're trying to achieve.

Companies and individuals alike have practical and commercial reasons for setting up a website. A website enables you to communicate with like-minded individuals or potential clients on a worldwide basis. If you're a creative talent of some kind, you can use a website to showcase your portfolio, offering online photographs, music tracks for download, or poetry. If you fancy yourself as a journalist, a blog enables you to get your opinion out there. If you own or work for a business, creating a website is often the most efficient means of marketing your company. And even if you just have a hobby, a website can be a great way of finding others who share your passion—while you may be the only person in town who likes a particular movie or type of memorabilia, chances are there are thousands of people worldwide who think the same, and a website can bring you all together. This is perhaps why the paper fanzine has all but died, only to be reborn online, where development costs are negligible and worldwide distribution is a cinch.

In practical terms, a website exists online all day, every day (barring the odd hiccup with ISPs), which certainly isn't the case with printed media, which is there one minute and in the recycle trash the next. Distribution is less expensive than sending out printed material—a thousand-page website can be hosted for $10 per month or less, but sending a thousand-page document to one person (let alone a thousand or several thousand) may cost more than that. Likewise, development (particularly corrections and updates) is often significantly cheaper, too. For example, if you want to rework a print brochure, you have to redesign it and then reprint it. Reworking a section of a website often means swapping out a few files, which is efficient and affordable. So, for large companies and individuals alike, the ability to have relevant information online in a form that can often be updated in mere minutes, thereby keeping all interested parties up-to-date, is hard to resist!

Audience requirements

This book centers on the design and technology aspects of web design, but close attention must always be paid to your potential audience. It's no good forcing design ideas that result in inappropriate visuals, unusable navigation to all but the most technically minded of people, and huge download times on your site's unsuspecting visitors.

Prior to creating a site, you must ascertain what your audience wants and expects in terms of content, design, and how the site will work (by way of talking to the relevant people, and also, if your budget allows, by using surveys and focus groups). You don't have to take all of your audience's ideas into account (after all, many will be contradictory), but be mindful of common themes and ensure they're not ignored.

Technical considerations must be researched. If you're targeting designers, you can be fairly sure that a large proportion of the audience will be using monitors set to a high resolution and millions of colors, and you can design accordingly. If your site is targeting mobile users, be mindful that it will be displayed on a wide range of devices. From tablets and smartphones with high-resolution Retina or PenTile technology displays to those with low-resolution LCD displays, mobile devices come in all shapes, sizes, and capabilities.

Determining the web browsers your audience members use is another important consideration. Although use of web standards (used throughout this book) is more likely to result in a highly compatible site, browser quirks still cause unforeseen problems; therefore, always check to see what browsers are popular with a site's visitors, and ensure you test in as many as you can. Sometimes you won't have access to such statistics, or you may just be after a "sanity check" regarding what's generally popular. A couple of useful places to research global web browser statistics are www.w3schools.com/browsers/browsers_stats.asp and www.upsdell.com/BrowserNews/. Note, though, that any statistics you see online are effectively guesswork and are not a definitive representation of the

Web as a whole; still, they do provide a useful, sizeable sample that's often indicative of current browser trends.

Although you might be used to checking browser usage and then, based on the results, designing for specific browsers, we'll be adhering closely to web standards throughout this book. When doing this, an "author once, work anywhere" approach is feasible, as long as you're aware of various browser quirks (many of which are explored in Chapter 9). Of course, you should still always ensure you test sites in as many browsers as possible, just to make sure everything works as intended.

Web design overview

Web design has evolved rapidly over the years. Initially, browsers were basic, and early versions of HTML were fairly limited in what they enabled designers to do. Therefore, many older sites on the Web are plain in appearance. Additionally, the Web was originally largely a technical repository, which is the reason for the boring layouts of many sites in the mid-1990s; after all, statistics, documentation, and papers rarely need to be jazzed up, and the audience didn't demand such things anyway.

As with any medium finding its feet, things soon changed, especially once the general public flocked to the Web. It was no longer enough for websites to be text-based information repositories. Users craved—demanded, even—color! Images! Excitement! Animation! Interaction! Even video and audio managed to get a foothold as compression techniques improved and connection speeds increased.

The danger of eye candy became all too apparent as the turn of the century approached: every site, it seemed, had a Flash intro, and the phrase "skip intro" became so common that it eventually spawned a parody website.

These days, site design has tended toward being more restrained, as designers have become more comfortable with using specific types of technologies for relevant and appropriate purposes. Therefore, you'll find beautifully designed HTML- and CSS-based sites sitting alongside highly animated Flash efforts. Also, with the increasing popularity of JavaScript and the introduction of CSS Transitions and HTML5 Canvas, Flash appears to be on the way out because Adobe has recently discontinued support for Flash on mobile devices.

Of late, special emphasis is being placed on usability and accessibility, and in the majority of cases, designers have cottoned to the fact that content must take precedence. However, just because web standards, usability, and accessibility are key, that doesn't mean design should be thrown out the window. As we'll see in later chapters, web standards do not have to come at the expense of good design—far from it. In fact, a strong understanding of web standards helps improve websites, making it easier for you to create cutting-edge layouts that work across platforms and are easy to update. It also provides you with a method of catering for obsolete devices.

Note: If you're relatively new to web design, you may be wondering about the best platform and software for creating websites. Ultimately, it matters little which platform you choose, as long as you have access to the most popular browsers for testing purposes (a list that I'd now include Apple's Safari in, alongside Chrome, Internet Explorer, Firefox, and Opera). Regarding software, there's an overview in Appendix E, but this isn't an exhaustive guide, so do your own research and find software to your liking.

Why WYSIWYG tools aren't used in this book

With lots of software available and this book being design-oriented, you might wonder why I'm not using WYSIWYG web design tools. This isn't because I shun such tools—it's more that in order to best learn how to do something, you need to start from scratch, with the foundations. Many web design applications make it tempting to "hide" the underlying code from you, and most users end up relying on the graphical interface. This is fine until something goes wrong and you don't know how to fix it.

Removing software from the equation also means we concentrate on the underlying technology that drives web pages, without the distraction of working out which button does what. It also ensures that the book will be relevant to you, regardless of what software you use or your current skill level. Therefore, I suggest you install a quality text editor to work through the exercises or set your web design application to use its code view. Once you're familiar with the concepts outlined in this book, you can apply them to your work, whatever your chosen application for web design. This level of flexibility is important, because you never know when you might have to switch applications—something that's relatively painless if you know how to design for the Web and understand technologies like CSS and HTML.

Introducing HTML5

The foundation of the majority of web pages is HyperText Markup Language, commonly known by its initials, HTML. A curious facet of the language is that it's easy to pick up the basics—anyone who's computer literate should be able to piece together a basic page after learning some tags—but it has enough flexibility and scope to keep designers interested and experimenting, especially when HTML is combined with Cascading Style Sheets (CSS), which we'll discuss later in this chapter.

The HTML5 syntax is designed to be simpler, more flexible, developer-friendly, and backward-compatible than HTML4 and XHTML. HTML5 introduces new features such as animation, offline capabilities, audio, advanced graphics, typography, transitions, and more, which yields a new class of web standards and replaces the need for proprietary technologies, like Flash and native mobile platforms.

Introducing the concept of HTML tags and elements

HTML documents are text files that contain tags, which are used to mark up HTML elements. These documents are usually saved with the `.html` file extension, although other extensions like `.htm` can be used.

The aforementioned tags are what web browsers use to display pages, and assuming the browser is well behaved (most modern ones are), the display should conform to standards as laid out by the World Wide Web Consortium (W3C), the organization that develops guidelines and specifications for many web technologies.

> Note: The W3C website is found at `www.w3.org`. The site offers numerous useful tools, including validation services against which you can check your web pages.

HTML tags are surrounded by angle brackets—for instance, <p> is a paragraph start tag. It's good practice to close tags once the element content or intended display effect concludes, and this is done with an end tag. End tags are identical to the opening start tags but with an added forward slash: /. A complete HTML element looks like this:

```
<p>Here is a paragraph.</p>
```

This element consists of the following:

- Start tag: `<p>`
- Content: `Here is a paragraph.`
- End tag: `</p>`

> Note: HTML doesn't have a hard-and-fast rule regarding the case of tags. If you look at the source code of HTML pages on the Web, you may see lowercase tags, uppercase tags, or, in the case of pages put together over a period of time, a mixture of the two. That said, it's still good practice with any markup language to be consistent, regardless of whether the rules are more flexible.

Nesting tags

There are many occasions when tags must be placed inside each other; this process is called *nesting*. One reason for nesting is to apply basic styles to text-based elements. Earlier, you saw the code for a paragraph element. We can now make the text bold by surrounding the element content with a `strong` element:

```
<p><strong>Here is a paragraph.</strong></p>
```

> *You might be used to using the bold element to make text bold, but it is a physical element that only amends the look of text rather than also conveying semantic meaning. Logical elements, such as strong, convey meaning and add styling to text and are therefore preferred. These will be covered in Chapter 3.*

Note that the strong tags are nested within the paragraph tags (<p></p>), not the other way around. That's because the paragraph is the parent element to which formatting is being applied. The paragraph could be made bold and italic by adding another element, emphasis (<em></em>), as follows:

```
<p><strong><em>Here is a paragraph.</em></strong></p>
```

In this case, the strong and em tags could be in the opposite order, because they're at the same level in the hierarchy. However, you must always close nested tags in the reverse order to that in which they're opened, as shown in the previous code block; otherwise, some browsers may not display your work as intended. For instance, the following should be avoided:

```
<p><strong><em>Here is a paragraph.</strong></em></p>
```

As previously mentioned, it's good practice to close tags in HTML—even though it's not a requirement for all elements, being sloppy in this area can lead to errors. Take a look at the following:

```
<p><strong><em>Here is a paragraph.</strong></p>
```

Here, the emphasis element isn't closed, meaning subsequent text-based content on the page is likely to be displayed in italics—so take care to close all your tags.

Web standards and HTML

HTML5 is an updated version of the HTML specification that has been around since 1997 and many of its features are already supported in today's browsers. The changes in HTML5 include a focus on semantic markup like the addition of the <header>, <footer>, <section>, and <article> elements and also the addition of the <canvas> element for displaying advanced interactive graphics and the <video> element for displaying video. Websites like html5please.com, caniuse.com, and of coarse the WC3 working draft (http://dev.w3.org/html5/html4-differences/) are great resources for finding out what has changed, what is new, or what is supported in each browser.

HTML5 markup can be defined in whatever way you want it to be. Uppercase, lowercase, quoted, unquoted, self-closing or not—it's your choice. The ultimate goal is semantic markup, ensuring the elements you choose and the style of your markup define the meaning of your content as closely as possible.

Evolution is another aspect that we have to deal with. Just as the survival of the fittest removes some species from nature, so too are tags (and attributes) unceremoniously dumped from the W3C specifications. Such tags and attributes are referred to as *deprecated*, meaning they are marked for removal from the standard and may not be supported in future browsers. In the case of HTML5 obsolete tags and attributes are still supported because of HTML5's backward-compatibility, it is still recommended that you do not use such tags and attributes because new implementations of browsers may choose not to support them.

Semantic markup

In the previous few subsections, you may have noticed specific elements being used for specific things. This is referred to as *semantic* markup and is a very important aspect of modern web design. Plenty of HTML elements exist, and each one has a clearly defined purpose (although some have more than one use). Because of the flexibility of markup languages, it's often possible to "wrongly" use elements, bashing your page into shape by using elements for design tasks they're not strictly suited for and certainly weren't originally designed for.

During the course of this book, we'll talk about semantics a fair amount. Ultimately, good semantic design enables you to simplify your markup and also provides the greatest scope for being able to style it with CSS (see the following section). By thinking a little before you code and defining your content with the correct markup, you'll end up with cleaner code and make it much easier for yourself in the long run when it comes to adding presentation to your content.

Introducing CSS

CSS is the W3C standard for defining the visual presentation for web pages. HTML was designed as a structural markup language, but the demands of users and designers encouraged browser manufacturers to support and develop presentation-oriented tags. These tags "polluted" HTML, pushing the language toward one of decorative style rather than logical structure. Its increasing complexity made life hard for web designers, and source code began to balloon for even basic presentation-oriented tasks. Along with creating needlessly large HTML files, things like font tags created web pages that weren't consistent across browsers and platforms, and styles had to be applied to individual elements—a time-consuming process.

The concept behind CSS was simple yet revolutionary: remove the presentation and separate design from content. Let HTML deal with structure, and use CSS for the application of visual presentation.

The idea caught on albeit slowly. The initial problem was browser support. At first, most browsers supported only a small amount of the CSS standard—and badly at that. But Internet Explorer 5 for Mac made great strides with regard to CSS support, and it was soon joined by other browsers fighting for the crown of standards king. These days, every up-to-date browser supports the majority of commonly used CSS properties and values, and more besides.

Another problem has been educating designers and encouraging them to switch from old to new methods. Benefits constantly need to be outlined and proven, and the new methods taught. Most designers these days style text with CSS, but many still don't use CSS for entire web page layouts, despite the inherent advantages in doing so. This, of course, is one of the reasons for this book: to show you, the designer, how CSS can be beneficial to you—saving you (and your clients) time and money—and to provide examples for various areas of web page design and development that you can use in your sites.

In this section, we'll look at separating content from design, CSS rules, CSS selectors and how to use them, and how to add styles to a web page.

Separating content from design

Do you ever do any of the following?

- Use tables for website layout

- Hack Photoshop documents to bits and stitch them back together in a web page to create navigation elements and more

- Get frustrated when any combination of the previous leads to unwieldy web pages that are a pain to edit

If so, the idea of separating content from design should appeal to you. On one hand, you have your HTML documents, which house content marked up in a logical and semantic manner. On the other hand, you have your CSS documents, giving you sitewide control of the presentation of your web page elements from a single source. Instead of messing around with stretching transparent GIFs and combining and splitting table cells, you can edit CSS rules to amend the look of your site, which is great for not only those times when things just need subtle tweaking but also when you decide everything needs a visual overhaul. After all, if presentation is taken care of externally, you can often just replace the CSS to provide your site with a totally new design.

Designers (and clients paying for their time) aren't the only ones to benefit from CSS. Visitors will, too, in terms of faster download times but also with regard to accessibility. For instance, people with poor vision often use screen readers to surf the Web. If a site's layout is composed of complex nested tables, it might visually make sense; however, the underlying structure may not be logical. View the source of a document, and look at the order of the content. A screen reader reads from the top to the bottom of the code and doesn't care what the page looks like in a visual web browser. Therefore, if the code compromises the logical order of the content (as complex tables often do), the site is compromised for all those using screen readers.

Accessibility is now very important in the field of web design. Legislation is regularly passed to strongly encourage designers to make sites accessible for web users with disabilities. It's likely that this trend will continue, encompassing just about everything except personal web pages. (However, even personal websites shouldn't be inaccessible.)

The rules of CSS

Style sheets consist of a number of rules that define how various web page elements should be displayed. Although sometimes bewildering to newcomers, CSS rules are simple to break down. Each rule consists of a selector and a declaration. The selector begins a CSS rule and specifies which part of the HTML document the rule will be applied to. The declaration consists of a number of property/value pairs that set specific properties and determine how the relevant element will look. In the following example, p is the selector, and everything thereafter is the declaration:

```
p {
  color: blue;
}
```

As you probably know, p is the HTML tag for a paragraph. Therefore, if we attach this rule to a web page (see the section "Adding styles to a web page" later in this chapter for how to do so), the declaration will be applied to any HTML marked up as a paragraph, thereby setting the color of said paragraphs to blue.

> Note: CSS property names are not case sensitive, but it's good to be consistent in web design—it's highly recommended to always use lowercase.

When you write CSS rules, you place the declaration within curly brackets: {}. Properties and values are separated by a colon (:), and property/value pairs are terminated by a semicolon (;). Technically, you don't have to include the final semicolon in a CSS rule, but most designers consider it good practice to do so. This makes sense—you may add property/value pairs to a rule at a later date, and if the semicolon is already there, you don't have to remember to add it.

If we want to amend our paragraph declaration and define paragraphs as bold, we can do so like this:

```
p {
  color: blue;
  font-weight:bold;
}
```

> Note: You don't have to lay out CSS rules as done in this section; rather, you can add rules as one long string. However, the formatting shown here is more readable in print. Note that in the files available for download, the formatting is changed slightly again: the property/value pairs and closing curly bracket are both tabbed inward, enabling rapid vertical scanning of a CSS document's selectors.

Types of CSS selectors

In the previous example, the most basic style of selector was used: an element selector. This defines the visual appearance of the relevant HTML tag. In the sections that follow, we'll examine some other regularly used (and well-supported) CSS selectors: class, ID, grouped, and contextual.

Class selectors

In some cases, you may want to modify an element or a group of elements. For instance, you may want your general website text to be blue, as in the examples so far, but some portions of it to be red. The simplest way of doing this is by using a class selector.

In CSS, a class selector's name is prefixed by a period (.), like this:

```
.warningText {
  color: red;
```

```
}
```

This style is applied to HTML elements in any web page the style sheet is attached to using the class attribute, as follows:

```
<h2 class="warningText">This heading is red.</h2>
<p class="warningText">This text is red.</p>
<p>This is a paragraph, <span class="warningText">and this text is
 red</span>.</p>
```

If you want a make a class specific to a certain element, place the relevant HTML tag before the period in the CSS rule:

```
p.warningText {
  color: red;
}
```

If you used this CSS rule with the HTML elements shown previously, the paragraph's text would remain red, but not the heading or span, because of the warningText class now being exclusively tied to the paragraph selector only.

Usefully, it's possible to style an element by using multiple class values. This is done by listing multiple values in the class attribute, separated by spaces:

```
<p class="warningText hugeText">
```

The previous example's content would be styled as per the rules .warningText and .hugeText.

ID selectors

ID selectors can be used only once on each web page. In HTML, you apply a unique identifier to an HTML element with the id attribute:

```
<p id="footer">&copy; 200X The Company. All rights reserved.</p>
```

To style this element in CSS, precede the ID name with a hash mark (#):

```
p#footer {
  padding: 20px;
}
```

In this case, the footer div would have 20 pixels of padding on all sides.

Essentially, then, classes can be used multiple times on a web page, but IDs cannot. Typically, IDs are used to define one-off page elements, such as structural divisions, whereas classes are used to define the style for multiple items.

Grouped selectors

Should you want to set a property value for a number of different selectors, you can use grouped selectors, which take the form of a comma-separated list:

```
h1, h2, h3, h4, h5, h6 {
  color: green;
}
```

In the preceding example, all the website's headings have been set to be green. Note that you're not restricted to a single rule for each element—you can use grouped selectors for common definitions and separate ones for specific property values, as follows:

```
h1, h2, h3, h4, h5, h6 {
  color: green;
}

h1 {
  font-size: 1.5em;
}

h2 {
  font-size: 1.2em;
}
```

> Note: If you define a property value twice, browsers render your web element depending on each rule's position in the cascade. See the section "The cascade" later in the chapter for more information.

Contextual selectors

This selector type is handy when working with advanced CSS. As the name suggests, contextual selectors define property values for HTML elements depending on context. Take, for instance, the following example:

```
<p>I am a paragraph.</p>
<p>So am I.</p>
<div id="navigation">
  <p>I am a paragraph within the navigation div.</p>
  <p>Another paragraph within the navigation div.</p>
</div>
```

You can style the page's paragraphs as a whole and then define some specific values for those within the navigation div by using a standard element selector for the former and a contextual selector for the latter:

```
p {
  color: black;
}

#navigation p {
  color: blue;
  font-weight: bold;
}
```

As shown, syntax for contextual selectors (#navigation p) is simple—you just separate the individual selectors with some whitespace. The two rules shown previously have the following result:

- The p rule colors the web page's paragraphs black.

- The #navigation p rule overrides the p rule for paragraphs within the navigation div, coloring them blue and making them bold.

By working with contextual selectors, it's possible to get very specific with regard to styling things on your website; we'll be using these selectors regularly.

Pseudo-selectors

This selector is defined with a colon preceding them. The most recognizable pseudo-selector would be hover used with links. For example, if you wanted to change a link's text color when your mouse hovers over it, you would define the following in your style sheet as follows:

```
a:hover {
  color: black;
}
```

Pseudo-selectors allow you to style your content dynamically and are incredibly powerful when combined with contextual and id selectors.

There are multiple different kinds of pseudo-selectors including structural, target, UI element states, negation, and links.

Attribute selectors

Attribute selectors allow you to target any element based on their attributes. Consider the following code:

```
<a href="http://www.apress.com">I am a link.</a>
```

Say you wanted to add the Apress logo before every link to Apress.com. You could update your markup with a class attribute to allow you to target each Apress link. This would be tedious, and you would have to remember to do this to every Apress link you add to your site. An easier option would be to use attribute selectors.

Using an attribute selector, you could target all Apress links and add a logo like the following:

```
a[href$='apress.com'] {
  content: url(logos/apress.png);
}
```

> Note: There are other types of selectors used for specific tasks. These will be covered as relevant throughout the book.

Adding styles to a web page

The most common (and useful) method of applying CSS rules to a web page is by using external style sheets. CSS rules are defined in a text document, which is saved with the file suffix .css. This document is attached to an HTML document in one of two ways, both of which require the addition of HTML elements to the head section.

The first method of attaching a CSS file is to use a link tag:

```
<link rel="stylesheet" href="mystylesheet.css">
```

Alternatively, import the style sheet into the style element:

```
<style type="text/css" media="screen">
@import url(mystylesheet.css);
</style>
```

The second of these methods was initially used to "hide" CSS rules from noncompliant browsers, thereby at least giving users of such devices access to the website's content, if not its design. In some browsers (notably Internet Explorer), however, this can cause a "flash" of unstyled content before the page is loaded. This flash doesn't occur when a link element is also present. In the full site designs in Chapter 10, you'll note that both methods are used—@import for importing the main style sheet for screen and link for linking to a print style sheet.

The style tag can also be used to embed CSS directly into the head section of a specific HTML document, like this:

```
<head>
<style type="text/css">
p {
   color: black;
}

#navigation p {
   color: blue;
   font-weight: bold;
}
</style>
</head>
```

You'll find that many visual web design tools create CSS in this manner, but adding rules to a style element is worth doing only if you have a one-page website or if you want to affect tags on a specific page, overriding those in an attached style sheet (see the next section for more information). There's certainly no point in adding styles like this to every page, because updating them would then require every page to be updated, rather than just an external style sheet.

The third method of applying CSS is to do so as an inline style, directly in an element's HTML tag:

```
<p style="color: blue;">This paragraph will be displayed in blue.</p>
```

As you can see, this method involves using the style attribute, and it's only of use in very specific, one-off situations. There's no point in using inline styles for all styling on your website—to do so would give few

15

benefits over the likes of archaic font tags. Inline styles also happen to be deprecated in XHTML 1.1, so they're eventually destined for the chop.

The cascade

It's possible to define the rule for a given element multiple times: you can do so in the same style sheet, and several style sheets can be attached to an HTML document. On top of that, you may be using embedded style sheets and inline styles. The cascade is a way of dealing with conflicts, and its simple rule is this:

The value closest to the element in question is the one that is applied.

In the following example, the second font-size setting for paragraphs takes precedence because it's closest to paragraphs in the HTML:

```
p {
    font-size: 1.1em;
}

p {
    font-size: 1.2em;
}
```

Subsequently, paragraphs on pages the preceding rule is attached to are rendered at 1.2em. If a similar rule were placed as an embedded style sheet below the imported/linked style sheet, that rule would take precedence, and if one were applied as an inline style (directly in the relevant element), then that would take precedence over all others.

> Note that it's possible to import or link multiple style sheets in a web page's *head* section. The cascade principle still applies; in other words, any rules in a second attached style sheet override those in the one preceding it.

CSS uses the concept of inheritance. A document's HTML elements form a strict hierarchy, beginning with html, and then branching into head and body, each of which has numerous descendant elements (such as title and meta for head, and p and img for body). When a style is applied to an element, its descendants—those elements nested within it—often take on CSS property values, unless a more specific style has been applied. However, not all CSS style properties are inherited. See the CSS reference section of this book for more details.

The CSS box model explained

The box model is something every designer working with CSS needs a full understanding of in order to know how elements interact with each other and also how various properties affect an element. Essentially, each element in CSS is surrounded by a box whose dimensions are automated depending on the content. By using width and height properties in CSS, these dimensions can be defined in a specific manner.

You can set padding to surround the content and add a border and margins to the box. A background image and background color can also be defined. Any background image or color is visible behind the content and padding but not the margin. The effective space an element takes up is the sum of the box dimensions (which effectively define the available dimensions for the box's contents), padding, border, and margins. Therefore, a 500-pixel-wide box with 20 pixels of padding at each side and a 5-pixel border will actually take up 550 pixels of horizontal space (5 + 20 + 500 + 20 + 5).

> Note that in some cases, margins between two elements "collapse," leading to only the larger margin value being used.

THE CSS BOX MODEL HIERARCHY

Content

Here's some sample content, constrained by the padding that's been applied. Here's some sample content, constrained by the padding that's been applied.

Border

Padding*

Background image

Background color

Margin*

* Transparent elements

© Jon Hicks (www.hicksdesign.co.uk)

Creating boilerplates

Every web page looks different, just as every book or magazine is different from every other one. However, under the hood there are often many similarities between sites, and if you author several, you'll soon note that you're doing the same things again and again. You can find many ready-made boilerplates online. One of the most popular ones is the HTML5 Boilerplate (html5boilerplate.com). This is a great starting point for any project you want to start. It includes many of the techniques discussed throughout this book such as cross-browser compatibility, mobile browser optimizations, progressive enhancement and graceful degradation, and more.

While the HTML5 Boilerplate is a great place to start, it is important to learn how to create your own boilerplates from scratch—starting points for all of your projects.

In the download files, available from the **Downloads** section of the friends of Apress website (www.apress.com), there are two boilerplates folders: basic-boilerplates and advanced-boilerplates. In basic-boiler plates, the basic.html web page is a blank HTML5 document, and in advanced-boilerplates, extended.html adds some handy structural elements that provide a basic page structure that's common in many web pages, along with some additions to the head section. (The former is used as a quick starting point for many of the tutorials in this book. The latter is perhaps a better starting point for a full website project.) The CSS-with-ToC.css document in advanced-boilerplates uses CSS comments to create sections in the document to house related CSS rules. This is handy when you consider that a CSS document may eventually have dozens of rules in it—this makes it easier for you to be able to find them quickly.

CSS comments look like this: /* this is a comment */. They can be single-line or multiple-line. In the advanced CSS boilerplate, a multiline comment is used for an introduction and table of contents:

```
/*

STYLE SHEET FOR [WEB SITE]
Created by [AUTHOR NAME]
[URL OF AUTHOR]

ToC

    1. defaults
    2. structure
    3. links and navigation
    4. fonts
    5. images

Notes

*/
```

Each section of the document is then headed by a lengthy comment that makes it obvious when a section has begun:

```
/* --------- 1. defaults  --------- */

* {
  margin: 0;
  padding: 0;     .
  }

body {
  }
```

As you can see, property/value pairs and the closing curly bracket are indented by two tabs in the document (represented by two spaces on this page), which makes it easier to scan vertically through numerous selectors. (Note that for the bulk of this book, the rules aren't formatted in this way, because indenting only the property/value pairs differentiates them more clearly in print; however, the download files all have CSS rules indented as per the recommendations within this section.) Comments can also be used for subheadings, which I tend to indent by one tab:

```
/* float-clearing rules */
.separator {
  clear: both;
  }
```

Although the bulk of the style sheet's rules are empty, just having a boilerplate to work from saves plenty of time in the long run, ensuring you don't have to key in the same defaults time and time again. Use the one from the download files as the basis for your own, but if you regularly use other elements on a page (such as pull quotes), be sure to add those, too; after all, it's quicker to amend a few existing rules to restyle them than it is to key them in from scratch.

> Tip: Along the same lines as boilerplates, you can save time by creating a snippets folder on your hard drive. Use it to store snippets of code—HTML elements, CSS rules, and so on—that you can reuse on various websites. Many applications have this functionality built in, so make use of it if your preferred application does.

To show you the power of CSS, we're going to work through a brief exercise using the boilerplates mentioned earlier. Don't worry about understanding everything just yet, because all of the various properties and values shown will be explained later in the book.

Creating, styling, and restyling a web page

Required files basic.html and CSS-default.css from the basic-boilerplates folder

What you'll learnHow to create, style, and restyle a web page

Completed files   creating-and-styling-a-web-page.html, creating-and-styling-a-web-page.css, creating-and-styling-a-web-page-2.html, and creating-and-styling-a-web-page-2.css, in the chapter 1 folder

1. Copy basic.html and CSS-default.css to your hard drive and rename them creating-and-styling-a-web-page.html and creating-and-styling-a-web-page.css.

2. Attach the style sheet. Type Creating and styling a web page in the title element to give the page a title, and then amend the @import value so that the style sheet is imported:

   ```
   <link rel="stylesheet" href="creating-and-styling-a-web-page.css">
   ```

3. Add some content. Within the wrapper div, add some basic page content, as shown in the following code block. Note how the heading, paragraph, and quote are marked up using a

heading element (<h1></h1>), paragraph element (<p></p>), and block quote element (<blockquote></blockquote>), rather than using styled paragraphs for all of the text-based content. This is semantic markup, as discussed briefly earlier in the chapter.

```
<div id="wrapper">
  <h1>A heading</h1>
  <p>A paragraph of text, which is very exciting&mdash;something
    that will live on through the generations.</p>
  <blockquote>
    <p>&ldquo;A quote about something, to make
      people go "hmmmm" in a thoughtful manner.&rdquo;</p>
    <cite>An inspirational book title.</cite>
  </blockquote>
  <p>Another paragraph, with equally exciting text; in fact, it&rsquo;s
    so exciting, we're not sure it&rsquo;s legal to print.</p>
</div>
```

> Note: The items with ampersands and semicolons, such as — and ”, are HTML entities—see Appendix C for more details.

4. Edit some CSS. Save and close the web page and then open the CSS document. Amend the body rule within the defaults section of the CSS. This ensures the text on the page is colored black and that the page's background color is white. The padding value ensures the page content doesn't hug the browser window edges.

```
body {
  font: 62.5%/1.5 Verdana, Arial, Helvetica, sans-serif;
  color: #000000;
  background: #ffffff;
  padding: 20px;
}
```

5. Style the wrapper. Add the following property values to the #wrapper rule to define a fixed width for it and then center it (via the margin property's auto value).

```
#wrapper {
  font-size: 1.2em;
  line-height: 1.5em;
  margin: 0 auto;
  width: 500px;
}
```

6. Style the text. Add the h1 rule as shown, thereby styling the level-one heading:

```
h1 {
  font: 1.5em/1.8em Arial, sans-serif;
  text-transform: uppercase;
}
```

7. Add the blockquote and blockquote p rules as shown. The former adds margins to the sides of the block quote, thereby making the text stand out more, while the latter (a contextual selector) styles paragraphs within block quotes only, making them italic and larger than standard paragraphs. Once you've done this, save your files and preview the web page in a web browser; it should look like the following image. (Don't close the browser at this point.)

```
blockquote {
  margin: 0 100px;
}
blockquote p {
  font-style: italic;
  font-size: 1.2em;

}
```

8. Duplicate creating-and-styling-a-web-page.css and rename it creating-and-styling-a-web-page-2.css. Open creating-and-styling-a-web-page.html, and amend the link value, linking to the newly created CSS document:

```
<link rel="stylesheet" href="creating-and-styling-a-web-page-2.css">
```

9. Open creating-and-styling-a-web-page-2.css, and switch the values of color and background in the first body rule.

```
body {
  font: 62.5%/1.5 Verdana, Arial, Helvetica, sans-serif;
  color: #ffffff;
  background: #000000;
  padding: 20px;
}
```

10. Replace the text-transform property/value pair from the h1 rule with color: #bbbbbb;. For the blockquote rule, make the following amendments, which add a border to the left and right edges, and some horizontal padding around the block quote's contents.

```
blockquote {
  margin: 0 100px;
  border-left: 3px solid #888888;
  border-right: 3px solid #888888;
  padding: 0 20px;
}
```

11. Finally, amend the blockquote p rule as shown:

```
blockquote p {
  font-weight: bold;
  font-size: 1.0em;
}
```

Refresh the web page in the browser, and you should see it immediately change, looking like that shown in the following image. Effectively, nothing in the web page was changed (you could have overwritten the rules in `creating-and-styling-a-web-page.css` rather than creating a duplicate style sheet); instead, the web page's design was updated purely by using CSS. (Note that in the download files, there are two sets of documents for this exercise—one with the design as per step 7, and the other as per step 11, the latter of which has the `-2` suffix added to the HTML and CSS document file names.)

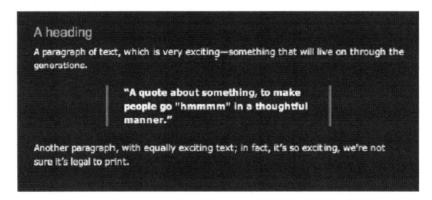

Although this was a very basic example, the same principle works with all CSS-based design. Create a layout in CSS and chances are that when you come to redesign it, you may not have to change much—or any—of the underlying code. A great example of this idea taken to extremes is css Media Queries (`www.mediaqueri.es`), whose single web page is radically restyled via dozens of submitted CSS documents.

Hillsong London

dConstruct 2012

Working with website content

Before we explore how to create the various aspects of a web page, we're going to briefly discuss working with website content and what you need to consider prior to creating your site. Technology and design aren't the only factors that affect the success of a website. The human element must also be considered. Most of the time, people use the Web to get information of some sort, whether for research purposes or entertainment. Typically, people want to be able to access this information quickly; therefore, a site must be structured in a logical manner. It's imperative that a visitor doesn't spend a great deal of time looking for information that should be easy to find. Remember, there are millions of sites out there, and if yours isn't up to scratch, it's easy for someone to go elsewhere.

> *Note: There are exceptions to the general rule of a website having a structured and logical design—notably sites that are experimental in nature or the equivalent of online art, thereby requiring exploration. In these cases, it may actually be detrimental to present a straightforward and totally logical site, but these cases are strictly a minority.*

In this section, we'll look specifically at information architecture and site maps, page layout, design limitations, and usability.

Information architecture and site maps

Before you begin designing a website, you need to collate and logically organize the information it's going to contain. A site map usually forms the basis of a site's navigation, and you should aim to have the most important links immediately visible. What these links actually are depends on the nature of your website, but it's safe to say that prominent links to contact details are a common requirement across all sites. A corporate website may also need prominent links to products, services, and a press area. The resulting site map for a corporate site might resemble the following illustration.

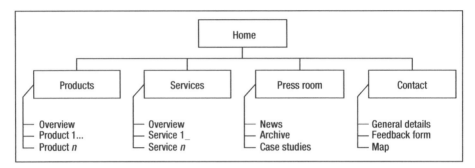

Here, the boxed links serve as the primary navigation and are effectively sections of the website. Underneath each boxed link is a list of subcategories or pages housed within that section. With this structure, it's easy for a newcomer to the site to work out where information is located. When working on site maps, try talking to people who might be interested in the site to get their reaction to your organization of the content. When working for a client, ensure that they sign off on the site map and that you get feedback on the site map from people at all levels in the company and, if possible, from the company's customers. In all cases, seek the opinions of both the technically minded and the relative computer novices, because each may have different ideas about how information should be structured. After all, most web designers are technically minded (or at least well versed in using a computer), and they often forget that most people don't use the Web as regularly as they do. In other words, what seems obvious to you might not be to the general public.

For larger sites, or those with many categories, site maps can be complex. You may have to create several versions before your site map is acceptable. Always avoid burying content too deep. If you end up with a structure in which a visitor has to click several times to access information, it may be worth reworking your site's structure.

Basic web page structure and layout

Once you've sorted out the site map, avoid firing up your graphics package. It's a good idea to sketch out page layout ideas on paper before working on your PC or Mac. Not only is this quicker than using graphics software, but it also allows you to compare many ideas side by side. At this stage, you shouldn't be too precious about the design—work quickly and try to get down as many ideas as possible. From there, you can then refine your ideas, combine the most successful elements of each, and then begin working on the computer.

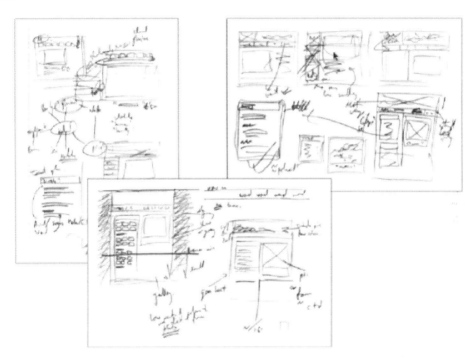

Although the Web has no hard-and-fast conventions, themes run throughout successful websites, many of which are evident in the following image of a version of my Snub Communications homepage.

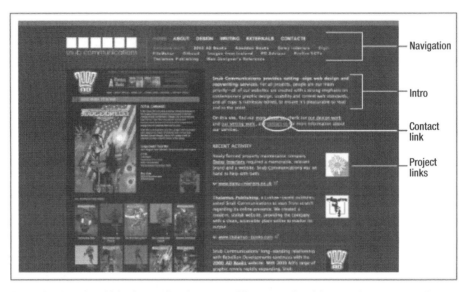

A website's navigation should be immediately accessible—you should never have to scroll to get to it. It's also a good idea to have a masthead area that displays the organization's corporate brand (or, if it's a personal site, whatever logo/identity you want to be remembered by, even if it's only a URL).

The homepage should include an introduction of some sort that briefly explains what the site is about, and it should have some pull-ins to other areas of the site. These pull-ins could be in the form of news items that link to recent product launches, completed projects, and so on.

Most websites require a method for people to contact the site owner, and at least one clear link to a contact page is essential.

Avoid constantly changing the design throughout the site. In print, this sometimes works well and provides variation within a book or magazine. Online, people expect certain things to be in certain places. Constantly changing the position of your navigation, the links themselves, and even the general design and color scheme often creates the impression of an unprofessional site and makes it harder to use.

Ultimately, however your site ends up, and whatever your design, you need to ensure your creation is as usable as possible. A good checklist—even if the points may seem entirely obvious—is as follows:

- Is the site easy to navigate?

- Is it easy for users to locate content on each page?

- Is it easy for users to find what they need on the site?

- Are download times kept to a minimum?

- Is the site suitable and relevant for its target audience?

- Does the site use familiar conventions?

If you can answer yes to all these things, then you should be on the right track!

> Note: Regarding conventions, it's important not to go overboard. For example, some web gurus are adamant that default link colors should always be used. I think that's sweet and quaint but somewhat archaic. As long as links are easy to differentiate from other text and styled consistently throughout the site, that's what matters.

Limitations of web design

Depending on your viewpoint, the inherent limitations of the Web are either a challenge or a frustration. Print designers often feel the latter and consider themselves hampered by the Web when compared to the relative freedom of print design. While print designers define the material their designs are displayed on, the Web comes in all shapes and sizes, from the tiny screen of a mobile phone to large, 1080p high-resolution displays. A web designer must consider each display resolution their site might be viewed on and also remember that browsers have different levels of support and implementations of HTML standards.

Columns take on a different role online compared to in print, because they're primarily used to display several areas of content with the same level of prominence. You don't use columns online to display continuous copy, unless you use just one column. If you use several columns, the visitor has to constantly scroll up and down to read everything.

There are other limitations when it comes to rendering text online. There are few web standard fonts (detailed in Chapter 3); serifs, which work well on paper, don't work so well online, and reading text on-screen is already harder than reading print, so complex page backgrounds should be avoided. HTML5 provides the ability to embed fonts into your page, but this again has its own set of limitations; browser providers implement this each using a different format and you must make considerations for older browsers and mobile browsers that do not support this powerful feature.

And then there are issues like not knowing what an end user's setup is and therefore having to consider monitor resolution and color settings, what browser is being used, and even the various potential setups of web browsers, not to mention mobile web browsers that offer their own set of limitations. Do you go for a liquid design, which stretches with the browser window; a fixed design, which is flanked by blank space at larger monitor resolutions; or a responsive design, which adapts to the available screen dimensions?

Don't worry, this isn't a pop quiz. These are questions that will be answered in this book, but I mention them now to get you thinking and realizing that planning is key with regard to web design. Because this is largely a book about concepts, ideas, and techniques, we won't return to talk about planning very much, which is why I'm drumming it in at this early stage.

Also, don't get disheartened by the previous limitations spiel. The Web is a truly magnificent medium, and for every downside there's something amazing to counter it. So what if the resolution is low? Nowhere else can you so effortlessly combine photography, video, sound, and text. Sure, it's all well and good to read a magazine, but the Web enables interaction, and navigation can be nonlinear, enabling you to link words within specific pieces to other articles on your website or elsewhere on the Internet. Don't get me wrong: the Web is a great thing. If it weren't, I wouldn't be interested in it, wouldn't be designing for it, and wouldn't be writing this book.

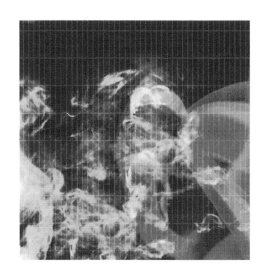

Chapter 2

Web Page Essentials

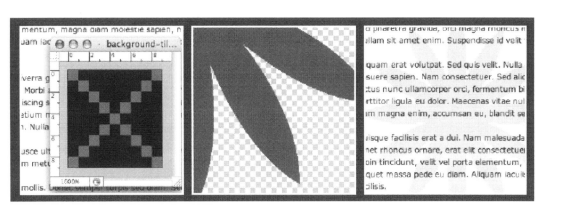

In this chapter:

- Creating HTML5 documents
- Understanding document type definitions
- Using `meta` tags
- Attaching external documents
- Working with the `body` section
- Using CSS for web page backgrounds
- Commenting your work

Starting with the essentials

You might wonder what's meant by this chapter's title: web page essentials. This chapter will run through everything you need to do with a web page prior to working on the layout and content, including creating the initial documents, attaching external documents to HTML files, and dealing with the head section of the web page. Little of this is a thrill with regard to visual design, which is why many designers ignore the topics we'll cover or stick their fingers in their ears, hum loudly, and wish it would all go away (and then probably get rather odd looks from nearby colleagues). However, as the chapter's title states, everything we'll be talking about is essential for any quality web page, even if you don't see exciting things happening visually.

This chapter also explores web page backgrounds, which, although they should be used sparingly and with caution, often come in handy. It's worth bearing in mind that some aspects discussed here will crop up later in the book. For example, CSS techniques used to attach backgrounds to a web page can be used to attach a background to any web page element (be that a `div`, table, heading, or paragraph). But before we get into any CSS shenanigans, we'll put our CSS cheerleading team on hold and look at how to properly construct an (X)HTML document.

HTML vs. XHTML

The HTML5 specification defines an abstract language for describing documents and applications and defines some APIs for interacting with what is known as the DOM HTML (or "the DOM" for short). There are various concrete syntaxes for this language, and two are HTML and XHTML

HTML (or HTML5) is the format suggested for most authors. It is compatible with most legacy web browsers. If a document is transmitted with an HTML MIME type, such as text/html, then it will be processed as an HTML document by web browsers.

XHTML (or XHTML5) is an application of XML. When a document is transmitted with an XML MIME type, such as application/xhtml+xml, then it is treated as an XML document by web browsers, to be parsed by an XML processor. Authors are reminded that the processing for XML and HTML differs; in particular, even minor syntax errors will prevent a document labeled as XML from being rendered fully, whereas they would be ignored in the HTML syntax.

Essentially, an XHTML5 page is a simple HTML5 document that has the following:

- *HTML doctype/namespace*: The <!DOCTYPE html> definition is optional, but it would be useful for preventing browser quirks mode.

- *XHTML well-formed syntax:*

  - *XML MIME type*: application/xhtml+xml. This MIME declaration is not visible in the source code, but it would appear in the HTTP Content-Type header that could be configured on the server.

  - *Default XHTML namespace*: <html xmlns="http://www.w3.org/1999/xhtml">.

It has been argued that the strict coding requirements of XHTML identify the structure of a document more clearly than HTML. In HTML, a browser assumes the location of a missing end tag to be the start tag of the next block element. In the example, <br /> is rendered after the paragraph in the XHTML document and as part of the paragraph in the HTML document.

It is recommended to use HTML and not XHTML, especially for beginners since the syntax can be more forgiving. Note that some server-side technologies might still favor XHTML output.

Document defaults

Both in HTML5 and in XHTML5, a blank document looks like the following code:

```
<!DOCTYPE html >
<html lang="en">
  <head>
    <title></title>
    <meta http-equiv="Content-type" content="text/html; charset=utf-8" />
  </head>
  <body>
  </body>
</html>
```

There are other character sets in use, too, for the likes of Hebrew, Nordic, and Eastern European languages, and if you're using them, the charset value would be changed accordingly. Although www.iana.org/assignments/character-sets provides a thorough character set listing and www.czyborra.com/charsets/iso8859.html contains useful character set diagrams, it's tricky to wade through it all, so listed here are some common values and their associated languages:

- *ISO-8859-1 (Latin1)*: Western European and American, including Afrikaans, Albanian, Basque, Catalan, Danish, Dutch, English, Faeroese, Finnish, French, Galician, German, Icelandic, Irish, Italian, Norwegian, Portuguese, Spanish, and Swedish.

- *ISO-8859-2 (Latin2)*: Central and Eastern European, including Croatian, Czech, Hungarian, Polish, Romanian, Serbian, Slovak, and Slovene.

- *ISO-8859-3 (Latin3)*: Southern European, including Esperanto, Galician, Maltese, and Turkish. (See also ISO-8859-9.)

- *ISO-8859-4 (Latin4)*: Northern European, including Estonian, Greenlandic, Lappish, Latvian, and Lithuanian. (See also ISO-8859-6.)

- *ISO-8859-5*: Cyrillic, including Bulgarian, Byelorussian, Macedonian, Russian, Serbian, and Ukrainian.

- ISO-8859-6: Arabic.

- *ISO-8859-7*: Modern Greek.

- ISO-8859-8: Hebrew.

- *ISO-8859-9 (Latin5)*: European. Replaces Icelandic-specific characters with Turkish ones.

- *ISO-8859-10* (Latin6*)*: Nordic, including Icelandic, Inuit, and Lappish.

For an overview of the ISO-8859 standard, see `http://en.wikipedia.org/wiki/ISO_8859`.

DOCTYPE declarations explained

The <!DOCTYPE> prolog identifies the type and version of HTML or XHTML in which the document is coded. In technical terms, <!DOCTYPE> specifies the type of document and the DTD that validates the document. The W3C provides a free online service at http://validator.w3.org/ that you can use to validate your documents.

All HTML and XHTML code should be validated. This verifies the code contains no coding errors. If there are errors, CSS selectors may fail to select elements as expected or may even select elements unexpectedly.

There are benefits to using XHTML. Validated XHTML documents are well-formed and have unambiguous structure. You can also use Extensible Stylesheet Language (XSLT) and XML Query Language (XQuery) processors to extract content and rearrange documents.

In the HTML4 era, there were two additional varieties of DOCTYPEs: strict and transitional. Strict removes all presentational elements and attributes, and transitional allows them. We do not recommend presentation elements and attributes, but the strict DOCTYPE may be too strict for some needs. For example, it prohibits the start attribute in ol and the value attribute in li, which are the only available means to control the numbering of an ordered list. The XHTML strict DOCTYPE also prohibits iframe.

The head section

The head section of a web page contains metadata content that sets up the presentation or behavior of the rest of the content, that sets up the relationship of the document with other documents, or that conveys other "out-of-band" information.

Page titles

Many designers are so keen to get pages online that they forget to provide a title for each page. Titles are added using the `title` element, as follows:

```
<title>Pro HTML5 and CSS3 Design</title>
```

The title is usually shown at the top of the browser window (and sometimes within the active tab, if you're using a browser that has a tabbed interface); the results of the previous code block are shown in the following image.

By default, web design software (for example, Adobe Dreamweaver) usually does one of the following things with regard to the title element:

- Adds no content

- Sets the `title` element's content as "Untitled Document"

- Sets the `title` element's content as the application's name

The first of these results in no title being displayed for the web page and is invalid XHTML, while the second means your page joins the legions online that have no title. The third option is just as bad: using your web page to advertise the application you used to create it. Therefore, add a title to every web page you create; in fact, make it one of the first things you do so you don't forget.

With regard to the content of your web page titles, bear in mind that this is often the most prominent thing returned in search engine results pages. Keep titles clear, concise, and utterly to the point. Use too many words, and the title will be clipped; use too few (or try to get arty with characters), and you may end up with something that stumps search engines and potential visitors, too.

Generally speaking, for the homepage at least, it's good to include the name of the site or organization, followed by an indication of the site's reason for existence (and author or location, if relevant). For instance, as shown in the following image, the InfoQ title includes the organization's name, followed by its mission statement.

InfoQ: Facilitating the spread of knowledge and innovation in ...
www.infoq.com/ - Cached
13 hours ago – **InfoQ**.com (Information Queue) is an independent online community focused on change and innovation in enterprise software development, ...

Some designers use the same title throughout their site. This is a bad idea—web page titles are used as visual indicators by visitors trawling bookmarks or their browser's history. This is why some tend to use titles as a breadcrumb navigation of sorts, showing where a page sits within the website's hierarchy, like this:

```
<title>Company name - Services - Service name</title>
```

meta tags and search engines

The Web was once awash with tips for tweaking `meta` tags. This was because although these tags are primarily there to provide information about the document, they were initially what most search engines used to categorize web pages and return results. It didn't take long for the shortfalls in the system to become apparent and for designers to abuse them, so many `meta` tags are today considered redundant.

Generally, search engines now trawl the content of the web page (including the contents of the `title` element), trying to match a user's search with the most important content on the page. This is why strong use of semantic markup is essential—by correctly utilizing headings, paragraphs, and other structural elements for text and by avoiding overuse of images for text content, modern search engines get a better handle on your content and can therefore, in theory, return more accurate results to users.

Tagging and other forms of metadata are also becoming an increasingly popular search engine aid, for both internal search engines—those within the site itself—and for the search engines that return results from the whole of the Internet. Both are a means of adding information to a website to aid users. Visual tags may show a number of keywords associated with a blog posting, for example, enabling a user to see whether something interests them by the size of the word; search engines will latch onto the keywords and the content of the piece itself. Metadata enables you to "embed" information in the page, aiding all manner of devices and potentially creating networks and links to like information. A form of metadata—microformats—is explored in Chapter 8.

Despite this, it's still worth being mindful of `meta` tags when creating web pages, for those search engines that still make use of them—just be aware that they're not nearly as important as they once were (with the possible exception of `description`).

Keywords and descriptions

Unless you're totally new to web design, it's likely you'll be aware of the `keywords` and `description` meta tags:

```
<meta name="keywords" content="keywords, separated, by, commas" />
<meta name="description" content="A short description about the Web
  site" />
```

The first of these tags, keywords, should contain a set of comma-separated tokens, each of which is a keyword relevant to the page that users might type into a search engine to find your site. Because of abuse (websites including thousands of words in the meta tag content in order to try to create a catchall in search engine results pages), such lists are rarely used these days. Instead, search engines tend to look at the entire content of a page to determine its relevance to someone's search. If you choose to include this element in your web page, 30 or fewer words and short phrases are sufficient.

The contents of the description's content attribute are returned by some search engines in a results page along with the web page's title. As with the title, keep things succinct; otherwise, the description will be cropped. Most search engines display a maximum of 200 characters, so 25 well-chosen words are just about all you can afford.

revisit-after, robots, and author

Other meta tags also use name and content attributes. These tags assist search engines. In the following example, the first tag provides an indication of how often they should return (useful for regularly updated sites), and the second tag states whether the page should be indexed.

```
<meta name="Revisit-After" content="30 Days" />
<meta name="robots" content="all,index" />
```

The content attribute of the robots meta tag can instead include the values noindex and none, in order to block indexing, and follow or nofollow, depending on whether you want search engine robots to follow links from the current page.

The author meta tag is of less use to search engines and typically includes the page author's name and home URL. Designers sometimes use it as a means to declare the author's name and details, but it has little use beyond that.

Attaching external documents

A web page—as in the (X)HTML document—is primarily designed to contain content that is structured in markup. Presentation should be dealt with via external CSS documents, and behavior should be dealt with via external scripting documents. Although it is possible to work with the likes of JavaScript and CSS within an HTML document, this goes against the modular nature of good web design. It's far easier to create, edit, and maintain a site if you work with separate files for each technology. (The exception is if your "site" is only a single page, therefore making it sensible to include everything in a single document.)

As already mentioned, HTML documents are text files that are saved with the suffix .html (or .htm). CSS and JavaScript files are also text documents, and their file suffixes are .css and .js, respectively. When you start a project, having already set the relevant DOCTYPE and added meta tags, it's a good idea to create blank CSS and JavaScript files and to attach them to your web page so you can then work on any element as you wish.

Attaching external CSS files: the link method

In the previous chapter, you were shown how to attach CSS to a web page (see the section "Adding styles to a web page" in Chapter 1); we'll briefly recap the process here. There are two methods of attaching an external CSS file: the link method and the @import method.

The link tag specifies a relationship between the linked document and the document it's being linked to. In the context of attaching a CSS file, it looks something like this:

```
<link rel="stylesheet" href="stylesheet.css" />
```

Possible attributes include the following:

- *rel*: Defines the relation from the parent document to the target

- *href*: The location of the target file

- *type*: The MIME type of the target document

- *media*: The target medium of the target document

The title attribute is also occasionally used with the link element, either to provide additional information or to be used as a "hook" for the likes of a style sheet switcher (see www.alistapart.com/stories/alternate/ for more information). Any style sheet lacking a title attribute (and a rel value of style sheet) is persistent—always affecting a document. These are by far the most common types of style sheets. A preferred style sheet also takes a title along with the rel attribute, and only one such style sheet can be used at a time—typically the first, with subsequent ones ignored. On pages that offer alternate style sheets (typically via a style switcher), the persistent styles are always used, and the first preferred is the additional default; the preferred styles, however, can be swapped out by selecting an alternative style sheet. (Note that in Firefox, you should avoid adding a title attribute to any style sheet for print, because otherwise the content may not print.)

In the previous example, the media attribute is set to all, specifying that this style sheet is intended for all devices. But it's feasible to attach multiple style sheets to a web page and set the media attribute of each one to a different type. For instance, in the following example, two CSS files are attached, one for screen and the other for printed output:

```
<link rel="stylesheet" href="stylesheet.css" type="text/css"
  media="screen" />
<link rel="stylesheet" href="printcss.css" type="text/css"
  media="print" />
```

There are other media types, including aural, braille, projection, and tv, but few are supported well. However, in Chapter 10, we'll look at style sheets for print, which is one of the alternatives to screen that is supported reasonably well in mainstream browsers.

Attaching CSS files: the @import method

A problem with the link method in the past was that obsolete browsers saw the style sheet but didn't understand it. This could result in garbled layouts—and often in unusable websites for those unfortunate enough to have to deal with such arcane web browsers. The solution was to hide the CSS from such browsers by using a command that they don't understand and so would ignore. This was often referred to as the @import method.

As shown in the following example, the `style` element is used to do this:
```
<style type="text/css" media="all">
@import url(stylesheet.css);
</style>
```

It is recommended to avoid using the @import method, especially since it might lead to performance issues in high-traffic sites (http://www.stevesouders.com/blog/2009/04/09/dont-use-import/ www.stevesouders.com/blog/2009/04/09/dont-use-import/) and with mobile users.

> *The CSS specifications permit the use of the style sheet location as a quoted string instead of enclosing it in url(). The method shown here is more commonly supported, though.*

Attaching CSS files: media queries

CSS has long supported media-dependent style sheets tailored for different media types. For example, a document may use sans-serif fonts when displayed on a screen and serif fonts when printed. screen and print are two media types that have been defined.

In the old days of HTML4, this could be written as follows:

<link rel="stylesheet" type="text/css" media="screen" href="sans-serif.css">

<link rel="stylesheet" type="text/css" media="print" href="serif.css">

With CSS3, media queries extend the functionality of media types by allowing more precise labeling of style sheets. A media query consists of a media type and zero or more expressions that check for the conditions of particular media features. By using media queries, presentations can be tailored to a specific range of output devices without changing the content itself. A media query is a logical expression that is either true or false. A media query is true if the media type of the media query matches the media type of the device where the user agent is running, and all expressions in the media query are true.

Here are a few examples:
```
<--! Devices of a certain media type ('screen') with certain feature (it must be a color
screen)-->
<link rel="stylesheet" media="screen and (color)" href="example.css" />

<!-- The same media query written in an @import-rule in CSS -->
@import url(color.css) screen and (color);
```

A shorthand syntax is offered for media queries that apply to all media types; the keyword all can be left out (along with the trailing and). In other words, the following are identical:
```
@media (orientation: portrait) { … }
@media all and (orientation: portrait) { … }
```

This way, designers and developers can create more complex queries that map their specific needs, like this one:

```
@media all and (max-width: 698px) and (min-width: 520px), (min-width: 1150px) {
  body {
    background: #ccc;
  }
}
```

There is a long list of media features that includes the following:

- width and device-width

- height and device-height

- orientation

- aspect-ratio and device-aspect-ratio

- color and color-index

- monochrome (if not a monochrome device, equals 0)

- resolution

- scan (describes the scanning process of output devices set to tv)

- grid (specifies whether the output device is grid or bitmap)

Attaching favicons and JavaScript

Favicons are those little icons you often see in your browser's address bar. They are attached using the link method discussed earlier, although you need to include only three attributes: rel, href, and type. The type value can change depending on the file type of your favicon. For example, image/png is fine if you've used a PNG.

```
<link rel="shortcut icon" href="favicon.ico" type="image/x-icon"/>
```

These days, favicons are almost ubiquitous, and they provide users with an additional visual clue to a site's identity. Although not particularly useful on their own, they can be handy when trawling through a large bookmarks list—you can look for the icon rather than the text. However, don't rely on them instead of a good web page title—they should merely be an additional tool in your arsenal. By default web browsers will search for a favicon.ico file in the root of a site, even if there is no link tag present.

Attaching a JavaScript file to a web page is similarly painless. You do so via the script element, as follows:

```
<script src="javascriptfile.js"></script>
```

> *JavaScript can be dynamically loaded in a page using a variety of techniques that are used in libraries called script loaders. These libraries bring performance improvements, such as nonblocking loading, but are beyond the scope of this book.*

Checking paths

When working with external files, ensure paths between files are complete and don't become broken as files are moved around; otherwise, your web page may lose track of the CSS and JavaScript, affecting its display and functionality. If you're using document-relative links (that is, links relative to the current document), remember to amend paths accordingly.

Here are a few examples of paths:

Path	Type	What it means
myfile.css	Relative path.	Look for the file in the same folder as the file that imports it.
/script/myscript.js	Relative path.	Look for the file in the folder scripts, which is in the same root folder as the file that imports it.
http://www.mysite.com/style.css	Absolute path.	Look for the file in this location.
/css/style.css	Absolute path.	Look for the file in the folder css, which is right under the root of the website.

The body section

The body element is used to define the body of a web page, and it contains the document's content. Technically the body tag is optional in HTML5 because HTML5 doesn't require the html, head, and body tags (browsers add them if missing). It is generally good practice to use the body element and avoid having content placed outside of it.

Although the body element has a number of possible attributes that can be included in its start tag, mostly for defining ids and classes, they should be avoided. This is because such things should be dealt with using CSS, which enables you to define values on a sitewide basis, rather than having to do so for each page.

Content margins and padding in CSS

Page margins and padding are easy to define using CSS. By setting these values once in an external file, you can update settings sitewide by uploading an amended style sheet rather than every single page on your site that has an amended body tag.

Furthermore, in terms of page weight, CSS is more efficient. If using old methods, to cater for all browsers, you set the following body attributes:

```
<body marginwidth="0" marginheight="0" topmargin="0" leftmargin="0"
  bottommargin="0" rightmargin="0">
```

The equivalent in CSS is the following:

```
body {
  margin: 0;
  padding: 0;
}
```

If a CSS setting is 0, there's no need to state a unit such as px or em.

The reason both `margin` and `padding` are set to 0 is because some browsers define a default padding value. Therefore, even if you set all body margins to 0, there would still be a gap around your page content. Setting both the margin and padding to 0 in the body rule ensures that all browsers display your content with no gaps around it.

Zeroing margins and padding on all elements

Although the previous block of code is clean and efficient, it isn't something we use in our websites. The reason for this is that browsers place default (and sometimes varying) margins around various elements other than the page's body, too. Therefore, our CSS boilerplates always include the following:

```
* {
  margin: 0;
  padding: 0;
}
```

The selector * is the universal selector, and the declaration therefore applies to all elements on the web page. In other words, add this rule to your CSS, and all default margins and padding for all elements are removed, enabling you to start from scratch in all browsers and define explicit values for those elements that need them.

Another way to makes browsers render all elements more consistently and in line with modern standards is to use a CSS reset kit. Some of the more popular ones are Eric Meyer's (http://meyerweb.com/eric/tools/css/reset/) and Yahoo's YUI 2 CSS Reset (http://developer.yahoo.com/yui/reset/). The goal of a reset style sheet is to reduce browser inconsistencies in things such as default line heights, margins and font sizes of headings, and so on.

An alternative to reset.css is normalize.css (http://necolas.github.com/normalize.css/), which normalizes styles for a wide range of HTML elements and corrects bugs and common browser inconsistencies. Users can just you the full normalize.css file or customize it to suit their needs.

Working with CSS shorthand for boxes

Both of the previous two code examples use CSS shorthand, and this is something that is useful to get to grips with in order to create the most efficient and easy-to-update CSS. The previous example showed how to set all margins and padding values to 0, and this was done in shorthand instead of writing out every single value. How CSS shorthand works for boxes is like this:

- *A single value (margin: 10px;)*: This is applied to all edges.

- *Two values (margin: 10px 20px;)*: The first setting (10px) is applied to the top and bottom edges. The second setting (20px) is applied to both the left and right edges (20px each, not in total).

- *Three values (margin: 10px 20px 30px;)*: The first setting (10px) is applied to the top edge. The second setting (20px) is applied to both the left and right edges. The third setting (30px) is applied to the bottom edge.

- *Four settings (margin: 10px 20px 30px 40px;)*: Settings are applied clockwise from the top (in other words, top: 10px; right: 20px; bottom: 30px; left: 40px).

Shorthand's benefits become obvious when comparing CSS shorthand with the equivalent properties and values written out in full. For instance, the following shorthand:

```
#box {
  margin: 0;
  padding: 0 100px;
}
```

looks like this when written out in full:

```
#box {
  margin-top: 0;
  margin-right: 0;
  margin-bottom: 0;
  margin-left: 0;
  padding-top: 0;
  padding-right: 100px;
  padding-bottom: 0;
  padding-left: 100px;
}
```

Whether you use shorthand is up to you. Some designers swear by it and others because of it. Some web design applications have options to "force" shorthand or avoid it entirely. We reckon it's a good thing: CSS documents are usually more logical and shorter because of shorthand. But if you don't agree, feel free to keep on defining margins and padding as relevant for every edge of every element.

Setting a default font and font color

As mentioned earlier, the body start tag was historically used to house attributes for dealing with default text and background colors, link colors, and background images. In CSS, link styles are dealt with separately (see Chapter 5). We'll look at how to apply backgrounds later in this chapter.

At this point, it's worth noting that, when working with CSS, the body selector is often used to set a default font family and color for the website. We'll discuss working with text in more depth in the next chapter, but for now, check out the following CSS:

```
body {
  font-family: Verdana, Arial, Helvetica, sans-serif;
  color: #000000;
  background-color: #ffffff;
}
```

This is straightforward. The `font-family` property sets a default font (in this case, Verdana) and fallback fonts in case the first choice isn't available on the user's system. The list should end with a generic family, such as `sans-serif` or `serif`, depending on your other choices. The fonts are separated by commas in the list, and if you're using multiple-word fonts, they must be quoted (`"Courier New"`, not `Courier New`).

The `color` property's value defines the default color of text throughout the site. In the preceding example, its value is `#000000`, which is the hexadecimal (hex) value for black (when defining colors in CSS, it's most common to use hex values, although you can use comma-separated RGB values if you want).

The color red can be specified in different ways:

- color: red (color name)
- color: #ff0000 (hex)
- color: rgb(255,0,0) (RGB value)

It's also advisable where possible to add a background color for accessibility; in this case, the background color is `#ffffff`—hex for white.

> *Although it's possible to set a default size (and other property values) for text in the* body *declaration, we'll leave that for now and instead explore how best to do so in the following chapter*

Web page backgrounds

Web page backgrounds used to be commonplace, but they became unpopular once designers figured out that visitors to web pages didn't want their eyes wrenched out by gaudy tiled background patterns. With text being as hard to read on-screen as it is, it's adding insult to injury to inflict some nasty paisley mosaic background (or worse) on the poor reader, too.

But, as affordable monitors continue to increase in size and resolution, designers face a conundrum. If they're creating a liquid design that stretches to fit the browser window, text can become unreadable, because the eye finds it hard to scan text in wide columns. And if they're creating a fixed-width design, large areas of the screen often end up blank. It's for the latter design style that backgrounds can be useful, both in drawing the eye to the content and providing some visual interest outside of the content area.

Like most things related to design, the use and style of backgrounds is subjective, but some rules are worth bearing in mind. The most obvious is that a background should not distract from your content. If you're using background images, keep them simple, and when you're using color, ensure that the contrast and saturation with the page's background color is fairly low but that the contrast with the text content over the background is very high. Also, unless you're using a subtle watermark, it's generally bad form to put complex images underneath text (a soft gradient or simple geometric shape can sometimes be OK, however). Also, because backgrounds are typically ancillary content, they should not significantly increase the loading time of the page.

Web page backgrounds in CSS

Backgrounds are added to web page elements using a number of properties, as described in the sections that follow.

background-color

This property sets the background color of the element. In the following example, the page's body background color has been set to #ffffff (which is hex for white):

```
body {
    background-color: #ffffff;
}
```

background-image

This property sets a background image for the relevant element:

```
body {
    background-image: url(background_image.jpg);
}
```

By using this CSS, you end up with a tiled background, as shown in the following image.

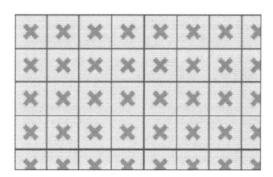

background-repeat

The properties explored so far mimic the range offered by deprecated HTML attributes, but CSS provides you with control over the background's tiling and positioning. The background-repeat property can take four values, the default of which is repeat, creating the tiled background just shown.

If background-repeat is set to no-repeat, the image is shown just once, as in the following illustration.

If this property is set to repeat-x, the image tiles horizontally only.

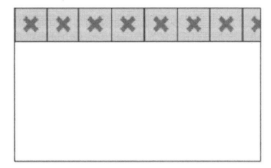

And if the property is set to repeat-y, the image tiles vertically only.

background-attachment

This property has two possible values: scroll and fixed. The default is scroll, in which the background works as normal, scrolling with the rest of the page. If you set the value to fixed, the background image remains stationary while the remainder of the page scrolls.

background-position

This property's values set the origin of the background by using two values that relate to the horizontal and vertical positions. The default background-position value is 0 0 (the top left of the web page).

Along with keywords (center, left, and right for horizontal positioning; center, top, and bottom for vertical positioning), you can use percentages and pixel values. It's possible to use a combination of percentages and pixel sizes, but you cannot mix keywords with either. Therefore, it's recommended that designers stick with using percentages and pixel values—after all, keyword positioning can be emulated with numbers anyway (left top being the same as 0 0, for instance). When setting values, they should always be defined in the order horizontal-vertical.

When using keywords, it's also recommended to use the order horizontal-vertical, because both percentage- and pixel-based background positioning use this order, and it's simpler to remember a single rule. In the following example, the background would be positioned on the left of the web page and positioned in the vertical center of the content:

```
body {
  background-image: url(background_image.gif);
  background-repeat: no-repeat;
  background-position: left center;
}
```

Again, when using percentages or pixel values, the first value relates to the horizontal position, and the second relates to the vertical. So, to create the equivalent of the keyword example, you'd use the following CSS:

```
body {
  background-image: url(background_image.gif);
  background-repeat: no-repeat;
  background-position:  0 50%;
}
```

Note, however, when using background-position with the body element, that browsers disagree slightly on where the background should be positioned vertically if the page content isn't taller than the viewing area. Internet Explorer and Safari assume the body is the full view area height when there's no content, thereby setting an image with a background-position value of 50% 50% directly in the center of the viewing area. Firefox and Opera instead assume the body has an effective height of 0, thereby placing the background vertically at the top of the view area (in fact, you see only the bottom half). For consistency across browsers in this case, you can define both background-position and background-attachment (as fixed), although this means the background will not scroll with the page content.

CSS shorthand for web backgrounds

As when defining margins and padding, you can use shorthand for web background values, bundling them into a single background property, although it's worth stating that the shorthand value overrides any previous settings in a CSS file for individual background properties. (For instance, if you use individual settings to define the background image and then subsequently use the shorthand for setting the color, the background image will most likely not appear.)

When using shorthand, you can set the values in any order. Here's an example:

```
body {
   background: #ffffff url(background_image.gif) no-repeat fixed 50%
     10px;
}
```

Generally speaking, it's best to use shorthand over separate background properties—it's quicker to type and easier to manage. You also don't have to explicitly define every one of the values; if you don't, the values revert to their defaults. Therefore, the following is acceptable:

```
body {
   background: #ffffff url(background_image.gif) no-repeat;
}
```

Because the background-attachment value hasn't been specified, this background would scroll with the page, and because the background-position value hasn't been defined, the background would be positioned at 0%, 0%—the top left of the browser window.

Gradients

A gradient is an image that smoothly fades from one color to another. These are commonly used for subtle shading in background images, buttons, and many other things. They can be used anywhere an image can, such as in the background-image or list-style-image properties.

```
.fancybox {
   background: linear-gradient(white, gray);
}
```

A *linear gradient* is created by specifying a gradient-line and then several colors placed along that line. The image is constructed by creating an infinite canvas and painting it with lines perpendicular to the gradient-line, with the color of the painted line being the color of the gradient-line where the two intersect. The first argument to the function specifies the gradient-line, which gives the gradient a direction and determines how color-stops are positioned.

Here are some examples:

```
linear-gradient(white, gray);
linear-gradient(to bottom, white, grey);
linear-gradient(180deg, white, grey);
```

In a radial gradient, rather than colors smoothly fading from one side of the gradient box to the other as with linear gradients, they instead emerge from a single point and smoothly spread outward in a circular or elliptical shape.

A *radial gradient* is specified by indicating the center of the gradient and the size and shape of the ending shape. Color stops are given as a list, just as for linear-gradient(). Starting from the center and progressing toward the ending shape, concentric ellipses are drawn and colored according to the specified color stops.

Here are some examples:

```
radial-gradient(yellow, green);
radial-gradient(ellipse at center, yellow 0%, green 100%);
```

In addition to the linear-gradient() and radial-gradient() functions, this spec defines repeating-linear-gradient() and repeating-radial-gradient()functions.

Web page background ideas

Before finishing up this section on web page backgrounds, we'll run through some examples that show the CSS and the result, along with the background image used. The files within the basic-boilerplates folder can be used as starting points for web pages and CSS documents. The images used in each case are in the chapter 2 folder of the download files, and they should be placed in the same folder as the HTML and CSS documents, unless you amend path values accordingly.

Rename the files as appropriate for each example, ensuring you import the relevant CSS file via the HTML document's @import line.

For the HTML document, add several paragraphs within the existing div element that has an id value of wrapper, as in the following code block (which, for space reasons, shows only a single truncated paragraph—add more than this!):

```
<div id="wrapper">
  <p>...</p>
</div>
```

In CSS, there are also some common elements to add to the boilerplate. For the #wrapper rule, add some padding to ensure the content within doesn't hug the box's edges, and add a background rule to color the box's background white. Also, the width value defines the width of the box's content, while the margin settings center the box horizontally. (The method will be discussed further in other chapters, but by setting 0 auto as the margin values, vertical margins are removed and horizontal margins are set to auto, which center the box horizontally in the browser window.)

```
#wrapper {
  padding: 18px;
  background: #ffffff;
  width: 500px;
  margin: 0 auto;
}
```

Note that in the download files, in order to keep things modular, there are two #wrapper rules in the CSS, and that's what's assumed in the previous code block. However, if you prefer, add the property/value pairs from the previous code block to the style sheet's existing #wrapper rule. The same is true for many of the rules, such as the body rules in the following sections.

Adding a background pattern

The following CSS can be used to add a patterned, tiled background to your web page:

```
body {
  background: #ffffff url(background-tile.gif);
}
```

The following screenshot shows a page with a diagonal cross pattern, although you could alternatively use diagonal stripes, horizontal stripes, squares, or other simple shapes.

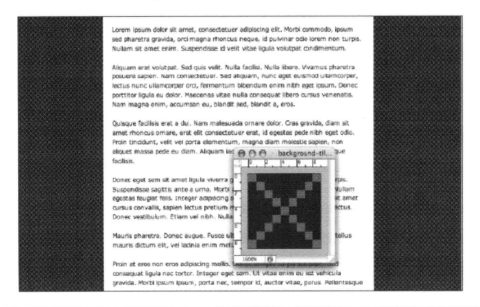

Note that if you remove many of the paragraphs from the web page, the white background color ends with the content, since in CSS a container's size by default only stretches to that of its content.

Drop shadows

The following image shows a page with a content area and drop shadow.

This effect was achieved by creating the depicted background image and tiling it vertically. In the body rule, the position was set to 50% 0 in order to position the background centrally on the horizontal axis. The background color of the web page is the same as the solid background on the image itself, so the image and color seamlessly blend.

```
body {
    background: #878787 url(background-drop-shadow.gif) 50% 0 repeat-y;
}
```

Regarding the white area of the image, this is 536 pixels wide. This is because the wrapper div's width was earlier set to 500 pixels, and its padding value was set to 18 pixels. As you will remember from the box model information from the previous chapter, padding is added to the dimensions of a box, so the overall width taken up by the wrapper div is 536 pixels (18 + 500 + 18 = 536).

A drop shadow that terminates with the content

In the previous example, the white background of the content area is part of the image. Therefore, if you remove most of the paragraphs in that example, the background stays as it is, tiling vertically to the height of the viewing area. Using a different method, you can instead have the background terminate with the content.

Some additional markup is needed, because of this method requiring two background images: one for the wrapper div (because, as per the white background in the "Adding a background pattern" section, you want the content area's background to stop when the content runs out) and one for a shadow for the bottom edge of the wrapper div (otherwise, the shadows at the side will just stop dead, resulting in something like what's shown in the following image).

In terms of markup, add an empty `div`, as shown in the following code block:

```
    ? accumsa'n eu, blandit sed, blandit a, eros.</p>
    <div class="contentFooter"><!-- x --></div>
  </div>
</body>
</html>
```

In CSS, for the drop shadows flanking the content area to stop where the content does, they need to be assigned to the wrapper `div`, not the web page's `body`. Therefore, you need to amend the `body` rule, removing the link to a background but retaining the color setting:

```
body {
  background: #878787;
}
```

The `#wrapper` rule needs updating in two ways. First, the new background image needs to be applied to the `div`—hence the new `background` property/value pair. However, because the drop shadows are now shown within the wrapper `div`, it needs to take up more horizontal space. Since the dimensions of the `div`'s content don't need changing, this is achieved by increasing the horizontal padding value. Also, because padding at the foot of the `div` is no longer required (the `contentFooter` `div` effectively takes care of padding at the bottom of the content area), the bottom padding value needs to be set to `0`. These padding values are done in shorthand, as per the method outlined in the "Working with CSS shorthand for boxes" section earlier in this chapter.

```
#wrapper {
  padding: 18px 36px 0;
  background: url(background-drop-shadow-2.gif) 50% 0 repeat-y;
  width: 500px;
  margin: 0 auto;
}
```

Finally, the `contentFooter` `div` needs styling. Its height is defined on the basis of the height of the background image (which is a slice of the Photoshop document shown in the following image). The background is applied to the `div` in the same way as in previous examples.

One major change, however, is the use of negative margins. The `contentFooter` `div` is nested within the wrapper, which has 36 pixels of horizontal padding. This means that the `contentFooter` `div` background doesn't reach the edges of the wrapper `div` by default, leaving whitespace on its left and right sides. By using margins equal to the negative value of this padding, the `div` can be "stretched" into place.

```
.contentFooter {
  height: 20px;
  background: url(background-drop-shadow-2-footer.gif) 50% 0;
  margin: 0 -36px;
}
```

As you can see, the horizontal value for margin is -36px, the negative of the horizontal padding value assigned to #wrapper. The addition of all these new rules results in the following image (which also shows the Photoshop image and exported GIF that makes up the background).

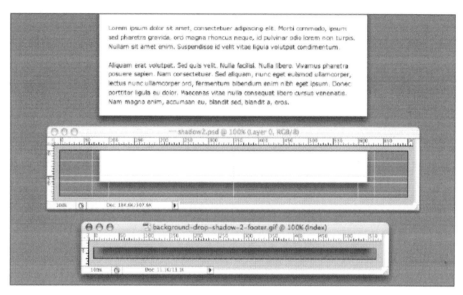

An alternate method for getting this effect would be to place the contentFooter div outside of the wrapper and then use the same method of aligning it:

```
.contentFooter {
  width: 500px;
  height: 20px;
  background: url(background-drop-shadow-2-footer.gif) 50% 0;
  padding: 0 36px;
  margin: 0 auto;
}
```

To ensure the background of the wrapper joins up with the shadow on the contentFooter div, a single pixel of bottom padding needs to be applied to the #wrapper rule:

```
#wrapper {
  padding: 18px 36px 1px;
  background: url(background-drop-shadow-2.gif) 50% 0 repeat-y;
  width: 500px;
  margin: 0 auto;
}
```

CSS3 shadows

The box-shadow property attaches one or more drop shadows on a box. The property is a comma-separated list of shadows, each specified by two to four length values, an optional color, and an optional insetkeyword.

```
div {
    width: 150px;
    height: 150px;
    border:5px solid blue;
    background-color:orange;
    margin: 30px;
    color: blue;
    text-align: center;
}
#box1 {
    box-shadow: rgba(0,0,0,0.4) 10px 10px;
}
#box2 {
    box-shadow: rgba(0,0,0,0.4) 10px 10px 0 10px
}
#box3 {
    box-shadow: rgba(0,0,0,0.4) 10px 10px inset
}
```

Plain image gradients

Tiled gradient images can be used to add depth and visual interest, without sapping resources (the example's image is less than 2 KB in size). The depicted example is based on the page from the "Drop shadows" section. The changes are an amendment to the background pair in the #wrapper rule, tiling the gradient image horizontally on the wrapper's background, and new padding settings, so the text doesn't appear over the gradient.

```
#wrapper {
    padding: 36px 18px 18px;
    background: #ffffff url(background-gradient.gif) repeat-x;
    width: 500px;
    margin: 0 auto;
}
```

Watermarks

Although it's common for sites to be centered in the browser window, many designers choose left-aligned sites that cling to the left edge of the browser window. Both design styles are perfectly valid, but in an era of rapidly increasing monitor resolutions, you can end up with a lot of dead space to the side of a fixed-width left-aligned design. And while some of you might be saying, "Well, create flexible-width designs, then!" some designs aren't suited to that, and text-heavy sites tend to work better with fairly narrow text columns, since most users find it hard to read very wide blocks of text.

All of this brings us to the final example in this chapter, which shows how to create watermarks for a web page. In the following screenshot, the wrapper div is to the left, with a background image to the right of this area.

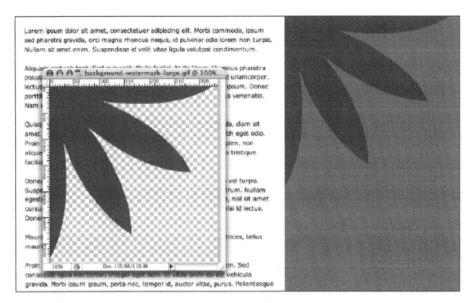

To achieve this effect, the margin property/value pair in the #wrapper rule has been removed, and the following rule has been added:

```
body {
  background: #878787 url(background-watermark-large.gif) no-repeat
    536px 0;
}
```

> As mentioned earlier in the chapter, this assumes you're adding a second *body* rule. You can, however, just add the *background* property/value pair to the existing *body* rule in the style sheet.

The image used is a transparent GIF, so the background color setting was made a medium-gray (#878787). The reasoning behind using a transparent GIF is explained in Chapter 4, but it relates to web browsers sometimes interpreting colors differently from graphics packages. Therefore, it's often easier to make the flat background color of a graphic transparent and then use the web page background color in place of it.

The repeat setting is set to no-repeat, because we don't want the image to tile. Finally, the background's position is set to 536px 0. The 0 setting means it hugs the top of the browser window, while the 536px setting means the image is placed at 536 pixels from the left. This is because the content area was earlier defined as 500 pixels wide with 18 pixels of padding, and 18 + 500 + 18 = 536.

As mentioned earlier, backgrounds can be added to any web page element. For instance, you can add a watermark to the wrapper div by using the following CSS:

```
#wrapper {
  padding: 18px;
```

```
background: #ffffff url(background-watermark.gif) no-repeat 20px
  20px;
width: 500px;
}
```

This adds the `background-watermark.gif` image to the background of the content `div` and positions it 20 pixels from the top and 20 pixels from the left. Again, `no-repeat` is used to stop the image from tiling.

In either case for the watermark backgrounds, the images scroll with the page content. However, watermarks can also work well as fixed backgrounds—this can be achieved by adding the `fixed` value to the `background` property in the `body` and `#wrapper` rules.

CSS3 patterns

The CSS3 gradient features that are described earlier are powerful enough to produce beautiful patterns. Web designer Lea Verou has assembled a nice CSS3 patterns gallery from many contributors (http://lea.verou.me/css3patterns).

Closing your document

At the start of this chapter, we examined basic HTML and XHTML documents. Regardless of the technology used, the end of the document should look like this:

```
  </body>
</html>
```

There are no variations or alternatives. A body end tag terminates the document's content, and an html end tag terminates the document. No web page content should come after the body end tag, and no HTML content should come after the html end tag (whitespace is fine, and it's common practice with server-side technologies to put functions after the html end tag—just don't put any HTML there).

Also, you must only ever have one body and one head in an HTML document, as well as a single html start tag and a single html end tag.

This is important stuff to bear in mind, and even if you think it's obvious, there are millions of pages out there—particularly those that utilize server-side includes and server-side languages—that include multiple body tags and head tags, have content outside the body tag, and have HTML outside the html tag.

Don't do this in your own work.

Naming your files

Each designer has their own way of thinking when it comes to naming files and documents. Personally, we like to keep document names succinct but obvious enough that we can find them rapidly via a trawl of the hard drive. Certain conventions, however, are key: all file names should avoid illegal characters (such as spaces), and it's good to be consistent throughout your site. We find that naming files in lowercase and replacing spaces with hyphens—`like-this-for-example.html`—works well.

> *Web designers have historically used underscores in place of spaces, but that causes problems with some search engines, some of which run-in keywords, effectively considering the words within the file name as one string. This doesn't happen with hyphens*

Commenting your work

The rules for HTML, CSS, and JavaScript comments are simple, but the actual characters used are different in each case.

HTML comments begin with `<!--` and end with `-->` and can run over multiple lines, as follows:

```
<!-- this is a comment in HTML -->
<!--
Multiple-line
HTML
comment
-->
```

In XHTML, double hyphens should not occur within the comment itself. Therefore, the following is not valid XHTML:

```
<!-- This is invalid -- as is the comment below -->
<!------------------------------------------------------->
```

The multiple-hyphen comment is commonly used by designers who favor hand-coding to separate large chunks of code within a document. When working in XHTML, you can replace the hyphens with a different character:

```
<!--oooooooooooooooooooooooooooooooooooooo-->
<!--=================================-->
```

CSS comments were covered in the "Creating boilerplates" section of Chapter 1, but we'll briefly look through them again; they're opened with `/*` and closed with `*/` and, like HTML comments, can run over multiple lines, as shown here:

```
/* This is a comment in CSS */
/*
Multiple-line
CSS
```

```
comment
*/
```

Multiple-line comments in JavaScript are the same as in CSS, but single-line comments are placed after double forward slashes:

```
// This is a single-line JavaScript comment.
```

Don't use comments incorrectly. CSS comments in an HTML document won't be problematic from a rendering standpoint—but they will be displayed. HTML comments in CSS can actually cause a CSS file to fail entirely.

> *Note: Along with enabling you to comment your work, comments can be used to disable sections of code when testing web pages.*

Quickly testing your code

You can easily test your HTML/CSS ideas with JsFiddle (http://jsfiddle.net), which includes an online editor for snippets build from HTML, CSS, and JavaScript. The code can then be shared with others, embedded in a blog, and so on.

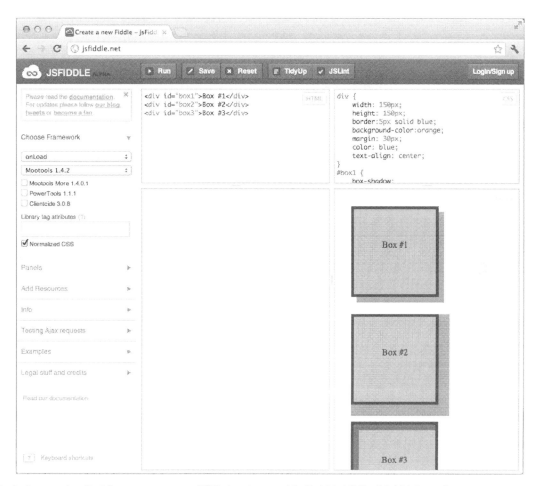

A similar service that focuses more on CSS development is Dabblet (http://dabblet.com).

Web page essentials checklist

Congratulations—you made it to the end of this chapter! We're aware that some of this one was about as much fun as trying to work out complex quadratic equations in your head, but as mentioned at the start, you need to know this stuff. Imagine designing a site and it suddenly not working the way you thought it would. It looks fine in your web design package and also in some web browsers, but it starts falling apart in others. Just removing an XML declaration might be enough to fix the site.

If you take the elements of this chapter and form them into a simple checklist, you won't have to risk displaying those wonderful "Untitled Documents" to the entire world (or inadvertently advertising the package you used to create the page). To make your life easier, you can refer to this checklist:

1. Ensure the relevant DOCTYPE declaration and namespace are in place.

2. Remove the XML declaration if it's lurking.

3. Add a `title` tag and some content within it.

4. Add a `meta` tag to define your character set.

5. If required, add `keywords` and `description` `meta` tags.

6. Attach a CSS file (or files).

7. Attach a JavaScript file (or files).

8. If your web editor adds superfluous `body` attributes, delete them.

9. Ensure there are no characters prior to the `DOCTYPE` declaration or after the `html` end tag.

10. Ensure no web page content appears outside the `body` element.

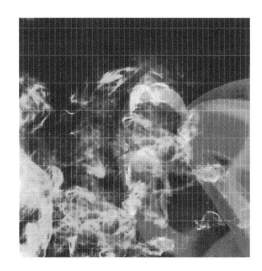

Chapter 3

Working With Type

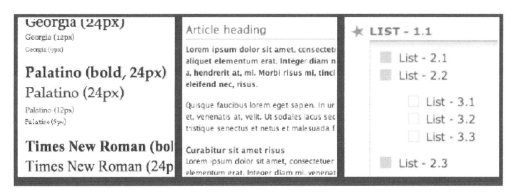

In this chapter:

- Working with semantic markup

- Defining font colors, families, and other styles

- Understanding web-safe fonts

- Creating drop caps and pull quotes

- Rapidly editing styled text

- Working to a grid

- Creating and styling lists

An introduction to typography

Words are important—not just what they say but how they look. To quote Ellen Lupton, from her book *Thinking with Type*, "Typography is what language looks like." Language has always been symbolic, although the origins of such symbols (of certain letterforms relating to, for example, animals) has largely been lost in written English; instead, we now have rather more abstract symbols designed for repetition on the page or screen.

However, from the early calligraphy that was created by hand through the movable type (invented in Germany by Johannes Gutenberg during the 15th century) that enabled mass-production printing via molded letterform casts to the most advanced desktop-publishing software available today, the ultimate aim of type has been one of record and information provision. In other words, type is important from a design standpoint because it needs to record whatever information is being written about, and that information needs to be easily retrievable by anyone who wants to understand it.

Like all aspects of design, typography has massively evolved over the years, particularly over the past couple of decades, where computers have enabled designers to more rapidly experiment with lettering. Despite this, many conventions formed much earlier still have a part to play:

- Myriad fonts exist, and each one has a different look and therefore a different "feel." You need to choose the most appropriate one for your purpose. (This is further complicated by there being only a certain number of web-safe fonts, as you'll learn later.)

- Headings, strap-lines/stand-firsts (the introductory line that introduces a piece of text, commonly used in editorial articles), and crossheads (short subheadings that break up areas of body copy) should stand out, and the prominence of each piece of text should be related to its level of importance (in other words, a crosshead shouldn't be more prominent than a main heading).

- Footnotes often use text smaller than the main body copy text to signify their lesser significance to the main text, but nonetheless they provide useful supplementary information.

- Decorative elements can be used to draw the reader's attention to specific parts of the text. Drop caps and initials—large initial letters, flamboyant in classical typography, but typically more restrained in modern work (see right)—enable a reader to rapidly navigate to the beginning of a piece of text. Pull quotes—quotes from the main body of the text, displayed in large lettering outside of context—are often used in magazine articles to

  L orem ipsur
  pharetra gr
  sit amet en
  pat. Sed quis velit. Ì
  Sed aliquam nunc

  draw a reader's attention to a particular article, highlighting particularly interesting quotes or information.

- Spacing is just as important as content. Kerning—the spacing between letter pairs—can be increased to add prominence to a heading. Leading—the amount of added vertical spacing between lines of text—can also be adjusted. Increasing leading from its default can make text more legible. In books, a baseline grid is often employed, ensuring that text always appears in the same place on each page. This means that the text on the opposite side of the paper doesn't appear in the gaps between the lines on the page you're reading. Baseline grids often make for extremely pleasing vertical rhythm and are regularly used in print publications; they're infrequently used online but can nonetheless be of use, making a page of text easier to read and navigate.

- Columns sometimes make a page easier to read, and this technique is routinely used by newspapers and magazines. Online, the recent ability to autoflow columns of text makes de facto text columns possible. This is impractical because not every browser supports it yet and because columns force users to scroll repeatedly, but the reasoning behind columns is still handy to bear in mind. Generally, it's considered easier to read text that has fairly narrow columns (although not too narrow—if there are too few characters, reading and comprehension slow down). Text that, for example, spans the entire width of a 23-inch monitor rapidly becomes tiring to read. There are no hard-and-fast rules when it comes to line length, although some go by the "alphabet-and-a-half" rule (39 characters per line), some advocate the "points-times-two" rule (double the point size and use the number for the number of characters), and others recommend a dozen or so words (or about 60 characters).

A few highly useful online resources for web typography can be found at the following locations:

- The Elements of Typographic Style Applied to the Web: www.webtypography.net/

- Five Simple Steps to Better Typography: www.markboulton.co.uk/journal/comments/five-simple-steps-to-better-typography/

- Five Simple Steps to Designing Grid Systems: www.markboulton.co.uk/journal/comments/five-simple-steps-to-designing-grid-systems/

When it comes to web design, some conventions are used, and others are ignored. In fact, while web designers take the utmost care to get layouts right, scant few give the same thought to text, merely choosing a font and arbitrarily setting other values, if they set them at all. Once, this could be excused, but CSS has enabled web type to come a long way, and although the same degree of control as print-based type isn't possible, you can do a lot more than just choose your preferred font for headings and body copy.

In this chapter, we'll take a look at the various components available when working on web-based type (including elements and CSS properties) and provide some exercises, the results from which you can use for the basis of your own sites' type. As a final note in this introduction, it's also worth mentioning spelling and grammar. Both of these are clearly way outside the scope of this book, but they're things designers tend to overlook. A site with a lot of grammatical and spelling errors, especially in larger text (such as headings and pull quotes), looks unprofessional. If in doubt when working on sites, consult (or get your client to consult) a copywriter.

> Note: There are a couple of books worth digging out for more information on typography and language. A decent primer on type design is Helen Lupton's Thinking with Type. For an entertaining (if not entirely accurate) history of the English language, read Bill Bryson's The Mother Tongue.

Styling text the old-fashioned way (or, why we hate font tags)

Styling text online used to be all about font tags. When Netscape introduced the font element—complete with size and color attributes—web designers wept tears of joy. When Microsoft announced it would go further, adding a face attribute (enabling you to specify the font family), web designers were giddy with anticipation. But things didn't go according to plan. Page sizes bloated as designers created pages filled with fonts of myriad sizes and colors. Web users looked on aghast, wondering whether giant, orange body copy was really the way to go and whether it was worth waiting twice as long for such abominations to download.

More important, it became apparent that font tags caused problems, including the following:

- Inconsistent display across browsers and platforms

- The requirement for font tags to be applied to individual elements

- Difficulty ensuring fonts were consistent sitewide, because of having to style individual elements

- HTML geared toward presentation rather than logical structure

- Large HTML documents because of all the extra elements

In addition, working with font tags is a time-consuming, boring process, and yet some (although, thankfully, increasingly few) web designers remain blissfully ignorant of such problems. In my opinion, if font tags weren't HTML elements, I'd suggest they be taken out back and shot. Today, there is no reason whatsoever to stick with them. Text can be rapidly styled sitewide with CSS, and, as you'll learn later in this chapter, CSS provides you with a greater degree of control than font tags ever did. More crucially, font tags encourage badly formed documents, with designers relying on inline elements to style things like headings, when there are perfectly good HTML elements better suited to that purpose.

HTML should be reserved for content and structure, and CSS for design. Web pages should be composed of appropriate elements for each piece of content. This method of working, called *semantic markup*, is what we're going to discuss next.

A new beginning: semantic markup

Essentially, *semantic markup* means "using the appropriate tag at the relevant time," and well-formed semantic markup is an essential aspect of any website. The following is an example of the wrong way of doing things—relying on font tags to create a heading and double line breaks (

) for separating paragraphs:

```
<font size="7" color="red" face="Helvetica">Article heading</font>
<br /><br />
Lorem ipsum dolor sit amet, consectetuer adipiscing elit. Sed aliquet
  elementum erat. Integer diam mi, venenatis non, cursus a,
  hendrerit at, mi.
<br /><br />
Quisque faucibus lorem eget sapien. In urna sem, vehicula ut, mattis
  et, venenatis at, velit. Ut sodales lacus sed eros.
```

Tags should always relate to the content so that if the styling is removed, there is always an indication of what role each element plays within the document structure and hierarchy—for instance, there would be no visual clues as to the importance of the heading. Also, the use of double line breaks (

) instead of paragraph tags means the "paragraphs" cannot be styled in CSS, because there's nothing to inform the web browser what the content actually is.

Instead, the example should be marked up like this:

```
<h1>Article heading</h1>
<p>Lorem ipsum dolor sit amet, consectetuer adipiscing elit. Sed
  aliquet elementum erat. Integer diam mi, venenatis non, cursus
  a, hendrerit at, mi.</p>
<p>Quisque faucibus lorem eget sapien. In urna sem, vehicula ut,
  mattis et, venenatis at, velit. Ut sodales lacus sed eros.</p>
```

Here, the heading is marked up with the relevant tags, and paragraph elements are used instead of double line breaks. This means the page's structural integrity is ensured, and the markup is logical and semantic. If the attached CSS styles are removed, the default formatting still makes obvious to the end user the importance of the headings and will visually display them as such.

In this section, we'll look at how to mark up paragraphs and headings, explore logical and physical styles, and discuss the importance of well-formed semantic markup.

Paragraphs and headings

With words making up the bulk of online content, the paragraph and heading HTML elements are of paramount importance. HTML provides six levels of headings, from h1 to h6, with h1 being the top-level heading. The adjacent image shows how these headings, along with a paragraph, typically appear by default in a browser.

```
<h1>Level one heading</h1>
<h2>Level two heading</h2>
<h3>Level three heading</h3>
<h4>Level four heading</h4>
<h5>Level five heading</h5>
<h6>Level six heading</h6>
<p>Default paragraph size</p>
```

By default, browsers put margins around paragraphs and headings. This can vary from browser to browser, but it can be controlled by CSS. Therefore, there's no excuse for using double line breaks to avoid default paragraph margins affecting web page layouts.

Level one heading

Level two heading

Level three heading

Level four heading

Level five heading

Level six heading

Default paragraph size

Despite the typical default sizes, level-five and level-six headings are not intended as "tiny text" but as a way to enable you to structure your document, which is essential, because headings help with assistive technology, enabling people who are visually disabled to efficiently surf the Web.

In terms of general usage, it's generally recommended to stick to just one h1 element per sectioning element, used for the section's primary heading. As discussed in Chapter 2, a sectioning element is an <article>, <nav>, <section>, or <aside>. The next level down—and the first level in a sidebar—would be h2, and then h3, and so on. Take care not to use too many heading levels, though; unless you're working on complex legal documents, you really shouldn't be getting past level four. If you are, look at restructuring your document.

Logical and physical styles

Once text is in place, it's common to add inline styles, which can be achieved by way of logical and physical styles. Many designers are confused by the difference between the two, especially because equivalents (such as the logical strong and physical b) tend to be displayed the same in browsers. The difference is that logical styles describe what the content is, whereas physical styles merely define what the content looks like. This subtle difference is more apparent when you take into account things like screen readers.

In the markup, I like to emphasize things; a screen reader emphasizes the text surrounded by the em tags. However, replace the em tags with i tags, and the screen reader won't emphasize the word, although in a visual web browser the two pieces of markup will almost certainly look identical.

Styles for emphasis (bold and italic)

Physical styles enable you to make text bold and <i>italic</i>, and these are the most commonly used inline physical styles. However, logical styles are becoming much more widespread (the majority of web design applications, such as Dreamweaver, now default to logical styles rather than physical ones).

Typically, strong emphasis emboldens text in a visual web browser, and emphasis italicizes text.

Deprecated and nonstandard physical styles

Many physical elements are considered obsolete, including the infamous blink (a Netscape "innovation" used to flash text on and off, amusingly still supported in Firefox). Some physical styles are deprecated: u (underline) and s (strikethrough; also strike) have CSS equivalents using the text-decoration property (text-decoration: underline, and text-decoration: line-through, respectively).

The small element

The small element is used to decrease the size of inline text (even text defined in pixels in CSS). An example of the use of small might be in marking up text that is semantically small print.

Note, however, that the change in size depends on individual web browsers, so it's important that you define specific values in CSS for the small element when used in context.

Subscript and superscript

This leaves two useful physical styles. The first, sub, renders as text subscript text. The second, sup, renders text as superscript text, respectively. These are useful for scientific documents, although there is a drawback: characters are displayed at the same size, defined by the browser. You can get around this by using a CSS tag selector and defining a new font size for each element. The following code shows how to do this, and the accompanying screenshot shows a default sup element (at the top of the image) and a CSS-styled sup element (at the bottom) in use.

```
sup {
font-size: 70%;
}
```

$$e=mc^2$$

$$e=mc^2$$

Logical styles for programming-oriented content

Several logical styles do similar jobs, are programming-oriented, and are usually displayed in a monospace font:

```
<code>Denotes a code sample.</code>
<kbd>Indicates text entered by the user.</kbd>
<samp>Indicates a programming sample.</samp>
```

The var element also relates to programming, signifying a variable. However, it is usually displayed in italics.

Block quotes, quote citations, and definitions

The blockquote element is used to define a lengthy quotation and must be set within a block-level element. Its cite attribute can be used to define the online location of quoted material. See the "Creating drop caps and pull quotes using CSS" section for more on using this element.

> *Note that some web design applications—notably, early versions of Dreamweaver—used the blockquote element to indent blocks of text, and this bad habit is still used by some designers. Don't do this. If you want to indent some text, use CSS.*

For shorter quotes that are inline, the q element can be used. This is also supposed to add language-specific quotes before and after the content between the element's tags. These quotes vary by browser—Firefox and Internet Explorer add "smart" quotes; Safari, Chrome, and Opera add "straight" quotes.

Finally, to indicate the defining instance of a term, you use the dfn element. This is used to draw attention to the first use of such a term and is also typically displayed in italics.

Abbreviations

Abbreviations assist with accessibility, enabling you to provide users with full forms of abbreviations and acronyms by way of the title attribute:

```
<abbr title="Cascading Style Sheets">CSS</abbr>
```

This has two uses. For one, it allows users with disabilities (using screen readers) to access the full form of the words in question. But anyone using a visual web browser can access the information, too, because title attribute contents are usually displayed as a tooltip when you hover your mouse over elements they're used on.

To further draw attention to an abbreviation or acronym, style the tag in CSS (using a tag selector), thereby making all such tags consistent across an entire website. The following code is an example of this, the results of which are shown in the example to the right (including the tooltip triggered by hovering over the abbr element, which has a title attribute).

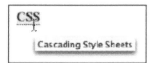

```
abbr {
  border-bottom: 1px dotted #000000;
  background-color: yellow;
}
```

> *Note: You can provide an additional aid to users by setting cursor to help in CSS for abbr elements. This changes the cursor to a question mark while hovering over the element.*

Elements for inserted and deleted text

The del and ins elements are used, respectively, to indicate deleted text and inserted text, typically in a manner akin to the tracking features of word-processing packages, although they do not include the tracking functionality. The del element usually appears in strike-through format, whereas ins usually appears underlined. Both accept cite and datetime attributes. The former enables you to define a URL that explains why text was inserted or deleted; the latter enables you to define the time and date that the text was amended—see the <ins> and <del> entries in Appendix A for accepted formats.

Note that these elements cannot be nested inside each other, for obvious reasons. The following is an example of their use:

```
<p>I <del>deleted this</del> and then <ins>inserted this</ins>.</p>
```

> I ~~deleted this~~ and then <u>inserted this</u>.

The default style of the ins element can prove problematic online. Because links are underlined by default, users may attempt to click text marked up as inserted text and wonder why nothing happens. It's a good idea to amend the tag's visual appearance by changing the underline color. This can be done by removing the default underline and replacing it with a bottom border, like so:

```
ins {
  text-decoration: none;
  border-bottom: 1px solid red;
}
```

The bottom border resembles an underline, although it appears lower than the default underline, which further differentiates inserted text from hypertext links.

The importance of well-formed markup

Many logical styles are rarely used online, because they look no different from text marked up using the likes of the i element. However, as mentioned earlier, physical appearance alone misses the point of HTML. Always using the most appropriate relevant element means that you can later individually style each element in CSS, overriding the default appearance if you want. If the likes of citations, defining instances, and variables are all marked up with i instead of cite, dfn, and var, there's no way of distinguishing each type of content and no way of manipulating their appearance on an individual basis. Well-formed markup involves more than ensuring visual flexibility, though. Use of the cite tag, for instance, enables you to manipulate the Document Object Model (DOM) to extract a bibliography or list of quotations from a page or even a full website. The ability to style logical tags like this with CSS is likely to be of increasing rather than diminishing importance.

The importance of end tags

While we're on the subject of well-formed markup, we'll revisit the importance of end tags. As mentioned earlier, XHTML demands that all tags be closed. Most browsers let you get away with ignoring some end tags, though, such as on paragraphs. Some designers may still have bad habits from working with HTML, for which many end tags are optional. Omit many others at your peril. For instance, overlook a heading element end tag, and a browser considers subsequent content to be part of the heading and displays it accordingly. As shown in the following image, two paragraphs are displayed as a heading because the earlier heading element lacks an end tag.

A heading, not closed

Lorem ipsum dolor sit amet, consectetuer adipiscing elit. Morbi commodo, ipsum sed pharetra gravida, orci magna rhoncus neque, id pulvinar odio lorem non turpis. Nullam sit amet enim. Suspendisse id velit vitae ligula volutpat condimentum. Aliquam erat volutpat. Sed quis velit. Nulla facilisi.

Nulla libero. Vivamus pharetra posuere sapien. Nam consectetuer. Sed aliquam, nunc eget euismod

A similar problem occurs when you accidentally omit end tags when using logical and physical elements. For instance, forget to close an emphasis element, and the remainder of the web page may be displayed in italics.

> *Note: Some designers when hand-coding create both start and end tags at the same time and then populate the element with content, ensuring end tags are not forgotten.*

Styling text using CSS

HTML is intended as a structural markup language, but the Web's increasing popularity meant it got "polluted" with tags designed for presentation. This made HTML more complex than it needed to be, and such tags soon became a headache for web designers trying to style page elements, such as text. In the bad ol' days (the end of the 1990s), you'd often see source code like this:

```
<font face="Helvetica" size="3" color="#333333"> This markup is
  <font size="+3"><small>really </small></font>bad, but it was sort of
  the norm in the 1990s.</font>
```

WYSIWYG tools would insert new tags to override previous ones, adding to the page weight and making it tough to ensure visual consistency sitewide. By and large, CSS eradicates these problems and enables far more control over text, as you'll see in the following sections.

This is a boon for graphic designers who used to loathe HTML's lack of typographical control. However, the level of freedom evident in print design still isn't quite so on the Web. Restrictions imposed by browsers and the screen must be taken into account, such as it being harder to read type on-screen than in print. This is largely related to resolution. Even magazines with fairly low-quality print tend to be printed at around 200 dpi or more—more than twice the resolution of a typical monitor. This means that very small text (favored by many designers, who think such small text looks neat) becomes tricky to read on-screen, because there aren't enough pixels to create a coherent image.

I'll note restrictions such as this at appropriate times during this section on styling text with CSS, thereby providing advice on striking a balance between the visual appearance and the practicality of web-based text.

Defining font colors

In CSS, the color property value defines the foreground color of the relevant CSS element, which for text sets its color. This can be set using hex, keywords, RGB, or RGBA. The following examples show each method in turn, and all have the same result: setting paragraphs to black.

```
p {
  color: #000000;
}
p {
  color: black;
}
p {
  color: rgb(0,0,0);
}
p {
  color: rgba(0,0,0,1);
}
```

Declaring colors using RGB is rare in web design—hex is most popular, especially because CSS supports so few keywords (see the section "Working with hex" in Chapter 4).

Remember to test your choices on both Windows and Mac, because there are differences in the default color space for each platform. In general terms, the Mac default display settings are brighter (or Windows is darker, depending on your outlook on life); if you use subtle dark tones on the Mac or very light tones on Windows, the result might be tricky to view on the other platform.

It is also a good idea to test on as many different monitors and devices available to you. While your site might display perfectly on an LCD monitor, it might not on a CRT. Smartphones and tablets are also becoming increasingly popular for viewing websites, and they have drastically different display technologies.

This should cause few problems with text, but some designers insist on rendering text with very little contrast to the background color, and this ends up being even harder to read on a different platform or monitor from the one on which it was created.

> *The main tip to keep in mind for color with regard to web-based text is simple: always provide plenty of contrast so that your text remains readable.*

Defining fonts

The font-family property enables you to specify a list of font face values, starting with your preferred first choice, continuing with alternates (in case your choice isn't installed on the user's machine), and terminating in a generic font family, which causes the browser to substitute a similar font (think of it as a last resort).

```
selector {
  font-family: preferred, "alterate 1", "alterate 2", generic;
}
```

The most common generic font family names are serif and sans-serif, although when you're using monospace fonts (such as Courier New), you should end your list with monospace.

Multiple-word font family names must be quoted (such as "Trebuchet MS" and "Times New Roman"). You can use single or double quotes—just be consistent. Single-word font family names should never be quoted. Examples of font-family in use are as follows:

```
h1 {
  font-family: Arial, Helvetica, sans-serif;
}
p {
  font-family: Georgia, "Times New Roman", Times, serif;
}
pre {
  font-family: Courier, "Courier New", Monaco, monospace;
}
```

> Note: *pre* is the element for preformatted text, used to display monospace text in an identical fashion to how it's formatted in the original HTML document. It's commonly used for online FAQs, film scripts, and the like.

Web-embedded fonts and web-safe fonts

Print designers have a world of fonts at their disposal, and now with the ability to embed any font you want into your website, web designers do as well. There is hope that web-embedded fonts will soon abolish the use of regular system fonts, which will enable a web designer to choose any typeface or font style they want. While all major browsers support embedding fonts, they don't all do it in the same way. It is important to include web-safe fonts as a fallback to keep your design consistent and prevent the layout of your design from breaking for mobile and older versions of major browsers. Web-safe fonts are fonts that are common across different operation systems such as Mac OS X, Windows, and Linux.

Over the next few pages, I'll provide an overview of different available fonts for the Web, but there are some handy online references that you should also bookmark. A page comparing fonts common to the Mac and Windows is available at `www.ampsoft.net/webdesign-l/WindowsMacFonts.html`, and `www.codestyle.org/css/font-family/sampler-Monospace.shtml` details available monospace fonts for various systems.

Embedding web fonts

Embedding web fonts allows web designers to use local or remotely hosted fonts in their designs without requiring the user to download the font. Using web-embedded fonts is easy and can be done by using the following CSS syntax:

```
@font-face {
  font-face: 'webfont';
  src: url('http://./') format('frmt')
}
selector {
  font-family: webfont;
  font-size: 22pt;
}
```

Since each major browser implements embedding web fonts using different formats, five different formats need to be included to ensure your font is displayed correctly across each browser. These formats are TrueType, OpenType, Embedded OpenType, Web Open Font Format, and SVG fonts. The bulletproof CSS syntax looks like this:

```
@font-face {
  font-family: Graublauweb;
  src: url('Graublauweb.eot'); /* IE9 Compatibility Modes */
  src: url('Graublauweb.eot?') format('eot'),   /* IE6-IE8 */
  url('Graublauweb.woff') format('woff'), /* Modern Browsers */
  url('Graublauweb.ttf')  format('truetype'), /* Safari, Android, iOS */
  url('Graublauweb.svg#svgGraublauweb') format('svg'); /* Legacy iOS */
}
```

Just like in print design, there are a number of commercial, freeware, and open source fonts, which can be embedded in your web design. Two great resources for free fonts are www.webfonts.info/ and www.google.com/webfonts.

As time goes on, legacy browsers and browsers that do not support web fonts will disappear, but until then, falling back to web-safe system fonts is key to having your website support these browsers.

Sans-serif fonts for the Web

Arial is a common font choice, largely because of its dominance on Windows. Its poor design makes it unreadable at small sizes and a poor choice for body copy, although it can be of use for headings. Mac users should be wary of choosing Helvetica—it's an excellent font, but it's not generally shipped with Windows. Although you can specify fallback fonts in CSS, again, there's little point in making your first choice something that the majority of people won't see.

> Note: Despite its lack of penetration on Windows, Helvetica is often used as a fallback sans-serif font, because of its prevalence on Linux.

Better choices for body copy are Verdana or Trebuchet MS. The former is typically a good choice, because its spacious nature makes it readable at any size. Its bubbly design renders it less useful for headings, though. Trebuchet MS is perhaps less readable, but it has plenty of character and is sometimes an interesting alternative, simply because it isn't used all that much online.

In recent times, Lucida variants have become popular, because of Apple using it not only as the default font in Mac OS X but also on its website. Despite Lucida Grande not being available for Windows, Lucida Sans Unicode is common and similar enough to be used as a first fallback. Usefully, Lucida is common on UNIX systems, meaning that sites using Lucida variants can look fairly similar textwise across all three major operating systems. Another pairing—albeit one that's less common—is Tahoma and Geneva, so use those with care, providing more generic fallbacks.

See the following images for a comparison of several sans-serif fonts on Mac (left) and Windows (right).

Arial (bold, 24px) Arial (24px) Arial (12px) Arial (9px)	**Arial (bold, 24px)** Arial (24px) Arial (12px) Arial (9px)
Lucida Grande (bold, 24px) Lucida Grande (24px) Lucida Grande (12px) Lucida Grande (9px)	**Lucida Grande (bold, 24px)** Lucida Grande (24px) Lucida Grande (12px) Lucida Grande (9px)
Trebuchet MS (bold, 24px) Trebuchet MS (24px) Trebuchet MS (12px) Trebuchet MS (9px)	**Trebuchet MS (bold, 24px)** Trebuchet MS (24px) Trebuchet MS (12px) Trebuchet MS (9px)
Verdana (bold, 24px) Verdana (24px) Verdana (12px) Verdana (9px)	**Verdana (bold, 24px)** Verdana (24px) Verdana (12px) Verdana (9px)

Serif fonts for the Web

Although popular in print, serif fonts fare less well online. If using serifs, ensure you render them large enough so that they don't break down into an illegible mess. Georgia is perhaps the best available web-safe serif, especially when used at sizes equivalent to 12 pixels and bigger, and it can be more suitable than a sans-serif if you're working with traditional subject matter or if you're attempting to emulate print articles (such as in the following screenshot of the online column Revert to Saved; www.reverttosaved.com).

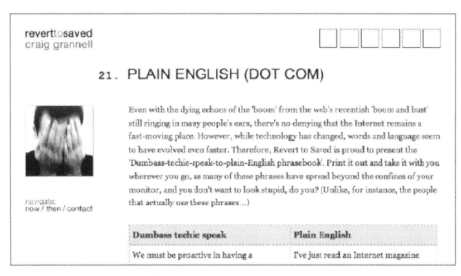

The other commonly available serif font, Times New Roman (Times being a rough equivalent on Linux systems), is inferior to Georgia but worth using as a fallback. Like Arial, its popularity is the result of its prevalence as a system font.

Elsewhere, Palatino is fairly common—installed by default on Windows (as Palatino Linotype) and available on Mac systems that have Classic or iWork installed. Mac owners with Office will also have the virtually identical Book Antiqua. That said, if using these fonts, you'll still need to fall back to safer serifs, as mentioned earlier.

See the following illustration for a comparison of serif fonts on Mac (left) and Windows (right).

Georgia (bold, 24px)
Georgia (24px)
Georgia (12px)
Georgia (9px)

Palatino (bold, 24px)
Palatino (24px)
Palatino (12px)
Palatino (9px)

Times New Roman (bold, 24px)
Times New Roman (24px)
Times New Roman (12px)
Times New Roman (9px)

Georgia (bold, 24px)
Georgia (24px)
Georgia (12px)
Georgia (9px)

Palatino Linotype (bold, 24px)
Palatino Linotype (24px)
Palatino Linotype (12px)
Palatino Linotype (9px)

Times New Roman (bold, 24px)
Times New Roman (24px)
Times New Roman (12px)
Times New Roman (9px)

Fonts for headings and monospace type

The remaining "safe" fonts are typically display fonts (for headings) or monospace fonts for when each character needs to be the same width—for example, when adding code examples to a web page.

Arial Black and Impact are reasonable choices for headings, although they must be handled with care. The bold version of Impact looks terrible (and isn't displayed at all in some browsers), and some browsers by default render headings in bold, so this must be overridden in CSS. Often, large versions of fonts mentioned in the previous two sections are superior.

Courier New is more useful and a good choice when you need a monospace font. Note that falling back to Courier for Linux is recommended. The pairing of Lucida Console (Windows) and Lucida Sans Typewriter or Monaco (Mac) may also be suitable for monospace work, if you're looking for a less "computery" feel.

Few other fonts are worth a mention, barring perhaps Comic Sans MS, which is inexplicably popular with novice web designers. To give the font its due, it is readable, but its quirky and unprofessional nature makes it unsuitable for most purposes (even comic artists eschew it in favor of personalized fonts).

The following image shows several of the fonts mentioned in this section, again with Mac versions on the left and Windows versions on the right.

Arial Black (bold, 24px)
Arial Black (24px)
Arial Black (12px)
Arial Black (9px)

Courier New (bold, 24px)
Courier New (24px)
Courier New (12px)
Courier New (9px)

Comic Sans MS (bold, 24px)
Comic Sans MS (24px)
Comic Sans MS (12px)
Comic Sans MS (9px)

Impact (bold, 24px)
Impact (24px)
Impact (12px)
Impact (9px)

Lucida Sans Typewriter
Lucida Sans Typewriter
Lucida Sans Typewriter
Lucida Sans Typewriter

Arial Black (bold, 24px)
Arial Black (24px)
Arial Black (12px)
Arial Black (9px)

Courier New (bold, 24px)
Courier New (24px)
Courier New (12px)
Courier New (9px)

Comic Sans MS (bold, 24px)
Comic Sans MS (24px)
Comic Sans MS (12px)
Comic Sans MS (9px)

Impact (bold, 24px)
Impact (24px)
Impact (12px)
Impact (9px)

Lucida Console
Lucida Console (24px)
Lucida Console (12px)
Lucida Console (9px)

Mac vs. Windows: anti-aliasing

When choosing fonts, it's worth noting that they look different on Mac and Windows. On Macs all browsers use the system default rendering engine called Core Text to render anti-alias on-screen text. On Windows, Internet Explorer 8 smooths type via the font-smoothing technology ClearType, while Internet Explorer 9 and 10 use the DirectWrite rendering engine

For body copy, font smoothing (or not) isn't a major problem; although some prefer aliased text and some prefer anti-aliased, both are fine, as long as the font size is large enough. However, when it comes to rendering large text—such as for headings—aliased text is significantly less visually pleasing.

> *Note: Aliased text is a simplified version of the original font, reduced to pixels made up of red, green, and blue subpixels. Anti-aliased text attempts to emulate the soft curves of the original font by introducing gray or colored pixels at the edges.*

Although arguments rage regarding which is the best method of displaying fonts on-screen, this is a moot point for web designers, because you don't control the end user's setup and therefore must be aware of each possibility.

Using images for text

Limitations imposed by how different browsers render both embedded and web-safe fonts lead some designers to seek out alternative methods of creating online type. It's common to use graphics (mostly GIFs, but sometimes Flash, because of its vector-based, scalable nature) for text. If you have to follow a corporate design style under pain of death, the ability to use graphics can be a lifesaver—after all, most browsers happily render images, and they can be marked up within heading elements, so you can control things like margins via CSS and also retain the structural integrity of your document.

However, graphical text has its share of problems:

- Some browsers do not enable you to resize graphical text in a browser.

- Because the Web is low-resolution, when a page is printed out, graphical text looks pixelated and of poor quality.

- Although GIF-based text tends to be small in terms of file size, it's still larger than HTML-based text.

- People using alternate browsers, such as screen readers, cannot "see" graphical text (although you can use the alt attribute to compensate).

- Graphical text cannot be copied and pasted.

- Graphical text cannot be read by search engines.

- Graphical text is a pain to update. To change a word, you must rework the original image and export and upload it, and if the image size has changed, you must edit the appropriate HTML documents and upload those, too.

In my opinion, graphics should be used as a last resort. A company's style can be made apparent by the use of a corporate logo and other imagery rather than by the use of a font. Also, never, ever render body copy as an image. There are many sites out there with body copy rendered as images, and quite frankly, every one of them makes me want to scream. Such sites are often full of typos (perhaps because amending them requires the entire graphic to be reworked, reexported, and uploaded again), cannot be printed at quality, and cannot be copied to a text editor. Some suggest this means the site's text is "secure." But this goes against one of the fundamental benefits of the Web: that people can share information and that it can be easily copied and sent on to others. Sure, this presents copyright implications, but everything online is subject to copyright anyway. Also, plenty of sites commit the cardinal sin of rendering things like contact details as a graphic—I'm sure their customers very much appreciate having to type such things out by hand rather than just being able to copy them into their digital address books.

Image-replacement techniques

If you need a greater degree of typographical control over a portion of text, such as the site's main heading, there is an option that enables you to include an image and also enable the text to remain in place, which is useful for users surfing the Web with screen readers. This is generally known as image replacement. Note that the technique should be used with care and sparingly—even from a basic practical standpoint, it doesn't make a great deal of sense to set all of your headings as images, simply because it takes time to create and export each one.

Of the techniques available for replacing images, the most common is to assign the relevant piece of text (usually a heading) a class value in HTML and also add a dummy span element before its content:

```
<h1 class="aFancyHeading"><span></span>A fancy heading</h1>
```

In an image editor, an image-based version of the heading is created and saved, and its dimensions are measured. Example files for this are a-fancy-heading.gif, image-replacement.css, and image-replacement.html, located in the chapter 3 folder. In the CSS file, you'll see rules created to define the dimensions of the heading (.aFancyHeading) and span (.aFancyHeading span). The heading's position value is set to relative, and the span element is then positioned in an absolute fashion, which ensures that it sits over the text-based heading's content. The width and height values ensure that the span (and therefore its background image) expands to fill its container. (Note that when used in conjunction with links, it's useful to also set display: block within the CSS rule so that the entire area becomes clickable and the cursor becomes a pointer—this is because some versions of Internet Explorer use the arrow pointer instead of the usual finger pointer. Alternatively, set cursor to pointer in CSS.) The overflow: hidden property/value pair ensures text doesn't peek out from behind the image—an issue that sometimes occurs in Internet Explorer or when text is resized. To deal with zoomed text in IE 7, it may also be necessary to set a pixel font-size value for the heading that's smaller than the height of the image.

> Note: Setting *overflow* to *hidden* can be an issue when this technique is used in conjunction with linked replaced elements, such as linked mastheads and logos. When tabbing through links, replaced elements that have an *overflow* setting of *hidden* will become displaced on receiving the focus, revealing the underlying text as well as the image overlaying it. Caution needs to be used here.

The following image shows a page using this technique with and without CSS.

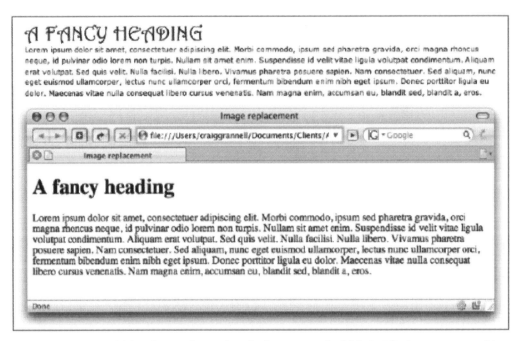

Some methods focus on hiding the text by setting display to none in CSS, but that can cause problems for screen readers, so avoid doing this. Others use text-indent to shift the text off of the page, although using absolute positioning with negative top and left coordinates is better—this prevents vertical space being taken up by the offset text, which is quite often noticeable, especially if margins haven't been controlled.

> *Note: Scalable Inman Flash Replacement (sIFR) is an alternative to replacing text with GIF images. Instead, it uses a combination of CSS, Flash, and JavaScript to switch out a block of text. Note that although this provides a great deal of typographic flexibility, it should still be used sparingly—pages where too much text is switched out using sIFR tend to be extremely sluggish. See sIFR Beauty (www.alvit.de/sifrbeauty/sifr-resources.php) for resources and Mike Davidson's site (www.mikeindustries.com/sifr/) for further information.*

Defining font size and line height

In theory, defining font sizes should be easy enough. You use the font-size property, and then you can set the value to an absolute size, a relative size, a length, or a percentage. For instance, you might set the following:

```
h1 {
  font-size: 20px;
}
p {
  font-size: 12px;
}
```

Alternatively, you might go for something like this:

```
h1 {
  font-size: 150%;
}
p {
  font-size: 90%;
}
```

Each method of sizing fonts has its advantages and disadvantages, which we'll briefly explore in this section of the book.

Setting text in pixels

Many designers specify font sizes in pixels, largely because pixels are the only measurement that allows you to be relatively certain that your text will look pretty much identical across various browsers and platforms (in the same way that sizing page sections in pixels enables you to keep output consistent). Unfortunately, unlike every other major browser on the market, Internet Explorer for Windows cannot resize pixel-based text, which creates an accessibility problem (although a user can choose to ignore font sizes via the little-known accessibility controls). Internet Explorer's `Text Size` menu only allows resizing of text sized using legacy methods, keywords, or relative units other than pixels. (Note that Internet Explorer 7 can zoom the entire page, but not the text alone.)

Therefore, if you decide to size text in pixels, ensure that your text is very readable. Test it on various people and listen to feedback. If complaints come your way regarding the fact that someone "had trouble reading the words" or rooted around for a microscope before giving up and playing solitaire, you need to increase your pixel size settings. The resulting page might not look quite as "designery," but at least people will be able to read it.

Setting text using keywords and percentages

A combination of keywords and percentages became fairly popular for a while on the Web. Available keyword values are xx-small, x-small, small, medium, large, x-large, and xx-large. A keyword is used to set the base value, using a body selector in CSS, and percentages are then used to set sizes for specific elements, such as headings, paragraphs, and lists. Here's an example:

```
body {
  font-size: small;
}
p {
  font-size: 93%;
(})
```

Keyword values don't compound, and most modern browsers set a lower limit, even on xx-small, so text tends never to enter the realm of the illegible.

Although Internet Explorer for Windows can resize text set with keywords (as can all other browsers), this method has several disadvantages. The most problematic from a design perspective is that percentage values aren't particularly consistent across browsers and platforms. Scaling tends to "jump" at fairly arbitrary percentage sizes, so while 93% may look the same in all browsers (using default font-size settings, at least), 94% may look like 100% in one and 93% in another. Also, it's often tricky to equate percentages with the pixel (or point) sizes typically used in mock-ups.

In Internet Explorer, fonts that are set to Small in the View➤Text Size menu can make keyword-set CSS text hard to read, but users can increase the text size by using a more sensible setting. Also, it's worth noting that this is up to user choice, and having a tiny minority of users screwing up their own settings and potentially ending up with unreadable text is better than the vast majority not being able to resize the text because its size is defined in pixels. Still, there's a better method for achieving this, as you'll see.

Setting text using percentages and ems

As mentioned, the problem with sizing text in pixels is that the text is not resizable in Internet Explorer. The main problem with using keywords and percentages is that the text size can be different across platforms and difficult to define—at least in terms of hitting a specific target size. This third method—and the one I typically use for websites I design—enables you to create font sizes that are targeted at a pixel size but are also resizable in Internet Explorer, since the measurements are relative units.

The system works by first setting a base font size of 62.5% using a body selector:

```
body {
  font-size: 62.5%;
}
```

Since most browsers have a default font size of 16 pixels, the previous rule then sets the default size to 62.5% of that value—in other words, 10 pixels. From here, ems can be used to define font sizes of specific elements, using values that are one-tenth the target pixel size:

```
h1 {
    font-size: 2.0em; /* will be the equivalent of 20px */
}
p {
    font-size: 1.2em; /* will be the equivalent of 12px */
}
```

The system isn't perfect—relative values defined in ems can be inherited, so if a list item is within another list item, the size of the nested item(s) may increase or decrease, depending on the value assigned to the parent. However, override rules can easily get around this problem (see "Dealing with font-size inheritance" later in the chapter), and the method generally leads to more satisfactory results from a design, control, and user point of view than either of the other two methods mentioned. It is worth noting, however, that this method is somewhat reliant on the user—if someone has changed the default font size in their browser, your design may not look as intended on their browser, since the value defined for body may be 62.5% of something other than 16 pixels. Still, few people muck around with their browser settings, and the general consensus in the industry is that the 62.5% method is the one to go for.

> Note: If using this method, ensure that the *font-size* setting of all text-oriented elements you use on the site is adjusted; otherwise, you'll end up with some illegible text set at 62.5% of the default font size. Also ensure you test your work at a range of text sizes in various browsers to ensure things still look OK if the text is zoomed in or out.

There is one other thing to bear in mind, though: Internet Explorer (again). Although the majority of browser-specific issues are left until Chapter 9 of this book, we'll make an exception now. Internet Explorer has problems with text zooming when the font size is set below 100%, so an additional rule is required:

```
html {
    font-size: 100%;
}
```

This doesn't adversely affect other browsers, so you'll find this rule in the boilerplate documents from the download files, even though it should technically be in the conditional comments documents.

Setting text using rems

CSS3 has introduced a new sizing unit called the *root em* unit. The rem unit solves the problem of inherited ems in nested items by being relative to the root element or the html element of your document.

In the case of rem units, you define a base font size using the html selector:

```
html {
    font-size: 62.5%;
}
```

All remaining font sizes can be defined as follows:

```
h1 { font-size: 1.4rem; }
p { font-size: 1.2rem; }
```

It is important to consider older browsers that do not support rem units. This can be done by defining a font size in pixel units as well as rem units.

```
h1 { font-size: 14px; font-size: 1.4rem; }
p { font-size: 12px; font-size: 1.2rem; }
```

Setting line height

Graphic designers will be familiar with leading, and the CSS line-height property enables you to set this. Generally speaking, it's a good idea to be fairly generous with leading for web pages, because text is harder to read on-screen than in print; by placing larger gaps between each line, the eye can more easily scan through large blocks of text.

When setting line-height, you have various options and can use a number, length, or percentage:

```
h1 {
  font-size: 14px;
  line-height: 20px;
}
h2 {
  font-size: 1.3em;
  line-height: 1.6em;
}
p {
  font-size: 1.1em;
  line-height: 1.5;
}
```

The difference between the font-size and line-height measurements is the leading value. Half the value is applied above the text and half below. Should you use a number alone, rather than a length or percentage, that value is multiplied by the font-size setting to define the line height. For example, if font-size is set to 10px and line-height is set to 1.5, the line-height value becomes 15px.

Many self-proclaimed web designers who have no graphic design experience ignore the line-height property, but, as mentioned earlier, it's essential for improving the legibility of a web page. In the following screenshots, the left images shows the default spacing, and the right one shows increased line height, resulting in increased legibility.

Defining font-style, font-weight, and font-variant

These three properties are straightforward. The first, font-style, enables you to set italic or oblique text. The former is often a defined face within the font, whereas the latter is usually computed. Typically, web browsers treat both the same, and only the italic value is in general use (except for the occasional use of normal—the default value—in order to override something set elsewhere).

An element's font-style is set like this:

```
h2 {
  font-style: italic;
}
```

The font-weight property is intended to make a font heavier or lighter, and despite the various available values, only bold and normal are in general use. This is detailed in full in the font-weight entry of Appendix D.

```
.introParagraph {
  font-weight: bold;
}
```

The font-variant property has three available values: normal (the default), small-caps, and inherit. The inherit value causes this element to use the font-variant settings of its parent element. Small caps are often used to deemphasize uppercase letters in abbreviations and acronyms and are similar in size to a typeface's lowercase characters. This property affects only lowercase letters, and the display of small caps varies across browsers and platforms—for example, older versions of Internet Explorer simply render such text entirely in normal caps (in other words, in standard uppercase letters).

When defining a font-face rule, it is important to set font-style and font-weight to normal to ensure that all browsers default to the same values. Webkit browsers need this definition, or else the font-face rule will ignore any weight or style commands applied to it.

CSS shorthand for font properties

The CSS properties discussed so far can be written in shorthand, enabling you to cut down on space and manage your CSS font settings with greater ease. Like other shorthand properties, some rules apply:

- Some browsers are more forgiving than others regarding required and optional values, but you should always specify the font-size and font-family values, in that order.

- Omitted values revert to default settings.

- The font-style, font-weight, and font-variant values, if included, should be placed at the start of the rule (in any order), prior to the font-size value.

- The font-size and line-height values can be combined using the syntax font-size/line-height (for example, 12px/16px for 12px font-size and 16px line-height).

A complete font declaration in shorthand could therefore look like this:

```
p {
  font: italic small-caps bold 100%/1.3em Arial, Helvetica,
    sans-serif;
}
```

The equivalent in longhand is the following:

```
p {
  font-style: italic;
  font-variant: small-caps;
  font-weight: bold;
  font-size: 100%;
  line-height: 1.3em;
  font-family: Arial, Helvetica, sans-serif;
}
```

As you can see, this is rather weightier!

An invalid font declaration is shown in the following code block. Here, the font-weight value (bold) is incorrectly placed after the font-family value, and the font-size value is missing.

```
p.invalid {
  font: Arial, Helvetica, sans-serif bold;
}
```

Controlling text element margins

By default, browsers place margins around block-level text-based elements (such as headings and paragraphs), which can be overridden by CSS. However, many designers get confused when dealing with margins, so a good rule of thumb is to first remove all element margins via the universal selector (see the "Zeroing margins and padding on all elements" section in Chapter 2 for more information).

```
* {
  margin: 0;
  padding: 0;
}
```

Once you've done this, you should primarily control spacing between text elements via the bottom margins:

```
h1, h2 {
  margin-bottom: 10px;
}
p {
  margin-bottom: 1em;
}
```

In the previous example, the margins below headings are small, enabling the eye to rapidly travel from the heading to the related body copy. The margin at the bottom of each paragraph is one character high.

Should you decide, after applying styles, that more room is required between paragraphs and subsequent headings, apply a top margin to the relevant level (or levels) of heading, but be aware that vertical margins collapse.

Later in the chapter, a few exercises will show how margins (along with various other settings) can affect the way a page looks and feels. Certainly, margin definitions shouldn't be throwaway—like in music, where the gaps are almost as important as the notes, the whitespace in typography is almost as important as the content.

Using text-indent for print-like paragraphs

Because of people's familiarity with nonindented paragraphs on the Web, the W3C recommends staying away from indented ones. However, there are times when designers yearn for a more print-based design, as in the following image.

For this effect, two things not previously discussed in this book are required: the text-indent CSS property and an adjacent sibling selector. This type of selector uses the syntax A+B, where B is the subject of the selector. For paragraph indentation, the CSS rule would look something like the following code block:

```
p+p {
  text-indent: 1.5em;
}
```

In plain English, this is saying, "If a paragraph follows another paragraph, indent the text by 1.5 ems." Therefore, paragraphs preceded by a different element, such as a heading, won't be indented, as is traditional in print.

> Note that prior to version 7, Internet Explorer didn't support adjacent sibling selectors, and so this effect won't work in version 6 or older of Microsoft's browser. A workaround would be to use a style sheet linked via a conditional comment to indent all paragraphs for Internet Explorer 6 and older. See the "Dealing with Internet Explorer bugs" section in Chapter 9 for more on conditional comments.

Setting letter-spacing and word-spacing

The letter-spacing and word-spacing properties work in the same way, taking length values or a default of normal. For letter-spacing, the value increases whitespace between characters, and for word-spacing, the defined value increases whitespace between words. Negative values are permitted, which cause characters or words to bunch together (or *kern*, if you're a graphic designer). A certain amount of experimentation is recommended if you decide to use these properties. Because the Web's resolution is low, subtle kerning changes are hard to achieve online, and the results often end up looking clunky. Also, spacing varies from platform to platform. One occasion when letter-spacing is worth experimenting with, however, is when styling headings for web pages: a small increase in the letter-spacing value can help further distinguish headings from body copy.

Examples of these properties in use are shown in the following code block:

```
h1 {
  letter-spacing: 3px;
}
h2 {
  word-spacing: 2px;
}
```

Controlling case with text-transform

The text-transform property enables you to change the case of letters within an element. Available values are capitalize, uppercase, lowercase, and none (the default). The uppercase and lowercase values force the text of the applied element into the relevant case regardless of the original content (for example, enabling you to override the case of the original content for ensuring that headings are consistent sitewide), whereas capitalize sets the first letter of each word in uppercase.

In the following example, the first heading is styled as uppercase, the second as lowercase, and the third as capitalize. Note that I wouldn't recommend such a mix of styles in a website—these rules are just examples of the properties in use.

Here's the HTML:

```
<h1>A heading</h1>
<h2>Another heading</h2>
<h3>A third heading</h3>
```

A HEADING

another heading

A Third Heading

Here's the CSS:

```
h1 {
  text-transform: uppercase;
}
h2 {
  text-transform: lowercase;
}
h3 {
  text-transform: capitalize;
}
```

Creating alternatives with classes and spans

It's common in web design to define alternatives to the rules set for tag selectors (h1, h2, p, and so on). This tends to happen most often in one of two situations. The first is when creating alternate styles for a portion of a web page. (As in print, it's often beneficial to use different text for sidebars and boxouts—stand-alone boxes on a magazine page, either housing supplementary information to the main article or entirely independent pieces that need to be visually distinct from other content on the page—and sidebars to ensure that each area of content is easy to distinguish from another.) In this situation, it's sensible to define a default rule for each element using an element selector and then create an override for the portion of the page that requires different text by using a contextual selector.

For example, imagine a typical web page that has a sidebar that's marked up as an aside with an id value of sidebar. You might use a different paragraph font in the sidebar to differentiate the text, like so:

```
p {
  font: 1.2em/1.5 Verdana, Arial, sans-serif;
  margin-bottom: 1em;
}
#sidebar p {
  font: 1.2em/1.5 Arial, sans-serif;
}
```

The other occasion where alternatives are required is when creating one-off styles to override an existing style. In such cases, you can define a class in the CSS and then use a class attribute to apply it to an element. Should you want only a portion of some text to take on the style, you can surround the selection with a span element and apply the class to that instead.

For example, if you wanted to create some "warning" text, you could use the following CSS:

```
.warning {
  color: #ff0000;
  font-size: 120%;
}
```

This can then be applied as follows:

```
<p class="warning">This paragraph takes on the styles defined in
  the warning class</p>
<p>Only <em class="warning">this portion</em> of this
  paragraph takes on the warningText class styles.</p>
```

Avoid overusing span elements, though. Text works best when it's consistent across the page.

> *Note that the preceding CSS style has a capital letter halfway through it—this case is known as* lowerCamelCase *and is a method of writing multiple-word style names, because spaces must be avoided in CSS. Take care if you do this, because styles are case sensitive. If you set a* class *attribute value to* warningtext *instead of* warningText, *many browsers fail to display the style, reverting to the default style for the relevant element. It is also important to remember that CSS styles can't begin with a number.* 1Style *will not work.*

Styling semantic markup

The exercises in this section will combine the elements discussed so far in this chapter, showing how to use the knowledge gained to style some semantic markup. Three different examples are on offer, showing how rapidly you can create great-looking text when working with CSS and also how you can easily restyle a page of text without touching the markup. The markup that you'll use is per that in the next code block, and the default web page, without any CSS applied, is shown to its right.

```
<article class="wrapper">
```

```
<h1>Article heading</h1>
<p>Lorem ipsum dolor sit amet,
consectetuer adipiscing elit. Sed
   aliquet elementum erat. Integer
   diam mi, venenatis non, cursus
   a, hendrerit at, mi. Morbi risus
   mi, tincidunt ornare, tempus
   ut, eleifend nec, risus.</p>
<p>Quisque faucibus lorem eget sapien.
   In urna sem, vehicula ut,
   mattis et, venenatis at, velit.
   Ut sodales lacus sed eros.
   Pellentesque tristique senectus et
   netus et malesuada fames
   ac turpis egestas.</p>
<h2>Curabitur sit amet risus</h2>
<p>Lorem ipsum dolor sit amet,
   consectetuer adipiscing elit. Sed
   aliquet elementum erat. Integer
   diam mi, venenatis non, cursus
   a, hendrerit at, mi. Morbi risus mi,
tincidunt ornare, tempus
   ut, eleifend nec, risus.</p>
<p>Quisque faucibus lorem eget sapien. In urna sem, vehicula ut,
   mattis et, venenatis at, velit. Ut sodales lacus sed eros.
   Pellentesque tristique senectus et netus et malesuada fames
   ac turpis egestas.</p>
<h3>Praesent rutrum</h3>
<p>Nam scelerisque dignissim quam. Ut bibendum enim in orci. Vivamus
   ligula nunc, dictum a, tincidunt in, dignissim ac, odio.</p>
<h3>Habitant morbid</h3>
<p>Nam scelerisque dignissim quam. Ut bibendum enim in orci. Vivamus
   ligula nunc, dictum a, tincidunt in, dignissim ac, odio.</p>
</article>
```

The code block is simple. The text has three levels of headings, with paragraphs between them. Everything is enclosed in an article element, which will be styled to restrict the width of its content. This makes it simpler to see how the leading—defined via line-height—is working out. If you were surfing at full-screen on a large monitor, the paragraphs might be shown on only a single line.

The default CSS document for these exercises has some rules common to all three examples. These are shown in the following code block:

```
* {
  margin: 0;
  padding: 0;
}

html {
```

```
    font-size: 100%;
}

body {
  padding: 20px;
  font-size: 62.5%;
}

.wrapper {
  margin: 0 auto;
  width: 400px;
}
```

The first rule, *, removes margins and padding from all elements, as discussed previously. The html and body rules set the default size of the text on the web page to 62.5%, as explained in the "Setting text using percentages and ems" section earlier in this chapter. Finally, the .wrapper rule defines a width for the wrapper article and therefore for its content.

Styling semantic markup: A basic example with proportional line heights

Required files   styling-semantic-text-starting-point.html and styling-semantic-text-starting-point.css from the chapter 3 folder

What you'll learn How to style headings and paragraphs using sans-serif fonts (Verdana for body copy and Arial for headings) and proportional, unitless line-height settings

Completed files   styling-semantic-text-1.html and styling-semantic-text-1.css from the chapter 3 folder

1. Define the font defaults. Using a body selector, define a default font for the web page, along with a default line-height value. Because this is a basic example, Verdana is used as the primary font, falling back to Arial and Helvetica. The unitless line-height value means that elements will have proportional line heights based on their font-size values, unless otherwise stated.

```
body {
  font-family: Verdana, Arial, Helvetica, sans-serif;
  line-height: 1.5;
}
```

> Note: In the CSS, you'll end up with two *body* selectors if you follow this to the letter—one for dealing with padding and setting the default font size to 62.5% and the other for defining the default *font-family* value for the page, along with the *line-height*. This enables these exercises to remain modular; in a real site, although it's acceptable to use selectors more than once, you should ensure property values and rules are correctly housed in the relevant section of your boilerplates—see Chapter 10 and Appendix D for more information on CSS management.

2. Define common settings for headings. In this example, the top two levels of headings will have the same font-family value. Therefore, it makes sense to use a grouped selector to define this property:

```
h1, h2 {
  font-family: Arial, Helvetica, sans-serif;
}
```

3. Define specific values for headings. How you style headings will depend on their purpose. For these exercises, h1 is the page heading, h2 is a subheading, and h3 is a crosshead to introduce a section of copy. With that in mind, the crosshead needs to be of similar size to the paragraphs, the main heading needs to be most prominent, and the subheading needs to be somewhere in between. Therefore, in the CSS, the h1 element has a font-size value of 2.5em, the h3 has a much smaller 1.2em, and the h2 has an in-between 2em.

```
h1 {
  font-size: 2.5em;
}
h2 {
  font-size: 2em;
}
h3 {
  font-size: 1.2em;
}
```

4. Style the paragraphs using the following rule. Whereas the space around headings is taken care of with the line-height setting defined in the body selector, that doesn't work for paragraphs, which must have distinct space between them. Therefore, along with a font-size property/value pair, a margin-bottom value sets the space between each paragraph to slightly more than the height of one character.

```
p {
  font-size: 1.1em;
  margin-bottom: 1.1em;
}
```

5. Refine the element spacing. At this point, the spacing is still a little suspect—the crossheads don't stand out enough. Therefore, add a margin-top value to the h3 rule; this provides a little extra space between paragraphs and level-three headings. (As mentioned earlier, vertical margins collapse, so the space between a paragraph with a bottom margin of 1.1em and a level-three heading with a top margin of 1.65em is 1.65em, not the sum of the two margins, which would be 2.75em.)

```
h3 {
  font-size: 1.2em;
  margin-top: 1.65em;
}

h3, p {
  margin-left: 1em;
}
```

The following image shows what your completed page should look like.

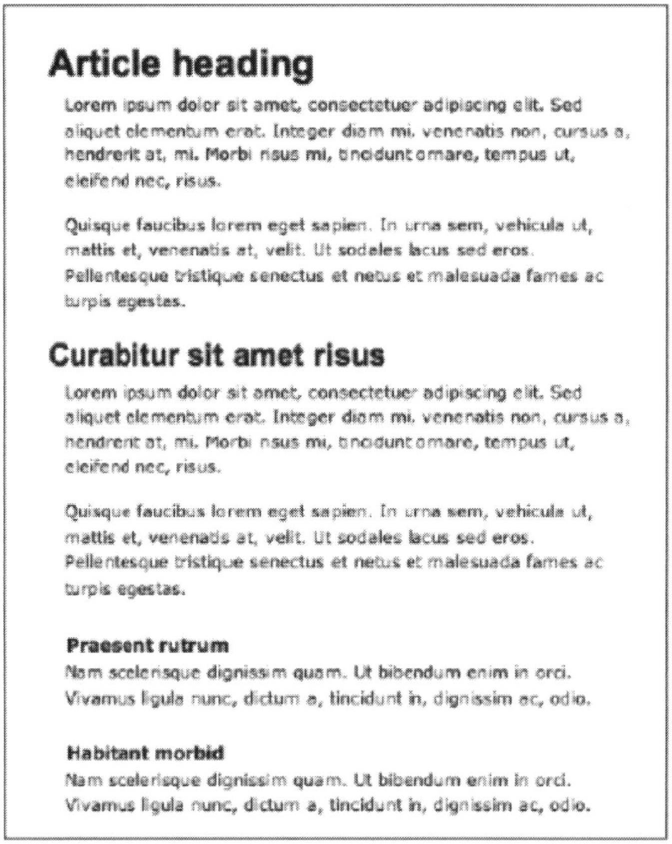

Required files   styling-semantic-text-starting-point.html and styling-semantic-text-starting-point.css from the chapter 3 folder

What you'll learn   How to create a contemporary-looking page of text using Lucida fonts, as per the text on Apple's website

Completed files styling-semantic-text-2.html and styling-semantic-text-2.css from the chapter 3 folder

1. Set the font defaults. As in the previous exercise, use a body rule to define the default font for the page, the first couple of choices of which are Lucida variants that are installed on Mac OS and Windows. Other fonts are provided for legacy or alternate systems.

```
body {
  font-family: "Lucida Grande", "Lucida Sans Unicode", Lucida, Arial,
    Helvetica, sans-serif;
  line-height: 1.5;
}
```

2. Style the main heading. An h1 rule is used to style the main heading. The restrictive value for line-height makes the leading value the height of one character of the heading, meaning there's no space underneath it. This means you can define an explicit padding-bottom value, followed by a border-bottom (here, 1 pixel, solid, and very light gray), followed by a margin-bottom value. The padding-bottom and margin-bottom values are the same, creating a very tight, clean feel for the heading. Elsewhere, the color setting knocks it back slightly so that it doesn't overpower the other content, and the font-weight value removes the default bold setting that browsers apply to headings. This helps the block of text appear light and clean.

```
h1 {
    font-size: 1.8em;
    line-height: 1em;
    padding-bottom: 7px;
    border-bottom: 1px solid #cccccc;
    margin-bottom: 7px;
    color: #666666;
    font-weight: normal;
}
```

> Tip: When removing the default bold style from headings, check them across platforms—on some Windows systems, nonbold headings can look a bit spindly, depending on the settings.

3. Style the other headings. For the next two heading levels, font-size values are assigned. In keeping with the modern style, the crossheads are the same size as the paragraph text (styled in the next step)—just displayed in bold; the subheading (h2) is slightly larger, making it a little more prominent. Again, the headings are colored to make them blend in a little more and not distract from the paragraph text.

```
h2, h3 {
    color: #333333;
}
h2 {
    font-size: 1.3em;
}
h3 {
    font-size: 1.2em;
    margin-top: 1.65em;
}
```

4. Style the paragraphs. The font-size setting is larger than that used on many websites (which typically tend toward 11 pixels, which would require a 1.1em value in this example), but this ensures clarity and, again, enhances the clean nature of the design.

```
p {
    font-size: 1.2em;
    margin-bottom: 1.2em;
}
```

5. The final rule—an adjacent sibling selector—styles the paragraph following the main heading, making the intro paragraph bold. It's colored a dark gray, rather than black, which would be overpowering and wreck the balance of the page.

```
h1+p {
  font-weight: bold;
  color: #222222;
}
```

The following image shows what your completed page should look like.

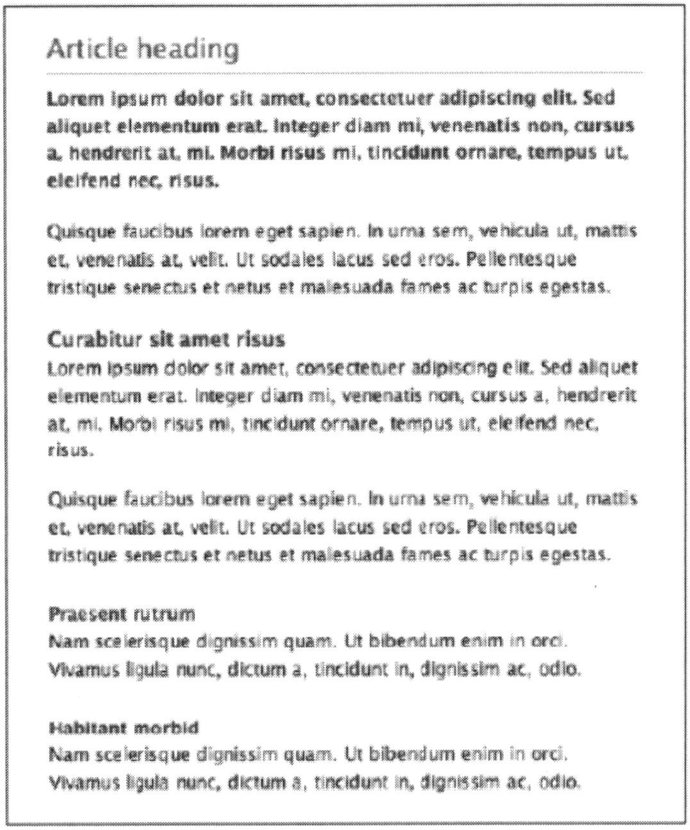

Required filesstyling-semantic-text-starting-point.html and styling-semantic-text-starting-point.css and styling-semantic-text baseline.gif from the chapter 3 folder

What you'll learn How to create a page of traditional-looking text as per a printed book. The text adheres strictly to a baseline grid, maintaining the page's vertical rhythm. This requires some extra calculations when it comes to defining line-height values.

Completed files styling-semantic-text-3.html and styling-semantic-text-3.css from the chapter 3 folder

1. Define a default font for the page. Using a body rule, a default font is chosen for the web page. This design primarily uses the Georgia font—a serif—to enhance the traditional feel.

```
body {
  font-family: Georgia, "Times New Roman", Times, serif;
}
```

2. At this point, it's also important to decide on a target line-height value for the page. For this example, it's going to be 18px.

3. Style the main heading. Here's where things get a little tricky. For these examples, we're working with relative units. As mentioned earlier in the chapter, the 62.5% method means that you can define font sizes by setting the font-size value to a setting in ems that's one-tenth of the target size in pixels. So, in the following code block, the h1 rule's font-size value of 1.8em means it's effectively displayed at 18 pixels (assuming the user hasn't messed around with their browser's default settings, again as mentioned earlier).

4. For the line-height value to hit the target of 18 pixels, it must therefore be 18 pixels or a multiple of it. However, when using ems, this value is relative to the font-size value. One em is equal to the height of one character, and since the font-size has been set to 1.8em (which is equivalent to 18 pixels), we set line-height to 1em. This makes the line-height of the h1 element the equivalent of 18 pixels.

5. Similar thinking is used to define the value for margin-bottom—this needs to be 18 pixels to keep the vertical rhythm going, so the value is set to 1em.

```
h1 {
  font-size: 1.8em;
  line-height: 1em;
  margin-bottom: 1em;
}
```

6. Style the subheading. For the subheading, the font-size value is set to 1.4em. To keep the line-height vertical rhythm going, you need to find the value that will multiply with the font-size setting to create 1.8 (since 1.8em is the equivalent of 18 pixels). You can get this by dividing 1.8 by the font-size value, which results in a line-height value of 1.2857142em. To keep the rhythm going, this setting can then be used for both the margin-top and margin-bottom values.

```
h2 {
  font-size: 1.4em;
  line-height: 1.2857142em;
  margin-top: 1.2857142em;
  margin-bottom: 1.2857142em;
}
```

7. However, what this serves to do is isolate the heading on its own line, rather than making it obviously lead to the subsequent paragraph. Two solutions exist for dealing with this. The first is simply to remove the bottom margin; the second is to create asymmetrical margins, making the top margin larger than the bottom one. To keep the entire space the element takes up strictly within the grid and not interrupt the vertical rhythm too much, it's sensible to take half the margin-bottom value and add it to the margin-top value.

```
h2 {
  font-size: 1.4em;
  line-height: 1.2857142em;
  margin-top: 1.9285713em;
  margin-bottom: 0.6428571em;
}
```

8. Style the crossheads and paragraphs. For this example, the crossheads and paragraphs are identical, save for the default styling on the headings that renders them in bold. The font-size value is 1.2em. Again, 1.8 is divided by the font-size figure to arrive at the line-height and margin values, both of which are set to 1.5em. Note that the h3 rule has no margin-bottom value, meaning that each level-three heading hugs the subsequent paragraph.

```
h3 {
  font-size: 1.2em;
  line-height: 1.5em;
  margin-top: 1.5em;
}

p {
  font-size: 1.2em;
  line-height: 1.5em;
  margin-bottom: 1.5em;
}
```

At this point, your page should look like the following image.

Article heading

Lorem ipsum dolor sit amet, consectetuer adipiscing elit. Sed aliquet elementum erat. Integer diam mi, venenatis non, cursus a, hendrerit at, mi. Morbi risus mi, tincidunt ornare, tempus ut, eleifend nec, risus.

Quisque faucibus lorem eget sapien. In urna sem, vehicula ut, mattis et, venenatis at, velit. Ut sodales lacus sed eros. Pellentesque tristique senectus et netus et malesuada fames ac turpis egestas.

Curabitur sit amet risus

Lorem ipsum dolor sit amet, consectetuer adipiscing elit. Sed aliquet elementum erat. Integer diam mi, venenatis non, cursus a, hendrerit at, mi. Morbi risus mi, tincidunt ornare, tempus ut, eleifend nec, risus.

Quisque faucibus lorem eget sapien. In urna sem, vehicula ut, mattis et, venenatis at, velit. Ut sodales lacus sed eros. Pellentesque tristique senectus et netus et malesuada fames ac turpis egestas.

Praesent rutrum

Nam scelerisque dignissim quam. Ut bibendum enim in orci. Vivamus ligula nunc, dictum a, tincidunt in, dignissim ac, odio.

Habitant morbid

Nam scelerisque dignissim quam. Ut bibendum enim in orci. Vivamus ligula nunc, dictum a, tincidunt in, dignissim ac, odio.

9. Add a (temporary) grid. When working on text that adheres to a baseline grid, it can help to create a tiled background image that you can use to check whether your measurements are accurate. The 18-pixel-high image file, styling-semantic-text-baseline.gif, has a single-pixel line at the bottom of the image. When applied to the wrapper article's background via the .wrapper rule (see the following code), a ruled background is shown. Although intended as a temporary design aid, you could retain the grid permanently, because it can help readers to rapidly skim text. However, the aid works only when a browser is using default settings—when the text is enlarged, the background image stays as it is, resulting in the grid of the image and the grid of the text being out of sync.

```
.wrapper {
  margin: 0 auto;
  width: 400px;
  background: url(styling-semantic-text-baseline.gif);
}
```

The following image shows how this image works behind the text styled in this exercise—as you can see, the vertical rhythm is maintained right down the page.

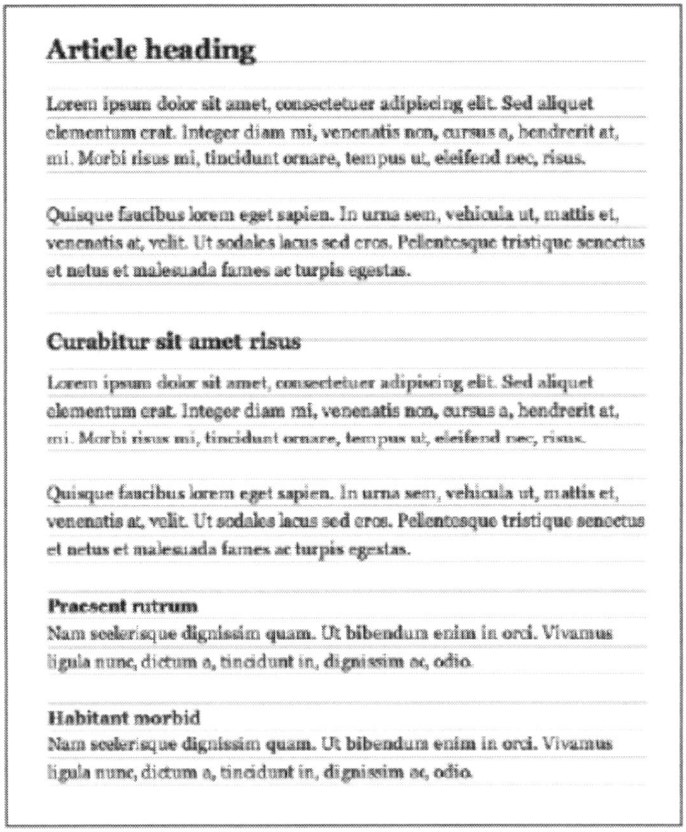

Creating drop caps and pull quotes using CSS

The previous exercise showed how something aimed primarily at the world of print design—a baseline grid—can actually work well online, and this section will continue that theme, showing how to use CSS to create drop caps and pull quotes. Drop caps—large letters typically used at the start of a printed article—are rare online, although they can be a useful way of drawing the eye to the beginning of the body copy. Pull quotes are more common, and while part of their use in print—taking a choice quote and making it stand out on the page to draw in the reader—is less effective online, pull quotes are still handy for highlighting a piece of text (such as a quote or idea) or for providing client quotes on a company website.

Creating a drop cap using a CSS pseudo-element

| Required files | styling-semantic-text-2.html and styling-semantic-text-2.css from the chapter 3 folder. |

What you'll learn   How to create a drop cap for a website and how to use the CSS float property. Any element can be floated left or right in CSS, and this causes subsequent content to wrap around it.

Completed files   drop-cap.html and drop-cap.css from the chapter 3 folder.

1. Create a new rule that targets the relevant character. For this, you can use a pseudo-element, first-letter, and the adjacent sibling selector created earlier in the "Styling semantic markup" section. See Appendix D for more on pseudo-elements.

```
h1+p:first-letter {

}
```

2. In plain English, this rule is saying, "Apply this rule to the first letter of the paragraph that follows the level-one heading."

3. Float the character and increase its size. Add a float: left property/value pair to float the first character in the paragraph to the left, which makes subsequent content wrap around it. Then set a large font-size value to increase the size of the character compared to the surrounding text.

```
h1+p:first-letter {
  float: left;
  font-size: 3em;
}
```

4. Finally, tweak the positioning. Define a line-height value and margin-top value to vertically position the character; you may need to experiment some when working on your own designs outside of this exercise, since the values required are somewhat dependent on the font-size setting. The margin-right setting provides some spacing between the drop cap and the subsequent text.

```
h1+p:first-letter {
  float: left;
  font-size: 3em;
  line-height: 1.0em;
  margin-top: -3px;
  margin-right: 0.15em;
}
```

> Note that you can use the *first-line* pseudo-element to target the first line of some text—for example, to make it bold, which is a commonly used design element in magazines.

Although this technique is the most straightforward one for working with drop caps, the results aren't entirely satisfactory. Because of the way different browsers deal with the first-letter pseudo-element, the display isn't particularly consistent across browsers and platforms—see the following two images, which show the results in Firefox and Safari. Therefore, if you want to use drop caps with more precision, it's best to fall back on a more old-fashioned but tried-and-tested method: the span element.

Article heading

L orem ipsum dolor sit amet, consectetuer adipiscing Sed aliquet elementum erat. Integer diam mi, vener non, cursus a, hendrerit at, mi. Morbi risus mi, tinci ornare, tempus ut, eleifend nec, risus.

Article heading

L orem ipsum dolor sit amet, consectetuer adipiscing Sed aliquet elementum erat. Integer diam mi, vener non, cursus a, hendrerit at, mi. Morbi risus mi, tincidun tempus ut, eleifend nec, risus.

Required files	styling-semantic-text-2.html, styling-semantic-text-2.css, quote-open.gif, and quote-close.gif from the chapter 3 folder
What you'll learn	How to create a magazine-style pull quote, which can draw the user's attention to a quote or highlight a portion of an article
Completed files	pull-quote.html and pull-quote.css from the chapter 3 folde

1. Add the HTML. The required markup for a basic pull quote is simple, centering around the blockquote element and nesting a paragraph within. Add the following to the web page, above the code <h2>Curabitur sit amet risus</h2>:

```
<blockquote>
  <p>This is the pull quote. It's really very exciting, so read it now!
  Lorem ipsum dolor sit amet, consectetuer adipiscing elit.</p>
</blockquote>
```

2. Style the blockquote element. Create a blockquote rule and use the background property to add the open quote image as its background. Set vertical margins that are larger than the margins between the paragraphs (to ensure that the pull quote stands out from the surrounding text) and the horizontal margins (to ensure that the pull quote doesn't span the entire column width, which also helps it visually stand out).

```
blockquote {
  background: url(quote-open.gif) 0 0 no-repeat;
  margin: 2.4em 2em;
}
```

3. Style the pull quote paragraph text. Using the contextual selector blockquote p, style the paragraph text within the blockquote element. Making the text bold and larger than the surrounding copy helps it stand out—but to ensure it doesn't become too distracting, knock back its color a little.

```
blockquote p {
  color: #555555;
  font-size: 1.3em;
  font-weight: bold;
  text-align: justify;
}
```

4. Use the background property to add the closing quote mark, which is added to the paragraph, since you can add only one background image to an element in CSS. The background's position is set to 100% 90%—far right and almost at the bottom. Setting it at the absolute bottom would

align the closing quote with the bottom of the leading under the last line of the paragraph text; setting the vertical position value to 90%, however, lines up the closing quote with the bottom of the text itself.

```
blockquote p {
  color: #555555;
  font-size: 1.3em;
  font-weight: bold;
  text-align: justify;
  background: url(quote-close.gif) 100% 90% no-repeat;
}
```

5. Tweak the positioning. If you test the page now, you'll see the paragraph content appearing over the top of the background images. To avoid this, padding needs to be applied to the quote mark to force its content inward but still leave the background images in place. Since the quote images are both 23 pixels wide, a horizontal padding value of 33px provides room for the images and adds an additional 10 pixels so that the content of the paragraph doesn't abut the quote marks. Finally, the default margin-bottom value for paragraphs is overridden (via a 0 value), since it's redundant here.

```
blockquote p {
  color: #555555;
  font-size: 1.3em;
  font-weight: bold;
  text-align: justify;
  background: url(quote-close.gif) 100% 90% no-repeat;
  padding: 0 33px;
  margin-bottom: 0;
}
```

The following image shows your pull quote page so far.

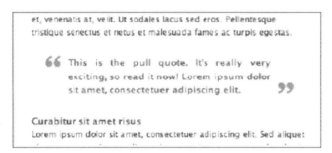

6. Next, credit the quotation. To add a credit to the quote, add another paragraph, with a nested cite element, inside which is the relevant content.

```
<blockquote>
  <p>This is the pull quote. It's really very exciting, so read it now!
  Lorem ipsum dolor sit amet, consectetuer adipiscing elit.</p>
  <p><cite>fredbloggs.com</cite></p>
</blockquote>
```

7. In CSS, add the following rule:

```
cite {
  background: none;
  display: block;
  text-align: right;
  font-size: 1.1em;
  font-weight: normal;
  font-style: italic;
}
```

8. Some of the property values in cite are there to override the settings from blockquote p and to ensure that the second paragraph's text is clearly distinguishable from the quote. However, at this point, both paragraphs within the blockquote element have the closing-quote background, so a final rule is required.

```
blockquote>p+p {
  background: none;
}
```

9. This fairly complex rule uses both a child selector (>) and an adjacent selector (+) and styles the paragraph that comes immediately after the paragraph that's a child element of the blockquote (which is the paragraph with the cite element). The rule overrides the background value defined in step 5 for paragraphs within the block quote. Note that this assumes the quote itself will be only a single paragraph. If you have multiparagraph quotes, you'll need to apply a class to the final paragraph and set the quote-close.gif image as a background on that, rather than on blockquote p.

Using classes and CSS overrides to create an alternate pull quote

Required files   pull-quote.html and pull-quote.css from the chapter 3 folder.

What you'll learn   How to use CSS classes to create alternatives to the default pull quote. In this example, you'll create a narrow pull quote that floats to the right of the body copy.

Completed files   pull-quote-2.html and pull-quote-2.css from the chapter 3 folder.

1. Amend the HTML. First, add a class to the blockquote element so that it can be targeted in CSS:

```
<blockquote id="fredBloggs">
```

2. Position the blockquote. Create a new CSS rule that targets the blockquote from the previous step by using the selector #fredBloggs. Set float and width values to float the pull quote and define its width.

```
#fredBloggs {
  float: right;
  width: 150px;
}
```

3. Remove the quote mark background image by setting background to none. Add the two border property/value pairs shown to visually separate the pull quote from its surroundings, drawing the eye to its content.

```
#fredBloggs {
  float: right;
  width: 150px;
  background: none;
  border-top: 5px solid #dddddd;
  border-bottom: 5px solid #dddddd;
}
```

4. Add padding and margins. First, add vertical padding to ensure that the pull quote's contents don't hug the borders added in the previous step. Next, define margin values, overriding those set for the default blockquote from the previous exercise. Because this alternate pull quote is floated right, there's no need for top and right margins, which is why they're set to 0; the bottom and left margin values are left intact.

```
#fredBloggs {
  float: right;
  width: 150px;
  background: none;
  border-top: 5px solid #dddddd;
  border-bottom: 5px solid #dddddd;
  padding: 10px 0;
  margin: 0 0 2em 2.4em;
}
```

5. Override the paragraph styles. The background and padding settings for the default blockquote style are no longer needed, so they're set to none and 0, respectively. Finally, text-align is set to center, which is appropriate for a narrow pull quote such as this.

```
#fredBloggs p {
  text-align: center;
  background: none;
  padding: 0;
}
```

6. Use pseudo-elements to add quotation marks before and after the blockquote contents.

```
#fredBloggs:before {
  content: open-quote;
}
#fredBloggs:after {
  content: close-quote;
}
```

Curabitur sit amet risus
Lorem ipsum dolor sit amet,
consectetuer adipiscing elit. Sed
aliquet elementum erat. Integer diam
mi, venenatis non, cursus a, hendrerit
at, mi. Morbi risus mi, tincidunt ornare,
tempus ut, eleifend nec, risus.

Quisque faucibus lorem eget sapien. In
urna sem, vehicula ut, mattis et,
venenatis at, velit. Ut sodales lacus sed
eros. Pellentesque tristique senectus et
netus et malesuada fames ac turpis egestas.

This is the pull quote.
It's really very
exciting, so read it
now! Lorem ipsum
dolor sit amet,
consectetuer
adipiscing elit.
Fred Bloggs

Adding reference citations

The blockquote element can have a cite attribute, and the content from this attribute can be displayed by using the following CSS rule:

```
blockquote[cite]:after {
  display : block;
  margin : 0 0 5px;
  padding : 0 0 2px 0;
  font-weight : bold;
  font-size : 90%;
  content : "[source: "" " attr(cite)"]";
}
```

Working with lists

This chapter concludes with the last of the major type elements: the list. We'll first look at the different types of lists—unordered, ordered, and definition—and also see how to nest them. Then we'll move on to cover how to style lists in CSS, list margins and padding, and inline lists.

Unordered lists

The unordered list, commonly referred to as a *bullet point list*, is the most frequently seen type of list online. The list is composed of an unordered list element (<ul></ul>) and any number of list items within, each of which looks like this (prior to content being added): <li></li>. An example of an unordered list follows, and the resulting browser display is shown to the right. As you can see, browsers typically render a single-level unordered list with solid black bullet points.

```
<ul>
  <li>List item one</li>
  <li>List item two</li>
  <li>List item 'n'</li>
</ul>
```

- List item one
- List item two
- List item 'n'

Ordered lists

On occasion, list items must be stated in order, whereupon an ordered list is used. It works in the same way as an unordered list, the only difference being the containing element, which is <ol></ol>.

```
<ol>
  <li>List item one</li>
  <li>List item two</li>
  <li>List item 'n'</li>
</ol>
```

1. List item one
2. List item two
3. List item 'n'

> Note: Web browsers automatically insert the item numbers when you use ordered lists. The only way of controlling numbering directly is via the *start* attribute, whose value dictates the first number of the ordered list.

Definition lists

A definition list isn't a straightforward list of items. Instead, it's a list of terms and explanations. This type of list isn't common online, but it has its uses. The list is enclosed in the definition list element (<dl></dl>), and within the element are terms and definitions, marked up with <dt></dt> and <dd></dd>, respectively. Generally speaking, browsers display the definition with an indented left margin, as in the following example:

```
<dl>
  <dt>Cat</dt>
  <dd>Four-legged, hairy animal, with an
    inflated sense of self-importance</dd>
  <dt>Dog</dt>
  <dd>Four-legged, hairy animal, often with
    an inferiority complex</dd>
</dl>
```

Cat
    Four-legged, hairy animal, with an inflated sense of self-importance

Dog
    Four-legged, hairy animal, often with an inferiority complex

Nesting lists

Lists can be nested, but designers often do so incorrectly, screwing up their layouts and rendering web pages invalid. The most common mistake is placing the nested list outside any list items, as shown in the following incorrect example:

109

```
<ul>
  <li>List item one</li>
  <ul>
    <li>Nested list item one</li>
    <li>Nested list item two</li>
  </ul>
  <li>List item two</li>
  <li>List item 'n'</li>
</ul>
```

Nested lists must be placed inside a list item, after the relevant item that leads into the nested list. Here's an example:

```
<ul>
  <li>List item one
      <ul>
         <li>Nested list item one</li>
         <li>Nested list item two</li>
      </ul>
  </li>
  <li>List item two</li>
  <li>List item 'n'</li>
</ul>
```

Always ensure that the list element that contains the nested list is closed with an end tag. Not doing so is another common mistake, and although it's not likely to cause as many problems as the incorrect positioning of the list, it can still affect your layout.

Styling lists with CSS

Lists can be styled with CSS, making it easy to amend item spacing or create custom bullet points. I tend to think bullet points work well for lists. They're simple and—pardon the pun—to the point. However, I know plenty of people would rather have something more visually interesting, which is where the list-style-image property comes in.

list-style-image property

The list-style-image property replaces the standard bullet or number from an unordered or ordered list with whatever image you choose. If you set the following in your CSS, the resulting list will look like that shown to the right. (Note that this is the nested list created earlier in this chapter.)

```
ul {
    list-style-image: url(bullet.gif);
}
```

Contextual selectors were first mentioned in Chapter 1 (see the section "Types of CSS selectors"). These enable you to style things in context, and this is appropriate when working with lists. You can style list items with one type of bullet and nested list items with another. The original rule stays in place but is joined by a second rule:

```
ul {
    list-style-image: url(bullet.gif);
}
ul ul {
    list-style-image: url(bullet-level-two.gif);
}
```

This second rule's selector is ul ul, which means that the declaration is applied only to unordered lists within an unordered list (that is, *nested* lists). The upshot is that the top-level list items remain with the original custom bullet, but the nested list items now have a different bullet graphic.

With this CSS, each subsequent level would have the nested list bullet point, but it's feasible to change the bullet graphic for each successive level by using increasingly complex contextual selectors.

> Note: When using custom bullet images, be wary of making them too large. Some browsers clip the bullet image, and some place the list contents at the foot of the image. In all cases, the results look terrible.

Dealing with font-size inheritance

Most of the font-size definitions in this chapter (and indeed, in this book) use relative units. The problem with using ems, however, is that they compound. For example, if you have a typical nested list like the one just shown and you define the following CSS, the first level of the list will have text sized at 1.5em; but the second-level list is a list within a list, so its font-size value will be compounded (1.5 $\times$ 1.5 = 2.25em).

```
html {
    font-size: 100%;
}
body {
    font-size: 62.5%;
    font-family: Verdana, Arial,
        Helvetica, sans-serif;
}
li {
    font-size: 1.5em;
}
```

111

The simple workaround for this is to use a contextual selector—li li—to set an explicit font-size value for list items within list items, as shown in the following rule:

```
li li {
   font-size: 1em;
}
```

With this, all nested lists take on the same font-size value as the parent list, which in this case is 1.5em.

list-style-position property

This property has two values: inside and outside. The latter is how list items are usually displayed: the bullet is placed in the list margin, and the left margin of the text is always indented. However, if you use inside, bullets are placed where the first text character would usually go, meaning that the text will wrap underneath the bullet.

list-style-type property

The list-style-type property is used to amend the bullets in an unordered or ordered list, enabling you to change the default bullets to something else (other than a custom image). In an unordered list, this defaults to disc (a black bullet), but other values are available, such as circle (a hollow disc bullet), square (a square bullet), and none, which results in no bullet points. For ordered lists, this defaults to decimal (resulting in a numbered list), but a number of other values are available, including lower-roman (i, ii, iii, and so on) and upper-alpha (A, B, C, and so on). A full list of supported values is in Appendix D.

Generally speaking, the values noted are the best supported, along with the upper and lower versions of roman and alpha for ordered lists. If a browser doesn't understand the numbering system used for an ordered list, it usually defaults to decimal. The W3C recommends using decimal whenever possible, because it makes web pages easier to navigate. I agree—things like alpha and roman are too esoteric for general use, plus there's nothing in the CSS specifications to tell a browser what to do in an alphabetic system after z is reached (although most browsers are consistent in going on to aa, ab, ac, and so on).

List-style shorthand

As elsewhere in CSS, there is a shorthand property for list styles, and this is the aptly named list-style property. An example of its use is shown in the following piece of CSS:

```
ul {
   list-style-type: square;
   list-style-position: inside;
   list-style-image: url(bullet.gif);
}
```

which can be rewritten as follows:

```
ul {
   list-style: square inside url(bullet.gif);
}
```

List margins and padding

Browsers don't seem to be able to agree on how much padding and margin to place around lists by default, and also how margin and padding settings affect lists in general. This can be frustrating when developing websites that rely on lists and pixel-perfect element placement. By creating a list and using CSS to apply a background color to the list and a different color to list items and then removing the page's padding and margins, you can observe how each browser creates lists and indents the bullet points and content.

In Gecko and Webkit browsers (for example, Mozilla Firefox), Chrome, Opera, and Safari, the list background color is displayed behind the bullet points, which suggests that those browsers place bullet points within the list's left padding (because backgrounds extend into an element's padding). Internet Explorer shows no background color there, suggesting it places bullet points within the list's left margin.

This is confirmed if you set the margin property to 0 for a ul selector in CSS. The list is unaffected in all browsers but Internet Explorer, in which the bullets abut the left edge of the web browser window. Conversely, setting padding to 0 makes the same thing happen in Gecko browsers, Safari, and Opera.

To get all browsers on a level playing field, you must remove margins and padding, which, as mentioned previously in this book, is done in CSS by way of the universal selector:

```
* {
margin: 0;
padding: 0;
}
```

With this in place, all browsers render lists in the same way, and you can set specific values as appropriate. For example, bring back the bullet points (which may be at least partially hidden if margins and padding are both zeroed) by setting either the margin-left or padding-left value to 1.5em (that is, set margin: 0 0 0 1.5em or padding: 0 0 0 1.5em). The difference is that if you set padding-left, any background applied to the list will appear behind the bullet points, but if you set margin-left, it won't. Note that 1.5em is a big enough value to enable the bullet points to display (in fact, lower values are usually sufficient, too—although take care not to set values too low, or the bullets will be clipped); setting a higher value places more space to the left of the bullet points.

Inline lists for navigation

Although most people think of lists as being vertically aligned, you can also display list items inline. This is particularly useful when creating navigation bars, as you'll see in Chapter 5. To set a list to display inline, you simply add display: inline; to the li selector. Adding list-style-type: none; to the ul selector ensures that the list sits snug to the left of its container (omitting this tends to indent the list items). Adding a margin-right value to li also ensures that the list items don't sit right next to each other. Here's an example:

```
ul {
  list-style-type: none;
}
li {
  display: inline;
  margin-right: 10px;
```

}

Thinking creatively with lists

The final part of this chapter looks at creating lists with a little panache. Although most lists are perfectly suited to straightforward bullet points, sometimes some added CSS and imagery can go a long way.

Creating better-looking lists

Required files	The HTML and CSS documents from the basic-boilerplates folder as a starting point, along with the images better-list-hollow-square.gif, better-list-shadow.gif, better-list-square.gif, and better-list-star.gif from the chapter 3 folder
What you'll learn	How to style a three-level list to look great, using background images and overrides
Completed files	better-looking-lists.html and better-looking-lists.css from the chapter 3 folder

1. Create the list. Within the HTML document's wrapper div, add the following code:

```
<ul>
  <li>List - 1.1
    <ul>
      <li>List - 2.1</li>
      <li>List - 2.2
        <ul>
          <li>List - 3.1</li>
          <li>List - 3.2</li>
          <li>List - 3.3</li>
        </ul>
      </li>
      <li>List - 2.3</li>
    </ul>
  </li>
</ul>
```

2. Amend the body rule. Add some padding to the body element so that page content doesn't hug the browser window edges during testing:

```
body {
  font: 62.5%/1.5 Verdana, Arial, Helvetica, sans-serif;
  padding: 20px;
}
```

3. Style the list elements. This kind of heavily styled list typically requires you to define specific property values at one level and then override them if they're not required for subsequent levels. This is done by adding the three rules in the following code block. For this example, the top level of the list (styled via ul) has a star background image that doesn't repeat (the 1px vertical value is used to nudge the image into place so it looks better positioned), and the list-style-type value of none removes the default bullet points of all lists on the page.

For the second level of lists (the first level of nesting), styled via ul ul, a horizontally tiling background image is added, giving the impression that the top-level list is casting a soft shadow. The border-left setting creates a soft boundary to the nested list's left, thereby enclosing the content. The padding value ensures that there's space around nested lists.

For the third level of lists (the second level of nesting—that is, a nested list within a nested list), styled via ul ul ul, no specific styles are required, but to deal with inherited styles from ul ul, background is set to none and border-left is set to 0. If this weren't done, third-level lists would also have the shadow background and dotted left-hand border.

```
ul {
  list-style-type: none;
  background: url(better-list-star.gif) 0 1px no-repeat;
}
ul ul {
  background: url(better-list-shadow.gif) repeat-x;
  border-left: 1px dotted #aaaaaa;
  padding: 10px;
}
ul ul ul {
  background: none;
  border-left: 0;
}
```

4. Style the list item elements. For the top-level list items, the li rule styles them in uppercase, adds some padding (to ensure the items don't sit over the background image applied in ul), and makes the text bold and gray. For the nested list items, the li li rule overrides the text-transform property, returning the text to sentence case, and adds a square gray bullet as a background image. The font-weight value is an override, and the color setting is darker than for the parent list's list items so that the nonbold text of the nested list items stand out. Finally, for the third-level list items, styled using the selector li li li, a background override provides a unique bullet point image (a hollow square).

```
li {
  text-transform: uppercase;
  padding-left: 20px;
  font-weight: bold;
  color: #666666;
}
li li {
  text-transform: none;
  background: url(better-list-square.gif) 0 2px no-repeat;
  font-weight: normal;
  color: #333333;
}
li li li {
  background: url(better-list-hollow-square.gif) 0 2px no-repeat;
}
```

✷ LIST - 1.1

  ▓ List - 2.1
  ▓ List - 2.2

    ☐ List - 3.1
    ☐ List - 3.2
    ☐ List - 3.3

  ▓ List - 2.3

Note: When creating lists such as this, don't overcomplicate things, and try to avoid going to many levels of nesting or combining ordered and unordered lists; otherwise, the selectors required for overrides become extremely complicated.

Required files	The HTML and CSS documents from the basic-boilerplates folder as a starting point

What you'll learn	How to style a list for displaying code online (complete with exercise headings and line numbers)

Completed files	display-code-online.html and display-code-online.css from the chapter 3 folder

1. Create the list. Code blocks require terminology and descriptions, meaning that a definition list can be used to mark them up. For this example, the code block from the preceding "List style shorthand" section will be used. Within the wrapper div, create a definition list and give it a class value of codeList. For the term, add a description of the code, and for the definition, add an ordered list, with each line of code within its own list item. Each line of code should also be nested within a code element.

```
<dl class="codeList">
  <dt>Writing out list styles in full</dt>
  <dd>
    <ol>
      <li><code>ul {</code></li>
      <li><code>list-style-type: square;</code></li>
      <li><code>list-style-position: inside;</code></li>
      <li><code>list-style-image: url(bullet.gif);</code></li>
      <li><code>}</code></li>
    </ol>
  </dd>
</dl>
```

2. Amend the body and #wrapper CSS rules, adding some padding to the former (so the content doesn't hug the browser window edges during testing) and a shorthand font definition to the latter (in place of existing content).

```
body {
  font: 62.5%/1.5 Verdana, Arial, Helvetica, sans-serif;
  padding: 20px;
}
#wrapper {
  font: 1.2em/1.5em 'Lucida Grande', 'Lucida Sans Unicode', Lucida,
    Arial, Helvetica,   sans-serif;
}
```

3. Style the list. Add the following rule, which adds a solid border around the definition list that has a codeList class value:

```
.codeList {
  border: 1px solid #aaaaaa;
}
```

4. Style the definition term element. Add the following rule, which styles the dt element. The rule colors the background of dt elements within any element with a class value of codeList and also adds some padding so the content of the dt elements doesn't hug their borders. The font-weight value of bold ensures the content stands out, while the border-bottom value will be used as a device throughout the other rules, separating components of the design with a fairly thin white line.

```
.codeList dt {
  background: #dddddd;
  padding: 7px;
  font-weight: bold;
  border-bottom: 2px solid #ffffff;
}
```

5. Style the list items within the ordered list by adding the following rule. The margin-left value places the bullets within the definition list, rather than outside of it.

```
.codeList li {
  background: #ffffff;
  margin-left: 2.5em;
}
```

> Note that in Internet Explorer, the bullets typically display further to the left than in other browsers. This behavior can be dealt with by overriding the *margin-left* value of *.codeList li* in an IE-specific style sheet attached using a conditional comment—see Chapter 9 for more on this technique.

6. Finally, style the code elements. The background value is slightly lighter than that used for the dt element, ensuring that each element is distinct. By setting display to block, the code elements stretch to fill their container (meaning that the background color also does this). The borders ensure that each line of code is visibly distinct, and the border-right setting essentially provides a border all the way around the code lines, seeing as the border-bottom setting in .codeList dt defines one at the top of the first line of code. The font is set to a monospace font, and the padding values place some space around the code, making it easier to read.

```
.codeList code {
  background: #eaeaea;
  display: block;
  border-bottom: 2px solid #ffffff;
  border-right: 2px solid #ffffff;
  font : 1.2em "Courier New", Courier, monospace;
  padding: 2px 10px;
}
```

Writing out list styles in full

```
1.  ul {
2.  list-style-type: square;
3.  list-style-position: inside;
4.  list-style-image: url(bullet.gif);
5.  }
```

That just about wraps things up for online type. After all that text, it's time to change track. In Chapter 4, you'll look at working with images on the Web, and in Chapter 5, you'll combine what you've learned so far and add anchors into the mix to create web navigation.

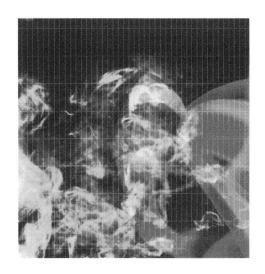

Chapter 4

Working With Images

In this chapter:

- Understanding color theory
- Choosing the best image format
- Avoiding common mistakes
- Working with images in HTML5

- Using `alt` text to improve accessibility

- Using CSS when working with images

- Displaying a random image from a selection

Introduction

Although text makes up the bulk of the Web's content, it's inevitable that you'll end up working with images at some point—that is, unless you favor terribly basic websites akin to those last seen in 1995. Images are rife online, comprising the bulk of interfaces, the navigation of millions of sites, and a considerable amount of actual content, too. As the Web continues to barge its way into every facet of life, this trend can only continue; visitors to sites now expect a certain amount of visual interest, just as readers of a magazine expect illustrations or photographs.

Like anything else, use and misuse of images can make or break a website—so, like elsewhere in this book, this chapter covers more than the essentials of working with HTML and CSS. Along with providing an overview of color theory, we've compiled a brief list of common mistakes that people make when working with images for the Web—after all, even the most dedicated web designers pick up bad habits without realizing it. Finally, at the end of the chapter, we'll introduce your first piece of JavaScript, providing you with a handy cut-out-and-keep script to randomize images on a web page.

Color theory

Color plays a massively important role in any field of design, and web design is no exception. Therefore, it seems appropriate to include in this chapter a brief primer on color theory and working with colors on the Web.

Color wheels

Circular color diagrams—commonly referred to as *color wheels*—were invented by Newton and remain a common starting point for creative types wanting to understand the relationship between colors and also for creating color schemes. On any standard color wheel, the three primary colors are each placed one-third of the way around the wheel, with secondary colors equally spaced between them—secondary colors being a mix of two primary colors. Between secondary and primary colors are tertiary colors, the result of mixing primary and secondary colors. Some color wheels blend the colors together, creating a continuous shift from one color to another, while others have rather more defined blocks of color; however, in all cases, the positioning is the same.

Additive and subtractive color systems

On-screen colors use what's referred to as an *additive* system, which is the color system used by light—where black is the absence of color and colored light is added together to create color mixes. The additive primaries are red, green, and blue (which is why you commonly hear RGB referring to the definition of screen colors). Mix equal amounts of red, green, and blue light, and you end up with white; mix secondaries from the primaries, and you end up with magenta, yellow, and cyan.

In print, a subtractive system is used, similar to that used in the natural world. This works by absorbing colors before they reach the eye—if an object reflects all light, it appears white, and if it absorbs all light, it appears black. Inks for print are transparent, acting as filters to enable light to pass through, reflect off the print base (such as paper), and produce unabsorbed light. Typically, the print process uses cyan, magenta, and yellow as primaries, along with a key color—black—since equal combination of three print inks tends to produce a muddy color rather than the black that it should produce in theory.

Although the technology within computers works via an additive system to display colors, digital-based designers still tend to work with subtractive palettes when working on designs (using red, yellow, and blue primaries), because that results in natural color combinations and palettes.

Creating a color scheme using a color wheel

Even if you have a great eye for color and can instinctively create great schemes for websites, it pays to have a color wheel handy. These days, you don't have to rely on reproductions in books or hastily created painted paper wheels. There are now digital color wheels that enable you to experiment with schemes, including Color Consultant Pro for the Mac (www.code-line.com/software/colorconsultantpro.html), shown in the following screenshot, and Color Wheel Pro (www.color-wheel-pro.com) and ColorImpact (www.tigercolor.com/Default.htm), both for Windows.

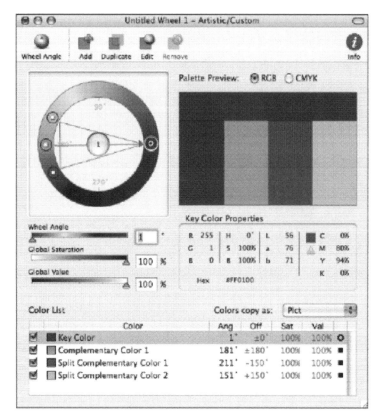

When working on color schemes and creating a palette for a website, various schemes are available for you. The simplest is a monochromatic scheme, which involves variations in the saturation (effectively the intensity or strength) of a single hue. Such schemes can be soothing—notably when based on green or blue—but also have a tendency to be bland, unless used with striking design and black and white. A slightly richer scheme can be created by using colors adjacent on the color wheel—this is referred to as an *analogous* scheme and is also typically considered harmonious and pleasing to the eye.

For more impact, a *complementary* scheme can be used, which uses colors on opposite sides of the color wheel (such as red/green, orange/blue, and yellow/purple); this scheme is often seen in art, such as a pointillist using orange dots in areas of blue to add depth. Complementary schemes work well because of a subconscious desire for visual harmony—an equal mix of complementary colors results in a neutral gray. Such effects are apparent in human color vision: if you look at a solid plane of color, you'll see its complementary color when you close your eyes.

A problem with a straight complementary scheme is that overuse of its colors can result in garish, tense design. A subtler but still attention-grabbing scheme can be created by using a color and the hues adjacent to the complementary color. This kind of scheme (which happens to be the one shown in the previous screenshot) is referred to as *split-complementary*.

Another scheme that offers impact—and one often favored by artists—is the *triadic* scheme, which essentially works with primary colors or shifted primaries (that is, colors equally spaced around the color wheel). The scheme provides plenty of visual contrast and, when used with care, can result in a balanced, harmonious result.

How colors "feel" also plays a part in how someone reacts to them—for example, people often talk of "warm" and "cool" colors. Traditionally, cooler colors are said to be passive, blending into backgrounds, while warmer colors are cheerier and welcoming. However, complexity is added by color intensity—a strong blue will appear more prominent than a pale orange. A color's temperature is also relative, largely defined by what is placed around it. On its own, green is cool, yet it becomes warm when surrounded by blues and purples.

Against black and white, a color's appearance can also vary. Against white, yellow appears warm, but against black, yellow has an aggressive brilliance. However, blue appears dark on white but appears luminescent on black.

The human condition also adds a further wrench in the works. Many colors have cultural significance, whether from language (cowardly yellow) or advertising and branding. One person may consider a color one thing (green equals fresh), and another may have different ideas entirely (green equals moldy). There's also the problem of color blindness, which affects a significant (although primarily male) portion of the population, meaning you should never rely entirely on color to get a message across. Ultimately, stick to the following rules, and you'll likely have some luck when working on color schemes:

- Work with a color wheel, and be mindful of how different schemes work.

- Use tints and shades of a hue, but generally avoid entirely monochromatic schemes—inject an adjacent color for added interest.

- Create contrast by adding a complementary color.

- Keep saturation levels and value levels the same throughout the scheme (a color's value increases the closer it is to white).

- Keep things simple—using too many colors results in garish schemes.

- Don't rely on color to get a message across—if in doubt about the effects of color blindness, test your design with a color blindness simulator application such as Color Oracle (http://colororacle.cartography.ch/).

- Go with your gut reaction—feelings play an important part when creating color schemes. What feels right is often a good starting point.

Working with hex

The CSS specifications support just 16 color names: aqua, black, blue, fuchsia, gray, green, lime, maroon, navy, olive, purple, red, silver, teal, white, and yellow. All other colors must be written in another format, such as RGB numbers or percentages—rgb(255,0,0) or rgb(100%,0%,0%)—or hexadecimal format, which tends to be most popular in online design. Note that to keep things consistent, it actually makes sense to write all colors—even the 17 with supported names—in hex. Colors written in hex comprise a hash sign followed by six digits. The six digits are comprised of pairs, representing the red, green, and blue color values, respectively:

- #XXxxxx: Red color value

- #xxXXxx: Green color value

- #xxxxXX: Blue color value

Because the hexadecimal system is used, the digits can range in value from 0 to f, with 0 being the lowest value (nothing) and f being the highest. Therefore, if we set the first two digits to full (ff) and the others to 0, we get #ff0000, which is the hex color value for red. Likewise, #00ff00 is green, and #0000ff is blue.

Of course, there are plenty of potential combinations—16.7 million of them, in fact. Luckily, any half-decent graphics application will do the calculations for you, so you won't have to work out for yourself that black is #000000 and white is #ffffff—just use an application's color picker/eyedropper tool, and it should provide you with the relevant hex value.

0to255.com offers a nice service to help web designers find variations of any color and quickly copy the hex code.

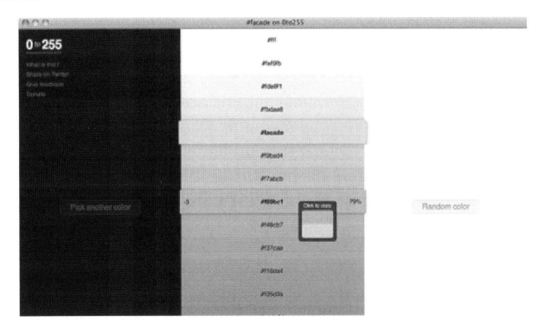

Note: When a hex value consists of three pairs, the values can be abbreviated. For example, the value #ffaa77 can be written #fa7. Some designers swear by this abbreviated form. I tend to use the full six-figure hex value because it keeps things consistent.

Web-safe colors

Modern PCs and Macs come with some reasonable graphics clout, but this wasn't always the case. In fact, many computers still in common use cannot display millions of colors. Back in the 1990s, palette restrictions were even more ferocious, with many computers limited to a paltry 256 colors (8-bit). Microsoft and Apple couldn't agree on which colors to use, so the web-safe palette was created, which comprises just 216 colors that are supposed to work accurately on both platforms without dithering. (For more information about dithering, see the "GIF" section later in this chapter.) Applications such as Photoshop have built-in web-safe palettes, and variations on the palette can be seen at www.visibone.com.

Colors in the web-safe palette are made up of combinations of RGB in 20% increments, and as you might expect, the palette is limited. Also discouraging, in the article "Death of the Websafe Color Palette?" on Webmonkey (www.webmonkey.com/00/37/index2a.html; posted September 6, 2000), David Lehn and Hadley Stern reported that all but 22 of these colors were incorrectly shifted in some way when tested on a variety of platforms and color displays—in other words, only 22 of the web-safe colors are actually totally web-safe.

The majority of people using the Web have displays capable of millions of colors, and almost everyone else can view at least thousands of colors. Unless you're designing for a very specific audience with known restricted hardware, stick with sRGB (the default color space of the Web—see www.w3.org/Graphics/Color/sRGB) and design in millions of colors. And consider yourself lucky that it's not 1995.

Choosing formats for images

To present images online in the best possible way, it's essential to choose the best file format when exporting and saving them. Although the save dialogs in most graphics editors present a bewildering list of possible formats, the Web typically uses just two: JPEG and GIF (along with the GIF89, or transparent GIF, variant), although a third, PNG, is finally gaining popularity, largely because of Internet Explorer 7 finally having offered full support for it.

JPEG

The Joint Photographic Experts Group (JPEG) format is used primarily for images that require smooth color transitions and continuous tones, such as photographs. JPEG supports millions of colors, and relatively little image detail is lost—at least when compression settings aren't too high. This is because the format uses lossy compression, which removes information that the eye doesn't need. As the compression level increases, this information loss becomes increasingly obvious, as shown in the following images. As you can see from the image on the right, which is much more compressed than the one on the left, nasty artifacts become increasingly dominant as the compression level increases. At extreme levels of compression, an image will appear to be composed of linked blocks (see the following two images, the originals of which are in the chapter 4 folder as tree.jpg and tree-compressed.jpg).

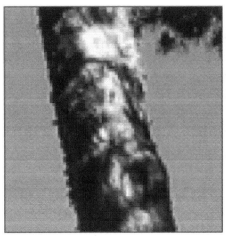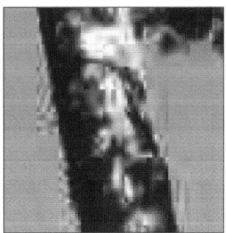

Although it's tricky to define a cutoff point, it's safe to say that for photographic work where it's important to retain quality and detail, 50 to 60% compression (40 to 50% quality) is the highest you should go for. Higher compression is sometimes OK in specific circumstances, such as for very small image thumbnails, but even then, it's best not to exceed 70% compression.

If the download time for an image is unacceptably high, you could always try reducing the dimensions rather than the quality; a small, detailed image usually looks better than a large, heavily compressed image. Also, bear in mind that common elements—that is, images that appear on every page of a website, perhaps as part of the interface—will be cached and therefore need to be downloaded only once. Because of this, you can get away with less compression and higher file sizes.

> *Note: Be aware that applications have different means of referring to compression levels. Some, such as Adobe applications, use a quality scale, in which 100 is uncompressed and 0 is completely compressed. Others, such as Paint Shop Pro, use compression values, in which higher numbers indicate increased compression. Always be sure you know which scale you're using.*

Some applications have the option to save progressive JPEGs. Typically, this format results in larger file sizes, but it's useful because it enables your image to download in multiple passes. This means that a low-resolution version will display rapidly and gradually progress to the quality you saved it at, allowing viewers to get a look at a simplified version of the image without having to wait for it to load completely.

GIF

Graphics Interchange Format (GIF) is in many ways the polar opposite of JPEG—it's lossless, meaning that there's no color degradation when images are compressed. However, the format is restricted to a maximum of 256 colors, thereby rendering it ineffective for color photographic images. Using GIF for such images tends to produce banding, in which colors are reduced to the nearest equivalent. A fairly extreme example of this is shown in the following illustration.

GIF is useful for displaying images with large areas of flat color, such as logos, line art, and type. As we mentioned in the previous chapter, you should generally avoid using graphics for text on your web pages, but if you do, PNG is the best choice of format, depending on the stylization of the text and whether it needs to be transparent.

Although GIF is restricted to 256 colors, it's worth noting that you don't have to use the same 256 colors every time. Most graphics applications provide a number of palette options, such as perceptual, selective, and web. The first of those, perceptual, tends to prioritize colors that the human eye is most sensitive to, thereby providing the best color integrity. Selective works in a similar fashion but balances its color choices with web-safe colors, thereby creating results more likely to be safe across platforms. Web refers to the 216-color web-safe palette discussed earlier. Additionally, you often have the option to lock colors, which forces your graphics application to use only the colors within the palette you choose.

Images can also be dithered, which prevents continuous tones from becoming bands of color. Dithering simulates continuous tones, using the available (restricted) palette. Most graphics editors allow for three different types of dithering: diffusion, pattern, and noise—all of which have markedly different effects on an image. Diffusion applies a random pattern across adjacent pixels, whereas pattern applies a half-tone pattern rather like that seen in low-quality print publications. Noise works rather like diffusion, but without diffusing the pattern across adjacent pixels. The following are four examples of the effects of dithering on an image that began life as a smooth gradient. The first image (1) has no dither, and the gradient has been turned into a series of solid, vertical stripes. The second image (2) shows the effects of diffusion dithering; the third (3), pattern; and the fourth (4), noise.

1   2   3   4

GIF89: The transparent GIF

The GIF89 file format is identical to GIF, with one important exception: you can remove colors, which provides a very basic means of transparency and enables the background to show through. Because this is not alpha transparency (a type of transparency that enables a smooth transition from solid to transparent, allowing for many levels of opacity), it doesn't work in the way many graphic designers expect. You cannot, for instance, fade an image's background from color to transparent and expect the web page's background to show through—instead, GIF89's transparency is akin to cutting a hole with a pair of scissors: the background shows through the removed colors only. This is fine when the "hole" has flat horizontal or vertical edges. But if you try this with irregular shapes—such as in the following image of the cloud with a drop shadow—you'll end up with ragged edges. In the example, the idea was to have the cloud casting a shadow onto the gray background. However, because GIFs can't deal with alpha transparency, we instead end up with an unwanted white outline. (One way around this is to export the image with the same background color as that of the web page, but this is possible only if the web page's background is a plain, flat color.)

Because of these restrictions, GIF89s are not used all that much these days. They do cling on in one area of web design, though: as spacers for stretching table cells in order to lay out a page. However, in these enlightened times, that type of technique must be avoided, since you can lay out precisely spaced pages much more easily using CSS.

PNG

For years, PNG (pronounced "ping," and short for Portable Network Graphics) lurked in the wilderness as a capable yet unloved and unused format for web design. Designed primarily as a replacement for GIF, the format has plenty to offer, including a far more flexible palette than GIF and true alpha transparency. Some have touted PNG as a JPEG replacement, too, but this isn't recommended—PNGs tend to be much larger than JPEGs for photographic images. For imagery with sharp lines, areas of flat color, or where alpha transparency is required, it is, however, a good choice.

The reason PNG was less common than GIF or JPEG primarily had to do with Internet Explorer. Prior to version 7, Microsoft's browser didn't offer support for PNG alpha transparency, instead replacing transparent areas with white or gray. Although a proprietary workaround exists (see Chapter 9's "Dealing with Internet Explorer bugs" section), it isn't intuitive, and it requires extra code. With post–version 6 releases of Internet Explorer finally supporting alpha transparency, PNG is a popular choice.

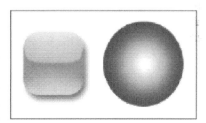

The three adjacent images highlight the benefit of PNG over GIF, as shown in a web browser. The first illustration shows two PNGs on a white background. The second illustration shows this background replaced by a grid. Note how the button's drop shadow is partially see-through, while the circle's center is revealed as being partially transparent, increasing in opacity toward its edge. The third illustration shows the closest equivalent when using GIFs—the drop shadow is surrounded by an ugly cutout, and the circle's central area loses its transparency. Upon closer inspection, the circle is also surrounded by a jagged edge, and the colors are far less smooth than those of the PNG.

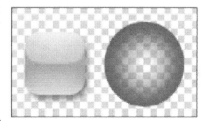

For more information about this format, checkout the PNG website at www.libpng.org/pub/png.

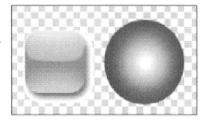

Other image formats

You may have worked on pages in the past and added the odd BMP or TIFF file or seen another site do the same. These are not standard formats for the Web, though, and while they may work fine in some cases, they require additional software in order to render in some browsers (in many cases, they won't render at all, or they'll render inconsistently across browsers). Furthermore, JPEG, GIF, and PNG are well-suited to web design because they enable you to present a lot of visual information in a fairly small file. Presenting the same in a TIFF or BMP won't massively increase the image's quality (when taking into account the low resolution of the Web), but it will almost certainly increase download times. Therefore, quite simply, don't use any formats other than JPEG, GIF, or PNG for your web images (and if you decide to use PNG transparency, be sure that your target audience will be able to see the images).

Common web image gaffes

The same mistakes tend to crop up again and again when designers start working with images. To avoid making them, read on to find out about some common ones (and how to avoid them).

Using graphics for body copy

Some sites use graphics for body copy on web pages in order to get more typographical control than CSS allows. However, using graphics for body copy causes text to print poorly—much worse than HTML-based text. Additionally, it means the text can't be read by search engines, can't be copied and pasted, and can't be enlarged, unless you're using a browser (or operating system) that can zoom—and even then it will be pixelated. If graphical text needs to be updated, it means reworking the original image (which could include messing with line wraps, if words need to be added or removed), reexporting it, and reuploading it.

As mentioned in the "Image-replacement techniques" section of Chapter 3, the argument is a little less clear-cut for headings (although I recommend using styled HTML-based text for those, too), but for body copy, you should always avoid using images.

Not working from original images

If it turns out an image on a website is too large or needs editing in some way, the original should be sourced to make any changes if the online version has been in any way compressed. This is because continually saving a compressed image reduces its quality each time. Also, under no circumstances should you increase the dimensions of a compressed JPEG. Doing so leads to abysmal results every time.

Overwriting original documents

The previous problem gets worse if you've deleted your originals. Therefore, be sure that you never overwrite the original files you're using. If resampling JPEGs from a digital camera for the Web, work with copies so you don't accidentally overwrite your only copy of that great photo you've taken with a much smaller, heavily compressed version. More important, if you're using an application that enables layers, save copies of the layered documents prior to flattening them for export—otherwise you'll regret it when having to make that all-important change and having to start from scratch.

Busy backgrounds

When used well, backgrounds can improve a website, adding visual interest and atmosphere—see the following image, showing the top of a version of the Snub Communications homepage. However, if backgrounds are too busy, in terms of complicated artwork and color, they'll distract from the page's content. If placed under text, they may even make your site's text-based content impossible to read. With that in mind, keep any backgrounds behind content subtle—near-transparent single-color watermarks tend to work best.

For backgrounds outside of the content area (as per the "Watermarks" section in Chapter 2), you must take care, too. Find a balance in your design and ensure that the background doesn't distract from the content, which is the most important aspect of the site.

Lack of contrast

It's common to see websites that don't provide enough contrast between text content and the background—for example, (very) light gray text on a white background, or pale text on an only slightly darker background. Sometimes this lack of contrast finds its way into other elements of the site, such as imagery comprising interface elements. This isn't always a major problem; in some cases, designs look stylish if a subtle scheme is used with care. You should, however, ensure that usability isn't affected—it's all very well to have a subtle color scheme, but not if it stops visitors from being able to easily find things like navigation elements or from being able to read the text.

Using the wrong image format

Exporting photographs as GIFs, using BMPs or TIFFs online, rendering soft and blotchy line art and text as a result of using the JPEG format—these are all things to avoid in the world of creating images for websites. See the section "Choosing formats for images" earlier in this chapter for an in-depth discussion of formats.

Resizing in HTML

When designers work in WYSIWYG editing tools, relying on a drag-and-drop interface, it's sometimes tempting to resize all elements in this manner (and this can sometimes also be done by accident), thereby compromising the underlying code of a web page. Where images are concerned, this has a detrimental effect, because the pixel dimensions of the image no longer tally with its width and height values. In some cases, this may lead to distorted imagery (as shown in the rather extreme example that follows); it may also lead to visually small images that have ridiculously large files sizes by comparison. In most cases, distortion of detail will still occur, even when proportion is maintained.

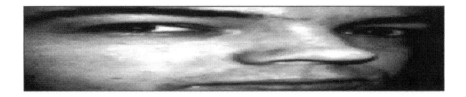

Note: There are exceptions to this rule, however, although they are rare. For instance, if you work with pixel art saved as a GIF, you can proportionately enlarge an image, making it large on the screen. Despite the image being large, the file size will be tiny.

Not balancing quality and file size

Bandwidth can be a problem in image-heavy sites—both in terms of the host getting hammered when visitor numbers increase and in terms of the visitors, many of whom may be stuck with slower connections than you having to download the images. Therefore, you should always be sure that your images are highly optimized in order to save on hosting costs and ensure that your website's visitors don't have to suffer massive downloads. (In fact, they probably won't—they'll more than likely go elsewhere.)

But this doesn't mean you should compress every image on your website into a slushy mess (and we've seen plenty of sites where the creator has exported JPEGs at what looks like 90% compression—"just in case").

Err on the side of caution, but remember: common interface elements are cached, so you can afford to save them at a slightly higher quality. Any image that someone requests (such as via a thumbnail on a portfolio site) is something they want to see, so these too can be saved at a higher quality because the person is likely to wait. Also, there is no such thing as an optimum size for web images. If you've read in the past that no web image should ever be larger than 50 KB, it's hogwash. The size of your images depends entirely on context, the type of site you're creating, and the audience you're creating it for.

Text overlays and splitting images

Some designers use various means to stop people from stealing images from their site and reusing them. The most common are including a copyright statement on the image itself, splitting the image into a number of separate images to make it harder to download, and adding an invisible transparent GIF overlay.

The main problem with copyright statements is that they are often poorly realized (see the following example), ruining the image with a garish text overlay. Ultimately, while anyone can download images from your website to their hard drive, you need to remember that if someone uses your images, they're infringing your copyright, and you can deal with them accordingly (and, if they link directly to images on your server, try changing the affected images to something text-based, like "The scumbag whose site you're visiting stole images from me").

As for splitting images into several separate files or placing invisible GIFs over images to try to stop people from downloading them, don't do this—there are simple workarounds in either case, and you just end up making things harder for yourself when updating your site. Sometimes you even risk compromising the structural integrity of your site when using such methods.

Stealing images and designs

Too many people appear to think that the Internet is a free-for-all, outside of the usual copyright restrictions, but this isn't the case: copyright exists on the Web just like everywhere else. Unless you have permission to reuse an image you've found online, you shouldn't do so. If discovered, you may get the digital equivalent of a slap on the wrist, but you could also be sued for copyright infringement.

Although it's all right to be influenced by someone else's design, you should also ensure you don't simply rip off a creation found on the Web—otherwise, you could end up in legal trouble or the subject of ridicule.

Working with images in HTML

The img element is used to add images to a web page. It's an empty tag, so it takes the combined start and end tag form with a trailing slash, as outlined in Chapter 1. The following code block shows an example of an image element, complete with relevant attributes:

```
<img src="sunset.jpg" height="200" width="400" alt="Sunset in
íReykjavík" />
```

Perhaps surprisingly, the height and width attributes are actually optional, although I recommend including them because they assist the browser in determining the size of the image before it downloads (thereby speeding up the process of laying out the page). The only two image element attributes required in HTML are src and alt. The first, src, is the path to the image file to be displayed; and the second, alt, provides some alternative text for when the image is not displayed.

> Note that this chapter's section on images largely concerns itself with inline images—the addition of images to the content of a web page. For an overview of using images as backgrounds, see the "Web page backgrounds" section of Chapter 2; for an overview of working with images within web navigation and with links in general, see Chapter 5.

Using alt text for accessibility benefits

Alternate text—usually referred to as *alt text*, after its attribute—is often ignored or used poorly by designers, but it's essential for improving the accessibility of web pages. Visitors using screen readers rely on the alt attribute's value to determine what an image shows. Therefore, always include a succinct description of the image's content and avoid using the image's file name, because that's often of little help. Ignoring the alt attribute not only renders your page invalid according to the W3C recommendations but also means that screen readers (and browsers that cannot display images) end up with something like this for output: [IMAGE][IMAGE][IMAGE]—not very helpful, to say the least.

Descriptive alt text for link-based images

Images often take on dual roles, being used for navigation purposes as well as additional visual impact. In such cases, the fact that the image is a navigation aid is likely to be of more significance than its visual appearance. For instance, many companies use logos as links to a homepage—in such cases, some designers would suggest using "Company X homepage" for the alt text, because it's more useful than "Company X."

Alternatively, stick with using the alt attribute for describing the image, and add a title attribute to the link, using that to describe the target. Depending on user settings, the link's title attribute will be read in the absence of any link text.

> Tip: If you don't have access to screen-reading software for testing *alt* text and various other accessibility aspects of a website, either install the text-based browser Lynx; run Opera in User mode, which can emulate a text browser; or try the Universal Access options on your computer such as Mac OS X with Voice Over options in Safari.

Null alt attributes for interface images

In some cases, images have no meaning at all (such as if they're a part of an interface), and there is some debate regarding the best course of action with regard to such images' alt values. Definitely never type something like spacer or interface element; otherwise, screen readers and text browsers will drive their users crazy relaying these values back to them. Instead, it's recommended that you use a null alt attribute, which takes the form alt="".

Null `alt` attributes are unfortunately not interpreted correctly by all screen readers; some, upon discovering a null `alt` attribute, go on to read the image's `src` value. A common workaround is to use empty `alt` attributes, which just have blank space for the value (`alt=" "`). However, the null `alt` attribute has valid semantics, so it should be used despite some screen readers not being able to deal with it correctly.

Alternatively, try reworking your design so that images without meaning are applied as background images to `div` elements, rather than placed inline.

Using alt and title text for tooltips

Although the W3C specifically states that `alt` text shouldn't be visible if the image can be seen, Internet Explorer ignores this, displaying `alt` text as a tooltip when the mouse cursor hovers over an image, as shown in the adjacent example.

Internet Explorer users are most likely accustomed to this by now, and, indeed, you may have used `alt` text to create tooltips in your own work. If so, it's time to stop. This behavior is not recommended by the W3C, and it's also not common across all browsers and platforms.

If an image requires a tooltip, most browsers display the value of a `title` attribute as one. In spite of this, if the text you're intending for a pop-up is important, you should instead place it within the standard text of your web page, rather than hiding it where most users won't see it. This is especially important when you consider that Firefox crops the values after around 80 characters, unlike some browsers, which happily show multiline tooltips.

Using CSS when working with images

In the following section, we're going to look at relevant CSS for web page images. You'll see how best to apply borders to images and wrap text around them, as well as define spacing between images and other page elements.

Applying CSS borders to images

You may have noticed earlier that we didn't mention the `border` attribute when working through the `img` element. This is because the `border` attribute is deprecated; adding borders to images is best achieved and controlled by using CSS. (Also, because of the flexibility of CSS, this means that if you want only a simple surrounding border composed of flat color, you no longer have to add borders directly to your image files.) Should you want to add a border to every image on your website, you could do so with the following CSS:

```
img {
  border: 1px solid #000000;
}
```

In this case, a 1-pixel solid border, colored black (#000000 in hex), would surround every image on the site. Using contextual selectors, this can be further refined. For instance, should you only want the images within a content area (marked up as a `div` with an `id` value of content) to be displayed with a border, you could write the following CSS:

```
div#content img {
  border: 1px solid #000000;
}
```

Alternatively, you could set borders to be on by default and override them in specific areas of the website via a rule using grouped contextual selectors:

```
img {
  border: 1px solid #000000;
}

#masthead img, #footer img, #sidebar img {
  border: 0;
}
```

Finally, you could override a global `border` setting by creating, for example, a `portfolio` class and then assigning it to relevant images. In CSS, you'd write the following:

```
.portfolio {
  border: 0;
}
```

And in HTML, you'd add the `portfolio` class to any image that you didn't want to have a border:

```
<img class="portfolio" src="sunset.jpg" height="200" width="400"
alt="A photo of a sunset" />
```

Clearly, this could be reversed (turning off borders by default and overriding this with, say, an `addBorder` style that could be used to add borders to specific images). Obviously, you should go for whichever system provides you with the greatest flexibility when it comes to rapidly updating styles across the site and keeping things consistent when any changes occur. Generally, the contextual method is superior for achieving this.

Although it's most common to apply borders using the shorthand shown earlier, it's possible to define borders on a per-side basis, as demonstrated in the "Using classes and CSS overrides to create an alternate pull quote" exercise in Chapter 3. If you wanted to style a specific image to resemble a Polaroid photograph, you could set equal borders on the top, left, and right, and a larger one on the bottom. In HTML, you would add a `class` attribute to the relevant image:

```
<img class="photo" src="sunset.jpg" height="300" width="300"
alt="Sunset photo" />
```

In CSS, you would write the following:

```
.photo {
  border-width: 8px 8px 20px;
  border-style: solid;
  border-color: #ffffff;
```

```
}
```

The results of this are shown in the image to the right. (Obviously, the white border shows only if you have a contrasting background—you wouldn't see a white border on a white background!)

Should you want to, you can also reduce the declaration's size by amalgamating the `border-style` and `border-color` definitions:

```
.photo {
  border: solid #ffffff;
  border-width : 8px 8px 20px;
}
```

Note that when you've used a contextual selector with an id value to style a bunch of elements in context, overriding this often requires the contextual selector to again be included in the override rule. In other words, a class value of .override would not necessarily override values set in #box img, even if applied to an image in the box div. In such cases, you'd need to add the id to the selector: #box .override.

There are other `border-style` values that can be used with images, as well. Examples include `dashed` and `dotted`; see the `border-style` entry in Appendix D (CSS Reference) for a full list. However, overdone decoration can distract from the image, so always ensure that your borders don't overpower your imagery.

Using CSS to wrap text around images

You can use the `float` and `margin` properties to enable body copy to wrap around an image. The method is similar to the pull quote example in the previous chapter, so we won't dwell too much on this. Suffice to say that images can be floated left or right, and margins can be set around edges facing body copy in order to provide some whitespace. For example, expanding on the previous example, you could add the following rules to ensure that the surrounding body copy doesn't hug the image:

```
.photo {
  border-width: 8px 8px 20px 8px;
  border-style: solid;
  border-color: #ffffff;
  float: right;
  margin-left: 20px;
  margin-bottom: 20px;
```

}

This results in the following effect shown in the following image.

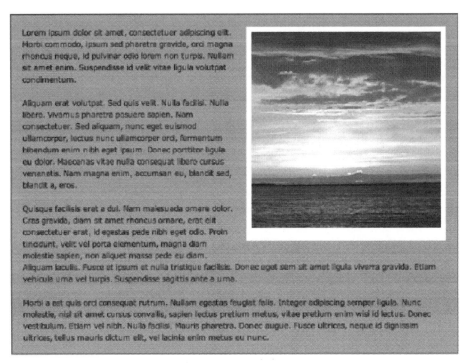

See `using-css-to-wrap-around-images.html`, `using-css-to-wrap-around-images.css`, and `sunset.jpg` in the `chapter 4` folder for a working example of this page.

Displaying random images

This section of the chapter looks at creating a simple system for displaying a random image from a selection. This has several potential uses, such as randomizing banners on a commercial website or giving the impression that a site is updated more often than it is by showing visitors some new content each time they arrive. Also, for portfolios, it's useful to present a random piece of work from a selection.

Prior to starting work, you need to prepare your images. Unless you're prepared for subsequent layout elements to shift upon each visit to the page, aim to export all your images with equal dimensions. Should this not be an option, try to keep the same height setting. Note, however, that you can use different file formats for the various images. It's good housekeeping to keep these images in their own folder, too; for this exercise, the images are placed within `assets/random-images`.

Creating a JavaScript-based image randomizer

Required files   The `image-randomizer-starting-point` folder from the `chapter 4` folder

1. Edit the HTML. Open randomizer.html. In the body of the web page, add the following img element. The src value is for the default image, and this is what's shown if JavaScript is unavailable. The id value is important—this is a hook for both the JavaScript function written in steps 4 through 6 and a CSS rule to add a border to the image.

```
<img src="assets/random-images/road.jpg" id="randomImage"
name="randomImage" height="300" width="300" />
```

2. Next, add an onload attribute to the body start tag, as shown in the following code block. Note that the value of this attribute will be the name of the JavaScript function.

```
<body onload="randomImage()">
```

3. In randomizer.js, create arrays for image file names and alt attribute values. For the former, only the image file names are needed, not the path to them (that will be added later). Note that the order of the items in the arrays must match; in other words, the text in the first item of the chosenAltCopy array should be for the first image in the chosenImage array.

```
var chosenImage=new Array();
chosenImage[0]="stream.jpg";
chosenImage[1]="river.jpg";
chosenImage[2]="road.jpg";

var chosenAltCopy=new Array();
chosenAltCopy[0]="A stream in Iceland";
chosenAltCopy[1]="A river in Skaftafell, Iceland";
chosenAltCopy[2]="A near-deserted road in Iceland";
```

4. Create a random value. The following JavaScript provides a random value:

```
var getRan=Math.floor(Math.random()*chosenImage.length);
```

5. Create a function. Add the following text to start writing the JavaScript function, which was earlier dubbed randomImage (see step 1's onload value). If you're not familiar with JavaScript, then note that content from subsequent steps must be inserted into the space between the curly brackets.

```
function randomImage()
{
}
```

6. Add JavaScript to set the image. By manipulating the Document Object Model (DOM), we can assign values to an element via its id value. Here, the line states to set the src attribute value of the element with the id value randomImage (that is, the image added in step 1) to the stated path value plus a random item from the chosenImage array (as defined via getRan, a variable created in step 3).

```
document.getElementById('randomImage').setAttribute
('src','assets/random-images/'+chosenImage[getRan]);
```

139

7. Add JavaScript to set the alt text. Setting the alt text works in a similar way to step 5, but the line is slightly simpler, because of the lack of a path value for the `alt` text:

```
document.getElementById('randomImage').setAttribute
('alt',chosenAltCopy[getRan]);
```

8. Style the image. In CSS, add the following two rules. The first removes borders by default from images that are links. The second defines a border for the image added in step 1, which has an `id` value of `randomImage`.

```
a img {
  border: 0;
}
#randomImage {
  border: solid 1px #000000;
}
```

Upon testing the completed files in a browser, each refresh should show a random image from the selection, as shown in the following screenshot. (Note that in this image, the `padding` value for `body` was set to `20px 0 0 20px` to avoid the random image hugging the top left of the browser window.)

There are a couple of things to note regarding the script. To add further images/alt text, copy the previous items in each array, increment the number in square brackets by one, and then amend the values—for example:

```
var chosenImage=new Array();
chosenImage[0]="stream.jpg";
chosenImage[1]="river.jpg";
chosenImage[2]="road.jpg";
chosenImage[3]="harbor.jpg";

var chosenAltCopy=new Array();
chosenAltCopy[0]="A stream in Iceland";
chosenAltCopy[1]="A river in Skaftafell, Iceland";
chosenAltCopy[2]="A near-deserted road in Iceland";
chosenAltCopy[3]="The harbor in Reykjavík ";
```

You'll also note that in this example the height and widths of the images are identical. However, these can also be changed by editing the script. For example, to set a separate height for each image, you'd first add the following array:

```
var chosenHeight=new Array();
chosenHeight[0]="200";
chosenHeight[1]="500";
chosenHeight[2]="400";
```

And you'd next add the following line to the function:

```
document.getElementById('randomImage').setAttribute
('height',chosenHeight[getRan]);
```

Remember, however, the advice earlier about the page reflowing if the image dimensions vary—if you have images of differing sizes, your design will need to take this into account.

Creating a PHP-based image randomizer

Required files   The image-randomizer-starting-point folder from the chapter 4 folder

What you'll learn   How to create an image randomizer using PHP

Completed files The image-randomizer-php folder in the chapter 4 folder

If you have access to web space that enables you to work with PHP, it's simple to create an equivalent to the JavaScript exercise using PHP. The main benefit is that users who disable JavaScript will still see a random image, rather than just the default. Note that you need some method of running PHP files to work on this exercise, such as a local install of Apache. Note also that prior to working through the steps, you should remove the HTML document's script element, and you should also amend the title element's value, changing it to something more appropriate.

1. Define the CSS rules. In CSS, define a border style, as per step 7 of the previous exercise, but also edit the existing paragraph rule with a font property/value pair, because in this example, you're going to add a caption based on the alt text value.

```
a img {
  border: 0;
```

```
}
#randomImage {
  border: solid 1px #000000;
}
p {
  font: 1.2em/1.5em Verdana, sans-serif;
  margin-bottom: 1.5em;
}
```

   2. Set up the PHP tag. Change the file name of randomizer.html to randomizer.php to make it a PHP document. Then, place the following on the page, in the location where you want the randomized image to go. Subsequent code should be placed within the PHP tags.

```
<?php
?>
```

   3. Define the array. One array can be used to hold the information for the file names and alt text. In each case, the alt text should follow its associated image.

```
$picarray = array("stream" => "A photo of a stream", "river" => "A
 photo of a river", "road" => "A photo of a road");
$randomkey = array_rand($picarray);
```

   4. Print information to the web page. Add the following lines to write the img and p elements to the web page, using a random item set from the array for the relevant attributes. Note that the paragraph content is as per the alt text. Aside from the caption, the resulting web page looks identical to the JavaScript example.

```
echo '<img src="assets/random-images/'.$randomkey.'.jpg"
alt="'.$picarray[$randomkey].'" width="300" height="300"
class="addBorder" />';

echo '<p>'.$picarray[$randomkey].'</p>';
```

   5. Use an include. This is an extra step of sorts. If you want to make your PHP more modular, you can copy everything within the PHP tags to an external document, save it (for example, as random-image.php) and then cut it into the web page as an include:

```
<?php
@include($_SERVER['DOCUMENT_ROOT'] . "/random-image.php");
?>
```

> For more on working with PHP, see *PHP Solutions: Dynamic Web Design Made Easy* by David Powers.

CSS image sprites

An *image sprite* is a collection of images put into a single image for performance issues. This way, a web page with many images can take a shorter time to load since it won't have to make multiple server requests. Using image sprites will reduce the number of server requests and save bandwidth. Spriting is a technique that originated from creating partially transparent graphics for use in video games.

The following shows one of the image sprites that Gmail uses in its UI.

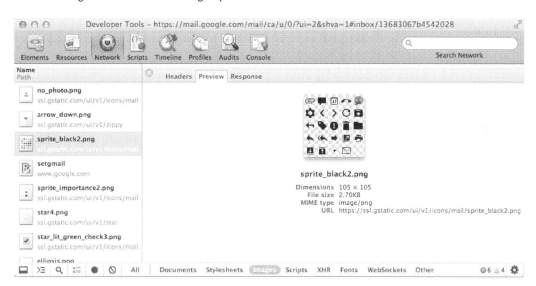

When Gmail is loaded, it won't load these images one by one but will rather load the whole master image at once. It may not sound like a significant improvement, but it is. CSS sprites reduce HTTP requests and the loading time of pages, which is the main reason they are often used on websites with heavy traffic.

Let's say you want to use three different images in a page:

```
<img src="first.png" style="width: 100px; height: 200px">
<img src="second.png" style="width: 300px; height: 300px">
<img src="third.png"  style="width: 25px; height: 50px">
```

You can use a service like csssprites.com to combine them in one master file and include them on the page in the following manner:

```
<style type="text/css">
    .sprite {
        background: url('master-file.png');
    }
</style>
```

```
<div class="sprite" style="background-position: -0px -0px; width: 100px; height:
200px"> </div>•
<div class="sprite" style="background-position: -0px -210px; width: 300px; height:
300px"> </div>•
<div class="sprite" style="background-position: -0px -520px; width: 25px; height:
50px"> </div>
```

The following shows how master-file.png looks (300x570px).

We hope you've found this chapter of interest and now feel you have a good grounding in working with images on the Web. It's amazing to think how devoid of visual interest the Web used to be in contrast to today, now that images are essential to the vast majority of sites. As we've mentioned before, the importance of images on the Web lies not only in content but in interface elements such as navigation—a topic we're covering in the next chapter.

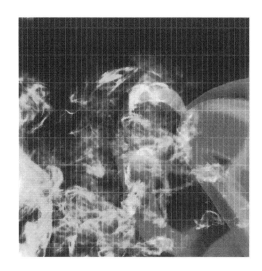

Chapter 5

Using Links and Creating Navigation

In this chapter:

- Introducing web navigation

- Creating links

- Controlling CSS link states

- Mastering the cascade

- Looking at links and accessibility

- Examining a JavaScript alternative to pop-ups

- Creating navigation bars

- Working with CSS-based rollovers

Introduction to web navigation

The primary concern of most websites is the provision of information. The ability to enable nonlinear navigation via the use of links is one of the main things that set the Web apart from other media. But without organized, coherent, and usable navigation, even a site with the most amazing content will fail.

During this chapter, we'll work through how to create various types of navigation. Instead of relying on large numbers of graphics and clunky JavaScript, we'll create rollovers that are composed of nothing more than simple HTML lists and a little CSS. And rather than using pop-up windows to display large graphics when a thumbnail image is clicked, we'll cover how to do everything on a single page.

Navigation types

There are essentially three types of navigation online:

- Inline navigation: General links within web page content areas

- Site navigation: The primary navigation area of a website, commonly referred to as a navigation bar

- *Search-based navigation*: A search box that enables you to search a site via terms you input yourself

Although I've separated navigation into these three distinct categories, lines blur, and not every site includes all the different types of navigation. Also, various designers call each navigation type something different, and there's no official name in each case, so in the following sections, I'll expand a little on each type.

Inline navigation

Inline navigation is one of the primary ways of navigating the Web, which, many moons ago, largely consisted of technical documentation. For instance, you can make specific words within a document link directly to related content. A great example of this is Wikipedia (www.wikipedia.org), the free encyclopedia.

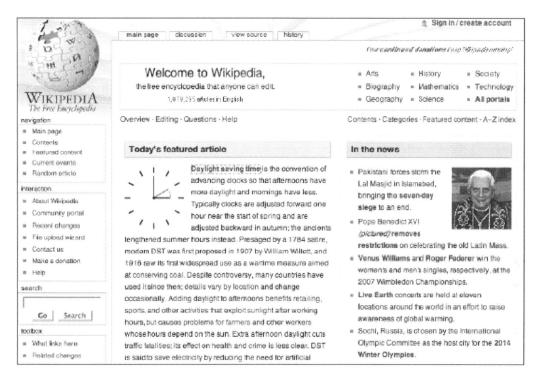

Site navigation

Wikipedia showcases navigation types other than inline. To the left, underneath the logo, is a navigation bar that is present on every page of the site, allowing users to quickly access each section. This kind of thing is essential for most websites—long gone are the days when users often expected to have to keep returning to a homepage to navigate to new content.

As Wikipedia proves, just because you have a global navigation bar, that doesn't mean you should skimp on inline navigation. In recent times, I've seen a rash of sites that say things like, "Thank you for visiting our website. If you have any questions, you can contact us by clicking the contact details link on our navigation bar." Quite frankly, this is bizarre. A better solution is to say, "Thank you for visiting our website. If you have any questions, please contact us" and to turn "contact us" into a link to the contact details page. This might seem like common sense, but not every web designer thinks in this way.

Search-based navigation

Wikipedia has a search box within its navigation sidebar. It's said there are two types of web users: those who eschew search boxes and those who head straight for them. The thing is, search boxes are not always needed, despite the claims of middle managers the world over. Indeed, most sites get by with well-structured and coherent navigation.

However, sites sometimes grow very large (typically those that are heavy on information and that have hundreds or thousands of pages, such as technical repositories, review archives, or large online stores like Amazon and eBay). In such cases, it's often not feasible to use only standard navigation elements to access information. Attempting to do so leads to users getting lost trying to navigate a huge navigation tree. Search is useful to users who know exactly what they are looking for and can be the deciding factor for the user when deciding between your website or another.

Unlike other types of navigation, search boxes aren't entirely straightforward to set up, requiring server-side scripting for their functionality. However, a quick trawl through a search engine provides many options, including Google Custom Search Engine (www.google.com/coop/cse/).

Creating and styling web page links

With the exception of search boxes, which are forms based on and driven by server-side scripting, online navigation relies on anchor elements. In its simplest form, an anchor element looks like this:

```
<a href="http://www.apress.com/">A link to the Apress website</a>
```

The href attribute value is the URL of the destination document, which is often another web page but can in fact be any file type (MP3, PDF, JPEG, and so on). If the browser can display the document type (either directly or via a plug-in), it does so; otherwise, it downloads the file (or brings up some kind of download prompt).

> Caution: Never omit end tags when working with links. Omitting </a> will cause most browsers to turn all subsequent content on the page into a link.

There are three ways of linking to a file: absolute links, relative links, and root-relative links. We'll cover these in the sections that follow, and you'll see how to create internal page links, style link states in CSS, and work with links and images. We'll also discuss enhanced link accessibility and usability, as well as link targeting.

Absolute links

The preceding example shows an absolute link, sometimes called a full URL, which is typically used when linking to external files (in other words, those on other websites). This type of link provides the entire path to a destination file, including the file transfer protocol, domain name, any directory names, and the file name itself. A longer example is as follows:

```
<a href="http://www.wireviews.com/lyrics/instar.html">Instar lyrics</a>
```

In this case, the file transfer protocol is http://, the domain is wireviews.com, the directory is lyrics, and the file name is instar.html.

Note: Depending on how the target site's web server has been set up, you may or may not have to include *www* prior to the domain name when creating this kind of link. It is a good idea to follow a link and see what the end result is before including it, to be on the safe side. An exception is if you're linking to a subdomain, such as *http://browsers.evolt.org.*

If you're linking to a website's homepage, you can usually leave off the file name, as in the earlier link to the Apress site, and the server will automatically pick up the default document—assuming one exists—which can be index.html, default.htm, index.php, index.asp, or some other name, depending on the server type. If no default document exists, you'll be returned a directory listing or an error message, depending on whether the server's permissions settings enable users to browse directories.

Relative links

A relative link is one that locates a file in relation to the current document. Taking the Wireviews example, if you were on the instar.html page, located inside the lyrics directory, and you wanted to link back to the homepage via a relative link, you would use the following code:

```
<a href="../index.html">Wireviews homepage</a>
```

The index.html file name is preceded by ../, which tells the web browser to move up one directory prior to looking for index.html. Moving in the other direction is done in the same way as with absolute links: by preceding the file name with the path. Therefore, to get from the homepage back to the instar.html page, you would write the following:

```
<a href="lyrics/instar.html">Instar lyrics</a>
```

In some cases, you need to combine both methods. For instance, this website has HTML documents in both the lyrics and reviews folders. To get from the instar.html lyrics page to a review, you have to go up one level and then down into the relevant directory to locate the file:

```
<a href="../reviews/alloy.html">Alloy review</a>
```

The base element when included in the head section of your web page allows you to set the default URL or target for all relative links.

```
<head>
<base href="http://www.wirereviews.com">
```

This allows you to define the relative links as follows:

```
<a href="index.html">Wireviews homepage</a>
<a href="lyrics/instar.html">Instar lyrics</a>
<a href="reviews/alloy.html">Alloy review</a>
```

Root-relative links

Root-relative links work in a similar way to absolute links but from the root of the website. These links begin with a forward slash, which tells the browser to start the path to the file from the root of the current website. Therefore, regardless of how many directories deep you are in the Wireviews website, a root-relative link to the homepage always looks like this:

```
<a href="/index.html">Homepage</a>
```

And a link to the `instar.html` page within the `lyrics` directory always looks like this:

```
<a href="/lyrics/instar.html">Instar lyrics</a>
```

This type of link therefore ensures you point to the relevant document without your having to type an absolute link or mess around with relative links and is, in my opinion, the safest type of link to use for linking to documents elsewhere on a website. Should a page be moved from one directory to one higher or lower in the hierarchy, none of the links (including links to style sheets and script documents) would require changing. Relative links, on the other hand, would require changing; and although absolute links wouldn't require changing, they take up more space and are less modular from a testing standpoint. If you're testing a site, you don't want to be restricted to the domain in question—you may want to host the site locally or on a temporary domain online so that clients can access the work-in-progress creation.

> Note: All paths in *href* attributes must contain forward slashes only. Some software—notably older releases from Microsoft—creates and permits backward slashes (for example, *lyrics\wire\154.html*), but this is nonstandard and does not work in non-Microsoft web browsers.

Internal page links

Along with linking to other documents, it's possible to link to another point in the same web page. This is handy for things like a FAQ (frequently asked questions) list, enabling the visitor to jump directly to an answer and then back to the list of questions, or for top-of-page links, enabling a user single-click access to return to the likely location of a page's masthead and navigation, if they've scrolled to the bottom of a long document.

When linking to other elements on a web page, you start by providing an `id` value for any element you want to be able to jump to. To link to that, you use a standard anchor element (`<a>`) with an `href` value equal to that of your defined `id` value, preceded by a hash symbol (#).

For a list of questions, you can have something like this:

```
<ul id="questions">
  <li><a href="#answer1">Question one</a></li>
  <li><a href="#answer2">Question two</a></li>
  <li><a href="#answer3">Question three</a></li>
</ul>
```

Later in the document, the first two answers might look like this:

```
<p id="answer1">The answer to question 1!</p>
<p><a href="#questions">Back to questions</a></p>
<p id="answer2">The answer to question 2!</p>
<p><a href="#questions">Back to questions</a></p>
```

As you can see, each link's href value is prefixed by a hash sign. When the link is clicked, the web page jumps to the element with the relevant id value. Therefore, clicking the Question one link, which has an href value of #answer1, jumps to the paragraph with the id value of answer1. Clicking the Back to questions link, which has an id value of #questions, jumps back to the list, because the unordered list element has an id of questions.

> Note: It's worth bearing in mind that the page jumps directly to the linked element only if there's enough room underneath it. If the target element is at the bottom of the web page, you'll see it plus a browser window height of content above.

Backward compatibility with fragment identifiers

In older websites, you may see a slightly different system for accessing content within a web page, and this largely involves obsolete browsers such as Netscape 4 not understanding how to deal with links that solely use the id attribute. Instead, you'll see a fragment identifier, which is an anchor tag with a name attribute, but no href attribute. For instance, a fragment identifier for the first answer is as follows:

```
<p><a id="answer1" name="answer1">Answer 1!</a></p>
```

The reason for the doubling up, here—using both the name and id attributes—is because the former is on borrowed time in web specifications, and it should therefore be used only for backward compatibility.

Top-of-page links

Internal page links are sometimes used to create a top-of-page/back-to-top link. This is particularly handy for websites that have lengthy pages—when a user has scrolled to the bottom of the page, they can click the link to return to the top of the document, which usually houses the navigation. The problem here is that the most common internal linking method—targeting a link at #top—fails in many browsers, including Firefox and Opera.

```
<a href="#top">Back to top</a>
```

You've likely seen the previous sort of link countless times, but unless you're using Internet Explorer or Safari, it's as dead as a dodo. There are various workarounds, though, one of which is to include a fragment identifier at the top of the document. At the foot of the web page is the Back to top link shown previously, and the fragment identifier is placed at the top of the web page:

```
<a id="top" name="top"></a>
```

This technique isn't without its problems, though. Some browsers ignore empty elements such as this (some web designers therefore populate the element with a single space); it's tricky to get the element right at the top of the page and not to interfere with subsequent content.

Two potential solutions are on offer. The simplest is to link the top-of-page link to your containing `div`—the one within which your web page's content is housed. For sites I create—as you'll see in Chapter 7—I typically house all content within a `div` that has an `id` value of `wrapper`. This enables me to easily control the width of the layout, among other things. In the context of this section of this chapter, the wrapper `div` also provides something for a top-of-page link to jump to. Clicking the link in the following code block would enable a user to jump to the top of the wrapper `div`, at (or very near to) the top of the web page.

```
<a href="#wrapper">Top of page</a>
```

Another solution is to nest a fragment identifier within a `div` and then style the `div` to sit at the top left of the web page. The HTML for this is the following:

```
<div id="topOfPageAnchor">
  <a id="top" name="top"> </a>
</div>
```

In CSS, you would then add the following:

```
div#topOfPageAnchor {
  position: absolute;
  top: 0;
  left: 0;
  height: 0;
}
```

Setting the `div`'s height to 0 means it takes up no space and is therefore not displayed; setting its positioning to `absolute` means it's outside the normal flow of the document, so it doesn't affect subsequent page content. You can test this by setting the background color of a following element to something vivid—it should sit tight to the edge of the container's edges.

Link states

By default, links are displayed underlined and in blue when viewed in a web browser. However, links have five states, and their visual appearance varies depending on the current state of the link. The states are as follows:

- `link`: The link's standard state, before any action has taken place
- `visited`: The link's state after having been clicked
- `hover`: The link's state while the mouse cursor is over it
- `focus`: The link's state while focused
- `active`: The link's state while being clicked

The `visited` and `active` states also have a default appearance. The former is displayed in purple and the latter in red. Both are underlined.

If every site adhered to this default scheme, it would be easier to find where you've been and where you haven't on the Web. However, most designers prefer to dictate their own color schemes rather than having blue and purple links peppering their designs. In my view, this is fine. Despite what some usability gurus claim, most web users these days probably don't even know what the default link colors are, and so hardly miss them.

Defining link states with CSS

CSS has advantages over the obsolete HTML method of defining link states. You gain control over the hover and focus states and can do far more than just edit the state colors—although that's what we're going to do first.

Anchors can be styled by using a tag selector:

```
a {
  color: #3366cc;
}
```

In this example, all anchors on the page—including links—are turned to a medium blue. However, individual states can be defined by using pseudo-class selectors (so called because they have the same effect as applying a class, even though no class is applied to the element):

```
a:link {
  color: #3366cc;
}
a:visited {
  color: #666699;
}
a:hover {
  color: #0066ff;
}
a:focus {
  background-color: #ffff00;
}
a:active {
  color: #cc00ff;
}
```

Correctly ordering link states

The various states have been defined in a specific order in the previous example: link, visited, hover, focus, active. This is because certain states override others, and those "closest" to the link on the web page take precedence.

There is debate regarding which order the various states should be in, so I can only provide my reasoning for this particular example. It makes sense for the link to be a certain color when you hover over it, and then a different color on the active state (when clicked), to confirm the click action. However, if you put the hover and active states in the other order (active, hover), you may not see the active one when the link is clicked. This is because you're still hovering over the link when you click it.

The focus state is probably primarily use keyboard users, so they won't typically see hover anyway. However, for mouse users, it makes logical sense to place focus after hover, because it's a more direct action. In other words, the link is selected, ready for activation during the focus state; but if you ordered

153

the states focus, hover, a link the cursor is hovering over would not change appearance when focused, which from a user standpoint is unhelpful.

> Tip: A simple way of remembering the basic state order (the five states minus *focus*) is to think of the words *love, hate: link, visited, hover, active*. If focus is included and my order is used, there's the slightly awkward (but equally memorable) *love her for always/love him for always: link, visited, hover, focus, active.*

However, there is a counter argument that recommends putting focus before hover so that when an already focused link (or potentially any other focused element for non-IE browsers) is hovered over, it will change from the focused state to indicate that it is now being hovered over. Ultimately, this is a chicken-and-egg scenario—do you want a hovered link to change from hover to focus to active? The focus will get lost somewhere in there until the link is depressed (and the active state removed), by which time the link will be in the process of being followed.

In the end, the decision should perhaps rest with how you're styling states and what information you want to present to the user, and often the focus state is a duplication of hover anyway, for the benefit of keyboard users. And on some occasions, it doesn't matter too much where it's put, if the styling method is much different from that for other states—for example, when a border is applied to focus, but a change of color or removal of underlines is used for the other states. However, if you decide on LVFHA or some other order, you'll have to make your own way of remembering the state order!

The difference between a and a:link

Many designers don't realize the difference between the selectors a and a:link in CSS. Essentially, the a selector styles all anchors, but a:link styles only those that are clickable links (in other words, those that include an href attribute) that have not yet been visited. This means that should you have a site with a number of fragment identifiers, you can use the a:link selector to style clickable links only, avoiding styling fragment identifiers, too. (This prevents the problem of fragment identifiers taking on underlines and also prevents the potential problem of user-defined style sheets overriding the a rule.) However, if you define a:link instead of a, you then must define the visited, hover, and active states; otherwise, they will be displayed in their default appearances. This is particularly important when it comes to visited, because that state is mutually exclusive to link and doesn't take on any of its styling. Therefore, if you set font-weight to bold via a:link alone, visited links will not appear bold (although the hover and active states will for unvisited links—upon the links being visited, they will become hover and active states for visited links and will be displayed accordingly).

Editing link styles using CSS

Along with changing link colors, CSS enables you to style links just like any other piece of text. You can define specific fonts; edit padding, margins, and borders; change the font weight and style; and also amend the standard link underline, removing it entirely if you want (by setting the text-decoration property to none).

```
a:link {
  color: #3366cc;
  font-weight: bold;
  text-decoration: none;
}
```

Removing the standard underline is somewhat controversial, even in these enlightened times, and causes endless (and rather tedious) arguments among web designers. My view is that it can be OK to do so, but with some caveats.

If you remove the standard underline, ensure your links stand out from the surrounding copy in some other way. Having your links in the same style and color as other words and not underlined is a very bad idea. The only exception is if you don't want users to easily find the links and click them (perhaps for a children's game or educational site).

A common device used by web designers is to recolor links in order to distinguish them from body copy. However, this may not be enough (depending on the chosen colors), because a significant proportion of the population has some form of color blindness. A commonly quoted figure for color blindness in Western countries is 8%, with the largest affected group being white males (the worldwide figure is lower, at approximately 4%). Therefore, a change of color (to something fairly obvious) and a change of font weight to bold often does the trick.

Whatever your choice, be consistent—don't have links change style on different pages of the site. Also, it's useful to reinforce the fact that links are links by bringing back the underline on the hover state. An example of this is shown below (see editing-link-styles-using-css.html and editing-link-styles-using-css.html in the chapter 5 folder of the completed files).

Lorem ipsum dolor sit amet, consectetuer adipiscing elit. Morbi commodo, ipsum sed pharetra gravida, orci magna rhoncus neque, id pulvinar odio lorem non turpis. Nullam sit amet enim. Suspendisse id velit vitae ligula volutpat condimentum. Aliquam erat volutpat. Sed quis velit. **Nulla facilisi**. Nulla libero. Vivamus pharetra posuere sapien. Nam consectetuer. Sed aliquam, nunc eget euismod ullamcorper, lectus nunc ullamcorper orci, fermentum bibendum enim nibh eget ipsum. Donec porttitor ligula eu dolor. Maecenas vitae nulla consequat libero cursus venenatis.

Links are bold and orange, making them stand out from surrounding text. On the hover state, the link darkens to red, and the standard underline returns. The second of those things is achieved by setting text-decoration to underline in the a:hover declaration. Note that even when presented in grayscale, such as in this book, these two states can be distinguished from surrounding text.

You can also combine pseudo-classes. For example, if you add the rules shown following to a style sheet (these are from the editing-link-styles-using-css documents), you'd have links going gray when visited but turning red on the hover state (along with showing the underline). Note that because the link and visited states are exclusive, the bold value for font-weight is assigned using the grouped selector. It could also be applied to individual rules, but this is neater.

```
a:link, a:visited {
  font-weight: bold;
}
a:link {
  color: #f26522;
  text-decoration: none;
}
a:visited {
  color: #8a8a8a;
}
a:hover {
  color: #f22222;
  text-decoration: underline;

}
a:active {
  color: #000000;
  text-decoration: underline;
}
```

If you decided that you wanted visited links to retain their visited color on the hover state, you could add the following rule:

```
a:visited:hover {
  color: #8a8a8a;
}
```

The :focus pseudo-class

The :focus pseudo-class enables you to define the link state of a focused link. Focusing usually occurs when tabbing to a link, so the :focus pseudo-class can be a handy usability aid.

The following example, used in editing-link-styles-using-css.css, turns the background of focused links yellow in compliant browsers:

```
a:focus {
  background: yellow;
}
```

Multiple link states: The cascade

A common problem web designers come up against is multiple link styles within a document. While you should be consistent when it comes to styling site links, there are specific exceptions, one of which is site navigation. Web users are quite happy with navigation bar links differing from standard inline links. Elsewhere, links may differ slightly in web page footers, where links are often displayed in a smaller font than that used for other web page copy; also, if a background color makes the standard link color hard to distinguish, it might be useful to change it (although in such situations it would perhaps be best to amend either the background or your default link colors).

A widespread error is applying a class to every link for which you want a style other than the default—you end up with loads of inline junk that can't be easily amended at a later date. Instead, with the careful use of `semantic elements` and unique `id`s on the web page and contextual selectors in CSS, you can rapidly style links for each section of a web page.

Styling multiple link states

Required files   XHTML-basic.html and CSS-default.css from the basic-boilerplates folder as a starting point

What you'll learn   How to use the cascade to set styles for links housed in specific areas of a webpage

Completed files   multiple-links-the-cascade.html and multiple-links-the-cascade.css from the chapter 5 folder

1. Add the basic page content structure shown following, placing it within the existing wrapper `div` of the boilerplate. This has three `sections`, which are the `navigation`, `content`, and `footer`, respectively. The navigation houses an unordered list that forms the basis of a navigation bar. The content is the content area, which has an inline link within a paragraph. The footer is sometimes used to repeat the navigation bar links, albeit in a simplified manner.

```
<nav>
  <ul>
    <li><a href="index.html">Homepage</a></li>
    <li><a href="products.html">Products</a></li>
    <li><a href="contact-details.html">Contact details</a></li>
  </ul>
</nav>
<div id="content">
  <p>Hello there. Our new product is a <a href="banjo.html">fantastic
    banjo</a>!</p>
</div>
<footer>
  <a href="index.html">Homepage</a> | <a href="products.html">
  Products</a> | <a href="contact-details.html">Contact
    details</a>
</footer>
```

> Note that the code block could be simplified, such as by dispensing with the navigation *div* and instead applying the relevant *id* value directly to the unordered list. However, this exercise aims to show how to create links in context, using a simplified web page layout that has specific areas for certain content types. See Chapters 7 and 10 for more on layout.

2. Add some padding to the existing body rule in the CSS to add some spacing around the page content:

```
body {
  font: 62.5%/1.5 Verdana, Arial, Helvetica, sans-serif;
  padding: 30px;
}
```

- Homepage
- Products
- Contact details
Hello there. Our new product is a fantastic banjo!

Homepage | Products | Contact details

3. Add some rules to define the main states for links on the web page. The following rules color links orange, change them to red on the hover state, make them gray on the visited state, and make them black on the active state.

```
a:link {
  color: #f26522;
}
a:visited {
  color: #8a8a8a;
}
a:hover {
  color: #f22222;
}
a:active {
  color: #000000;
}
```

4. Next, style the navigation links. Contextual selectors are used to style the links within the navigation div.

```
nav a, nav a:visited {
  text-decoration: none;
  font-weight: bold;
  color: #666666;
  text-transform: uppercase;
}
nav a:hover {
  text-decoration: underline;
}
```

The first rule removes the underline from all links within the navigation div, renders them in bold and uppercase, and colors them a medium gray. The second rule brings back the underline on the hover state.

> *You'll note that the visited state is the same as the standard state in the previous code block. While I don't recommend doing this for links in a page's general content area, or for pages that have a lot of navigation links, I feel it's acceptable for sites that have a small number of navigation links, where it's not likely a visitor will need notification regarding which pages or sections have been accessed.*

5. Style the footer links. Add another contextual selector to style the footer links, making them smaller than links elsewhere on the page:

```
footer a:link, footer a:visited {
  font-size: 0.8em;
}
```

- HOMEPAGE
- PRODUCTS
- CONTACT DETAILS
Hello there. Our new product is a fantastic banjo!

Homepage | Products | Contact details

And there we have it: three different link styles on the same page, without messing around with classes.

Enhanced link accessibility and usability

We've already touched on accessibility and usability concerns during this chapter, so we'll now briefly run through a few attributes that can be used with anchors (and some with area elements—see the "Image Maps" section later in the chapter) to enhance your web page links.

The title attribute

Regular users of Internet Explorer may be familiar with its habit of popping up alt text as a tooltip. This has encouraged web designers to wrongly fill alt text with explanatory copy for those links that require an explanation, rather than using the alt text for a succinct overview of the image's content. Should you require a pop-up, add a `title` attribute to your surrounding a element to explain what will happen when the link is clicked. The majority of web browsers display its a value when the link is hovered over for a couple of seconds (see right).

```
<a href="large-image.html" title="Click to view a larger image">
<img src="image.jpg" alt="This is some text that explains what
  the image is" width="400" height="300" /></a>
```

Using accesskey and tabindex

I've bundled the `accesskey` and `tabindex` attributes because they have similar functions—that is, enabling keyboard access to various areas of the web page. Most browsers enable you to use the Tab key to cycle through links, although if you end up on a web page with dozens of links, this can be a soul-destroying experience. (And before you say "So what?" you should be aware that many web users cannot use a mouse. You don't have to be severely disabled or elderly to be in such a position either—something as common as repetitive strain injury affects plenty of people's ability to use a mouse. It can also be faster to use if your hands are already on the keyboard.)

The `accesskey` attribute can be added to anchor and `area` elements. It assigns an access key to the link, whose value must be a single character. In tandem with your platform's assigned modifier key (Alt for Windows and Ctrl for Mac), you press the key to highlight or activate the link, depending on how the browser you're using works.

```
<a href="index.html" accesskey="/">Home page</a>
```

An ongoing problem with access keys is that the shortcuts used to activate them are mostly claimed by various technologies, leaving scant few characters. In fact, research conducted by WATS.ca (www.wats.ca/show.php?contentid=32) concluded that just three characters were available that didn't clash with anything at all: /, \, and]. This, combined with a total lack of standard access key assignments/bindings, has led to many accessibility gurus conceding defeat, admitting that while there's a definite need for the technology, it's just not there yet.

The `tabindex` attribute has proved more successful. This is used to define the attribute's value as anything from -1 (which excludes the element from the tabbing order, which can be useful) to 32767, thereby setting its place in the tab order, although if you have 32,767 tabbable elements on your web page, you really do need to go back and reread the earlier advice on information architecture (see Chapter 1). Note that tab orders needn't be consecutive, so it's wise to use tabindex in steps of ten, so you can later insert extra ones without renumbering everything. Before HTML5 the tabindex attribute was valid only on form and link elements, HTML5 has changed this making it valid on any element.

What's logical to some people—in terms of tab order—may not be to others, so always ensure you test your websites thoroughly, responding to feedback.

Skip navigation links

Designers who work with CSS layouts tend to focus on information structure, rather than blindly putting together layouts in a visual editor. This is good from an accessibility standpoint, because you can ensure information is ordered in a logical manner by checking its location in the code. However, when considering alternate browsers, it's clear that some of the information on the page will be potentially redundant. For example, while a user surfing with a standard browser can ignore the masthead and navigation in a split second, rapidly focusing on the information they want to look at, someone using a screen reader will have to sit through the navigation links being read out each time, which can prove extremely tedious if there are quite a few links.

Various solutions exist to help deal with this problem, and although you can use CSS to reorder the page information (most commonly by placing the code for the masthead at the end of the HTML document and then using absolute positioning to display it at the top when the page is viewed in a browser), it's more common to use what's typically referred to as skip navigation.

Creating a skip navigation link

Required files	skip-navigation-starting-point.html and skip-navigation-starting-point.css from the chapter 5 folder as a starting point

What you'll learn	How to create some basic skip navigation

Completed files	skip-navigation-completed.html and skip-navigation-completed.css from the chapter 5 folder

1. Examine the web page. Successful skip navigation relies in part on semantic and logical document structure. Open skip-navigation-starting-point.html, and you'll see it's a basic web page, with all of the page's content—title, navigation, and main content—contained within a wrapper div; next is a masthead div, containing a heading and a few links. Under the masthead div is a content div, which, suitably enough, houses the page's main content. The beginning of the content is immediately visible, even on monitors with low resolutions, but for users of screen readers, the site's name and navigation links will be read out every single time a page is accessed—a tedious process for the user.

A VERY SIMPLE WEBSITE

Home page   About us   Contact details

Lorem ipsum dolor sit amet, consectetuer adipiscing elit. Morbi commodo, ipsum sed pharetra gravida, orci magna rhoncus neque, id pulvinar odio lorem non turpis. Nullam sit amet enim. Suspendisse id velit vitae ligula volutpat condimentum. Aliquam erat volutpat. Sed quis velit. Nulla facilisi. Nulla libero. Vivamus pharetra posuere sapien. Nam consectetuer. Sed aliquam, nunc eget euismod ullamcorper, lectus nunc ullamcorper orci, fermentum bibendum enim nibh eget ipsum. Donec porttitor ligula eu dolor. Maecenas vitae nulla consequat libero cursus venenatis. Nam magna enim accumsan eu, blandit sed, blandit a, eros.

2. Immediately after the body element start tag, add a nav element with an id value of skipLink, which is a hook to later style the element and its link using CSS. The href value for the anchor is set to #content. As you will remember from earlier in the chapter, this will make the page jump to the element with an id value of content when the link is clicked (that is, the content div in this example's case).

```
<nav id="skipLink">
  <a href="#content">Skip to content</a>
</nav>
```

3. Test the web page. Already, the benefits of this are apparent. You can use Opera's User mode or View ➤ Page Style ➤ No Style in Firefox to temporarily remove the CSS and emulate a text browser (roughly equating to the content available to screen readers)—see the following left image. Click the skip to content link, and the page will jump to the web page's content—see the right image. Even with three links, this proves useful, but if the site has a couple of dozen links, this improves usability for screen reader users no end.

Styling a skip navigation link

Required files	skip-navigation-completed.html and skip-navigation-completed.css from the chapter 5 folder as a starting point
What you'll learn	How to style skip navigation
Completed files	skip-navigation-styled.html and skip-navigation-styled.css from the chapter 5 folder

When skip navigation is styled, it's common to set the container (in this case, the skipLink one) to display: none, thereby making it invisible. This is all well and good in theory, but some screen readers render CSS, meaning that your cunning skip navigation won't be accessible. Therefore, this exercise will show how to hide the skip navigation within the existing page design. (Note that, depending on your site and target audience, you may want to leave the skip navigation visible to aid users whose sight is fine but who have difficulty with motor tasks. That said, the exercise still shows how to style skip navigation in general and should therefore prove useful regardless.)

1. Style the skipLink nav. Remove the skipLink nav from the document flow (thereby meaning it won't affect the positioning of any other element) by setting position to absolute in a CSS rule targeting the element (see the following code snippet); Chapter 7 has more information on positioning div elements. The top and right values define the nav's position in relation to its parent element (which in this case is body—effectively the entire browser window view area). The settings place the nav inside the masthead.

```
#skipLink {
position: absolute;
top: 30px;
right: 30px;
}
```

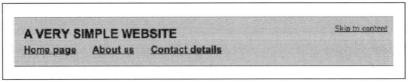

2. Make the link invisible—via the use of contextual selectors you can set the link's color to blend with that of the web page element it's positioned over. You can also use the :hover and :focus pseudo-classes mentioned earlier in this chapter to make the link visible on the hover and focus states.

```
#skipLink a:link, #skipLink a:visited {
  color: #cecece;
}
#skipLink a:hover, #skipLink a:focus {
  color: #000000;
}
```

Enhancing skip navigation with a background image

Required files	skip-navigation-completed.html, skip-navigation-completed.css, and skip-navigation-down-arrow.gif from the chapter 5 folder
What you'll learn	How to create skip navigation that sits centrally at the top of the web page and is invisible but that displays a rollover effect during the hover and focus states
Completed files	skip-navigation-background-image.html, skip-navigation-background-image.css, and skip-navigation-down-arrow.gif (unchanged during the tutorial) from the chapter 5 folder

1. Position the skipNav nav. Add the following link to remove the skipNav nav from the document flow, and position it at the top of the web page. The width and

text-align property values stretch the div to the full width of the browser window and center the text horizontally, respectively.

```
#skipLink {
  position: absolute;
  top: 0;
  left: 0;
  width: 100%;
  text-align: center;
}
```

2. Style the skip navigation link. Add the following rule to style the link within the skipLink nav. By setting display to block, the active area of the link stretches to fill its container, thereby effectively making the entire containing div clickable. The padding-bottom setting is important, because this provides space at the bottom of the div for displaying the background image used for the hover state, added in the next step. The color value is black (#000000) at this point, which ensures that the text fits happily within the space available above the page content. (This may change for users with nondefault settings, but for the default and first zoom setting, it'll be fine.)

```
#skipLink a:link, #skipLink a:visited {
  display: block;
  color: #000000;
  font: 1.0em Arial, Helvetica, sans-serif;
  padding-top: 5px;
  padding-bottom: 20px;
}
```

3. Recolor the skip navigation link. Change the color property so that the link blends into the background.

```
#skipLink a:link, #skipLink a:visited {
  display: block;
  color: #fefefe;
  font: 1.0em Arial, Helvetica, sans-serif;
  padding-top: 5px;
  padding-bottom: 20px;
}
```

4. Define the hover and focus states. Add the following rule to set the style for the hover and focus states. This essentially makes the text visible (via the color setting) and defines a background image—a wide GIF89 image with a downward-facing arrow at its center now appears when the user places their mouse cursor over the top of the web page.

```
#skipLink a:hover, #skipLink a:focus {
  color: #000000;
  background: url(skip-navigation-down-arrow.gif) 50% 100% no-repeat;
}
```

Link targeting

Although a fairly common practice online, link targeting—using the `target` attribute (see the following code for an example), typically to open a link in a new window—is not without its problems and should be avoided.

```
<a href="a-web-page.html" target="_blank">Open in a new window</a>
```

While some argue that this practice is beneficial, enabling users to look at external content and return to your site, what it actually does is take control of the browser away from users. After all, if someone actually wants to open content in a new window or tab, they can do so using keyboard commands and/or contextual menus. More important, opening documents in new windows breaks the history path. For many, this might not be a huge issue, but for those navigating the Web via a screen reader, pop-ups are a menace. New content opens up and is deemed to not be of interest, and the back function is invoked. But this is a new window, with its own blank history. Gnashing of teeth ensues. There's also the problem that you can't guarantee what will happen when this attribute is used anyway—many users configure browsers to suppress new windows, either forcing them to open in a new tab or over the top of the current page. In HTML5 the target attribute is no longer deprecated but because of the previously stated reasons its use is strongly discouraged.

Links and images

Although links are primarily text-based, it's possible to wrap anchor tags around an image, thereby turning it into a link:

```
<a href="a-link.html"><img src="linked-image.gif" width="40"
  height="40" /></a>
```

Some browsers border linked images with whatever link colors have been stated in CSS (or the default colors, if no custom ones have been defined), which looks nasty and can displace other layout elements. Historically, designers have gotten around this by setting the border attribute within an img element to 0, but this has been deprecated. Therefore, it's best to use a CSS contextual selector to define images within links as having no border.

```
a img {
  border: 0;
}
```

Clearly, this can be overridden for specific links. Alternatively, you could set an "invisible" border (one that matches the site's background color) on one or more sides and then set its color to that of your standard hover color when the user hovers over the image. This would then provide visual feedback to the user, confirming that the image is a link.

```
a img {
  border: 0;
  border-bottom: 1px solid #ffffff;
}

a:hover img {
  border-bottom: 1px solid #f22222;
}
```

In any case, you must always have usability and accessibility at the back of your mind when working with image-based links. With regard to usability, is the image's function obvious? Plenty of websites use icons instead of straightforward text-based navigation, resulting in frustrated users if the function of each image isn't obvious. People don't want to learn what each icon is for, and they'll soon move on to competing sites. With regard to accessibility, remember that not all browsers can zoom images, and so if an image-based link has text within it, ensure it's big enough to read easily. Whenever possible, offer a text-based alternative to image-based links, and never omit `alt` and `title` attributes (discussed earlier in this chapter). The former can describe the image content and the latter can describe the link target (in other words, what will happen when the link is clicked).

Therefore, the example from earlier becomes the following:

```
<a href="a-link.html"><img title="Visit our shop"
  src="linked-image.gif" width="40" height="40"
  alt="Shopping trolley" /></a>
```

Adding pop-ups to images

On occasion, when a user hovers their mouse cursor over an image, you might like to add a pop-up that's a little more flamboyant than what a `title` attribute can provide. Using CSS, you can add a fully stylable pop-up to an image, when the user moves their cursor over it. Note, however, that this technique should be used sparingly, and you should never rely on users accessing this information, unless you make it clear that the pop-up exists—for example, you could use it for a game, showing the answer to a question when the user mouses over an image. (However, if something is extremely important for your users to see immediately, don't hide it away in a pop-up—display it in plain sight.) The following walk-through shows you how to use pop-ups in such a way.

Adding a pop-up to an image

Required files   XHTML-basic.html and CSS-default.css from the basic-boilerplates folder as a starting point, along with the two image files add-a-pop-up-image.jpg and add-a-pop-up-pop-up.jpg from the chapter 5 folder

What you'll learn   How to create a totally CSS-based pop-up that can be applied to an image

Completed files   add-a-pop-up.html and add-a-pop-up.css in the chapter 5 folder, along with the two images, which remain unchanged

1. Create a container for the pop-up. Add the div shown following to the web page, within the wrapper; the div will act as a container for the pop-up.

```
<div id="popupContainer">
</div>
```

2. Add the main image in the usual fashion, placing it inside the div created in step 1.

```
<img src="add-a-pop-up-image.jpg" alt="Landscape" width="500"
  height="375" />
```

3. Add a link and pop-up content. Surround the image with a dummy link, and then add a span element immediately after the image. Within this, place the pop-up content, which can contain text and even other images. Text can be styled within inline elements (strong, em, and anchors, for example). In this example, the span contains an image, which will be floated right, and some text (which is truncated for space reasons—the completed version in the download files is longer). To ensure that the floated image is "cleared," making the span's background appear behind it once styled, a clearFix class is added to the span start tag, and an associated CSS rule is created (in step 10). More on this float-clearing technique, along with floats and clears in general, is given in Chapter 7.

```
<a href="#"><img src="add-a-pop-up-to-an-image.jpg" alt="Landscape"
  width="500" height="375" /><span class="clearFix"><img
  src="add-a-pop-up-pop-up.jpg" alt="Winter shot" width="126"
  height="215" />
The text for the pop-up goes here…</span></a>
```

> *Note: Because you can't place paragraphs within a span element, you need to stick to a single block of text or split paragraphs with double line breaks (

), despite the iffy semantics of doing that.*

4. Set defaults. At this stage, the page content is displayed in a linear fashion—large image followed by small image followed by text—so some CSS is now needed. In the CSS document, add some padding to the existing body element, ensuring the page content doesn't hug the browser window edges when you're testing the page.

```
body {
  font: 62.5%/1.5 Verdana, Arial, Helvetica, sans-serif;
  padding: 20px;
}
```

5. Give the images a border. Add the following rule to apply a thin gray border to the images on the page.

```
img {
  border: 1px solid #666666;
}
```

6. Define the pop-up area size. Add the following rule to define the size of the pop-up area (the width setting defines its width and display: block stretches the active area of the link to the size of its container—the image). The other settings override link defaults, making the text within the div and anchor black and not underlined.

```
#popupContainer a:link, #popupContainer a:visited {
  position: relative;
  display: block;
  width: 500px;
  text-decoration: none;
  color: #000000;
}
```

7. Make the pop-up invisible. Add the following rule to make the pop-up initially not display on-screen (that is, outside of the viewing area of the browser).

```
#popupContainer a span {
  position: absolute;
  left: -10000px;
  top: -10000px;
}
```

8. Style the span element. The following rule styles the span element during the hover state. The display property value of block defines the pop-up as a block-level element, rather than an inline one, while the position setting of relative overrides that set in the previous step (as do the left and top values). The width setting defines a width for the pop-up. The negative margin-top setting pulls the pop-up upward, so it no longer sits under the main image. The value is the same as the height of the main image minus the vertical offset required. (If it were set to the height of the main image, the pop-up would sit flush to the top of the image during the hover state, which looks cluttered.) The margin-left value provides a horizontal offset, while the padding value places some padding within the span, so its contents don't hug its borders. The other settings style colors and fonts.

```
#popupContainer a:hover span, #popupContainer a:focus span,
  #popupContainer a:active span {
  display: block;
  position: relative;
  left: 0;
```

```
    top: 0;
    width: 360px;
    color: #000000;
    font: 1.1em/1.5 Arial, Helvetica, sans-serif;
    margin-top: -335px;
    margin-left: 50px;
    padding: 20px;
    background-color: #e0e4ef;
    border: 1px solid #666666;
}
```

> Note: The selector for step 8's code block offers three alternate routes for users to access the pop-up: the *hover* state (for mouse users), the *focus* state (for keyboard users), and the *active* state (for Internet Explorer keyboard users, since that browser doesn't yet support *:focus*).

9. Next, a rule is needed to float the image within the span. The margin settings ensure that the image doesn't hug the text-based content.

```
#popupContainer a:hover span img, #popupContainer a:focus span img,
  #popupContainer a:active span img {
  border: 1px solid #666666;
  float: right;
  margin-left: 15px;
  margin-bottom: 5px;
}
```

10. Apply the clearFix rule. Floated elements are outside the standard document flow. Therefore, if there's little text, the image appears to stick out of the span box, as shown in the following example.

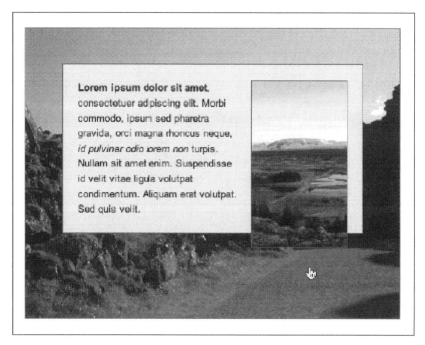

This can be fixed by adding the following rule (this technique is fully explained in Chapter 7):

```
.clearFix:after {
  content: ".";
  display: block;
  height: 0;
  clear: both;
  visibility: hidden;
}
```

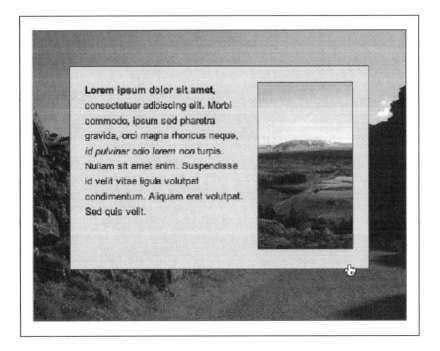

Image maps

Image maps enable you to define multiple links within a single image. For example, if you have a weather map, you could use an image map to link to each region's weather forecast; or if you had a picture of your office, you could use an image map to make each of the objects clickable, leading to pages explaining more about each of them. Clickable regions within image maps can be fairly basic—rectangles or circles— or complex polygonal shapes. Note that there are both server-side and client-side versions of image maps—server-side image maps are now considered obsolete and pose accessibility problems, and even client-side image maps tend to be avoided by most designers, although use of alt text can help them become reasonably accessible.

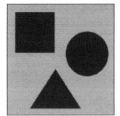

Regardless of the complexity of the image and the defined regions, the method of creating an image map remains the same. To the right is the image used in this section to show how a basic image map is created. It contains three geometric shapes that will be turned into clickable hot-spots.

The image is added to the web page in the usual way (and within a block element, since img is an inline element), but with the addition of a usemap attribute, whose value must be preceded by a hash sign (#).

```
<div id="wrapper">
  <img src="image-map-image.gif" alt="Shapes" width="398" height="398"
    usemap="#shapes" />
</div>
```

The value of the usemap attribute must correlate with the name and id values of the associated map element. Note that the name attribute is required for backward compatibility, whereas the id attribute is mandatory.

```
<map id="shapes" name="shapes">
</map>
```

The map element acts as a container for specifications regarding the map's active areas, which are added as area elements.

```
<map id="shapes" name="shapes">
  <area title="Access the squares page." shape="rect"
    coords="29,27,173,171" href="square.html" alt="A square" />
  <area title="Access the circles page" shape="circle"
    coords="295,175,81" href="circle.html" alt="A circle" />
  <area title="Access the triangles page" shape="poly"
    coords="177,231,269,369,84,369" href="triangle.html"
    alt="A triangle" />
</map>
```

Each of the preceding area elements has a shape attribute that corresponds to the intended active link area:

- rect defines a rectangular area; the coords (coordinates) attribute contains two pairs that define the top-left and bottom-right corners of the rectangle in terms of pixel values (which you either take from your original image or guess, should you have amazing pixel-perfect vision).

- circle is used to define a circular area; of the three values within the coords attribute, the first two define the horizontal and vertical position of the circle's center, and the third defines the radius.

- poly enables you to define as many coordinate pairs as you wish, which allows you to define active areas for complex and irregular shapes—in the previous code block, there are three pairs, each of which defines a corner of the triangle.

Creating image maps is a notoriously tedious process, and it's one of the few occasions when I advise using a visual web design tool, if you have one handy, which can be used to drag out hot-spots. However, take care not to overlap defined regions—this is easy to do, and it can cause problems with regard to each link's active area. If you don't have such a tool handy, you'll have to measure out the coordinates in a graphics package.

> Note that some browsers will place a border around the image used for an image map. This can be removed by using CSS to set the image's border to 0 (either via applying a *class* to the image or via a contextual selector).

Faking images maps using CSS

Although there's no direct equivalent to image maps in CSS, you can fashion a similar effect by creating block-level anchors (rather like the one in the pop-up example). The most common way of structuring this "fake" image map is by using an unordered list, placing links within each list item, and using absolute positioning to set the locations of the links. Further CSS trickery can be used to make all hot-spots visible when the mouse cursor is placed over the image and to change the image on the rollover state.

In the following exercise, a picture of three sheep minding their own business is going to be used for the fake image map. When you mouse over the image, all three hot-spots will be shown (as a 1-pixel, black border). Placing the cursor over a hot-spot will then turn that portion of the grayscale image into color (by way of placing a second image as a background on the hot-spot), along with showing a caption.

> Note: As you might imagine, with CSS being based around boxes, the technique tends to work best with highly regular, box-shaped rollover areas.

SHEEP TWO

Hover your mouse cursor over the sheep!

Using CSS to create a fake image map with rollovers

Required files   basic.html and CSS-default.css from the basic-boilerplates folder, along with image files fake-image-map-color.jpg and fake-image-map-gray.jpg from the chapter 5 folder.

What you'll learn   How to fake an image map using CSS, which will enable two levels of rollover.

Completed files   fake-image-map.html and fake-image-map.css in the chapter 5 folder, along with the image files, which are unchanged

1. Add the structure for the fake image map. In the body of the HTML document, add the following code, which structures the content for the fake image map. Note how the unordered list has a unique `class` value and how each of the list items has a `class` value referring to the hot-spot relating to a specific item on the image.

```
<ul class="sheepImageMap">
  <li class="sheepOne"><a href="#"><span>Sheep one</span></a></li>
  <li class="sheepTwo"><a href="#"><span>Sheep two</span></a></li>
  <li class="sheepThree"><a href="#"><span>Sheep three</span></a></li>
</ul>
<p>Hover your mouse cursor over the sheep!</p>
```

2. Set page defaults. Add some padding to the existing body rule:

```
body {
  font: 62.5%/1.5 Verdana, Arial, Helvetica, sans-serif;
  padding: 20px;
}
```

3. Add the following rule to style the unordered list. The `font` and `text-transform` property values define the font styles for the captions. The `background` value defines the grayscale image as the background for the list, and the `width` and `height` values ensure the list's dimensions are the same as that of the background image. The `position` property is set to `relative` because this enables the list item positioning to then be set from the top left of the unordered list, rather than from the top left of the browser window.

```
.sheepImageMap {
  font: 1.0em/1 Arial, Helvetica, sans-serif;
  text-transform: uppercase;
  background: url(fake-image-map-gray.jpg);
  width: 500px;
  height: 375px;
  position: relative;
  margin-bottom: 10px;
}
```

Hover your mouse cursor over the sheep!

4. Style the links. By setting `display` to `block`, the links stretch to fit their container (the list items). The `text-indent` setting is used to massively offset the indent of the text within the links, effectively making the text invisible by default, but keeping the element itself visible and clickable. The `text-decoration` value of none turns off the default underline for the links.

```
.sheepImageMap a {
  display: block;
  text-indent: -100000px;
  text-decoration: none;
}
```

> Note: In some circumstances, offsetting using *text-indent* can lead to minor layout issues. This wouldn't be a problem in the layout being created here, but with more finely tuned layouts, it could—because of some browsers keeping the space taken up by the element's height available to it and thus forcing subsequent content to appear below where it's meant to be by an equivalent amount. In cases like those, absolute positioning and offsetting both vertically and horizontally works well.

5. Set hot-spot borders. Utilizing the `:hover` pseudo-class, the following rule makes it so that when the list is hovered over, the three hot-spots show a 1-pixel border:

```
.sheepImageMap:hover .sheepOne, .sheepImageMap:hover .sheepTwo,
  .sheepImageMap:hover .sheepThree {
  border: 1px solid #000000;
}
```

6. Add the following rule to style the list items, removing the default bullet point (via the `list-style` value of none) and defining them to be positioned in an absolute manner and displayed as block elements.

```
.sheepImageMap li {
  list-style: none;
  position: absolute;
  display: block;
}
```

7. Create the first hot-spot. In a graphics package, four values are required for each hot-spot: its width, its height, and the distance from the top and left corners. These are then translated, respectively, into the `width`, `height`, `left`, and `top` values in a rule applied to the relevant hot-spot:

```
.sheepOne {
  width: 80px;
  height: 104px;
  left: 60px;
  top: 50px;
}
```

Two more rules complete the effect. The first ensures the relevant anchor has the correct height (note how the `height` value is the same as in the previous rule):

```
.sheepOne a {
  height: 104px;
}
```

The second rule sets the color version of the image to be displayed as a background on the hover state (as in, when the user mouses over the hot-spot area, the relevant area is displayed in color). By default, the top left of the image will be shown, and so negative positioning values are used to pull it into place. Note how these are the negatives of the values defined for `left` and `top` in the `.sheepOne` rule, minus 1 further pixel. The reason for the extra pixel is to take into account the 1-pixel border defined in step 5. If the borders weren't used (although they are handy, since they show all the hot-spots), the positioning values would just be the direct negatives of the `left` and `top` values from `.sheepOne`.

```
.sheepOne a:hover {
  background: url(fake-image-map-color.jpg) -61px -51px;
}
```

Hover your mouse cursor over the sheep!

> Note that the *a* selector is used in this exercise rather than *a:link*. Because the rules are
> strictly based on context—anchors within the defined areas of the fake image map—this
> is acceptable, and it saves having to use both *:link* and *:visited* selectors.

8. Create the other hot-spots. The other two hot-spots are created in the same way as the first one in step 7. Again, the positioning values in the hover states are negative values minus 1 of the left and top values in the rules that defined the dimensions and positions of the hot-spots.

```
.sheepTwo {
  width: 200px;
  height: 126px;
  left: 141px;
  top: 108px;
}
.sheepTwo a {
  height: 126px;
}
.sheepTwo a:hover {
  background: url(fake-image-map-color.jpg) -142px -109px;
}
.sheepThree {
  width: 68px;
  height: 38px;
  left: 418px;
```

```
  top: 19px;
}
.sheepThree a {
  height: 38px;
}
.sheepThree a:hover {
  background: url(fake-image-map-color.jpg) -419px -20px;
}
```

9. Add styles for the captions. In step 4, the text-indent property was set to a huge negative value, which made the text effectively disappear. To bring it back on the hover state, add the following rule to your CSS, which also colors the text in white:

```
.sheepImageMap a:hover {
  text-indent: 0;
  color: #ffffff;
}
```

10. At this stage, the text still doesn't stand out enough. Therefore, add the following rule, which styles the span elements wrapped around the text in each list item, setting a background color and adding some padding around the content:

```
.sheepImageMap a:hover span {
  padding: 2px;
  background-color: #000000;
}
```

11. This looks fine, but with some further absolute positioning, these captions can be positioned elsewhere within the hot-spot. By adding the bolded rules shown following, the captions are positioned at the bottom right of the hot-spots, as shown in the original example screenshot before the start of the exercise.

```
.sheepImageMap a:hover span {
  padding: 2px;
  background-color: #000000;
  position: absolute;
  bottom: 0;
  right: 0;
}
```

> Note: Pre-version 7, Internet Explorer didn't respond to :hover unless it was used on a link. Because of this, the borders will not appear in that browser, causing a 1-pixel "jog" up and left when you mouse over a hot-spot. You can get around this by applying the border to the following rules (via a conditional style sheet): .sheepOne a:hover, .sheepTwo a:hover, and .sheepThree a:hover.

Enhancing links with JavaScript

In this section, we're going to use a little JavaScript, showing some methods of providing enhanced interactivity and functionality to links. Note that in all cases, a non-JavaScript backup (or fallback) to essential content is required for those who choose to surf the Web with JavaScript disabled. In all cases, JavaScript can be added either to external JavaScript files attached to your HTML documents (which is the preferred method; see the section "Attaching favicons and JavaScript" in Chapter 2) or in a script element within the head of the HTML page:

```
<script>
    (script goes here)
</script>
```

Specifically, we'll look at pop-up windows, swapping images using JavaScript, and toggling div visibility with JavaScript.

Creating a pop-up window

Pop-up windows are mostly an annoyance, especially when automated and when they remove browser controls. However, they are occasionally useful, such as for providing a user with brief access to terms and conditions without interrupting a checkout process. Some portfolio sites also use pop-up windows to display larger versions of images (although we'll later see a better method of creating an online gallery).

Should you require a pop-up window of your very own, the JavaScript is simple:

```
function newWindow()
{
  window.open("location.html");
}
```

And this HTML calls the script using the onclick attribute:

```
<a href="location.html" onclick="newWindow(); return false;">Open a
  new window!</a>
```

Note how the href attribute still has a value, which caters to users with JavaScript disabled (loading the document into the current window). The return false part of the onclick value ensures the href value is ignored for browsers with JavaScript activated (otherwise both the original and pop-up windows would display with the new web page).

Creating a system to open windows with varied URLs requires only slight changes to both script and HTML. The script changes to this:

```
function newWindow(webURL)
{
  window.open(webURL);
}
```

The HTML changes to this:

```
<a href="location-one.html" onclick="newWindow('location-one.html');
 return false;">Open location one in a new window!</a>
<a href="location-two.html" onclick="newWindow('location-two.html');
 return false;">Open location two in a new window!</a>
```

Note how the target location is now within the single quotes of the onclick value. This could be any file name, and the link type can be absolute, relative, or root-relative. To provide a warning when a pop-up is opened (as recommended by Web Content Accessibility Guidelines [WCAG]), you can add a single line to the JavaScript:

```
function newWindow(webURL)
{
  alert("You are about to open a new window.");
  window.open(webURL);
}
```

It's also possible to control the settings of a pop-up window. To do so, the script needs to be amended as follows:

```
function newWindow(webURL)
{
  alert("You are about to open a new window.");
  var newWin = window.open(webURL,"new_window",
   "toolbar,location,directories,
   status,menubar,scrollbars,resizable,
   copyhistory,width=300,height=300");
  newWin.focus();
}
```

The values within the set of quotes that begin "toolbar, location... enable you to set the pop-up window's dimensions and appearance. There must be no whitespace in the features list, and it must all be on one line. Most of the items are self-explanatory, but some that may not be are location, which defines whether the browser's address bar is visible, and directories, which defines whether secondary toolbars such as the links bar are visible. Note that if you specify one or more of these, any you don't specify will be turned off—therefore, you must specify all the features you want in the pop-up window.

Now, a word of warning: as alluded to earlier, having control of the web browser wrenched away from them makes some users want to kick a puppy. Therefore:

- Never use JavaScript to pop up windows without the user knowing that it's going to happen. (The integrated alert mentioned earlier is one thing, but you should always also mention next to the relevant link that a pop-up will be created if the link is clicked.)

- Never create a site that automatically pops up a window and removes the window controls.

- Never use a pop-up window unless it's absolutely necessary.

Some designers might argue about aesthetics and for the clean nature of a browser window at full-screen, devoid of its controls, but there are no real reasons for using pop-up windows in this manner other than that; there are, however, counterarguments, such as taking control from the user, the general annoyance factor, a full-screen window suddenly covering everything else, and so on. Ultimately, pop-ups and nonrequested new windows are a very bad thing, and since most browsers block them, you should avoid using them.

Creating an online gallery

As mentioned earlier, there's a better way of creating an online gallery than using pop-up windows when thumbnails are clicked. Instead, JavaScript can be used to swap out an image that's on a web page, replacing it with another, as shown in the following exercise.

Switching images using JavaScript

Required files   gallery-starting-point folder in the chapter 5 folder

What you'll learn   How to create a basic online gallery that enables you to easily switch the main image by clicking on thumbnails

Completed files   gallery-completed folder in the chapter 5 folder

1. Add the script. Create a new text document and save it as gallery.js in the same folder as the files from the gallery-starting-point folder. Add the following to it:

```
function swapPhoto(photoSRC) {
  document.images.imgPhoto.src = "assets/" + photoSRC;
}
```

Be aware of the case-sensitive nature of JavaScript and also the path to the images, which is set here as assets/.

2. Add the main image. This requires an id attribute that correlates with the one provided in step 1 (imgPhoto). Leave off the height and/or width attributes if your images have varied dimensions. If your images have one identical dimension (such as the same widths), include that, but omit the other. (The img is placed within a div so that the document conforms to XHTML Strict. This also enables the gallery width to be defined later in CSS.)

```
<div id="wrapper">
  <img src="assets/image-1.jpg" width="500" height="375" id="imgPhoto"
    alt="Main photo" />
</div>
```

3. Add thumbnails. In each case, the swapPhoto value is the file name of the image to be loaded. Remember that the path to the images was defined in step 1, so it's not needed here. The href value links directly to the full-size image to accommodate users who have disabled JavaScript.

```
<a href="assets/image-1.jpg" onclick="javascript:swapPhoto
('image-1.jpg'); return false;"><img src="assets/image-1-t.jpg"
```

```
  alt="sheep" width="100" height="75" /></a>
<a href="assets/image-2.jpg" onclick="javascript:swapPhoto
('image-2.jpg'); return false;"><img src="assets/image-2-t.jpg"
  alt="hillside" width="100" height="75" /></a>
```

4. Add some CSS. To the gallery.css file, add the following rules, the first of which sets a width value for the wrapper div, and the second of which removes the default border from image-based links.

```
#wrapper {
  width: 500px;
}
a img {
border: 0;
}
```

And that's all there is to it. The solution is elegant and doesn't require pop-up windows. Instead, users can see thumbnails on the same page as the main image, making navigation through the portfolio that much easier. For those users who don't have JavaScript, the values in the href attributes ensure they still get access to the full-size images, too.

Adding captions to your image gallery

Required files	The gallery-completed folder from the chapter 5 folder.

What you'll learn	Without context, some pictures are meaningless, so this exercise shows how to take the gallery created in the previous exercise and add a caption to each image.

Completed files	The gallery-captions folder in the chapter 5 folder.

1. Edit the script. Add the elements shown in bold to your script (in gallery.js). These will enable you to target an element on the page with an id value of caption, loading new text into it when a thumbnail is clicked.

```
function swapPhoto(photoSRC,theCaption) {
  var displayedCaption = document.getElementById("caption");
  displayedCaption.firstChild.nodeValue = theCaption;
  document.images.imgPhoto.src = "assets/" + photoSRC;
}
```

2. Add a caption. Under the main image in the gallery.html file, add a paragraph with an id value of caption, along with the caption text for the default image.

```
<img src="assets/image-1.jpg" width="500" height="375" id="imgPhoto"
  alt="Main photo" />
<p id="caption">Some sheep, grazing.</p>
```

3. Edit the thumbnails. For each thumbnail, add some caption text, as shown following. Ensure that there's a comma between the two swapPhoto values you now have.

```
<a href="assets/image-1.jpg" onclick="javascript:swapPhoto
('image-1.jpg','Some sheep, grazing.'); return false;"><img
  src="assets/image-1-t.jpg" alt="sheep" width="100"
  height="75" /></a>
```

> Note: Some characters are invalid for captions, because they terminate the script early. If you want to add a single quote mark (often used as an apostrophe online, when "smart" quotes aren't being used), you must escape the character first, using a backslash, like so: \'. If you want to add a double quote mark, you need to define it as an HTML entity: ".

Automated gallery scripts

The kind of script mentioned in the previous exercise is great for creating a gallery fine-tuned to your specific website: you can control the styles and positioning with ease. However, there are a number of ready-made scripts online, one of the best of which is Lightbox2 (www.huddletogether.com/projects/lightbox2/), by Lokesh Dhakar. The script is highly automated, darkening the screen and providing next/previous buttons, along with the capability to rapidly add captions.

The hillside at Uffington.

In terms of setup, you attach the various scripts and the CSS file from the download files and check the paths to the included images (which can be replaced, if you don't like the defaults). You then simply add rel="lightbox" to any link or thumbnail that's to be used to activate the lightbox script. The optional title element enables you to add a caption.

```
<a href="assets/image-1.jpg" rel="lightbox" title="The caption"><img
  src="assets/image-1-t.jpg" alt="thumbnail" width="100"
  height="75" /></a>
```

It's also possible to add more complex captions, including links, by using character entities to encode the ‹, ›, and " characters when adding HTML. (See Appendix C for more on entities.)

```
<a href="assets/image-1.jpg" rel="lightbox" title="The caption - &lt;
 a href=&quot;http://www.a-website.com&quot;&gt;Link content
&lt;/a&gt;"><img src="assets/image-1-t.jpg" alt="thumbnail"
  width="100" height="75" /></a>
```

Usefully, groups of images can be defined just by adding square brackets and a group name, directly after lightbox in the rel value. This automates the inclusion of **prev** and **next** buttons, along with providing an image count (such as "Image 4 of 10") for the current group.

```
<a href="assets/image-1.jpg" rel="lightbox[groupName]" title="The
  caption"><img src="assets/image-1-t.jpg" alt="thumbnail"
  width="100" height="75" /></a>
<a href="assets/image-2.jpg" rel="lightbox[groupName]" title="The
  second caption"><img src="assets/image-2-t.jpg" alt="thumbnail"
  width="100" height="75" /></a>
<a href="assets/image-3.jpg" rel="lightbox[groupName]" title="The
  third caption"><img src="assets/image-3-t.jpg" alt="thumbnail"
  width="100" height="75" /></a>
```

The following image shows how the site looks (this example is from Pinkflag.com's gallery in the **look** section). If you're fine with the look of the gallery (although some of its elements can be restyled and tweaked in CSS) and its popularity (it's used on a lot of sites these days), it can save a bit of time, and it's also very easy for clients to update themselves. For a more unique take, you'll need to get your hands dirty with your own code.

Note that some may consider the behavior of Lightbox2 at odds with user expectations, because the browser back button returns you to the previous page you visited, rather than closing the lightbox. In my opinion, this is logical—after all, Lightbox2 is internal page content, not a separate page. However, if you'd like to override the default behavior and have the back button on the browser close the lightbox, instructions are available from www.cloversignsblog.com/2007/06/fixing-the-back-button-in-lightbox/.

Collapsible page content

The DOM enables you to access and dynamically control various aspects of a web page, and this allows you to use a nifty little trick to toggle the visibility of divs. This has numerous uses, from providing a method of hiding "spoiler" content unless someone wants to see it to various navigation-oriented uses, which will be more fully explored later in the chapter.

Setting up a collapsible div	
Required files	The collapsible-div-starting-point folder from the chapter 5 folder
What you'll learn	How to create a collapsible div
Completed files	The collapsible-div-completed folder from the chapter 5 folder

1. Examine the script. Open collapsible-div.js. The code enables you to target any div with a unique id value. Each time the script is run, it determines whether the display value of the div is set to block (which makes it visible). If it is, the value is set to none, thereby making it invisible. If it isn't set to block (which means it's set to none), the script sets the value to block.

```
function swap(targetId){
  if (document.getElementById)
  {
    target = document.getElementById(targetId);
    if (target.style.display == "block")
    {
      target.style.display = "none";
    }
    else
    {
      target.style.display = "block";
    }
  }
}
```

2. Add a link. Add the code block shown following—when clicked, the link will toggle the hidden content. The value within the onclick attribute (hiddenDiv, in this case) is the id value of the div that this link will toggle.

```
<p><a href="#" title="Toggle section" onclick="toggleDiv('hiddenDiv');
 return false;">Toggle div!</o>
```

3. Add a div, and give it an id value equal to the onclick value from the previous step. Within the div, add whatever content you want. The style attribute makes the div initially hidden.

```
<p><a href="#" title="Toggle section" onclick="toggleDiv('hiddenDiv');
 return false;">Toggle div!</a></p>
<div id="hiddenDiv" style="display: none;">
<p>Initially hidden content goes here.</p>
</div>
```

A combination of the previous two exercises can be seen in action in a previous version of my Images from Iceland website—see www.snubcommunications.com/iceland/. This site expands on the div toggler by also toggling the arrow images when a section is toggled, and it shows what you can do with some straightforward JavaScript, some decent photographs, and a bit of imagination.

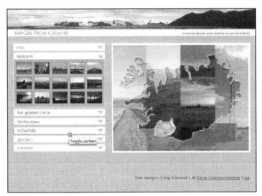

Enhancing accessibility for collapsible content

Although the old version of the Images from Iceland site looks good, it has a problem in common with the previous exercise: when JavaScript is disabled, the initially hidden content is inaccessible. The Iceland site was quickly knocked together a number of years back and has been superseded with a new site, but for any site developed today, there should be no excuses.

In the previous exercise, the hidden content is set to be hidden by default, and the display property is toggled via the JavaScript function. What therefore needs to be done is to make the content visible by default and then override this, making it invisible, but only if the user has JavaScript. The first thing to do is remove the style attribute from the following line of code:

```
<div id="hiddenDiv" style="display: none;">
```

Next, a style sheet is created (named javascript-overrides.css for this example), with a rule that targets the relevant div and sets display to none.

```
#hiddenDiv {
  display: none;
}
```

Finally, amendments are made to the JavaScript file, adding some lines that attach the new JavaScript document to the web page:

```
var cssNode = document.createElement('link');
cssNode.setAttribute('rel', 'stylesheet');
cssNode.setAttribute('type', 'text/css');
cssNode.setAttribute('href', 'javascript-overrides.css');
document.getElementsByTagName('head')[0].appendChild(cssNode);
```

The results of this are the following:

- If a user has JavaScript enabled, javascript-overrides.css is loaded, applying the display value of none to the togglable div.

- If a user has JavaScript disabled, javascript-overrides.css is not loaded, meaning the togglable div contents are visible.

See the `collapsible-div-accessible` folder within the `chapter 5` folder for reference files.

Modularizing the collapsible content script

Although the previous script works perfectly well for a single `div`, it's awkward if you want to use several `div`s over the course of a page. That's how the old Images from Iceland site works, and I had to keep track of `id` names and values while constructing it. However, it is possible to make a toggler strip more modular, although this relies on keeping document structure very strict as far as the collapsible sections go. The files for this section are in the `collapsible-div-modular` folder within the `chapter 5` folder.

The JavaScript is similar to that in the previous example.

```
function toggle(toggler) {
  if(document.getElementById) {
    targetElement = toggler.parentNode.nextSibling;

    if(targetElement.className == undefined) {
      targetElement = toggler.parentNode.nextSibling.nextSibling;
    }

    if (targetElement.style.display == "block") {
      targetElement.style.display = "none";
    }
    else {
      targetElement.style.display = "block";
    }
  }
}
```

The main change is that instead of targeting a `div` with a specific `id` value, the script targets an element in relation to the one being used as a toggler, by way of the `parentNode`/`nextSibling` JavaScript properties.

If you look at the HTML document, you'll see that the parent of the anchor element is the `p` element. What the next sibling element is depends on the browser—Internet Explorer just looks for the next element in the document (`div`), but other browsers count whitespace as the next sibling.

```
<p><a href="#" title="Toggle section" onclick="toggle(this); return
  false;">Toggle div 1!</a></p>
<div class="expandable">
  <p>Initially hidden content (div 1) goes here.</p>
</div>
```

It would be possible to get around this by stripping whitespace. However, a line in the JavaScript makes this unnecessary.

```
if(document.getElementById) {
  targetElement = toggler.parentNode.nextSibling;

if(targetElement.className == undefined) {
  targetElement = toggler.parentNode.nextSibling.nextSibling;
}
```

The first line of the previous code block sets the target to the next sibling of the parent element of the link. In Internet Explorer this works, but other browsers find only whitespace. Therefore, the second line essentially says, "If you find whitespace (undefined), then set the target to the next sibling on." It's a bit of a workaround, but it's only one line of JavaScript.

The JavaScript also includes the method used in the preceding "Enhancing accessibility for collapsible content" section to make the togglable sections initially invisible in JavaScript-enabled browsers only. Note that the related CSS is slightly different from that shown in the previous section—instead of hidden content being in a div with an id value of hiddenDiv, it's now in multiple divs, all of which have a class value of expandable. Therefore, the selector in the CSS rule has been updated accordingly:

```
.expandable {
  display: none;
}
```

Toggle div 1!	Toggle div 1!
Initially hidden content (div 1) goes here.	Initially hidden content (div 1) goes here.
Toggle div 2!	Toggle div 2!
	Initially hidden content (div 2) goes here.

This system enables you to use as many collapsible divs as you like on the page, and you don't have to set id values—the toggling is essentially automated. However, as mentioned earlier, you must ensure that your structure remains the same for each area that can be toggled; otherwise, the script won't find the correct element to make visible or invisible when the links are clicked.

How to find targets for collapsible content scripts

If you want to change your document structure when using the script from the previous section in this chapter, you need to find the parent/sibling path, in Internet Explorer and in other browsers. If you have a good grasp of JavaScript, this should be simple; however, if you don't—or you just want to sanity-check your values—it's simple to find out what an element's parent is, what it's next sibling is, and various combinations thereof.

First, give your clickable element a unique id value:

```
<p><a id="linkToggler" href="#" title="Toggle section"
  onclick="toggle(this); return false;">Toggle div 1!</a></p>
```

Elsewhere within the web page, add the following script:

```
<script>
    alert(document.getElementById("linkToggler").nodeName);
</script>
```

Before .nodeName, add whatever combination of .parentNode and .nextSibling you like—here's an example:

```
<script>
    alert(document.getElementById("linkToggler").parentNode.
        •nextSibling.nextSibling.nodeName);
</script>
```

When you load the web page in a browser, an alert message will be displayed. This will detail what the target element is, based on the path defined in the previous code block.

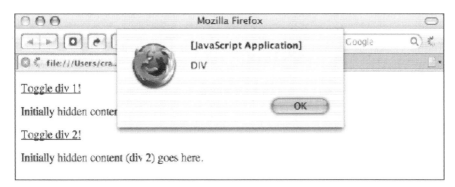

In this section, you've seen a bare-bones, unstyled version of how to work with collapsible content. Later in the chapter, this method will be used to create collapsible sections for a navigation bar.

Creating navigation bars

The chapter has so far largely concentrated on inline navigation, so we'll now turn our attention to navigation bars. Before getting immersed in the technology, you need to decide what names you're going to use for your navigation bar's items. When designing the basic structure of the site, content should be grouped into categories, and this is often defined by what the user can do with it. It therefore follows that navigation bar links tend to be one of the following:

- Action-based (buy now, contact us, read our history)

- Site audience–based (end users, resellers, employees)

- Topic-based (news, services, contact details)

Whenever possible, keep to one of the preceding categories rather than mixing topics and actions. This sits easier with readers. Navigation links should also be succinct, to the point, and appropriate to the brand and tone of the website.

In this section, we'll cover using lists for navigation, styling list-based navigation bars, working with inline lists, and creating graphical navigation bars with rollover graphics.

Using lists for navigation bars

Think back to what we've covered to this point about semantic markup. Of the HTML elements that exist, which is the most appropriate for a navigation bar? If you said, "a table," go to the back of the class. Using tables for navigation bars might be a rapid way of getting them up and running, but it's not structurally sound. When looked at objectively, navigation bars are essentially a list of links to various pages on the website. It therefore follows that HTML lists are a logical choice to mark up navigation bars.

When creating the initial pass of the website, just create the list as it is, along with all the associated pages, and let people play around with the bare-bones site. This enables users to get a feel for its structure, without getting distracted by content, colors, and design. However, sooner or later, you're going to want to make that list look a little fancier.

Much of the remainder of this chapter is concerned with CSS and how it can be used to style lists. From a plain HTML list, you can rapidly create exciting visual designs—and ones that are easy to update, both in terms of content and design. After all, adding another navigation link is usually just a matter of adding another list item.

The nav element

HTLM5 has introduced a new element that provides a semantic way for grouping together links used for major navigation. As you saw previously in this chapter the nav element was used for skip links. Since these links are for accessibility this is considered major navigation. Some other areas of your site that can be considered major navigation and should therefore use the nav element include main navigation, pagination links, breadcrumbs, and a table of contents.

Using HTML lists and CSS to create a button-like vertical navigation bar

Required files- `basic.html` and `CSS-default.css` from the `basic-boilerplates` folder.

What you'll learn   How to create a vertically aligned navigation bar and how to style it with CSS to create a 3D-like effect for each of the list items.

Completed files   The vertical-navigation-bar folder in the chapter 5 folder

1. Create the list structure. Add the following code block to create the structure of the navigation bar. By using nested lists, you can provide the navigation bar with a hierarchical structure (and you can style each level in CSS). In this example, the list has two levels. (Refer to Chapter 3 for an overview of correctly formatting lists.) This list is nested within a `div` with an `id` value of navigation, which we'll later take advantage of by using contextual selectors. (For this example, dummy `href` values of # are being used, but in a live site, always check that your links lead somewhere!)

```
<nav>
  <ul>
    <li>
      <a href="#">Section one</a>
      <ul>
        <li><a href="#">A link to a page</a></li>
        <li><a href="#">A link to a page</a></li>
```

```
      <li><a href="#">A link to a page</a></li>
      <li><a href="#">A link to a page</a></li>
    </ul>
  </li>
  <li>
    <a href="#">Section two</a>
    <ul>
      <li><a href="#">A link to a page</a></li>
      <li><a href="#">A link to a page</a></li>
      <li><a href="#">A link to a page</a></li>
      <li><a href="#">A link to a page</a></li>
    </ul>
  </li>
  <li>
    <a href="#">Section three</a>
    <ul>
      <li><a href="#">A link to a page</a></li>
      <li><a href="#">A link to a page</a></li>
      <li><a href="#">A link to a page</a></li>
      <li><a href="#">A link to a page</a></li>
    </ul>
  </li>
  </ul>
</nav>
```

2. Add some padding to the body element, so page content doesn't hug the browser window edges. Also, add the background-color pair shown following:

```
body {
font: 62.5%/1.5 Verdana, Arial, Helvetica, sans-serif;
padding: 20px;
background-color: #aaaaaa;
}
```

3. Style the list. Add the following rule to remove the default bullet points from unordered lists within the navigation div, define a width for the lists, and also set the default font style.

```
nav ul {
  list-style-type: none;
  width: 140px;
  font: 1.2em/1 Arial, Helvetica, sans-serif;
}
```

4. Set an override for nested lists. As you can see from the previous image, the nested links have much larger text. This is because font sizes in ems are inherited, and therefore the font size within the nested lists ends up at 1.2ems multiplied by 1.2ems. By adding the following rule, the font size of nested lists is reset to 1em, making nested lists look the same as top-level lists.

```
nav ul ul {
  font-size: 1em;
}
```

5. Style the buttons. Use a contextual selector to style links within the navigation container (that is, the links within this list). These styles initially affect the entire list, but you'll later override them for level-two links. Therefore, the styles you're working on now are intended only for level-one links (which are for sections or categories). This first set of property/value pairs turns off the default link underline, sets the list items to uppercase, and defines the font weight as bold.

```
nav a:link, nav a:visited {
  text-decoration: none;
  text-transform: uppercase;
  font-weight: bold;
}
```

6. Set button display and padding. Still within the same rule, set the buttons to display as block, thereby making the entire container an active link (rather than just the link text). Add some padding so the links don't hug the edge of the container.

```
nav a:link, nav a:visited {
  text-decoration: none;
  text-transform: uppercase;
  font-weight: bold;
  display: block;
  padding: 3px 12px 3px 8px;
}
```

7. Define colors and borders. Define the button background and foreground colors, setting the former to gray and the latter to white. Then add borders to create a 3D effect. Borders can be styled individually. By setting the left and top borders to a lighter shade than the background and setting the right and bottom borders to a darker shade, a 3D effect is achieved. (Don't use black and white, because it will make the result is too harsh.)

```
nav a:link, nav a:visited {
  text-decoration: none;
  text-transform: uppercase;
  font-weight: bold;
  display: block;
  padding: 3px 12px 3px 8px;
  background-color: #666666;
  color: #ffffff;
  border-top: 1px solid #dddddd;
  border-right: 1px solid #333333;
  border-bottom: 1px solid #333333;
  border-left: 1px solid #dddddd;
}
```

8. Define other link states. The hover state is defined by just changing the background color, making it slightly lighter.

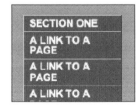

```
nav a:hover {
  background-color: #777777;
}
```

The `active` state enables you to build on the 3D effect: the padding settings are changed to move the text up and left by 1 pixel, the background and foreground colors are made slightly darker, and the border colors are reversed.

```
nav a:active {
  padding: 2px 13px 4px 7px;
  background-color: #444444;
  color: #eeeeee;
  border-top: 1px solid #333333;
  border-right: 1px solid #dddddd;
  border-bottom: 1px solid #dddddd;
  border-left: 1px solid #333333;
}
```

9. Style nested list item links. The selector `#navigation li li a` enables you to style links within a list item that are themselves within a list item (which happen to be in the navigation container). In other words, you can create a declaration for level-two links. These need to be differentiated from the section links, which is the reason for the following rule setting them to lowercase and `normal` font weight (instead of `bold`). The padding settings indent these links more than the section links, and the background and foreground colors are different, being very dark gray (almost black) on light gray rather than white on a darker gray.

```
nav li li a:link, nav li li a:visited {
  text-decoration: none;
  text-transform: lowercase;
  font-weight: normal;
  padding: 3px 3px 3px 17px;
  background-color: #999999;
  color: #111111;
}
```

10. Style nested item `hover` and `active` states. This is done in the same way as per the section links, changing colors as appropriate and again reversing the border colors on the `active` state.

```
nav li li a:hover {
  background-color: #aaaaaa;
}
nav li li a:active {
  padding: 2px 4px 4px 16px;
  background-color: #888888;
  color: #000000;
  border-top: 1px solid #333333;
  border-right: 1px solid #dddddd;
  border-bottom: 1px solid #dddddd;
  border-left: 1px solid #333333;
}
```

The navigation bar is now complete, and as you can see from the following images (which depict, from left to right, the `default`, `hover`, and `active` states), the buttons have a tactile feel to them. Should this not be to your liking, it's easy to change the look of the navigation bar because everything is styled in CSS. To expand on this design, you could introduce background images for each state, thereby making the navigation bar even more graphical. However, because you didn't simply chop up a GIF, you can easily add and remove items from the navigation bar, just by amending the list created in step 1. Any added items will be styled automatically by the style sheet rules.

Creating a vertical navigation bar with collapsible sections

Required files   The files from vertical-navigation-bar in the chapter 5 folder

What you'll learn   How to take the navigation bar created in the previous exercise and make its sections collapsible

Completed files   vertical-navigation-bar-collapsible in the chapter 5 folder

1. Set up the JavaScript. Create a new JavaScript document and attach it to the HTML file via a script element in the head of the document. (In the example files, this document has been named vertical-navigation-bar.js.) First, add the JavaScript lines first shown in the "Enhancing accessibility for collapsible content" section:

```
var cssNode = document.createElement('link');
cssNode.setAttribute('rel', 'stylesheet');
cssNode.setAttribute('type', 'text/css');
cssNode.setAttribute('href', 'javascript-overrides.css');
document.getElementsByTagName('head')[0].appendChild(cssNode);
```

Next, add the toggler script shown in the "Modularizing the collapsible content script" section, but amend the target element as shown:

```
function toggle(toggler) {
  if(document.getElementById) {
  targetElement = toggler.nextSibling;
```

```
  if(targetElement.className == undefined) {
  targetElement = toggler.nextSibling.nextSibling;
  }
if (targetElement.style.display == "block")
  {
  targetElement.style.display = "none";
  }
  else
  {
  targetElement.style.display = "block";
  }
  }
}
```

> Note that if you wanted to toggle different kinds of elements on your page, the two
> scripts shown so far in this chapter would clash. Therefore, you would need to create
> two different functions, with different names; for example, you could change all instances
> of *toggle(toggler)* in this exercise to *toggleNav(toggler)*.

2. Amend the list. To each top-level navigation link, add the `onclick` attribute, as shown following. And to each second-level list that you initially want to be invisible, add the `class` attribute shown. For any list you want to be visible, instead add `style="display: block;"`.

```
<li>
  <a href="#" onclick="toggle(this); return false;">Section one</a>
  <ul class="collapsibleList">
    <li><a href="#">A link to a page</a></li>
    <li><a href="#">A link to a page</a></li>
    <li><a href="#">A link to a page</a></li>
    <li><a href="#">A link to a page</a></li>
  </ul>
</li>
```

3. Add a style sheet. Create and save the style sheet document javascript-overrides.css, and add the following rule to initially hide any lists with the `collapsibleList` class value in JavaScript-enabled browsers.

```
#navigation ul.collapsibleList {
  display: none;
}
```

The following images show the results (which depict, from left to right, the default, hover, and active states).

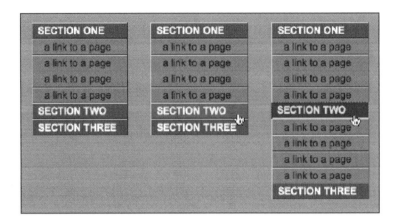

Working with inline lists

By default, list items are displayed in a vertical fashion, one under the other. However, this behavior can be overridden in CSS, enabling you to create inline lists. This is handy for website navigation, since many navigation bars are horizontally oriented. Some designers mark up horizontal navigation up by using strings of links separated by vertical bars or spaces:

```
<a href="link.html">A link</a> | <a href="link.html">A link</a> |
  <a href="link.html">A link</a>
```

However, a horizontal navigation bar is still a list of links, and so semantically should be marked up in the same way as the vertical navigation bar in the previous exercise. In this section, you'll find out how to work with inline lists, discovering how to create breadcrumb navigation, CSS-only "tabbed" navigation, and various graphical navigation bars, complete with rollover effects—all without relying on JavaScript.

Creating breadcrumb navigation

Required files	basic.html and CSS-default.css from the basic-boilerplates folder, along with double-arrow.gif from navigation-images within the chapter 5 folder

What you'll learn	How to create breadcrumb navigation by using a list styled in CSS. Breadcrumb links show the path you've taken to the current document

Completed files	The breadcrumb-navigation folder in the chapter 5 folder

1. Add the list. In the HTML document, add the following code for the breadcrumbs. Note that the last item signifies the current page—this is why it's not a link.

```
<nav id="breadcrumbs"><ul>
  <li><a href="#">Home page</a></li>
  <li><a href="#">Reviews</a></li>
  <li><a href="#">Live gigs</a></li>
  <li>London, 2008</li>
</ul></nav>
```

2. Add some body padding. Add a `padding` value to the existing body rule.

```
body {
  font: 62.5%/1.5 Verdana, Arial, Helvetica, sans-serif;
  padding: 20px;
}
```

3. Style the list by adding the following rule. The `font-size` setting specifies the font size for the list items, and the `margin-bottom` setting adds a margin under the list.

```
#breadcrumbs ul {
  font-size: 1.2em;
  margin-bottom: 1em;
}
```

4. Add the following rule to style the list items. By setting `display` to `inline`, list items are stacked horizontally. The `background` value sets `double-arrow.gif` as the background to each list item (ensure it's in the same directory as the CSS document, or modify the path accordingly); the positioning values ensure the background is set at 0 horizontally and 50% vertically, thereby vertically centering it at the left—at least once `no-repeat` is set, which stops the background tiling. Finally, the `padding` value sets padding at the right of each list item to `10px`, ensuring items don't touch the subsequent background image; the left padding value of `15px` provides room for the background image, ensuring the list item text doesn't sit on top of it.

```
#breadcrumbs ul li {
  display: inline;
  background: url(double-arrow.gif) 0 50% no-repeat;
  padding: 0 10px 0 15px;
}
```

> *Note that when list items are displayed inline, the default bullet points are not displayed. This is one reason why the bullets in this example are background images, although we also wanted something more visually relevant, right-facing arrows showing the path direction.*

>> Home page   >> Reviews   >> Live gigs   >> London, 2008

5. Remove the first bullet. As the trail is leading from the first item, it shouldn't have a bullet. This can be dealt with via a simple, standards-compliant rule that removes the background from only the list item that is the first child of the unordered list (that is, the first list item in the list):

```
#breadcrumbs ul li:first-child {
  background: none;
}
```

Creating a simple horizontal navigation bar

Required files	The graphical-navigation-starting-point folder from the chapter 5 folder

What you'll learn	How to create a good-looking navigation bar, entirely based on HTML text and styled using CSS.

Completed files	The simple-horizontal-navigation-bar folder in the chapter 5 folder

1. Examine the web page. The web page for this exercise—graphical-navigation.html—is designed for flexibility when it comes to styling elements on the page, making it easy to change elements without touching the markup (this page is used with a few modifications in subsequent exercises, too).

The page's contents are placed within a wrapper div, within which are the masthead and content divs. The latter contains some paragraphs, and the former includes a navContainer div, which houses a nav element, which in turn houses the unordered list shown in the following code block. (This nesting of divs isn't required for all sites—often you can get away with a single nav element around the navigation list; however, having an additional wrapper or two is often useful for more complex layouts.)

The list is an unordered list. The main difference from previous lists is the inclusion of an id value for each list item. For horizontal lists, especially those that will be highly styled, this is worth doing, because it enables you to work all manner of CSS trickery later, which can benefit the web page. (In fact, some of the techniques can be applied to vertical lists, too.)

```
<ul>
  <li id="homePageLink"><a href="#">Home page</a></li>
  <li id="servicesPageLink"><a href="#">Services</a></li>
  <li id="customerSupportPageLink"><a href="#">Customer support</a>
  </li>
  <li id="contactDetailsPageLink"><a href="#">Contact details</a></li>
</ul>
```

2. Edit the body and p rules. This design is going to have a classic feel, so in the CSS file, edit the body rule to amend the font set, add a light gray background, and amend the p rule to change the font size.

```
body {
font: 62.5%/1.5 Georgia, "Times New Roman", Times, serif;
background: #dddddd;
}
p {
  font-size: 1.3em;
  margin-bottom: 1em;
}
```

3. Style the structural divs. First, add a rule to style the wrapper div, as shown in the following code block. This sets a fixed width for the div, centers it horizontally, and applies borders on all edges except the top one. The background value provides a white background for the page's content.

(Note that there's plenty of explanation about page layout in Chapter 7.) For the content area, add some horizontal padding by adding the #content rule shown in the following code block.

```
#wrapper {
  width: 700px;
  margin: 0 auto;
  border-right: 1px solid #898989;
  border-bottom: 1px solid #898989;
  border-left: 1px solid #898989;
  background: #ffffff;
}
#content {
  padding: 0 15px;
}
```

4. Style the navigation container by adding the following rule to style the navContainer div. In this rule, the font style for the navigation bar's links is set, and the text-align value centers the content horizontally. The padding value applies some padding at the top and bottom of the navContainer div, ensuring its content doesn't hug its edges—in design, the space is often as important as the content, so don't cram things in.

```
#navContainer {
  font: 1.1em/1 Georgia, "Times New Roman", Times, serif;
  background: #d7d7d7;
  text-align: center;
  padding: 7px 0px;
  border-top: 1px solid #898989;
  border-bottom: 1px solid #898989;
  margin-bottom: 10px;
}
```

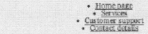

Lorem ipsum dolor sit amet, consectetuer adipiscing elit. Morbi commodo, ipsum sed pharetra gravida, orci magna rhoncus neque, id pulvinar odio lorem non turpis. Nullam sit amet enim.

Suspendisse id velit vitae ligula volutpat condimentum. Aliquam erat volutpat. Sed quis velit. Nulla facilisi. Nulla libero. Vivamus pharetra posuere sapien. Nam consectetuer. Sed aliquam, nunc eget euismod ullamcorper, lectus nunc ullamcorper orci, fermentum bibendum enim nibh eget ipsum.

5. Style the list items. Now that the structure is styled, it's time to get cracking on the list. First, add a rule to remove the default bullets from the unordered list within the navigation div.

```
#navigation ul {
  list-style: none;
}
```

Next, set the list items to display inline, as with the breadcrumbs. Add some horizontal padding, and also, as shown, add a border to each item's right edge, which will act as a visual separator, making each link more distinct.

```
#navigation li {
  display: inline;
  padding: 0px 9px;
  border-right: 1px solid #aaaaaa;
}
```

If you test the page at this point, you'll see that all the links have a right-edge border—not a terrible crime—but from a design standpoint, the one at the far right shouldn't have one (after all, separators are needed only between pairs of links). Luckily, because of the id values applied to the list items earlier, each one can be individually styled, which also means an override can be applied to a specific link. In this case, add the following rule, which removes the border from the list item with an id value of contactDetailsPageLink:

```
#navigation #contactDetailsPageLink {
  border-right: none;
}
```

6. The last thing to do is style the links. The following rules set the link text to uppercase, removing the default underline and coloring them black by default. The links are then gray on the visited state, have an underline on the hover state, and are red on the active state.

```
#navigation a:link, #navigation a:visited {
  text-transform: uppercase;
  text-decoration: none;
}
#navigation a:link {
  color: #000000;
}
#navigation a:visited {
  color: #222222;
}
#navigation a:hover {
  text-decoration: underline;
}
#navigation a:active {
  color: #ff0000;
}
```

Note: In this example, the color of the navigation links—which have no underline—is the same as the body copy. While this would be a very bad idea for inline links, it's fine for the navigation links, because they're obviously distinct from the text elsewhere on the page, due to the background color and horizontal line that separates the navigation area from the content area

Creating a CSS-only tab bar that automates the active page

Required filesThe `graphical-navigation-starting-point` folder from the chapter 5 folder

What you'll learn   How to create a tab-style navigation bar, using only CSS for styling (no images)

Completed files   The css-only-tab-bar folder in the chapter 5 folder

1. Edit the body element—in the HTML page, edit the body start tag, adding the `class` value shown. Its significance will be explained later.

```
<body id="homePage">
```

2. Edit the body rule. In the CSS document, amend the body rule as shown to add a light gray background:

```
body {
  font: 62.5%/1.5 Verdana, Arial, Helvetica, sans-serif;
  background: #dddddd;
}
```

3. Style structural `divs`. Add the following #wrapper rule, which defines a set width for the page, centers it, and sets the background color to white.

```
#wrapper {
  width: 700px;
  margin: 0 auto;
  background: #ffffff;
}
```

Next, style the content `div` by adding the following rule, which adds a border to all edges but the top one and defines internal padding:

```
#content {
  padding: 15px 15px 0;
  border-right: 1px solid #898989;
  border-bottom: 1px solid #898989;
  border-left: 1px solid #898989;
}
```

These rules work slightly differently from those in the previous exercise. We want the content borders to start right under the navigation, which is why the padding is being applied to the top of the content `div`, rather than a margin below the `navContainer` `div`.

4. Style the navContainer div. Add the following rule to style the navContainer div. The font settings define a size and family. Avoid setting a line-height value, because that makes it much harder to line up the tabs with the borders later. The padding value applies some padding above the soon-to-be-created tabs, and the border-bottom value finally surrounds all edges of the content div with a border. Because the wrapper div has a white background, this currently shows through the navContainer div, and so a background setting is applied, using the same background color value as applied to the body element.

```
#navContainer {
  font: 1.1em Arial, Helvetica, sans-serif;
  text-align: center;
  padding: 20px 0 0;
  border-bottom: 1px solid #909090;
  background: #dddddd;
}
```

5. Style the list. Add the following rule to style the list. The bottom padding value (5px here) adds padding to the bottom of the list and needs to be equivalent to the padding value you want to be under the text in each tab.

```
#navigation ul {
  padding: 0 0 5px;
}
```

Next, style the list items to make them display inline.

```
#navigation li {
  display: inline;
}
```

6. Add the following rule to style the links. Most of the property values should be familiar by now. Note how the border value applies a border to each link; this, in tandem with the background value, gives all the links the appearance of background tabs. The padding setting provides space around the link contents (and note how the vertical padding value is the same as the bottom padding value in step 5), and the margin-right setting adds some space between each tab.

```
#navigation a:link, #navigation a:visited {
  text-transform: uppercase;
  text-decoration: none;
```

```
    color: #000000;
    background: #bbbbbb;
    border: 1px solid #898989;
    padding: 5px 10px;
    position: relative;
    margin-right: 5px;
}
```

As per the previous exercise, the unwanted right-hand value for the rightmost tab (in this case, the margin-right setting) can be overridden by using a contextual selector that takes advantage of the id values defined in the HTML document's unordered list items.

```
#navigation #contactDetailsPageLink a:link, #navigation
```

```
    #contactDetailsPageLink a:visited {
    margin-right: 0;
}
```

7. Style other link states. Add the following two rules to define the other link states. The first makes the text slightly lighter when a link has been visited. The second brings back the default underline on the hover state, along with making the link's background slightly lighter.

```
#navigation a:visited {
    color: #222222;
}
#navigation a:hover {
    text-decoration: underline;
    background: #cccccc;
}
```

8. Create page-specific overrides. Remember back in step 1, when you defined an id value for the body element? This can now be used to automate the active tab via the following rule:

```
#homePage #homePageLink a:link, #homePage #homePageLink a:visited,
    #servicesPage #servicesPageLink a:link, #servicesPage
    #servicesPageLink a:visited, #customerSupportPage
    #customerSupportPageLink a:link, #customerSupportPage
    #customerSupportPageLink a:visited, #contactDetailsPage
    #contactDetailsPageLink a:link, #contactDetailsPage
    #contactDetailsPageLink a:visited {
    background: #ffffff;
    border-bottom-color: #ffffff;
}
```

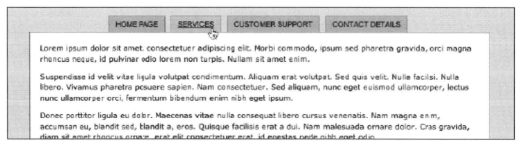

The declaration is simple: a white background is applied, and the bottom border color is changed to white. The grouped selector is more complex, so I'll start by explaining the first contextual selector, which is #homePage #homePageLink a:link. What this means is, "Apply the declaration to the link within an element with an id of homePageLink that's in an element with an id of homePage." In the page you've been working on, the body element has an id of homePage, and the first list element in the unordered list has an id of homePageLink. Therefore, the link within this list item is automatically given the style, making it look like the active tab (since the background blends directly into the content area).

The other selectors in the grouped selector behave in the same way (in each case for the link and visited styles); so if, for example, you change the id value of the body start tag in the HTML document to customerSupportPage and then refresh the web page, you'll see the third link become the active tab.

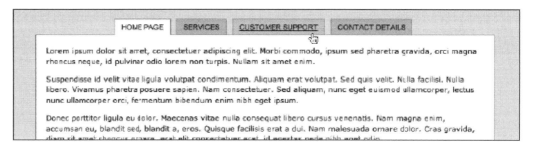

Graphical navigation with rollover effects

Working with text and CSS alone is fine, but designers are creative types and tend to like working with graphics. Many enjoy creating more visually arresting navigation bars, which make use of imagery and rollovers. Historically, such systems have required a number of images (three or more per tab) and the use of JavaScript. However, it's possible to use CSS, the same unordered list as used for the previous two exercises, and just a single image to create a graphical navigation bar, as shown in the next exercise.

Using CSS backgrounds to create a navigation bar		
Required files image.gif from	The graphical-navigation-starting-point folder and css-tab-rollover-	
	the navigation-images folder in the chapter 5 folder	

What you'll learn	How to create a graphical navigation bar with four different states, driven by CSS, without using any JavaScript

| Completed files | The graphical-navigation-bar folder in the chapter_5 folder |

For this exercise, graphical tabs will be created, using a single GIF image that contains four variations on the graphic: three are for link states for which styles will be defined (active, hover, and then link and visited, which share an image); the other is to flag the current page. By applying this image as a background to links and then amending its vertical positioning on each state, only the relevant portion of the image will be shown. This technique is called *CSS sprites* and is used to limit the number of files that have to be loaded into your page. This is great for updating a site (you need to amend only a single image) and also from a bandwidth standpoint (one image deals with every tab and every state—no need for preloading anything), and it's easy to implement.

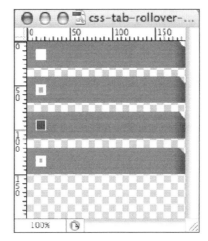

1. Edit the body element. Like in the previous exercise, edit the body start tag, adding the id value shown.

```
<body id="homePage">
```

2. Style the structural divs. This page's structure is simple, as are the CSS rules required to style it. The #wrapper rule sets a fixed width (which is four times the width of one of the tabs) and centers the design in the browser window. The #masthead rule adds some padding at the top of the masthead, so the tabs won't hug the top of the browser window.

The #navContainer rule has a bottom border (to firmly separate the navigation from the other page content) and a defined height, which is the height of a tab. The height setting is useful, because these tabs will be floated, meaning they're outside of the standard document flow. By giving the container a fixed height, the border is shown in the right place; without the height definition, the border would be displayed at the top of the navContainer div, because as far as browsers are concerned, floated elements technically don't take up any height within the standard document flow.

Finally, the #content rule gives that area a background color and some padding.

```
#wrapper {
  width: 740px;
  margin: 0 auto;
}
#masthead {
  padding-top: 20px;
}
#navContainer {
  height: 30px;
  border-bottom: 5px solid #ad3514;
}
#content {
  padding: 10px;
  background-color: #eeeeee;
}
```

    3.   Remove the default bullet points from the list items by adding the following rule:

```
#navigation ul {
list-style-type: none;
}
```

    4.   Style list items. Items within the list are styled to float left. The background value includes the location of the rollover image, with additional settings being no-repeat (to stop it from tiling), and then 0 and 0, to ensure the relevant portion of the rollover image is seen by default. The width and height values are the same as that of the image: 185px and 30px, respectively.

```
#navigation li {
  float: left;
  background: url(css-tab-rollover-image.gif) no-repeat 0 0;
  width: 185px;
  height: 30px;
}
```

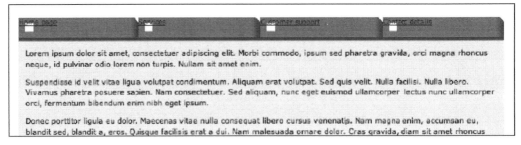

    5.   Next, style the links. The text is rendered in white, in uppercase, and in Arial, and the default underlines are removed. Setting display to block makes the entire link container into an active link, thereby making the navigation bar work in the traditional manner (rather than just the text being active). Finally, the padding settings position the text correctly over the background images.

The height setting, combined with the padding top setting of 9px, adds up to the height of the container—30px. Without this, the space underneath the text would not be active.

```
#navigation a:link, #navigation a:visited {
  font: bold 1.1em Arial, Helvetica, sans-serif;
  text-transform: uppercase;
  color: #ffffff;
  text-decoration: none;
  display: block;
  height: 21px;
  padding: 9px 0px 0px 30px;
}
```

6. Style other link states. For the hover and active states, you define which portion of the rollover graphic is supposed to be visible. This is done via background position values. The first of these remains 0, because you always want to see the image from its far left. The vertical reading depends on where the relevant portion of the image appears in the rollover graphic.

If you check css-tab-rollover-image.gif in an image editor, you'll see the hover state graphic is 40 pixels from the top and the active state graphic is 80 pixels from the top. This means the image needs to be vertically moved −40 pixels and −80 pixels for the hover and active states, respectively. Therefore, the rules for these states are as follows:

```
#navigation a:hover {
  background: url(css-tab-rollover-image.gif) 0 -40px;
}
#navigation a:active {
  background: url(css-tab-rollover-image.gif) 0 -80px;
}
```

7. Define the active section state. As per step 8 of the previous exercise, the active state graphic can be set. In this case, this is done by displaying the fourth state in the rollover image via the following rule:

```
#homePage #homePageLink a:link, #homePage #homePageLink a:visited,
  #servicesPage #servicesPageLink a:link, #servicesPage
  #servicesPageLink a:visited, #customerSupportPage
  #customerSupportPageLink a:link, #customerSupportPage
  #customerSupportPageLink a:visited, #contactDetailsPage
  #contactDetailsPageLink a:link, #contactDetailsPage
  #contactDetailsPageLink a:visited {
  background: url(css-tab-rollover-image.gif) 0 -120px;
}
```

Again, you can change the id value of the body element to one of the other list item id values to change the active section link.

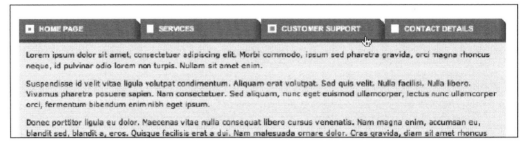

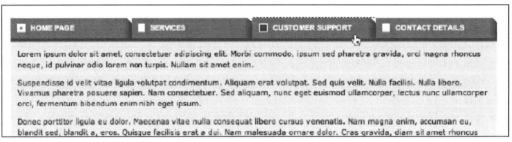

Using a grid image for multiple link styles and colors

Required files	The files from the `graphical-navigation-bar` folder and `css-rollover-grid.gif` from the `navigation-images` folder in the chapter 5 folder
What you'll learn	How to amend the previous exercise in order to create a different tab for each link—still by using a single image
Completed files	The graphical-navigation-bar-grid folder in the chapter 5 folder

Taking the previous exercise's completed files as a starting point, along with `css-rollover-grid.gif`, which will be used as the rollover image, you're now going to have a different tab for each link. This will be done via more background positioning and by making use of the list item `id` values to create rules with contextual selectors specific to each item. Naturally, the rollover image contains all of the states for the rollover images.

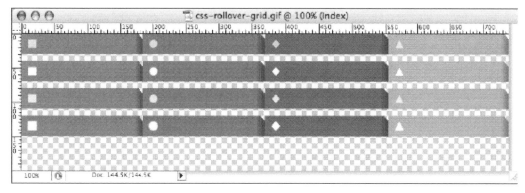

1. Amend the list item style. To apply the new background to the list items, amend the #navigation li rule:

```
#navigation li {
  float: left;
  display: inline;
  width: 185px;
  height: 30px;
  background: url(css-rollover-grid.gif) no-repeat 0 0;
}
```

2. Amend the navContainer div border. Because the tabs are now multicolored, the orange border at the bottom of the navContainer div won't look good, so change it to dark gray.

```
#navContainer {
  height: 30px;
  border-bottom: 5px solid #333333;
}
```

3. Set specific background positions. Each tab now requires a separate background position to show the relevant portion of the background image for each tab. Again, negative margins are used to pull the image into place in each case. (Because the different colors aren't obvious in grayscale, the tabs also have unique icons at the far left.) These rules should be placed after the #navigation a:link, #navigation a:visited rule.

```
#navigation #homePageLink {
  background-position: 0 0;
}
#navigation #servicesPageLink {
  background-position: -185px 0;
}
#navigation #customerSupportPageLink {
  background-position: -370px 0;
}
#navigation #contactDetailsPageLink {
  background-position: -555px 0;
}
```

4. Edit the active-page state for each tab. The correct portion of the image needs to show when a tab is the active page, and this is done by replacing the rule from step 6 of the previous exercise with the following four rules, which should be placed after the rules added in the previous step.

```
#homePage #homePageLink a:link, #homePage #homePageLink a:visited {
  background: url(css-rollover-grid.gif) 0 -120px;
}
#servicesPage #servicesPageLink a:link, #servicesPage
  #servicesPageLink a:visited {
  background: url(css-rollover-grid.gif) -185px -120px;
}
#customerSupportPage #customerSupportPageLink a:link,
  #customerSupportPage #customerSupportPageLink a:visited {
  background: url(css-rollover-grid.gif) -370px -120px;
}
#contactDetailsPage #contactDetailsPageLink a:link,
  #contactDetailsPage #contactDetailsPageLink a:visited {
  background: url(css-rollover-grid.gif) -555px -120px;
}
```

5. Finally, the two rules for the hover and active states need to be replaced by four rules each—one for each tab. Again, negative margin values are used to display the relevant portion of the background image for each state for each image. Add these rules after those from the previous step.

```
#navigation li#homePageLink a:hover {
  background: url(css-rollover-grid.gif) 0 -40px;
}
#navigation li#servicesPageLink a:hover {
  background: url(css-rollover-grid.gif) -185px -40px;
}
#navigation li#customerSupportPageLink a:hover {
  background: url(css-rollover-grid.gif) -370px -40px;
}
#navigation li#contactDetailsPageLink a:hover {
  background: url(css-rollover-grid.gif) -555px -40px;
}

#navigation li#homePageLink a:active {
  background: url(css-rollover-grid.gif) 0 -80px;
}
#navigation li#servicesPageLink a:active {
  background: url(css-rollover-grid.gif) -185px -80px;
}
#navigation li#customerSupportPageLink a:active {
  background: url(css-rollover-grid.gif) -370px -80px;
}
#navigation li#contactDetailsPageLink a:active {
  background: url(css-rollover-grid.gif) -555px -80px;
}
```

Once again, change the id value of the body element to amend the active section link.

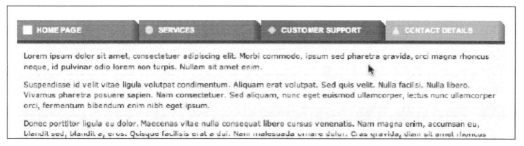

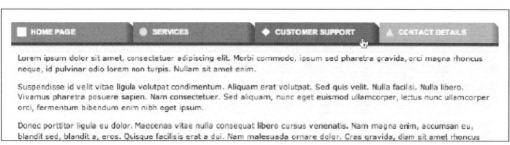

Creating graphical tabs that expand with resized text

Required files	The files from the graphical-navigation-bar folder, and the images css-tab-rollover-image-left.gif and css-tab-rollover-image-right.gif from the navigation-images folder from the chapter 5 folder
What you'll learn	How to amend the result from the "Using CSS backgrounds to create a navigation bar" exercise, enabling the tabs to expand, resizing with their content
Completed files	graphical-navigation-bar-sliding-doors in the chapter 5 folder

With both of the graphical tab exercises so far, there is a problem: when the text is resized, the tabs don't resize with it.

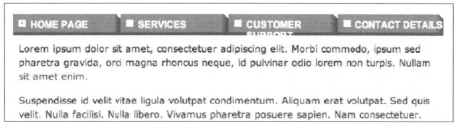

This can be dealt with using a technique typically referred to as "sliding doors." This requires two images in place of the original background image tab—one for its left part and one for the right part, with enough vertical repetition to expand horizontally. With wider links, more of the right image will be displayed.

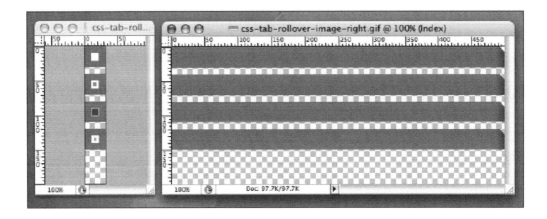

> *Note that the increase in flexibility in this method is only horizontal. If you need more flexibility vertically, increase the height of each "state" in the graphical tabs, remove the* height *values from both* #navigation li *and* #navigation a:link, #navigation a:visited, *and add a* padding-bottom *value to the latter of those two rules.*

1. Amend the list. To the list items, apply the css-tab-rollover-image-left.gif background image, and add a padding-left value that's the same width as the image. This provides the left side of each tab. The reason for the padding value is so that the right side of the tab (applied to the link) doesn't overlap the left image.

```
#navigation li {
  float: left;
  background: url(css-tab-rollover-image-left.gif) no-repeat 0 0;
  padding-left: 30px;
  height: 30px;
}
```

2. Amend the link style. Because the padding at the left of the link is now dealt with by the previous rule, there's no need for a padding-left value in #navigation a:link, #navigation a:visited. However, because the link now stretches with the content, a padding-right value is required, to stop the tab content in each case from hugging the edge of the tab. This explains the amended values for the padding property. For the background property, the image file name is amended, along with its horizontal position, which is now at the far right (100%).

```
#navigation a:link, #navigation a:visited {
  font: bold 1.1em Arial, Helvetica, sans-serif;
  text-transform: uppercase;
  color: #ffffff;
  text-decoration: none;
  display: block;
  height: 21px;
  padding: 9px 30px 0px 0px;
  background: url(css-tab-rollover-image-right.gif) no-repeat 100% 0;
}
```

3. With this technique, the left portion of the tab is no longer an active link. It's therefore usually recommended to keep the left image as narrow as possible. In this example, the left image is 30 pixels wide, but this was used to show how to convert a standard graphical navigation bar into one where the tabs can expand—it's not recommended for the graphical design of such a system. However, this means the hover and current page states need amending; otherwise, there's no feedback. Therefore, for #navigation a:hover, set text-decoration to underline, and delete everything else within the rule; and for the large, complex rule at the end, set color: #fff200; as the sole property/value pair in the declaration.

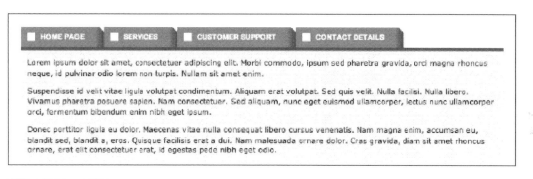

Creating a two-tier navigation menu

Required files   The files from the graphical-navigation-bar folder and the images active-section-tab-background.gif and sub-navigation-background-tile.gif from the navigation-images folder from the chapter 5 folder.

What you'll learn   How to create a two-tier navigation system, with different backgrounds and styles for each tier. This is another method for dealing with navigation text resizing, and it's also useful for larger websites, providing a place for subnavigation.

Completed files   two-tier-navigation in the chapter 5 folder.

1. Edit the body element. In the HTML page, give the body start tag an id value of homePage.

```
<body id="homePage">
```

2.   Add some subnavigation. Open the HTML document and add another list for subnavigation, directly after the navigation div.

```
<div id="subNavigation">
  <ul>
    <li><a href="#">Sub-nav one</a></li>
    <li><a href="#">Sub-nav two</a></li>
    <li><a href="#">Sub-nav three</a></li>
    <li><a href="#">Sub-nav four</a></li>
    <li><a href="#">Sub-nav five</a></li>
    <li><a href="#">Sub-nav six</a></li>
    <li><a href="#">Sub-nav seven</a></li>
  </ul>
</div>
```

3.   Amend the body rule. In the CSS document, edit the body rule to add a dark gray background color and some padding at the top of the document.

```
body {
  font: 62.5%/1.5 Verdana, Arial, Helvetica, sans-serif;
  background: #333333;
  padding-top: 20px;
}
```

4.   Style the structural divs—add the following three rules to style the three main structural divs. Adding a light gray bottom border to the masthead makes the transition between the vibrant navigation to the black-text-on-white-background content area less harsh.

```
#wrapper {
  width: 750px;
  margin: 0 auto;
  background-color: #ffffff;
  border: 1px solid #555555;
}
#masthead {
  border-bottom: 8px solid #cccccc;
}
#content {
  background: #ffffff;
  padding: 10px;
}
```

5.   Add the following two rules to remove list defaults, center list content, and display list items inline.

```
#navContainer ul {
  text-align: center;
}
#navContainer li {
  display: inline;
}
```

6. Style the navigation div and its links. Add the following three rules to style the navigation div and the links within. The padding settings work as per the earlier exercises in this chapter: again, the vertical padding must be kept constant between the container and the links, which is why the vertical padding is being set to 6px in both cases. Note the hover color—a bright yellow, designed to stand out against both the black background of the main navigation bar and the orange background of the subnavigation and highlighted tab.

```
#navigation {
  background: #111111;
  padding: 6px 0;
}
#navigation a:link, #navigation a:visited {
  font: bold 1.2em Arial, Helvetica, sans-serif;
  color: #ffffff;
  text-decoration: none;
  padding: 6px 10px;
}
#navigation a:hover {
  color: #ffd800;
}
```

7. Style the active page link. Using one of those grouped contextual selectors we seem to like so much in this chapter, set a rule to style the active page link. In this case, a background image is tiled horizontally and set to sit at the bottom of the links. A background color is also defined, which is handy for if the text is zoomed—if no background color were defined, the image might run out, leaving the navigation div's background color to show through instead. This rule, however, ensures that the background will always have some color, regardless of the font size. The color setting itself was taken from the top pixel of the background image, so it blends seamlessly with said image.

```
#homePage #homePageLink a:link, #homePage #homePageLink a:visited,
  #servicesPage #servicesPageLink a:link, #servicesPage
  #servicesPageLink a:visited, #customerSupportPage
  #customerSupportPageLink a:link, #customerSupportPage
  #customerSupportPageLink a:visited, #contactDetailsPage
  #contactDetailsPageLink a:link, #contactDetailsPage
  #contactDetailsPageLink a:visited {
  background: #28b767 url(active-section-tab-background.gif)
```

```
  0 100% repeat-x;
  border-top: 1px solid #ca8d5c;
}
```

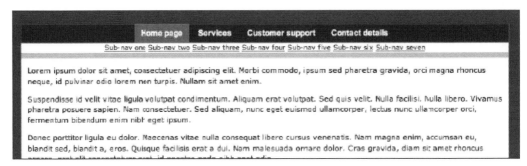

8. Add the following three rules to style the subnavigation. Here, a background image is tiled horizontally behind the entire subNavigation div, and it works in a similar way to the one used in step 7, blending into a background color if the text is zoomed, dramatically changing the div's height. The border-bottom setting provides a darker base to the navigation, which works better than having the light gray masthead border directly beneath it. The margin-top setting pulls the entire subNavigation div up two pixels, which stops the layout from splitting at some levels of text zoom.

```
#subNavigation {
  margin-top: -2px;
  background: #b76628 url(sub-navigation-background-tile.gif) 0 100%
    repeat-x;
  border-bottom: 1px solid #6b6b6b;
  padding: 6px 0;
}
#subNavigation a:link, #subNavigation a:visited {
  font: bold 1.1em Arial, Helvetica, sans-serif;
  color: #ffffff;
  text-decoration: none;
  padding: 6px 10px;
}
#subNavigation a:hover {
  color: #ffd800;
}
```

As you can see from the following images, this navigation bar deals really well with increased text sizes—only when the text is absolutely massive does it not work entirely as expected, although, crucially, it still remains usable.

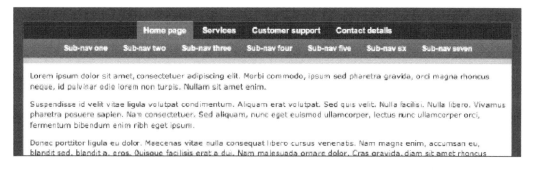

> Caution: The *subNavigation div* in this technique sometimes suffers from the *hasLayout* bug in Internet Explorer 6. See Chapter 9 for a method of dealing with *hasLayout*.

Creating a drop-down menu

Required files	Files from the graphical-navigation-bar folder and drop-down-menu-background.gif (which is a crop of the list item background image) from the navigation-images folder in the chapter 5 folder
What you'll learn	How to work with an existing CSS-based navigation menu and convert it into a drop-down menu
Completed files	The drop-down-menu folder in the chapter 5 folder

The next type of navigation we're going to explore in this chapter is the drop-down menu. In part popularized by operating systems such as Windows and Mac OS, drop-down menus are convenient for storing plenty of links in a relatively small space. However, use them with caution, because the second tier of navigation is initially hidden from view, unlike in the previous exercise's system, where it was visible. However, with drop-downs, all second-tier navigation is available from the menu.

1. Edit the web page. For any link you want to have a drop-down menu spawn from, nest an unordered list in its parent list item, as per the example in the following code block.

```
<li id="servicesPageLink">
  <a href="#">Services</a>
  <ul>
    <li><a href="#">Drop-down link one</a></li>
    <li><a href="#">Drop-down link two</a></li>
    <li><a href="#">Drop-down link three</a></li>
    <li><a href="#">Drop-down link four</a></li>
  </ul>
</li>
```

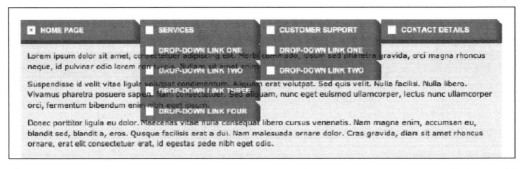

2. Create the drop-downs. Test your page now, and it will look odd because nested list items pick up the styles for the standard list items. To start dealing with this, add position: relative; to the #navigation li rule, which will enable nested absolute-positioned elements to take their top and left values from their containers rather than the page as a whole. Then, after the existing rules in the CSS, add the #navigation li ul rule shown in the following code block. By setting position to absolute and left to a large negative value, the nested lists (in other words, the drop-down menus) are placed offscreen by default but are still accessible to screen readers. Adding the top border helps visually separate the nested list from its parent button.

```
#navigation li ul {
  border-top: 1px solid #ad3514;
  width: 185px;
  position: absolute;
  left: -10000px
}
```

3. Next, add the following rule to bring the nested lists back when you hover the cursor over the parent list item. Upon doing so, the list item's descendant list's display value is set to block, and it's displayed directly underneath the parent item.

```
#navigation li:hover ul  {
  display: block;
  left: 0;
}
```

4. Style nested list items and links. Add the following rule to replace the default background for list items with one specifically for the drop-down menus. The `border-bottom` value visually separates each of the list items.

```
#navigation li li {
  background: url(drop-down-menu-background.gif) repeat-y;
  border-bottom: 1px solid #ad3514;
}
```

5. Next, add the following rule to style nested list item links, overriding the `text-transform` and padding values of top-level list items.

```
#navigation li li a:link, #navigation li li a:visited {
  text-transform: none;
  padding-left: 10px;
}
```

6. The final step is to override the `hover` and `active` states. For this example, the `background` value for top-level lists is overridden and the background image removed (meaning the `hover` state for nested list links has no unique background). To make the `hover` state stand out, the links are given a vibrant left border. This also moves the text inward by the width of the border.

```
#navigation li li a:hover, #navigation li li a:active {
  background: none;
  border-left: 5px solid #f7bc1d;
}
```

These property values are common to both states, apart from the border color (orange for the `hover` state and red for the `active` state, roughly matching the colors applied to the top-level tab icons in the same states, although the orange is brighter for the drop-downs so that they stand out more); therefore, add the following rule to change only the left border's color on the `active` state:

```
#navigation li li a:active {
  border-left-color: #ed1c24;
}
```

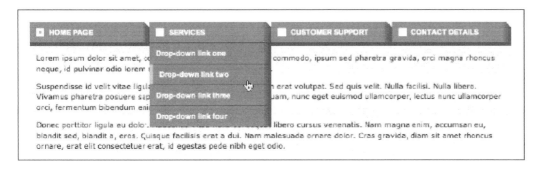

> Note: If you decide to create drop-down menu–based navigation, avoid copying an operating system's menu style, because this may confuse visitors using that operating system and irritate visitors using a rival system. The exception to this rule is if you're creating a site that centers around nostalgia for the days where operating systems used to come on floppy disks. One such site—an amusing Mac OS System 7 look-alike—can be found at *http://myoldmac.net/*.

Creating a multicolumn drop-down menu

Required files	The drop-down-menu folder from the chapter 5 folder.

What you'll learn	How to create a multicolumn drop-down menu, based on the code from the previous exercise

Completed files	The drop-down-menu-multi-column folder in the chapter 5 folder

The final example in this chapter is a multicolumn drop-down menu. These are increasingly common, enabling sites to provide a lot of links in a drop-down that simply wouldn't fit on the screen if they were listed vertically. For an example of such a drop-down in action (although one that uses a different method), visit `www.2000adonline.com/books/` and hover over the `Books List` link.

1. Edit the HTML to remove the existing nested lists. Then, for the multicolumn drop-down, decide which link you want it to spawn from and place an unordered link in its parent list item, with a single list item of its own. Within that list item, place the unordered lists for the columns in the drop-down, one after the other. Note that if some columns have fewer items, they must still have the same number of list items. However, list items can be left empty, despite this technically being a presentational hack. (Note that HTML Tidy might have problems with this and trim the empty list items. If you use that tool, add a nonbreaking space as the list's content.)

```
<li id="servicesPage">
  <a href="#">Services</a>
  <ul>
    <li>
      <ul>
        <li><a href="#">Drop-down link 1.1</a></li>
        <li><a href="#">Drop-down link 1.2</a></li>
        <li><a href="#">Drop-down link 1.3</a></li>
```

```
        <li><a href="#">Drop-down link 1.4</a></li>
      </ul>
      <ul>
        <li><a href="#">Drop-down link 2.1</a></li>
        <li><a href="#">Drop-down link 2.2</a></li>
        <li></li>
        <li></li>
      </ul>
      <ul>
        <li><a href="#">Drop-down link 3.1</a></li>
        <li><a href="#">Drop-down link 3.2</a></li>
        <li><a href="#">Drop-down link 3.3</a></li>
        <li></li>
      </ul>
    </li>
  </ul>
</li>
```

2. Next, edit the nested list. The list that contains the three lists that form the columns of the drop-down needs styling. Having larger borders on multicolumn drop-downs is a good idea, because it enables users to focus on the contents more easily, which is the reason for the amended border setting in the following code block. The other change is to the width setting, which must be a multiple of three (here, it's set to 465px, meaning that each column will be 155 pixels wide). With multicolumn drop-downs, it's best to avoid making each column the same width as a tab; otherwise, the result will look strange.

```
#navigation li ul {
  border: 2px solid #ad3514;
  width: 465px;
  position: absolute;
  left: -10000px
}
```

3. Now, the list item within the nested list needs amending. For the previous exercise, the #navigation li li rule dealt with the list items in the drop-down, but here it's primarily for the container of the three columns. Therefore, the height and width settings need to be set to auto to enable the list item to stretch to fit its nested items. The background image is superfluous, so it's replaced by a flat color, and the border-bottom pair is removed—the borders will be moved to list items within the columns.

```
#navigation li li {
  background: #d27448;
  height: auto;
  width: auto;
}
```

4. The link rules should be styled next. Since the links are now one level deeper in the list, instances of li li in the selectors are changed to li li li. In this example, this change isn't technically necessary, but it always pays to keep your selectors as precise and accurate as possible. For the link and visited states, padding settings for the top-level links are overridden, as are width and

height settings. For the other states, the border used for the hover and active effects is replaced by a change in background color. Note that the rule that originally had both the hover and active states in the selector (#navigation li li a:hover, #navigation li li a:active) now requires only the hover state (#navigation li li li a:hover), because the rules have nothing in common.

```
#navigation li li li a:link, #navigation li li li a:visited {
  text-transform: none;
  padding: 10px;
  width: 135px;
  height: auto;
}

#navigation li li li a:hover {
  background: #ad3514; !important;
}
#navigation li li li a:active {
  background: #ed1c24;
}
```

5. Style the column list items. Add a rule to define a width and height for the column list items, along with a bottom border. The last of those things makes it easier to scan the rows within the list, while the width and height settings ensure that the layout isn't affected if the list items have no links within. (If the width and height settings were omitted, the list items within the columns would show their bottom borders only underneath their content's width—and not at all if they were empty.) The height setting is defined in ems rather than pixels, because this makes it possible for the list items to stretch vertically if the web page's text is resized.

```
#navigation li li li {
width: 155px;
height: 3em;
border-bottom: 1px solid #ad3514;
}
```

6. Finally, add a rule to float and define a width for the lists that comprise the containers for the list items styled in the previous step.

```
#navigation ul ul ul {
  border: 0;
  width: 155px;
  float: left;
  position: relative;
}
```

Note: Although the drop-down examples work in currently shipping browsers, neither works as is in Internet Explorer 6, because that browser doesn't enable you to do anything with the *hover* state unless it's on a link. To cater for that browser, JavaScript must be used as a backup.

The dos and don'ts of web navigation

So, that's the end of our navigation chapter. Before we move on to working with layout, here are a few succinct tips regarding designing web navigation.

Do

- Use appropriate types of navigation.

- Provide alternate means of accessing information.

- Ensure links stand out.

- Take advantage of link states to provide feedback for users.

- Get the link state order right (link, visited, hover, active).

- Use styled lists for navigation.

- Use CSS and as few images as possible (preferably one) for rollovers.

Don't

- Add search boxes just for the sake of it.

- Use deprecated body attributes.

- Style navigation links like normal body copy.

- Use image maps unless absolutely necessary.

- Open new windows from links or use pop-ups.

- Use clunky JavaScript for rollovers.

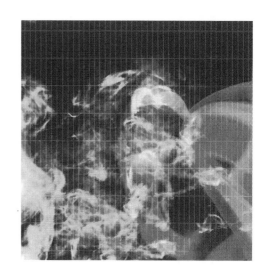

Chapter 6

Tables: How Nature (and the W3C) Intended

A playlist of great music	
Time	Artist
3:34	Wire
3:18	Worm Is Green
6:07	Silo
4:48	Fischerspooner
3:21	Bloc Party
3:58	Cansei De Ser Sexy (CSS)
3:45	Tom Vek
5:05	Björk
4:21	Charlotte Hatherley
4:04	The Delgados

Templates	6:07
Emerge	4:48
Banquet	3:21
Alala	3:58
I Ain't Saying My Goodbyes	3:45
Jóga	5:05
Kim Wilde	4:21
Witness	4:04
Feel Good Inc.	3:41
Returning Wheel	3:26
P.E.T.R.O.L.	6:21
Pweization	3:08

Banquet	3:21
Alala	3:58
I Ain't Saying My Goodbyes	3:45
Jóga	5:05
Kim Wilde	4:21
Witness	4:04
Feel Good Inc.	3:41
Returning Wheel	3:26
P.E.T.R.O.L.	6:21
Pweization	3:08
Betrayed	3:05
When The Sun Hits	4:47
Little Fyre	4:20

In this chapter:

- Introducing how tables work

- Using borders, padding, and spacing

- Creating accessible tables

- Enhancing tables with CSS

- Designing tables for web page layout

The great table debate

Tables were initially intended as a means of displaying tabular data online, enabling web designers to rapidly mark up things such as price lists, statistical comparisons, specification lists, spreadsheets, charts, forms, and so on (the following example shows a simple table, taken from www.infoq.com).

Option	Adoption Ready	Importance	Votes	Details
Big Data	69%	67%	65	Heatmap
NoSQL	73%	75%	72	Heatmap
Cross Platform Mobile	68%	64%	54	Heatmap
Continuous Delivery	78%	73%	63	Heatmap
GPU Programming	59%	57%	52	Heatmap
Cloud Open Standards	55%	56%	50	Heatmap
Hybrid Clouds	54%	57%	46	Heatmap
Cloud Dev & Test	67%	66%	50	Heatmap
Node.js	58%	62%	54	Heatmap
Event–driven Architectures	73%	74%	58	Heatmap
HTML5	82%	84%	65	Heatmap
Google Dart	43%	51%	56	Heatmap
Scala	60%	71%	55	Heatmap
Clojure	58%	69%	49	Heatmap
Functional Programming	70%	73%	62	Heatmap
DevOps	71%	74%	52	Heatmap
Lean / Kanban	73%	74%	49	Heatmap
UX for Devs	60%	70%	42	Heatmap
Scrum	70%	76%	48	Heatmap

It wasn't long, however, before web designers realized that you could place any web content within table cells, and this rapidly led to web designers chopping up Photoshop layouts and piecing them back together in table-based web pages, often by using automated tools.

The strong will of CSS advocates, who typically shout that tables are evil, sometimes leads designers to believe that tables should be ditched entirely. However, that's not the case at all. As mentioned, tables have a specific purpose in HTML, and it's one that's still valid. Therefore, the bulk of this chapter is going to look at tables in the context for which they're intended: the formatting of tabular data. Web page layout will be looked at in the next chapter, which concentrates on CSS layout.

How tables work

In this section, we're going to look at how tables are structured and some of the table element's attributes, which enable you to define the table's dimensions and borders, along with the spacing, padding, and alignment of its cells.

Tabular data works via a system of rows and columns, and HTML tables work in the same way. The table element defines the beginning and end of a table. Within the table element are table row elements (<tr></tr>), and nested within those are table cell elements (<td></td>). The actual content is placed inside the td elements. Therefore, a simple table with two rows containing two cells each is created like this:

```
<table>
  <tr><td>Cell one</td><td>Cell two</td></tr>
  <tr><td>Cell three</td><td>Cell four</td></tr>
</table>
```

> Note: Always ensure that you include all end tags when working with tables. If you began working with HTML in the mid-1990s, you may have learned that it's OK to omit the odd end tag from tables or table cells. However, not only does this result in invalid XHTML, but some browsers won't render tables accurately (or at all) when end tags are omitted. Furthermore, there's evidence to suggest some search engines can't properly index pages that contain broken tables.

Adding a border

You can place a border around table cells by using the border attribute and setting its value to 1 or greater. The adjacent example shows how this looks in a web browser.

HTML borders for tables have a kind of 3D effect and tend to look clunky and old-fashioned. If you want to add a border to a table, this is best done in CSS.

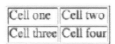

Cell spacing and cell padding

In addition to amending the border size, it's possible to change the amount of padding within a table's cells, as well as the spacing between all the cells in a table. This is done with the cellpadding and cellspacing attributes, respectively. In the rather extreme example that follows, cellpadding is set to 20, cellspacing to 40, and border to 5, so that each can be differentiated with ease (see the subsequent screenshot). As you can see, cellspacing affects not only the spacing between the cells but also the distance between the cells and the table's edges. The CSS property border-spacing is intended to do the same thing as cellspacing.

```
<table cellpadding="20" cellspacing="40" border="5">
  <tr><td>Cell one</td><td>Cell two</td></tr>
  <tr><td>Cell three</td><td>Cell four</td></tr>
</table>
```

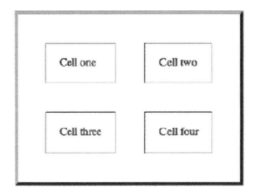

You might be thinking that designwise, this example sucks, and you'd be right. The chunk-o-vision 3D border isn't particularly tasteful. However, you can omit the border attribute and use CSS to style borders instead—see the "Styling a table" section later on in this chapter. That section also details how to set padding in CSS, which provides you with sitewide control over cell padding. CSS also gives you much finer control over the individual elements in a table—whereas the inline HTML attributes impose a one-style-fits-all straightjacket.

Spanning rows and cells

It's sometimes necessary for data to span multiple rows or columns. This is achieved via the rowspan and colspan attributes, respectively. In the following table, the first row has three cells. However, in the second row, the first cell spans two rows, and the second cell spans two columns. This means the second row lacks a third cell, and the third row also has only two cells (whose contents align with the second and third cells of the top row). See the following screenshot of the table to help make sense of this.

```
<table border="1" cellpadding="2">
  <tr>
    <td>A cell</td>
    <td>Another cell</td>
    <td>Yet another cell!</td>
  </tr>
  <tr>
    <td rowspan="2">A cell that spans two rows</td>
    <td colspan="2">A cell that spans two columns</td>
  </tr>
  <tr>
    <td>Another cell</td>
    <td>The last cell</td>
```

```
    </tr>
  </table>
```

A cell		Another cell	Yet another cell!
A cell that spans two rows		A cell that spans two columns	
		Another cell	The last cell

> Note: In the preceding HTML, the cell elements are indented to make it easier for you to make them out. This wasn't done earlier in the chapter. Either method of writing markup is fine—it's up to you. Note, however, that if you use images within table cells, this extra whitespace in the HTML sometimes causes layouts to break and must therefore be deleted.

Take care when spanning rows or columns with a cell, because it's easy to add extra cells accidentally. For instance, in the preceding example, it would be easy to absentmindedly add a third cell to both the second and third rows—however, doing so appends the extra cells to the end of the table (see the following example), which looks bad and—more important—makes little structural sense. Also, some screen readers have difficulty handling such data, often assigning the wrong headers to various pieces of data (see the "Creating accessible tables" section later in the chapter for information on table headers).

A cell		Another cell	Yet another cell!	
A cell that spans two rows		A cell that spans two columns		This shouldn't be here
		Another cell	The last cell	A wrongly added cell

etting dimensions and alignment

As you can see from the examples so far, browsers by default set cell sizes to the smallest possible values that are large enough to accommodate the contents and any cell padding settings defined. Although this is suitable for the majority of purposes, designers tend to want more visual control over layouts.

Longtime designers may be well-versed in the practice of using height and width attributes to control table and cell dimensions, but beware. The width attribute is fine to use on table start tags (the possible values of which are a number denoting the width in pixels of the table, and a percentage, which is a percentage of the parent element's size). However, the height attribute is nonstandard and fails in many web browsers, which might come as something of a shock to those people who enjoy centering content in a browser window by using a table. On the other hand, the CSS height property works as expected.

> Take care when using visual web design applications: many of them add deprecated elements to tables if you manually drag the cells around. Use your favored application's preferences to turn off this feature; otherwise, you'll end up with obsolete and redundant markup.

Vertical alignment of table cell content

If you set your table's width to a small value or if you have a lot of content in one cell and relatively little in an adjacent one, something else becomes apparent: web browsers vertically align content in the middle of cells. (Generally, horizontal alignment is, as with other text, to the left.) See the image on the right for an example.

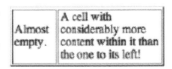

Historically, designers have used the `valign` attribute to override this vertical-centering behavior—the attribute can be added to a row or cell start tag and set to top: `valign="top"`. Other values are `middle` (the default) and `bottom`, the results of which are shown in the adjacent screenshot.

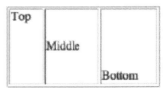

The problem with `valign` is that it's presentational markup and shouldn't really be used; in fact, because it's an obsolete attribute—which means it can't be used if you're creating proper HTML5—you should instead work with the CSS alternative, the `vertical-align` property, which provides practically identical results.

As an example of `vertical-align` in use, say you wanted all cells within a table that had a `class` value of `priceList` to be vertically aligned to the top; you could add the following rule to your CSS:

```
table.priceList td {
  vertical-align: top;
}
```

This results in the same effect as `valign="top"`, as discussed earlier. Likewise, you can set the `vertical-align` property to `middle`, `bottom`, and various other values, as outlined in Appendix D.

That's pretty much where many web designers leave tables; however, there are other elements and attributes that should be used when creating tables, which will be covered in the following sections.

Creating accessible tables

Many web designers ignore all but the most basic elements when working with tables, and in doing so they end up with output that causes problems for screen readers. By correctly and carefully structuring and formatting a table, not only will users of screen readers benefit, but you as a designer will also have far more control over its visual appearance. Additionally, extendable browsers like Firefox can also enable you to use the table data in other ways, including outside of the browser. For example, the TableTools2 plug-in (`https://addons.mozilla.org/en-US/firefox/addon/tabletools2/`) enables sorting, filtering, and exporting of tabular data from a web page. A properly formatted table will enhance this, making the table even more useful. Adding a few extra elements and attributes to your table is a win-win situation, and it's surprising to note how few designers bother with anything other than rows and cells in their tables.

aptions and summaries

Two seldom-used table additions that enable you to provide explanations of a table's contents are the caption element and the summary attribute. The former is usually placed directly after the table start tag and enables you to provide a means of associating the table's title with the table itself. Obviously, this also helps users—particularly those with screen readers. After reading the caption, the screen reader will go on to read the table headers (see the "Using table headers" section later in this chapter). Without the caption, the table's contents might be relatively meaningless.

By default, most browsers center captions horizontally, and some set their contents in bold type, but these default styles can be overridden with CSS.

The summary attribute, which is invisible in browsers, is used by screen readers to give the user an overview of the table's contents prior to accessing the content. The contents of the summary attribute should be kept succinct, highlighting the most important aspects of the table contents, letting the user know what to anticipate.

Many suggest that summaries should be included on all tables, but this isn't necessarily the case. A summary should be used only when it performs the task for which it's designed: to make available a succinct summary of data within a table. Should you be using tables for layout (which I don't recommend), there's little point including summaries within each layout table. After all, someone using a screen reader is hardly going to jump for joy upon hearing, for the umpteenth time, "This table is used for laying out the web page." Summaries should save time, not waste it.

sing table headers

The table header cell element (`<th></th>`) performs a similar function to the standard table cell but is useful with regard to accessibility. Imagine a long data table comprised solely of standard cells. The first row likely contains the headers, but because they're not differentiated, a screen reader might treat them as normal cells, read them once, and then continue reading the remainder of the data. (If it doesn't do this, it still has to assume which cells are headers, and it might guess wrong.) When using table headers, the data is usually read in context (header/data, header/data, and so on), enabling the user to make sense of everything. Things can be sped up slightly by using the abbr attribute—long table headers can be cut down, reducing what needs to be repeated when a table's data is being read. An example of table header cells and a row of data cells follows:

```
<th>Country</th><th abbr="Capital">Capital city</th>
<td>France</td><td>Paris</td>
```

In this case, a screen reader should read the headers and then provide them with the data of each cell (Country: France, Capital: Paris, and so on). But even with screen-based browsers, the inclusion of headers proves beneficial for users, because table header cell content by default is styled differently from data cell content, meaning the two cell types can be easily differentiated.

Although headers are often at the top of a table, they may also be aligned down the left side. Therefore, you also need to specify whether the header provides header information for the remainder of the row, column, row group, or column group that contains it. This can be done with the `scope` attribute, which is added to the table header start tag and given the relevant value (`row`, `col`, `rowgroup`, or `colgroup`). It's also possible to use the `headers` attribute in conjunction with `id` values. See the following "Scope and headers" section for more information.

Row groups

Row group elements are almost never used, the main reason being a supposed lack of browser support. The three possible row group elements—`<thead></thead>`, `<tbody></tbody>`, and `<tfoot></tfoot>`— enable browsers to support the scrolling of the body area of long tables, with the head and foot of the table remaining fixed. Furthermore, when tables are printed, the aforementioned elements enable the table head and foot to be printed on each page.

Although browser support comes up short in some areas, we still recommend using row groups, because they encourage you as a designer to think about the structure of the tables you're creating. Also, although browsers don't do all they might with the elements, they still recognize them, which means they can be used as selectors in CSS, enabling you to set separate styles for the head, body, and foot data.

When using row groups, you can have one or more `tbody` elements and zero or one `thead` and `tfoot` elements. They should be ordered with the head first, foot second, and body/bodies third, thereby enabling the browser to render the foot prior to receiving all of the data. Note, however, that despite this order in HTML, browsers visually render the row groups in the order you'd expect: head, body, and foot.

Scope and headers

Although table header cells provide a means of differentiating headers and other data, a direct means of associating one with the other can be added via the use of various attributes. For simple data tables, the `scope` attribute, added to table headers, provides an indication of which data a heading refers to. For example, in the previous code block, the table is oriented in columns—the headers are above their associated data. Therefore, adding a `scope` attribute to the header cells, with a value of `col`, clearly defines this relationship, and this is something that comes in handy for screen readers.

```
<th scope="col">Country</th><th scope="col">Capital city</th>
<td>France</td><td>Paris</td>
```

If the alignment of the table were changed, with the headers at the left, the `row` value would instead be used.

```
<th scope="row">Country</th><td>France</td>
<th scope="row">Capital city</th><td>Paris</td>
```

Note that if a table header contains `colspan` or `rowspan` attributes—for example, if a header, such as `food`, spanned two columns (thereby having the attribute/value pair `colspan="2"`) and had underneath two further headings, such as `fruit` and `vegetables`— you could set `scope="colgroup"` in the table header start tag. The equivalent is true for headers with a `rowspan` attribute, whereupon the `scope` value changes to `rowgroup`. In such cases, you also need to use the `colgroup/rowgroup` elements.

These are positioned between the `caption` and `thead` of the table (see the following code, and see the following section for an overview of the various structural elements of tables combined).

```
<colgroup span="2"></colgroup >
<colgroup span="2"></colgroup >
<thead>
  <tr>
    <th scope="colgroup" colspan="2">Fruit</th>
    <th scope="colgroup" colspan="2">Vegetable</th>
  </tr>
  <tr>
    <th scope="col">Citrus</th>
    <th scope="col">Berry</th>
    <th scope="col">Root</th>
    <th scope="col">Legume</th>
  </tr>
</thead>
```

For more complex tables that have intricate structures, using many colspans or rowspans, where it wouldn't be immediately obvious where the relationship lies between a data cell and a header, you can use `id` values and the `headers` element. Each table header cell should be assigned a unique id value. Each table data cell that refers to one or more headers requires a `headers` element. The value of the `headers` element is the `id` or `ids` that the cell data refers to. Even for simpler data tables, this method can work well—see the following code block for how our fruit and vegetables table snippet works with `id` and `headers`.

```
<thead>
  <tr>
    <th id="fruit" colspan="2">Fruit</th>
    <th id="vegetables" colspan="2">Vegetable</th>
  </tr>
  <tr>
    <th id="citrus">Citrus</th>
    <th id="berry" >Berry</th>
    <th id="root" >Root</th>
    <th id="legume" >Legume</th>
  </tr>
</thead>

<tbody>
  <tr>
    <td headers="fruit citrus">Lemon</td>
    <td headers="fruit berry">Blueberry</td>
    <td headers="vegetable root">Potato</td>
    <td headers="vegetable legume">Pea</td>
  </tr>
</tbody>
```

Note that the code blocks in this section are here to highlight the attributes and elements being discussed—they should not be seen as examples of complete tables.

Building a table

You're now going to build a table, taking into account all of the information mentioned so far. This will be based on an iTunes playlist.

#	Name	Time	Artist	Album	Play Count
1	In The Art Of Stopping	3:34	Wire	Send	5
2	Electron John	3:18	Worm Is Green	Push Play	43
3	Templates	6:07	Silo	Instar	11
4	Emerge	4:48	Fischerspooner	Fischerspooner #1	24
5	Banquet	3:21	Bloc Party	Silent Alarm	25
6	Alala	3:58	Cansei De Ser Se...	Cansei De Ser Sexy	10
7	I Ain't Saying My Goodbyes	3:45	Tom Vek	We Have Sound	42
8	Jóga	5:05	Bjork	Homogenic	26
9	Kim Wilde	4:21	Charlotte Hatherley	Grey Will Fade	18
10	Witness	4:04	The Delgados	The Great Eastern	10
11	Feel Good Inc.	3:41	Gorillaz	Demon Days	21
12	Returning Wheel	3:26	Malka Spigel	Hide	14
13	P.E.T.R.O.L.	6:21	Orbital	PI (OST)	10
14	Pweization	3:08	Pop Will Eat Itself...	Karmadrome	12
15	Betrayed	3:05	Project Noise	Listen to me	31
16	When The Sun Hits	4:47	Slowdive	Souvlaki	2
17	Little Eyes	4:20	Yo La Tengo	Summer Sun	29

As you can see from the screenshot, the playlist lends itself well to being converted to an HTML table. At the top is the table head, which details each column's data type (song name, time, and so on). And although there's no table foot, you can simply add some information regarding whose choice of music this is—something of a signature—although the table foot can also be used to provide a succinct summary of the table's contents, akin to the value of the summary attribute discussed earlier.

Building the table	
Required files	XHTML-basic.html from the basic-boilerplates folder as a starting point, along with building-the-table-body.txt from the chapter 6 folder
What you'll learn	How to create a table
Completed files	building-the-table.html in the chapter 6 folder

1. Structure the `table` element. To emulate the structure of the iTunes playlist, set the table's width to a percentage value. This means the table will stretch with the browser window. As explained earlier, you should also use the `summary` attribute to succinctly detail what the table is all about.

```
<table width="90%" border="1" cellspacing="0"
Ísummary="Music selected by Craig Grannell, with details of song,
  playing time, artist, album and play count.">
</table>
```

> Strictly speaking, the *border* attribute should be omitted. However, prior to adding CSS rules, it's a handy way to more prominently show the table's structure in a browser. Note also the use of *cellspacing*—without this, most browsers place gaps between the table cells of unstyled tables.

2. Add a caption. Immediately after the table start tag, add a `caption` element to provide the table with a title.

```
<caption>A playlist of great music</caption>
```

3. Add the basic table structure. Use row groups to provide the table with its basic structure.

```
<thead>
</thead>
<tfoot>
</tfoot>
<tbody>
</tbody>
```

> Remember that row groups must be added in the order outlined in the previous "Row groups" section.

4. Using table header cell elements, add the content for the table head (the column headers) as in the following code block, remembering to include relevant `scope` attribute/value pairs:

```
<thead>
  <tr>
    <th scope="col">Song Name</th>
    <th scope="col">Time</th>
    <th scope="col">Artist</th>
    <th scope="col">Album</th>
    <th scope="col">Play Count</th>
  </tr>
</thead>
```

There's no need to add any styling—not even `strong` tags. By default, most browsers display table header cell content in bold (and centered) to differentiate it from table data; also, in the following section, you'll be using CSS to style everything, anyway.

> *Note: It's always best to keep your HTML as simple as possible and do any styling in CSS. This reduces page load times and means that you have a greater degree of control. It also means that people without the ability to view CSS see the browser defaults, which are sensible and clear.*

5. Add table foot content. As mentioned, the footer for this table is to essentially be a signature, stating who's at fault for this selection of music. Because this is a single line of text that could potentially span the entire table width, simply include a single table cell, set to span five rows (using the colspan attribute).

```
<tfoot>
  <tr><td colspan="5">Music selection by:
    www.snubcommunications.com</td></tr>
</tfoot>
```

6. Add table body content. Finally, add the table's body content via the usual method, using table row and table cell elements. This table will have nearly 20 rows, so to save on trees, only the first two rows are detailed in the following printed code block—you can add all the others in the same way, or just copy across the content of building-the-table-body.txt from the download files, to save inputting the data yourself.

```
<tbody>
  <tr>
    <td>In The Art Of Stopping</td>
    <td>3:34</td>
    <td>Wire</td>
    <td>Send</td>
    <td>3</td>
  </tr>
  <tr>
    <td>Electron John</td>
    <td>3:18</td>
    <td>Worm Is Green</td>
    <td>Push Play</td>
    <td>42</td>
  </tr>
</tbody>
```

> *Tip: Take care that your table body content aligns correctly with your table headers. Badly formed tables are one thing, but when the headers and data don't correlate, the table is useless.*

The following image shows the table so far.

A playlist of great music				
Song Name	Time	Artist	Album	Play Count
In The Art Of Stopping	3:34	Wire	Send	3
Electron John	3:18	Worm Is Green	Push Play	42
Templates	6:07	Silo	Instar	9
Emerge	4:48	Fischerspooner	Fischerspooner #1	23
Banquet	3:21	Bloc Party	Silent Alarm	23
Alala	3:58	Cansei De Ser Sexy (CSS)	Cansei De Ser Sexy	6
I Ain't Saying My Goodbyes	3:45	Tom Vek	We Have Sound	40
Jóga	5:05	Björk	Homogenic	24
Kim Wilde	4:21	Charlotte Hatherley	Grey Will Fade	16
Witness	4:04	The Delgados	The Great Eastern	9
Feel Good Inc.	3:41	Gorillaz	Demon Days	20
Returning Wheel	3:26	Malka Spigel	Hide	13
P.E.T.R.O.L.	6:21	Orbital	Pi (OST)	8
Pweization	3:08	Pop Will Eat Itself (PWEI)	Karmadrome	11
Betrayed	3:05	Project Noise	Listen to me	31
When The Sun Hits	4:47	Slowdive	Souvlaki	1
Little Eyes	4:20	Yo La Tengo	Summer Sun	28
Music selection by: www.snubcommunications.com				

This table is not pretty, but it's structurally sound, and it includes all the relevant elements to at least help make it accessible. As you can see, the addition of the caption and table header cells also makes a difference. If you're unsure of this, look at the following screenshot of the same table, with plain table data cells throughout and no caption.

Song Name	Time	Artist	Album	Play Count
In The Art Of Stopping	3:34	Wire	Send	3
Electron John	3:18	Worm Is Green	Push Play	42
Templates	6:07	Silo	Instar	9
Emerge	4:48	Fischerspooner	Fischerspooner #1	23
Banquet	3:21	Bloc Party	Silent Alarm	23
Alala	3:58	Cansei De Ser Sexy (CSS)	Cansei De Ser Sexy	6
I Ain't Saying My Goodbyes	3:45	Tom Vek	We Have Sound	40
Jóga	5:05	Björk	Homogenic	24
Kim Wilde	4:21	Charlotte Hatherley	Grey Will Fade	16
Witness	4:04	The Delgados	The Great Eastern	9
Feel Good Inc.	3:41	Gorillaz	Demon Days	20
Returning Wheel	3:26	Malka Spigel	Hide	13
P.E.T.R.O.L.	6:21	Orbital	Pi (OST)	8
Pweization	3:08	Pop Will Eat Itself (PWEI)	Karmadrome	11
Betrayed	3:05	Project Noise	Listen to me	31
When The Sun Hits	4:47	Slowdive	Souvlaki	1
Little Eyes	4:20	Yo La Tengo	Summer Sun	28
Music selection by: www.snubcommunications.com				

All the information might be there, but it's harder to pick out the headers, and users will have to rely on body copy elsewhere to discover what the data in the table represents.

Styling a table

Flip back over the past few pages and you might notice that the table doesn't exactly bear a striking resemblance to the iTunes playlist as yet. But then, we're only halfway through building the table. Now it's time to start styling it using CSS.

Adding borders to tables

As mentioned earlier, it's a good policy to avoid using the default HTML table border. It looks ugly and old-fashioned, and it's a far cry from a clean, flat, 1-pixel border. You might think it's a straightforward process to add CSS borders to a table—logically, it makes sense to simply add a `border` property/value pair to a grouped selector that takes care of both the table headers and table data cells.

```
th, td {
  border: 1px solid #c9c9c9;
}
```

But this doesn't work. As the screenshot to the right shows, this method results in the correct single-pixel border around the edge of the table but creates double-thick borders everywhere else. This is because the borders don't collapse by default, meaning that the right border of one cell sits next to the left border of an adjacent cell, and so on.

Designers have historically gotten around this by using a rule to define a style for the top and left borders of the table and another to define a style for the right and bottom borders of table cells. However, there's a perfectly good property that deals with the double-border syndrome: `border-collapse`. When this property, with a value of `collapse`, is applied to the `table` element via an element selector, borders collapse to a single border wherever possible. The other available `border-collapse` property value, which reverts borders to their "standard" state, is `separate`.

```
table {
  border-collapse: collapse;
}
```

With this brief explanation of table borders completed, we'll now move into exercise mode and style the table.

Styling the playlist table		
Required files table-starting-	styling-the-playlist-table-starting-point.html, styling-the-playlist-table-starting-	
	point.css, and table-header-stripe.gif from the chapter 6 folder	
What you'll learn	How to style a table	
Completed files chapter 6	styling-the-playlist-table.html and styling-the-playlist-table.css in the	
	folder (along with the GIF image, which isn't amended)	

1. Set things up. If they still exist, remove the border, cellpadding, and cellspacing attributes within the table start tag. Add the universal selector rule (*) to remove margins and padding, as shown a bunch of times already in this book. Also, set the default font by using the html and body rules, as detailed in Chapter 3 of this book. Because we're creating a playlist based on the iTunes interface, it may as well be a little more Apple-like, which is why we're using Lucida variants as the primary fonts. Note that the padding value in the body rule is there to ensure that the table doesn't hug the browser window when you're previewing the page.

```
* {
  padding: 0;
  margin: 0;
}
html {
  font-size: 100%;
}
body {
  font: 62.5%/1.5 "Lucida Grande", "Lucida Sans Unicode", Arial,
    Helvetica, sans-serif;
  padding: 20px;
}
```

2. Style the table borders. As per the "Adding borders to tables" section, style the table borders.

```
table {
  border-collapse: collapse;
}
th, td {
  border: 1px solid #c9c9c9;
}
```

3. Style the caption. The borders have been dealt with already, so the next step is to style the caption, which currently lacks impact. The caption is effectively a title, and titles should stand out. Therefore, place some padding underneath it, set font-weight to bold, font-size to 1.3em, and text-transform to uppercase. Note that, in the following code block, CSS shorthand is used for three values for setting padding; as you may remember from Chapter 2, the three values set the top, horizontal (left and right), and bottom values, respectively, meaning the caption will have 0px padding everywhere except at the bottom, where the padding will be 5px.

```
caption {
  font-weight: bold;
  font-size: 1.3em;
  text-transform: uppercase;
  padding: 0 0 5px;
}
```

A PLAYLIST OF GREAT MUSIC				
Song Name	Time	Artist	Album	Play Count
In The Art Of Stooping	3:34	Wire	Send	3
Electron John	3:18	Worm Is Green	Push Play	42
Te modistae	6:07	Side	meter	0

4. Style the header cells. To make the header cells stand out more, apply the CSS rule outlined in the following code block. The url value set in the background property adds a background image to the table headers, which mimics the subtle metallic image shown in the same portion of the iTunes interface; the 0 50% values vertically center the graphic; and the repeat-x setting tiles the image horizontally. From a design standpoint, the default centered table heading text looks iffy, which is why we added a text-align property set to left. These settings ensure that the table header contents stand out from the standard data cell content.

```
th {
  background: url(table-header-stripe.gif) 0 50% repeat-x;
  text-align: left;
}
```

5. Set the font and pad the cells. At the moment, the table cell text hugs the borders, so it needs some padding; the text is also too small to comfortably read, so its size needs increasing. This is dealt with by adding font-size and padding pairs to the th, td rule, as shown here:

```
th, td {
  border: 1px solid #c9c9c9;
  font-size: 1.1em;
  padding: 1px 4px;

}
```

A PLAYLIST OF GREAT MUSIC

Song Name	Time	Artist	Album	Play Count
In The Art Of Stopping	3:34	Wire	Send	3
Electron John	3:18	Worm Is Green	Push Play	42
Templates	6:07	Silo	Instar	9
Emerge	4:48	Fischerspooner	Fischerspooner #1	23
Banquet	3:21	Bloc Party	Silent Alarm	23
Alala	3:58	Cansei De Ser Sexy (CSS)	Cansei De Ser Sexy	6
I Ain't Saying My Goodbyes	3:45	Tom Vek	We Have Sound	40
Joga	5:05	Björk	Homogenic	24
Kim Wilde	4:21	Charlotte Hatherley	Grey Will Fade	16
Witness	4:04	The Delgados	The Great Eastern	9
Feel Good Inc.	3:41	Gorillaz	Demon Days	20
Returning Wheel	3:26	Marka Spigel	Hide	13
P.E.T.R.O.L.	6:21	Orbital	Pi (OST)	8
Pweization	3:08	Pop Will Eat Itself (PWEI)	Karmadrome	11
Betrayed	3:05	Project Noise	Listen to me	31
When The Sun Hits	4:47	Slowdive	Souvlaki	1
Little Eyes	4:20	Yo La Tengo	Summer Sun	28

Music selection by: www.snubcommunications.com

6. Style the footer. The footer content needs to be easy to differentiate from the other data cells; you can achieve this by setting a background color for the entire row within the tfoot element and by making the color of the text have less contrast. Also, centering the text and making it smaller than text within the other data cells ensures it doesn't distract from the main content in the table. Centering it also provides some balance, because the caption is also centered.

```
tfoot {
  background-color: #dddddd;
  color: #555555;
}
  tfoot td {
  font-size: 1.0em;
  text-align: center;
}
```

> In Chapter 3, we warned against using text with low contrast against a background graphic. In the case of the table's footer in this exercise, the contrast is lower than for other text, but it's still readable; also, the content is not a huge chunk of body copy— it's only a single line of text.

dding separator stripes

One of iTunes's best visual features (and something seen in usable tables all over the Internet, but more often in print and in applications) is missing from the completed table: colored separator stripes, which assist you in rapidly scanning rows of data. Although you could conceivably add a class (setting a background color) to alternating rows, such a solution is poor when creating a static site—if you had to add a row in the middle of the table, you'd need to update every subsequent table row start tag, which is hardly efficient.

David Miller's article "Zebra Tables" on A List Apart (see www.alistapart.com/articles/zebratables/) offers a far more elegant solution. This was later reworked by Matthew Pennell (www.thewatchmakerproject.com), whose article "Stripe Your Tables the OO Way" (www.thewatchmakerproject.com/journal/309/stripe-your-tables-the-oo-way) offers the lowdown on his technique, including an improved version of his script at www. thewatchmakerproject.com/zebra.html.

Applying separator stripes

Required files	styling-the-playlist-table.html, styling-the-playlist-table.css, table-header-stripe.gif, and styling-the-playlist-table-stripes.js from the chapter 6 folder

What you'll learn	How to add separator stripes to a table

Completed files	styling-the-playlist-table-stripes.html and styling-the-playlist-table-stripes.css in the chapter 6 folder (along with the GIF image and JavaScript document, neither of which is amended)

1. Link to the JavaScript document. Taking things up from the completed table from the previous exercise (also available in the download files as styling-the-playlist-table.html and styling-the-playlist-table.css), add a script element in the HTML document's head section to link to the JavaScript file styling-the-playlist-table.js. Note that the JavaScript document is also available in the download files.

```
<script src="styling-the-playlist-table-stripes.js"
  type="text/javascript"></script>
```

2. Give the table a unique id. For the script to do its work, the table start tag must be given a unique id value. This must match the value given in styling-the-playlist-table.js in the onload function. Therefore, add the id attribute and value shown in the following code block:

```
<table id="playlist1" width="90%" border="0" summary="A playlist of
• great music, selected by www.snubcommunications.com.">
```

3. In the JavaScript, the relevant code that matches this is already defined, as shown in the following code block:

```
window.onload = function() {
  zebraTable.stripe('playlist1');
}
```

4. Assign a separator stripe style. The script creates alternating table rows, which are given a class value of alt. This can then be styled in CSS by using a rule with the selector tbody tr.alt td:

```
tbody tr.alt td {
  background: #e7edf6;
}
```

5. The previous code block styles the background of alternate rows in a light blue.

6. Define a table row hover state. The script also provides a hover state, making it easy for users to highlight entire table rows by placing the mouse cursor over one of the row's cells. This is styled using the rule shown in the following code block. Note that both background and color settings are defined, which pretty much reverse the standard colors (white on blue, rather than black on a light color). This makes the highlighted row stand out more and is the same device applications tend to use. Also note that there are two selectors here. The first is for compliant browsers, which apply :hover rules to more than just anchors. The second is a fallback for older versions of Internet Explorer (before version 7), which didn't do this.

```
tbody tr:hover td, tbody tr.over td {
  background: #5389d7;
  color: #ffffff;
}
```

7. Remove some horizontal borders. With the stripes in place, the top and bottom borders of table cells in the tbody area are now redundant. Therefore, remove them by adding the following rule:

```
tbody td {
  border-top: 0;
  border-bottom: 0;
}
```

Your table should now look like the following image.

Song Name	Time	Artist	Album	Play Count
In The Art Of Stopping	3:34	Wire	Send	3
Electron John	3:18	Worm Is Green	Push Play	42
Templates	6:07	Silo	Instar	9
Emerge	4:48	Fischerspooner	Fischerspooner #1	23
Banquet	3:21	Bloc Party	Silent Alarm	23
Alala	3:58	Cansei De Ser Sexy (CSS)	Cansei De Ser Sexy	6
I Ain't Saying My Goodbyes	3:45	Tom Vek	We Have Sound	40
Jóga	5:05	Björk	Homogenic	24
Kim Wilde	4:21	Charlotte Hatherley	Grey Will Fade	16
Witness	4:04	The Delgados	The Great Eastern	9
Feel Good Inc.	3:41	Gorillaz	Demon Days	20
Returning Wheel	3:26	Malka Spigel	Hide	13
P.E.T.R.O.L.	6:21	Orbital	Pi (OST)	8
Pweization	3:08	Pop Will Eat Itself (PWEI)	Karmadrome	11
Betrayed	3:05	Project Noise	Listen to me	31
When The Sun Hits	4:47	Slowdive	Souvlaki	1
Little Eyes	4:20	Yo La Tengo	Summer Sun	28

A PLAYLIST OF GREAT MUSIC

Music selection by: www.snubcommunications.com

To add stripes to more tables, just assign each one a unique id value and then add another line to the window.onload function in the JavaScript document, as per the instructions in this exercise. For example, if you added a table with an id value of playlist2, the line of JavaScript to add to the function would be ZebraTable.stripe('playlist2');.

Adding separator stripes with PHP

If you're creating a table from data stored in a database, automating separator stripes is a relatively simple process. After the PHP for retrieving data and the opening table markup (including headers), you add the following:

```
$alternate = TRUE;
while ($row = mysql_fetch_object($sqlresult)) :
  if($alternate) :
    $class = ' class="alt"';
    $alternate = FALSE;
  else :
    $class = "";
    $alternate = TRUE;
  endif;

  echo '<tr'.$class.'>';
  echo '<td>' . $row->field1 . '</td>';
  echo '<td>' . $row->field2 . '</td>';
  echo '</tr>';
endwhile;
```

This is then followed by the markup to close the table. Note that in this example, the alt class value is applied to alternate table rows, so the CSS from the previous exercise should still work fine.

dding separator stripes with the :nth-child selector

CSS3 includes selectors that let us pick out the rows we want to style. The nth-child selector targets elements in a document tree that have a certain number of siblings before it. Where n is an integer, :nth-child(an+b) would match the element that has an+b-1 siblings before it. In this scenario, n is basically a counter, b represents the counter's starting place, and a is the positions of the elements we match after that.

For the separator stripes, we need to target only odd or even elements:

```
/* targets even */
tr:nth-child(2n) {
   background: #e7edf6;
}
* targets odd */
tr:nth-child(2n+1) {
   background: #5389d7;
   color: #ffffff;
}
```

ables for layout

This section is going to be brief, because you should avoid using tables for layout or even components of a layout (excepting tabular data, obviously). There are exceptions—for instance, some web designers consider tables acceptable for laying out forms. However, generally speaking, tables are less accessible than CSS, harder to maintain and update, are slow to render in browsers, and they don't print particularly well. More importantly, once you know how to create CSS-based layouts, you'll mostly find working with tables for layout frustrating and clunky.

A common way of creating tabular layouts is to chop up a Photoshop layout and use images to stretch table cells to the correct size. (As mentioned earlier, table cells expand to the dimensions of their content.) Many designers then use a 1-pixel invisible GIF89 (often referred to as a spacer or shim) to force content into position or stretch table cells to a certain size. Because the 1-pixel GIF is a tiny file that's cached, it can be used hundreds of times without impacting download times. However, spacer and table layout usage pretty much destroys the idea of a semantic Web. Because so much of the layout is defined via inline HTML, updating it requires amendments to every page on the site (which must also be uploaded and tested in each case), rather than the simple editing and uploading of an external CSS file.

It is possible to combine CSS and tables—something that's usually referred to as a *transitional* layout, although one might argue that the "transition" from tables to CSS layouts should now be considered a historic event. Such layouts are usually created to ensure layout-based backward compatibility with obsolete devices. This direction should be taken only when the target audience is known to definitely include a significant number of users of very obsolete browsers and also when the layout is paramount to the working of the site (rather than just the content). When working on such a layout, there are a few golden rules:

- *Avoid nesting tables whenever possible*: Although tables can be nested like any other HTML element, doing so makes for a web page that is slow to render and nightmarish to navigate for a screen reader. (Obviously, there are exceptions, such as if you need to present a table of tabular data within your layout table.)

- *Structure the information on the page logically*: When designers use tables (particularly those exported from a graphics package), they have a tendency to think solely about how the page looks rather than its underlying code. However, it's important to look at how the information appears in the HTML, because that's how a screen reader will see it. The content should still make sense with regard to its flow and order even if the table is removed entirely. If it doesn't, you need to rework your table. (You can use Opera's User mode to temporarily disable tables to find out how your information is ordered without them. Chris Pederick's Web Developer toolbar for Firefox [www.chrispederick.com/work/web-developer/] offers similar functionality via **Miscellaneous ◊ Linearize Page**.) Ensure that content is immediately available; if it isn't, provide a link that skips past extraneous content, such as the masthead and navigation—otherwise, people using screen readers will be driven bonkers. (See www.w3.org/TR/WAI-WEBCONTENT/ for more on web content accessibility guidelines.)

- *Avoid deprecated attributes*: For instance, there's little point in setting the table's height to 100% when many web browsers ignore that rule (or need to be in quirks mode to support it).

- *Use CSS whenever possible to position elements*: To give an example—if you're working with a three-cell table and want the middle cell's content to begin 100 pixels from the top of the cell, don't use a spacer GIF. Instead, provide the cell with a class or unique ID, and use CSS padding.

> Note: The last two of these rules are primarily concerned with ensuring that if you design for legacy browsers, you don't compromise your work for more modern efforts.

As we keep hammering home, CSS is the way to go for high-quality, modern web page layouts, and tables should be left for the purpose for which they were designed—formatting data. The arguments that rumbled on for a few years after the 1990s came to a close—that browsers didn't support enough CSS to make CSS layouts possible and that visual design tools such as Dreamweaver couldn't cope with CSS layouts—are now pretty much moot. Even the previous major release of the worst offender (yes, we're talking about Internet Explorer 6) has more than adequate support for the vast majority of CSS layouts, and anything shipping today is more than capable of dealing with CSS.

Having said that, in March 2011, the W3C HTML Working Group decided that designers may put role=presentation on a table element so it can be used (in a conforming way) for presentational purposes (http://lists.w3.org/Archives/Public/public-html/2011Mar/0245.html).

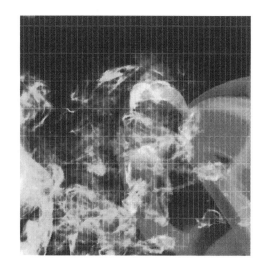

Chapter 7

Page Layouts with CSS

In this chapter:

- Explaining CSS workflow
- Positioning web page elements with CSS
- Creating boxouts and sidebars
- Creating column-based layouts
- Amending layouts, depending on body class settings

- Creating scrollable content areas

Layout for the Web

Although recent years have seen various institutions offer web-oriented courses, the fact remains that many web designers are not "qualified" *per se*. What I mean by this is that plenty of them have come from some sort of design or technology background related to—but not necessarily a part of—the Web. Therefore, we often see print designers moving over to the Web through curiosity or sheer necessity and technologists dipping their toes into the field of design.

This accounts for the most common issues seen in web layouts: many designers coming from print try to shoehorn their knowledge into their website designs, despite the Web being a very different medium from print. Conversely, those with no design knowledge lack the basic foundations and often omit design staples. Even those of us who've worked with the Web almost from the beginning and who also come from a design or arts background sometimes forget that the best sites tend to be those that borrow the best ideas from a range of media and then tailor the results to the desired output medium.

In this section, we'll take a brief look at a few layout techniques: grids and boxes, columns, and fixed vs. liquid design.

Grids and boxes

Like print-oriented design, the basis of web page design tends to be formed from grids and boxes. Regardless of the underlying layout technology (previously, tables; then, CSS; and now HTML5 and CSS3), web pages are formed of rectangular areas that are then populated with content.

Grid layouts can add visual rhythm to guide your user's eye, making your design look clean and ordered, and provide consistency. They enable stability and structure into which you can easily drop new elements and rearrange existing ones without the time and energy it would take to do so in a nongrid layout.

A grid is a division of layout with vertical and horizontal guidelines that incorporate margins, spaces, and columns for organizing your content. The grid container should be evenly divisible. For example, a 960-pixel total width is a good starting point, because it provides a massive amount of scope for divisions (960 is divisible by 2, 3, 4, 5, 6, 8, 10, 12, 15, 16, 20, 24, 30, 32, 40, 48, 60, 64, 80, 96, 120, 160, 192, 240, 320, and 480).

That said, too many columns can result in excessive complexity, so when working on initial grid designs, stick to about a dozen columns. The reason for working with 12 columns (rather than, say, seven or ten) is because of the flexibility it affords you in being able to divide the layout evenly (2 x 6, 3 x 4) and also in various other combinations.

A good rule of thumb for web design is to keep things relatively simple. Plan the layout on paper prior to going near any design applications, and simplify the structure as much as possible. Always design with mobile and legacy browsers in mind, and use progressive enhancement to add the advanced styles supported by desktop browsers. A typical web page contains as few as three or four structural areas (such as masthead, navigation, content, and footer areas), which can then be styled to define their relationship with each other and the page as a whole.

Working with columns

The vast majority of print media makes heavy use of columns. The main reason for this is that the eye generally finds it easier to read narrow columns of text than paragraphs that span the width of an entire page. However, when working with print, you have a finite and predefined area within which to work, and by and large, the "user" can see the entire page at once. Therefore, relationships between page elements can be created over the entire page, and the eye can rapidly scan columns of text.

On the Web, things aren't so easy. Web pages may span more than the screen height, meaning that only the top portion of the page is initially visible. Should a print page be translated directly to the Web, you may find that some elements essential for understanding the page's content are low down the page and not initially visible. Furthermore, if using columns for text and content, you may end up forcing the user to scroll down and up the page several times.

Therefore, web designers tend to eschew columns—but let's not be too hasty. It's worth bearing in mind something mentioned earlier: the eye finds it tricky to read wide columns of text. Therefore, it's often good practice to limit the width of body copy on a website to a comfortable reading width. Also, if you have multiple pieces of content that you want the user to be able to access at the same time, columns can come in handy. This can be seen in the following screenshots from the Smashing Magazine website (www.smashingmagazine.com/about/).

As you can see, the main, central column of the About page provides an overview of the website. To the right is the sitewide search and multiple advertisements; and to the left is a sidebar that contains the main and subnavigation for the website. This provides text columns that are a comfortable, readable width and enables faster access to information than if the page content were placed in a linear, vertical fashion.

Fixed vs. fluid

As already mentioned in this book, the Web is a unique medium in that end users have numerous different systems for viewing the web page. When designing for print, the dimensions of each design are fixed, and although television resolutions are varied (PAL, NTSC, HDTV), those designing for the screen work within a fixed frame—and regardless of the size of the screen, the picture content is always the same.

On the Web, there is an endless supply of new browser dimensions and resolutions, from a tiny mobile screen at 320px to a high-definition 1080p widescreen monitor at 2560px or higher. This presents a web designer with many challenges, and the decision to use one layout over another should be determined by the capabilities of the devices used by your target audience.

Later in the chapter, you'll see various methods for creating strict, fixed-layout skeletons; liquid designs; and combinations of the two. Some of these will then be turned into full-page designs in Chapter 10.

Fixed layouts

A fixed-width layout is a static layout whose width is set to a specific value, in pixels. Fixed-width sites are beneficial in that they enable you to position elements exactly on a web page, and its proportions remain the same no matter what the user's browser resolution is. However, because they don't expand with the browser window, fixed-width sites restrict you to designing for the lowest common screen size for your intended audience, meaning that people using larger resolutions see an area of blank space (or a background pattern).

Fixed-width websites are easier to design and maintain, since you translated what you designed on paper to the screen. They give the designer greater control over how content is floated, they allow for planned whitespace, and they are more predictable since the layout doesn't change when the browser is resized.

While the fixed-width layout is the most common layout used on the Web today, it is not ideal for the modern Web since it doesn't take advantage of the available space in the browser window and it won't adapt to the smaller browser dimensions and resolution of mobile devices, making it extremely difficult to read and navigate your content.

Fluid layouts

A fluid or liquid layout is designed by using percentage-based widths so that the design can adapt to the dimensions of the browser. These layouts take more time and energy to plan, because you need to foresee issues that might happen at each browser dimension you want to support. The benefit of a fluid design is that it's irrelevant what resolution the end user's machine has—the design stretches to fit. The drawback is that when designing, you have to be mindful that web page elements move, depending on each end user's monitor resolution and/or browser window size. You therefore cannot place elements with pixel-perfect precision.

Fluid layouts can mix fixed and percentage width columns to create unique configurations with the goal being to display as much horizontal content as you can fit on the screen.

ogical element placement

Besides the ability to rapidly edit CSS-based layouts, the greatest benefit when using CSS is the emphasis on accessibility, partly because it encourages the designer to think about the structure of the document and therefore logically plazce the elements within the web page (first comes the masthead, then the navigation, then the content, and so on). Each element is then styled to suit.

The logical placement of each element in the web page's structure results in improved document flow. And if you're scratching your head, wondering what on Earth I'm talking about, let me explain. A web page should still make sense if you remove all formatting and design elements. This is how a screen reader sees the page—it simply reads from the top of the HTML page downward. While some newer screen readers can interpret some CSS, it is still best to assume that they can't. This is because the capabilities of screen readers varies greatly, and how they interpret some CSS values can cause them to behave incorrectly. When working with CSS, the structure of the web page isn't compromised.

Vorkflow for CSS layouts

This section—and, indeed, much of this chapter—shows how straightforward creating CSS layouts can be, so long as you carefully plan what you're going to do. Upon working through the chapter, the benefits of a CSS-based system will become obvious, including the following: rapidly editing a website's entire visual appearance from a single, external file; fine-tuning the placement of elements; and creating flowing, accessible pages.

reating a page structure

We've covered semantic markup—that is, using HTML elements for the purpose for which they were created. This theme continues when working with CSS-based layouts. When working with CSS, you need to be aware of the structure of your web page from the start. That way, you can create structural elements with id values that relate to their purpose and then style them to suit.

One of the weaknesses of HTML4 and XHTML was that the ability to define the meaning of your content through your markup was severely limited. In the past, for basic page structure, you would most likely work with the div element. Custom classes assigned to your div elements defined meaning to your content. The problem with this solution is that different designers could have a different word for the same thing, such as *header* or *masthead*. This makes it difficult for applications such as search engines to parse your content and determine its meaning.

While divs are still heavily used for page structure, HTML5 has brought us semantic structural elements such as header, footer, article, nav, and aside. These tags provide a standard way of defining the meaning of your content and have been reviewed in detail in Chapter 2.

ox formatting

The box model is mentioned elsewhere in this book (see Chapter 2 and Appendix D), and this is a timely place for a recap, because the box model is something that confuses some web designers.

In CSS, every element is considered to be within its own box, and you can define the dimensions of the content and then add padding, a border, and a margin to each edge as required, as shown in the following image.

THE CSS BOX MODEL HIERARCHY

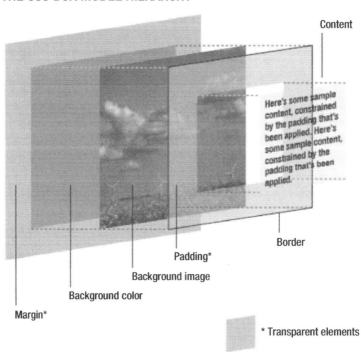

© Jon Hicks (www.hicksdesign.co.uk)

This is one of the trickiest things to understand about the CSS box model: padding, borders, and margins are added to the set dimensions of the content, and so the sum of these elements is the overall space that they take up. In other words, a 100-pixel-wide element with 20 pixels of padding will take up an overall width of 140 pixels, not 100 pixels with 20 pixels of padding within.

You can force browsers to respect the width you set by applying box-sizing: border-box to all elements:

`* { -moz-box-sizing: border-box; -webkit-box-sizing: border-box; box-sizing: border-box; }`

This is supported by all modern browsers without a vendor prefix with the exception of Firefox.

Note that the top and bottom margins on adjacent elements collapse, meaning that the overall box dimensions aren't necessarily fixed, depending on your design. For instance, if you set the bottom margin to 50px on an element and you have a top margin of 100px on the element below it, the effective margin between the two elements will be 100 pixels, not 150 pixels.

CSS layouts: a single box

In the remainder of this chapter, we'll walk through a number of common CSS layout techniques, which can be combined to form countless layouts. In Chapter 10, these skeleton layouts will form the basis of various full web page layouts, which will also integrate techniques shown elsewhere in the book (such as navigation bars).

The starting point for any layout is a single box, which this section concentrates on. I typically refer to these as *wrappers* (and accordingly provide said divs with an id value of wrapper); you can think of them as site containers, used to define a width for the site or set a fixed-size design in the center of the browser window.

Creating a fixed-width wrapper

Required files	Files from the basic-boilerplates folder as a starting point
What you'll learn	How to create a fixed-width div
Completed files	create-a-fixed-width-wrapper in the chapter 7 folder

1. Set things up. Rename the boilerplate documents to create-a-fixed-width-wrapper.html and create-a-fixed-width-wrapper.css. Link the CSS document to the web page by amending the url value of the style element.

```
<link rel="stylesheet" id="fixed-width-wrapper-css" href="create-a-fixed-width-wrapper.css"
type="text/css" media="screen">
```

2. Add some content. The web page already has a div element with an id of wrapper. Within it, add a bunch of paragraphs and test the web page. You'll see that the content stretches with the browser window and goes right up to its edges—this is a basic liquid design. If the browser window is very wide, this makes the content all but unreadable.

3. Restrict the wrapper's width. In CSS, add the following rule:

```
#wrapper {
  width: 600px;
  margin: 0 auto;
```

```
}
```

The `width` setting defines a width in pixels for the wrapper `div`. The `margin` setting provides automatic margins to the left and right of the `div`, which has the effect of centering the layout in the browser window, as shown in the following screenshot.

Adding padding, margins, and backgrounds to a layout

Required files-Files from `add-starting-point` in the `chapter 7` folder as a starting point

What you'll learn   How to add style to a fixed-width `div`

Completed files   `add-completed` in the `chapter 7` folder

1. Add a page background. In the `add-starting-point` folder, there are two images, both of which are gradients. One is a black gradient, fading toward gray at its bottom edge; this is intended for a page background. Add this by adding the following rule to the style sheet (after the `add your code below` comment):

```
body {
  background: #4d4d4d url(page-background.gif) repeat-x;
}
```

2. The `repeat-x` value ensures that the background tiles horizontally only; the color value #4d4d4d is the color of the bottom pixel of the gradient image, ensuring the gradient seamlessly blends with the web page background.

> *Note that in some examples in this book, selectors are used multiple times, such as body here, as described in the cascade section of Chapter 1. This is perfectly acceptable, although if you want to merge rules, you can—just be mindful of the cascade if you do so.*

3. Add a border to the wrapper. Amend the #wrapper rule to add a border around the wrapper. Note that the wrapper in this example sits flush with the top edge of the browser window view area, so no top border is needed. That's why the border-top pair is added, overriding the previous rule for the top border only.

```
#wrapper {
  width: 600px;
  margin: 0 auto;
  border: 2px solid #777777;
  border-top: 0;
}
```

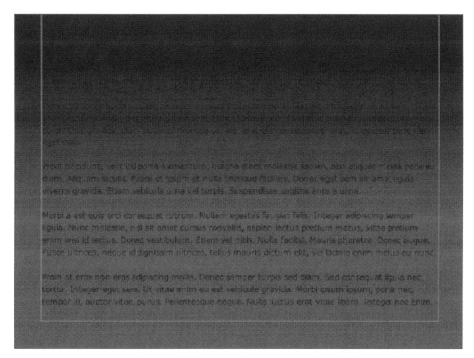

4. Add a wrapper background. If you test the page now, the background shows behind all of the page's content, thereby making it unreadable. Therefore, add the background pair to the rule, which sets a background color for the wrapper div and also sets the second image in the add-starting-point folder (a white-to-light-gray vertical gradient) to tile horizontally at the bottom of the div:

```
#wrapper {
  width: 600px;
  margin: 0 auto;
  border: 2px solid #777777;
  border-top: 0;
  background: #ffffff url(wrapper-background.gif) 0 100% repeat-x;
}
```

5. Add some padding. Test the page now, and you'll see two major layout errors commonly seen on the Web. First, the content hugs the edges of the `div`, which makes it hard to read and also looks cluttered, despite the `div` being 600 pixels wide. Second, the text at the bottom of the `div` is displayed over the gradient—it's still readable, but it looks a little messy. By adding padding (more to the bottom edge, to account for the gradient), these issues are dealt with:

```
#wrapper {
  width: 600px;
  margin: 0 auto;
  border: 2px solid #777777;
  border-top: 0;
  background: #ffffff url(wrapper-background.gif) 0 100% repeat-x;
  padding: 20px 20px 50px;
}
```

Lorem ipsum dolor sit amet, consectetuer adipiscing elit. Morbi commodo, ipsum sed pharetra gravida, orci magna rhoncus neque, id pulvinar odio lorem non turpis. Nullam sit amet enim.

Suspendisse id velit vitae ligula volutpat condimentum. Aliquam erat volutpat. Sed quis velit. Nulla facilisi. Nulla libero. Vivamus pharetra posuere sapien. Nam consectetuer. Sed aliquam, nunc eget euismod ullamcorper, lectus nunc ullamcorper orci, fermentum bibendum enim nibh eget ipsum.

Donec porttitor ligula eu dolor. Maecenas vitae nulla consequat libero cursus venenatis. Nam magna enim, accumsan eu, blandit sed, blandit a, eros. Quisque facilisis erat a dui. Nam malesuada ornare dolor. Cras gravida, diam sit amet rhoncus ornare, erat elit consectetuer erat, id egestas pede nibh eget odio.

Proin tincidunt, velit vel porta elementum, magna diam molestie sapien, non aliquet massa pede eu diam. Aliquam iaculis. Fusce et ipsum et nulla tristique facilisis. Donec eget sem sit amet ligula viverra gravida. Etiam vehicula urna vel turpis. Suspendisse sagittis ante a urna.

Morbi a est quis orci consequat rutrum. Nullam egestas feugiat felis. Integer adipiscing semper ligula. Nunc molestie, nisl sit amet cursus convallis, sapien lectus pretium metus, vitae pretium enim wisi id lectus. Donec vestibulum. Etiam vel nibh. Nulla facilisi. Mauris pharetra. Donec augue. Fusce ultrices, neque id dignissim ultrices, tellus mauris dictum elit, vel lacinia enim metus eu nunc.

Proin at eros non eros adipiscing mollis. Donec semper turpis sed diam. Sed consequat ligua nec tortor. Integer eget sem. Ut vitae enim eu est vehicula gravida. Morbi ipsum ipsum, porta nec, tempor id, auctor vitae, purus. Pellentesque neque. Nulla luctus erat vitae libero. Integer nec enim.

Note that because of the padding and borders added to this div, it now takes up 644 pixels of horizontal space, due to the 20-pixel horizontal padding values and the 2-pixel borders. To return the overall width to 600 pixels, subtract the 44 pixels from the width setting, reducing it to 556px.

Creating a maximum-width layout

Required filesFiles from add-completed in the chapter 7 folder as a starting point

What you'll learn   How to create a div with a maximum width

Completed files   max-width-example in the chapter 7 folder

1. Amend a rule. Replace the `width` pair in the `#wrapper` rule with the `max-width` pair shown following. This works much like you'd expect: the design works in a liquid manner, up until the point at which the content area's width (this does `not` include the padding and borders) is the value defined for `max-width`, whereupon the layout becomes fixed.

```
#wrapper {
  max-width: 800px;
  margin: 0 auto;
  border: 2px solid #777777;
  border-top: 0;
  background: #ffffff url(wrapper-background.gif) 0 100% repeat-x;
  padding: 20px 20px 50px;
}
```

2. Amend the body rule. At small browser widths, the design fills the browser window. If you still want some space around the wrapper, even when the browser window is narrow, all you need do is amend the body rule, adding some horizontal padding.

```
body {
  background: #4d4d4d url(page-background.gif) repeat-x;
  padding: 0 30px;
}
```

> Note that it's possible to use the *min-width* property to set the minimum width of a *div*. In all cases when using *max-width* and *min-width*, be sure to test the usability of your design at a wide range of browser window sizes.

Using absolute positioning to center a box onscreen

| Required files | Files from basic-boilerplates in the chapter 7 folder as a starting point |

| What you'll learn | How to center a div within the browser window |

| Completed files | center-a-box-on-screen in the chapter 7 folder |

The final exercise in this section shows how to center a box within the browser window, horizontally and vertically. Note that this kind of layout isn't particularly flexible, because it needs the containing wrapper to have a fixed width and height. Therefore, take care when using this device, because if your page has plenty of content, your users may be forced to scroll a lot.

1. Add a few paragraphs of text to the web page, placing them inside the wrapper div.

2. Add some backgrounds and style the wrapper div.

```
body {
  background: #666666;
}
#wrapper {
  background: #ffffff;
  border: 4px solid #000000;
  padding: 20px;
  width: 400px;
  height: 300px;
```

}

Lorem ipsum dolor sit amet, consectetuer adipiscing elit. Morbi commodo, ipsum sed pharetra gravida, orci magna rhoncus neque, id pulvinar odio lorem non turpis. Nullam sit amet enim.

Suspendisse id velit vitae ligula volutpat condimentum. Aliquam erat volutpat. Sed quis velit. Nulla facilisi. Nulla libero. Vivamus pharetra posuere sapien. Nam consectetuer. Sed aliquam, nunc eget euismod ullamcorper, lectus nunc ullamcorper orci, fermentum bibendum enim nibh eget ipsum.

Donec porttitor ligula eu dolor. Maecenas vitae nulla consequat libero cursus venenatis. Nam magna enim, accumsan eu, blandit sed, blandit a, eros. Quisque facilisis erat a dui. Nam malesuada ornare dolor. Cras gravida, diam sit amet rhoncus ornare, erat elit consectetuer erat, id egestas pede nibh eget odio.

3. Position the div. Set the wrapper div's position value to absolute, and set the top and left values to 50%. This sets the top-left position of the div to the center of the browser window.

```
#wrapper {
  background: #ffffff;
  border: 4px solid #000000;
  padding: 20px;
  width: 400px;
  height: 300px;
  position: absolute;
  top: 50%;
  left: 50%;
}
```

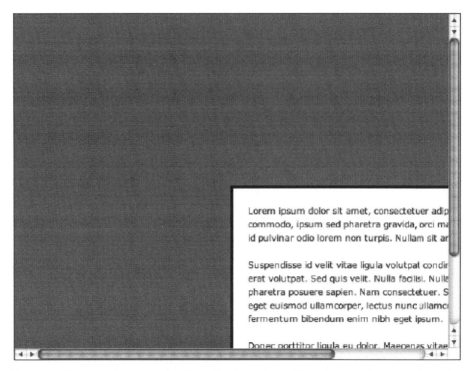

4. Use negative margins. Clearly, the div is not positioned correctly as yet, and that's—as mentioned in the previous step—because absolute positioning and the top and left values specify the position of the top left of the element they're applied to. To place the div centrally, negative top and left margins are used to pull it into place, the values of which are half the width or height, depending on the margin in question. For the margin-left value, you need the negative of half the horizontal space the div takes up, which is found by adding its width, horizontal padding, and horizontal margin values (4 + 20 + 400 + 20 + 4 = 444), dividing by two (222), and making the number negative (−222). Similarly, the margin-top value is the sum of the vertical dimensions (300px height, two lots of 20px padding and two lots of 4px borders, which comes to 344px) divided by 2 and made negative.

```
#wrapper {
  background: #ffffff;
  border: 4px solid #000000;
  padding: 20px;
  width: 400px;
  height: 300px;
  position: absolute;
  top: 50%;
  left: 50%;
  margin-left: -222px;
  margin-top: -172px;
}
```

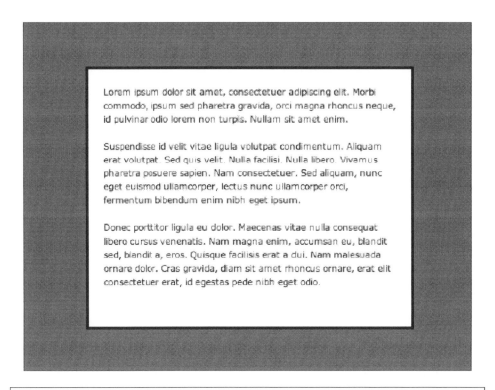

Note that if you use this kind of layout and have too much content for your wrapper, it will spill out of it. See later in the chapter for dealing with this issue by creating scrollable areas for page content.

Nesting boxes: boxouts

Boxouts are design elements commonly used in magazines, but they can, in principle, also be used on the Web. A boxout is a box separate from other page content that is often used to house images, captions, and other ancillary information. In magazines, these may be used for supporting text, alternate features, or magazine mastheads (with contributor information). Online, this enables you to immediately present content that's complementary to the main text.

The elements aside and figure are perfect for boxouts. A figure should be used when the content is related to the main content but is not meant to stand alone without it. An aside should be used when the content can stand alone without the main content to support it.

In the following screenshot of the HTML5 Rocks website (www.html5rocks.com/en/features/offline), a boxout is used to house demos of the offline feature, with a link to a page containing the full demo.

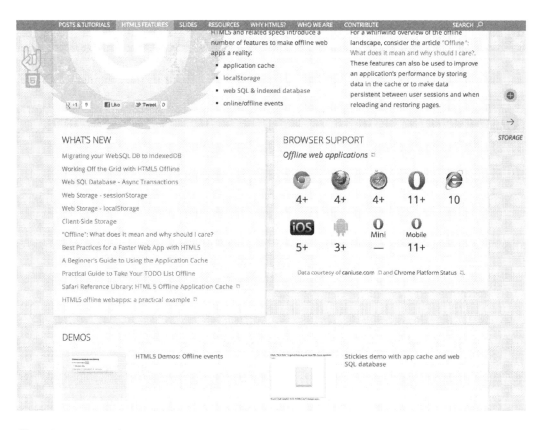

The float property

Mastering the `float` property is key to creating CSS-based web page layouts. It enables you to position an element to the left or right of other web page content, which then wraps around it.

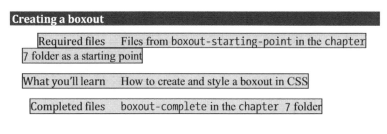

Creating a boxout

> **Required files** Files from boxout-starting-point in the chapter 7 folder as a starting point
>
> **What you'll learn** How to create and style a boxout in CSS
>
> **Completed files** boxout-complete in the chapter 7 folder

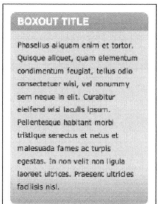

BOXOUT TITLE

Phasellus aliquam enim et tortor. Quisque aliquet, quam elementum condimentum feugiat, tellus odio consectetuer wisi, vel nonummy sem neque in elit. Curabitur eleifend wisi laculis ipsum. Pellentesque habitant morbi tristique senectus et netus et malesuada fames ac turpis egestas. In non velit non ligula laoreet ultrices. Praesent ultricies facilisis nisl.

As mentioned earlier, boxouts can be handy on web pages for displaying ancillary content simultaneously with the main text (rather than having supporting text following the main content). Like any other `element`, a boxout can also be styled, which is what this exercise will show how to do. Steps 1 through 3 show you how to create a basic, plain boxout, and step

4 onward shows how to style it. The final boxout will look like that shown in the image to the right: the corners are rounded; the plain background of the content area darkens slightly at its base; and the heading is on a colored background with a gradient (not obvious in a grayscale book, but if you check out the completed files, you'll see it's orange) and a white stripe beneath it to help make the boxout's heading and content distinct.

1. Examine the web page. Open `boxout.html` and look at the page's `body` content. The content of the web page is within a wrapper `div`. The bulk of the page content is a bunch of paragraphs. The boxout is an `aside` `element` with a `class` value of `boxout`, and this is placed before the content the boxout is supposed to float right of. (In other words, by placing the boxout before the other content, the other content will wrap around it once the boxout is floated.)

2. Style the wrapper and body. The `boxout-starting-point` folder contains the images from the "Adding padding, margins, and backgrounds to a layout" exercise earlier in this chapter, so add the `body` and `#wrapper` rules from that exercise to style the page's general layout.

```css
body {
  background: #4d4d4d url(page-background.gif) repeat-x;
}
#wrapper {
  width: 600px;
  margin: 0 auto;
  border: 2px solid #777777;
  border-top: 0;
  background: #ffffff url(wrapper-background.gif) 0 100% repeat-x;
  padding: 20px 20px 50px;
}
```

3. Position the boxout. To do so, you need to float it right and assign it a fixed width—if no width is set, the boxout will span the width of its container, which in this case would be the width of the wrapper `div`. Margin values at the bottom and left ensure that the boxout doesn't hug content that wraps around it.

```css
.boxout {
  float: right;
  display: block;
  width: 180px;
  margin: 0 0 20px 20px;
}
```

Lorem ipsum dolor sit amet, consectetuer adipiscing elit. Morbi commodo, ipsum sed pharetra gravida, orci magna rhoncus neque, id pulvinar odio lorem non turpis. Nullam sit amet enim.

Suspendisse id velit vitae ligula volutpat condimentum. Aliquam erat volutpat. Sed quis velit. Nulla facilisi. Nulla libero. Vivamus pharetra posuere sapien. Nam consectetuer. Sed aliquam, nunc eget euismod ullamcorper, lectus nunc ullamcorper orci, fermentum bibendum enim nibh eget ipsum.

Donec porttitor ligula eu dolor. Maecenas vitae nulla consequat libero cursus venenatis. Nam magna enim, accumsan eu, blandit sed, blandit a, eros. Quisque facilisis erat a dui. Nam malesuada ornare dolor. Cras gravida, diam sit amet rhoncus ornare, erat elit consectetuer erat, id egestas pede nibh eget odio.

Proin tincidunt, velit vel porta elementum, magna diam molestie sapien, non aliquet massa pede eu diam. Aliquam iaculis. Fusce et ipsum et nulla tristique facilisis. Donec eget sem sit amet ligula viverra gravida. Etiam vehicula urna vel turpis. Suspendisse sagittis ante a urna.

Boxout title

Phasellus aliquam enim et tortor. Quisque aliquet, quam elementum condimentum feugiat, tellus odio consectetuer wisi, vel nonummy sem neque in elit. Curabitur eleifend wisi iaculis ipsum. Pellentesque habitant morbi tristique senectus et netus et malesuada fames ac turpis egestas. In non velit non ligula laoreet ultrices. Praesent ultricies facilisis nisl.

4. Add a background. As shown earlier, the boxout has a background, and this is added by applying a CSS gradient to the boxout that blends into a solid background color. Finally, padding values are added to ensure that the boxout content doesn't go right up to the edge of the background.

Boxout title

Phasellus aliquam enim et tortor. Quisque aliquet, quam elementum condimentum feugiat, tellus odio consectetuer wisi, vel nonummy sem neque in elit. Curabitur eleifend wisi iaculis ipsum. Pellentesque habitant morbi tristique senectus et netus et malesuada fames ac turpis egestas. In non velit non ligula laoreet ultrices. Praesent ultricies facilisis nisl.

```
.boxout {
  float: right;
  width: 180px;
  margin: 0 0 20px 20px;
  padding: 0 10px;
  display: block;
  background-color: #e1e1e1;
  background-image: -webkit-gradient(linear, 0% 0%, 0% 100%,
from(#e1e1e1), to(#b5b5b5));
 background-image: -webkit-linear-gradient(top, #e1e1e1, #b5b5b5);
  background-image:    -moz-linear-gradient(top, #e1e1e1, #b5b5b5);
       background-image:     -ms-linear-gradient(top, #e1e1e1, #b5b5b5);
       background-image:     -o-linear-gradient(top, #e1e1e1, #b5b5b5);
}
```

5. The boxout header now needs styling, which will add the second part of the background. A contextual selector is used for this, ensuring that the style applies only to level-two headings within an element with a `class` value of `boxout`. The first three pairs in the rule style the header font (see Chapter 3 for more on styling type); a background CSS gradient has been applied as in step 4.

```
.boxout h2 {
  font: bold 1.2em Arial, Helvetica, sans-serif;
  text-transform: uppercase;
  color: #ffffff;
  background-color: #d7932a;
        background-image: -webkit-gradient(linear, 0% 0%, 0% 100%, from(#e3b46a), to(#d7932a));
        background-image: -webkit-linear-gradient(top, #e3b46a, #d7932a);
        background-image:    -moz-linear-gradient(top, #e3b46a, #d7932a);
        background-image:    -ms-linear-gradient(top, #e3b46a, #d7932a);
        background-image:     -o-linear-gradient(top, #e3b46a, #d7932a);
}
```

6. Position the header. If you test the page, you'll see that the header has a gap at its left and right. This is because the header is within the boxout `aside`, which has 10 pixels of padding on its left and right edges. By applying negative margins of the same value to the header, the horizontal space it takes up is increased to span the entire width of the boxout. Some padding is then added to ensure that the heading text doesn't hug its container's edges. Next, the `bottom-border` setting shown following adds a single-pixel white line under the header.

```
.boxout h2 {
  font: bold 1.2em Arial, Helvetica, sans-serif;
  text-transform: uppercase;
  color: #ffffff;
  background-color: #d7932a;
        background-image: -webkit-gradient(linear, 0% 0%, 0% 100%, from(#e3b46a), to(#d7932a));
        background-image: -webkit-linear-gradient(top, #e3b46a, #d7932a);
        background-image:    -moz-linear-gradient(top, #e3b46a, #d7932a);
        background-image:    -ms-linear-gradient(top, #e3b46a, #d7932a);
        background-image:     -o-linear-gradient(top, #e3b46a, #d7932a);
  margin: 0 -10px 10px;
  padding: 5px 10px;
  border-bottom: 1px solid #ffffff;
}
```

7. A final rule styles paragraphs within the boxout, differentiating them from other text.

```
.boxout p {
  font-size: 0.9em;
}
```

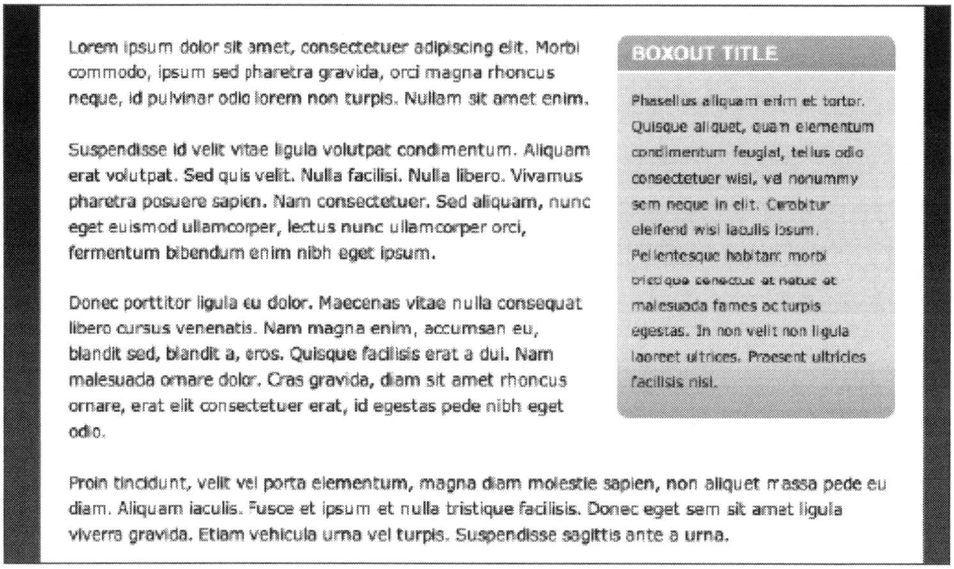

Note that because of the way the header's background is styled, using a CSS gradient that stretches to fill the available space, there's no chance of the background running out, even if the page's text is massively zoomed (see the following image). Although the vast majority of users will never use such settings, it always pays to see how well your sites fare when very atypical settings are used in the browser. While some problems will be tricky to get around, others just require a little lateral thinking, as shown here.

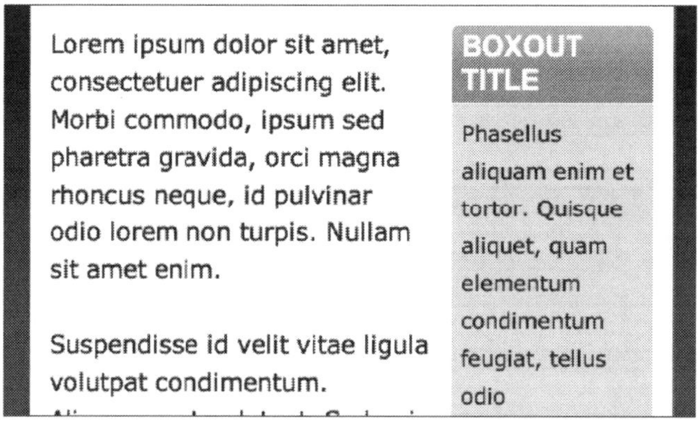

Advanced layouts with multiple boxes and columns

The layouts so far in this chapter have laid the foundation, showing you how to get to grips with creating a wrapper for site content and then nesting a div within the wrapper, providing a little added scope for layout. In this section, you're going to find out how to fashion the basic building blocks of more complex layouts, working with two and then three or more structural divs, finding out how they can be styled using

CSS. In all cases, try to think in a modular fashion, because the methods for creating the basic building blocks shown can be combined in many different ways to create all sorts of layouts.

One of the main reasons for working with two structural `divs` is to create columns on a web page. Although columns of the sort found in newspapers and magazines should be avoided online, columns can be useful when you're working with various types of content. For instance, you may offer current news in one column and an introduction to an organization in another. Using columns makes both sets of information immediately available. If a linear layout is instead used, you'll need to decide which information you want the user to see first and which information will initially be out of sight. The general principle of columns is about more than written site content, though. For example, you could use one column to house a vertical navigation bar and another to contain thumbnail images relating to an article.

Working with two structural divs

In the following exercise, you'll work with two structural `divs`, seeing how seemingly small changes to CSS rules can make a major difference to the layout of the web page. This will highlight the flexibility of web layouts, showing how quickly you can build pages and also how easy it is to experiment with designs and make edits and rapid changes should they be required.

Manipulating two structural divs for fixed-width layouts	
Required files	Files from two-divs-starting-point in the chapter 7 folder as a starting point
What you'll learn	How to use two structural divs to create various types of fixed-width layouts, including two-column designs
Completed files	two-divs-fixed-complete in the chapter 7 folder

1. Examine the code. Open `two-divs.html`, and you'll see a simple page layout. A level-one heading is followed by the first `div`, with an `id` value of `divOne`. This is then followed by a second `div`, which has an `id` value of `divTwo`. Both `divs` have a level-two heading and some paragraphs within. Some initial styles are also in the style sheet, defining the fonts and placing 20 pixels of padding around the page's content (via the `padding` pair in the `body` rule) so the page content doesn't hug the browser window edge.

Working with two divs

Div one

Lorem ipsum dolor sit amet, consectetuer adipiscing elit. Morbi commodo, ipsum sed pharetra gravida, orci magna rhoncus neque, id pulvinar odio lorem non turpis. Nullam sit amet enim.

Suspendisse id velit vitae ligula volutpat condimentum. Aliquam erat volutpat. Sed quis velit. Nulla facilisi. Nulla libero. Vivamus pharetra posuere sapien. Nam consectetuer. Sed aliquam, nunc eget euismod ullamcorper, lectus nunc ullamcorper orci, fermentum bibendum enim nibh eget ipsum.

Donec porttitor ligula eu dolcr. Maecenas vitae nulla consequat libero cursus venenatis. Nam magna enim, accumsan eu, blandit sed, blandit a, eros. Quisque facilisis erat a dui. Nam malesuada ornare dolor. Cras gravida, diam sit amet rhoncus ornare, erat elit consectetuer erat, id egestas pede nibh eget odio.

Div two

Proin tincidunt, velit vel porta elementum, magna diam molestie sapien, non aliquet massa pede eu diam. Aliquam iaculis. Fusce et ipsum et nulla tristique facilisis. Donec eget sem sit amet ligula viverra gravida. Etiam vehicula urna vel turpis. Suspendisse sagittis ante a urna.

Morbi a est quis orci consequat rutrum. Nullam egestas feugiat felis. Integer adipiscing semper ligula. Nunc molestie, nisl sit amet cursus convallis, sapien lectus pretium metus, vitae pretium enim wisi id lectus. Donec vestibulum. Etiam vel nibh. Nulla facilisi. Mauris pharetra. Donec augue. Fusce ultrices, neque id dignissim ultrices, tellus mauris dictum elit, vel lacinia enim metus eu nunc.

Proin at eros non eros adipiscing mollis. Donec semper turpis sed diam. Sed consequat ligula nec tortor. Integer eget sem. Ut vitae enim eu est vehicula gravida. Morbi ipsum ipsum, porta nec, tempor id, auctor vitae, purus. Pellentesque neque. Nulla luctus erat vitae libero. Integer nec enim.

---

2. Add the background colors. When initially working on CSS layouts and hand-coding, it's often useful to apply background colors to your main structural `divs`. This enables you to more easily see their edges and how they interact. Therefore, add the following rules to your CSS:

```
#divOne {
  background: #dddddd;
}
#divTwo {
  background: #aaaaaa;
}
```

3. If you test the web page at this point, you'll see the `divs` are positioned in a basic linear fashion. The gap between the two occurs because the paragraphs have margins assigned on their bottom edges—therefore, the gap is from the margin of the top `div`'s last paragraphs.

Working with two divs

Div one

Lorem ipsum dolor sit amet, consectetuer adipiscing elit. Morbi commodo, ipsum sed pharetra gravida, orci magna rhoncus neque, id pulvinar odio lorem non turpis. Nullam sit amet enim.

Suspendisse id velit vitae ligula volutpat condimentum. Aliquam erat volutpat. Sed quis velit. Nulla facilisi. Nulla libero. Vivamus pharetra posuere sapien. Nam consectetuer. Sed aliquam, nunc eget euismod ullamcorper, lectus nunc ullamcorper orci, fermentum bibendum enim nibh eget ipsum.

Donec porttitor ligula eu dolor. Maecenas vitae nulla consequat libero cursus venenatis. Nam magna enim, accumsan eu, blandit sed, blandit a, eros. Quisque facilisis erat a dui. Nam malesuada ornare dolor. Cras gravida, diam sit amet rhoncus ornare, erat elit consectetuer erat, id egestas pede nibh eget odio.

Div two

Proin tincidunt, velit vel porta elementum, magna diam molestie sapien, non aliquet massa pede eu diam. Aliquam iaculis. Fusce et ipsum et nulla tristique facilisis. Donec eget sem sit amet ligula viverra gravida. Etiam vehicula urna vel turpis. Suspendisse sagittis ante a urna.

Morbi a est quis orci consequat rutrum. Nullam egestas feugiat felis. Integer adipiscing semper ligula. Nunc molestie, nisl sit amet cursus convallis, sapien lectus pretium metus, vitae pretium enim wisi id lectus. Donec vestibulum. Etiam vel nibh. Nulla facilisi. Mauris pharetra. Donec augue. Fusce ultrices, neque id dignissim ultrices, tellus mauris dictum elit, vel lacinia enim metus eu nunc.

Proin at eros non eros adipiscing mollis. Donec semper turpis sed diam. Sed consequat ligula nec tortor. Integer eget sem. Ut vitae enim eu est vehicula gravida. Morbi ipsum ipsum, porta nec, tempor id, auctor vitae, purus. Pellentesque neque. Nulla luctus erat vitae libero. Integer nec enim.

Note that for an actual website, you should use *id* (and *class*) values relevant and appropriate to the content within them, as evidenced by *wrapper* and *boxout* earlier in this chapter. The values of *divOne* and *divTwo* are used in this exercise to enable you to easily keep track of each one.

---

4. Make the divs flush to each other. By adding padding-bottom values equal to the margin-bottom value for paragraphs, you can make the div backgrounds flush to subsequent content.

```
#divOne {
  background: #dddddd;
  padding-bottom: 1.5em;
}
#divTwo {
  background: #aaaaaa;
  padding-bottom: 1.5em;
}
```

Working with two divs

Div one

Lorem ipsum dolor sit amet, consectetuer adipiscing elit. Morbi commodo, ipsum sed pharetra gravida, orci magna rhoncus neque, id pulvinar odio lorem non turpis. Nullam sit amet enim.

Suspendisse id velit vitae ligula volutpat condimentum. Aliquam erat volutpat. Sed quis velit. Nulla facilisi. Nulla libero. Vivamus pharetra posuere sapien. Nam consectetuer. Sed aliquam, nunc eget euismod ullamcorper, lectus nunc ullamcorper orci, fermentum bibendum enim nibh eget ipsum.

Donec porttitor ligula eu dolor. Maecenas vitae nulla consequat libero cursus venenatis. Nam magna enim, accumsan eu, blandit sed, blandit a, eros. Quisque facilisis erat a dui. Nam malesuada ornare dolor. Cras gravida, diam sit amet rhoncus ornare, erat elit consectetuer erat, id egestas pede nibh eget odio.

Div two

Proin tincidunt, velit vel porta elementum, magna diam molestie sapien, non aliquet massa pede eu diam. Aliquam iaculis. Fusce et ipsum et nulla tristique facilisis. Donec eget sem sit amet ligula viverra gravida. Etiam vehicula urna vel turpis. Suspendisse sagittis ante a urna.

Morbi a est quis orci consequat rutrum. Nullam egestas feugiat felis. Integer adipiscing semper ligula. Nunc molestie, nisl sit amet cursus convallis, sapien lectus pretium metus, vitae pretium enim wisi id lectus. Donec vestibulum. Etiam vel nibh. Nulla facilisi. Mauris pharetra. Donec augue. Fusce ultrices, neque id dignissim ultrices, tellus mauris dictum elit, vel lacinia enim metus eu nunc.

Proin at eros non eros adipiscing mollis. Donec semper turpis sed diam. Sed consequat ligula nec tortor. Integer eget sem. Ut vitae enim eu est vehicula gravida. Morbi ipsum ipsum, porta nec, tempor id, auctor vitae, purus. Pellentesque neque. Nulla luctus erat vitae libero. Integer nec enim.

5. Float the `divs` to make columns. By adding `width` values and floating both `divs` in the same direction, the `divs` stack horizontally, thereby creating columns.

```
#divOne {
  background: #dddddd;
  padding-bottom: 1.5em;
  float: left;
  width: 350px;
}
#divTwo {
  background: #aaaaaa;
  padding-bottom: 1.5em;
  float: left;
  width: 250px;
}
```

Working with two divs

Div one

Lorem ipsum dolor sit amet, consectetuer adipiscing elit. Morbi commodo, ipsum sed pharetra gravida, orci magna rhoncus neque, id pulvinar odio lorem non turpis. Nullam sit amet enim.

Suspendisse id velit vitae ligula volutpat condimentum. Aliquam erat volutpat. Sed quis velit. Nulla facilisi. Nulla libero. Vivamus pharetra posuere sapien. Nam consectetuer. Sed aliquam, nunc eget euismod ullamcorper, lectus nunc ullamcorper orci, fermentum bibendum enim nibh eget ipsum.

Donec porttitor ligula eu dolor. Maecenas vitae nulla consequat libero cursus venenatis. Nam magna enim, accumsan eu, blandit sed, blandit a, eros. Quisque facilisis erat a dui. Nam malesuada ornare dolor. Cras gravida, diam sit amet rhoncus ornare, erat elit consectetuer erat, id egestas pede nibh eget odio.

Div two

Proin tincidunt, velit vel porta elementum, magna diam molestie sapien, non aliquet massa pede eu diam. Aliquam iaculis. Fusce et ipsum et nulla tristique facilisis. Donec eget sem sit amet ligula viverra gravida. Etiam vehicula urna vel turpis. Suspendisse sagittis ante a urna.

Morbi a est quis orci consequat rutrum. Nullam egestas feugiat felis. Integer adipiscing semper ligula. Nunc molestie, nisl sit amet cursus convallis, sapien lectus pretium metus, vitae pretium enim wisi id lectus. Donec vestibulum. Etiam vel nibh. Nulla facilisi. Mauris pharetra. Donec augue. Fusce ultrices, neque id dignissim ultrices, tellus mauris dictum elit, vel lacinia enim metus eu nunc.

Proin at eros non eros adipiscing mollis. Donec semper turpis sed diam. Sed consequat ligula nec tortor. Integer eget sem. Ut vitae enim eu est vehicula gravida. Morbi ipsum ipsum, porta nec, tempor id, auctor vitae, purus. Pellentesque neque. Nulla luctus erat vitae libero. Integer nec enim.

Note how each div only stretches to fill its content. Later, you'll find out how to mimic full-height columns by using a background image (creating what are known as faux columns).

6. Switch the column order. You can switch the stack direction by amending the float values, changing left to right. This can be useful for when you want information to be displayed in a certain order on-screen but in a different order in code. For example, your main content might be on the right and a sidebar on the left on-screen, but screen readers would go through the main content before the sidebar.

7. Note that floats start stacking from the edge of their container, which in this case is 20 pixels in from the browser window edge. For more control over the overall layout, columns can be placed in a wrapper, which will be discussed later in the chapter.

```
#divOne {
  background: #dddddd;
  padding-bottom: 1.5em;
  float: right;
  width: 350px;
}
#divTwo {
  background: #aaaaaa;
  padding-bottom: 1.5em;
  float: right;
  width: 250px;
}
```

Working with two divs

Div two

Proin tincidunt, velit vel porta elementum, magna diam molestie sapien, non aliquet massa pede eu diam. Aliquam iaculis. Fusce et ipsum et nulla tristique facilisis. Donec eget sem sit amet ligula viverra gravida. Etiam vehicula urna vel turpis. Suspendisse sagittis ante a urna.

Morbi a est quis orci consequat rutrum. Nullam egestas feugiat felis. Integer adipiscing semper ligula. Nunc molestie, nisl sit amet cursus convallis, sapien lectus pretium metus, vitae pretium enim wisi id lectus. Donec vestibulum. Etiam vel nibh. Nulla facilisi. Mauris pharetra. Donec augue. Fusce ultrices, neque id dignissim ultrices, tellus mauris dictum elit, vel lacinia enim metus eu nunc.

Proin at eros non eros adipiscing mollis. Donec semper turpis sed diam. Sed consequat ligula nec tortor. Integer eget sem. Ut vitae enim eu est vehicula gravida. Morbi ipsum ipsum, porta nec, tempor id, auctor vitae, purus. Pellentesque neque. Nulla luctus erat vitae libero. Integer nec enim.

Div one

Lorem ipsum dolor sit amet, consectetuer adipiscing elit. Morbi commodo, ipsum sed pharetra gravida, orci magna rhoncus neque, id pulvinar odio lorem non turpis. Nullam sit amet enim.

Suspendisse id velit vitae ligula volutpat condimentum. Aliquam erat volutpat. Sed quis velit. Nulla facilisi. Nulla libero. Vivamus pharetra posuere sapien. Nam consectetuer. Sed aliquam, nunc eget euismod ullamcorper, lectus nunc ullamcorper orci, fermentum bibendum enim nibh eget ipsum.

Donec porttitor ligula eu dolor. Maecenas vitae nulla consequat libero cursus venenatis. Nam magna enim, accumsan eu, blandit sed, blandit a, eros. Quisque facilisis erat a dui. Nam malesuada ornare dolor. Cras gravida, diam sit amet rhoncus ornare, erat elit consectetuer erat, id egestas pede nibh eget odio.

8. Add padding and margins. Switch the right values for float back to left, and then change the padding-bottom properties to padding, adding values for the top and horizontal edges. A margin-right setting for #divOne provides a gap between the two divs.

```
#divOne {
  background: #dddddd;
  padding: 10px 10px 1.5em;
  float: left;
  width: 350px;
  margin-right: 10px;
}
#divTwo {
  background: #aaaaaa;
  padding: 10px 10px 1.5em;
  float: left;
  width: 250px;
}
```

Working with two divs

Div one

Lorem ipsum dolor sit amet, consectetuer adipiscing elit. Morbi commodo, ipsum sed pharetra gravida, orci magna rhoncus neque, id pulvinar odio lorem non turpis. Nullam sit amet enim.

Suspendisse id velit vitae ligula volutpat condimentum. Aliquam erat volutpat. Sed quis velit. Nulla facilisi. Nulla libero. Vivamus pharetra posuere sapien. Nam consectetuer. Sed aliquam, nunc eget euismod ullamcorper, lectus nunc ullamcorper orci, fermentum bibendum enim nibh eget ipsum.

Donec porttitor ligula eu dolor. Maecenas vitae nulla consequat libero cursus venenatis. Nam magna enim, accumsan eu, blandit sed, blandit a, eros. Quisque facilisis erat a dui. Nam malesuada ornare dolor. Cras gravida, diam sit amet rhoncus ornare, erat elit consectetuer erat, id egestas pede nibh eget odio.

Div two

Proin tincidunt, velit vel porta elementum, magna diam molestie sapien, non aliquet massa pede eu diam. Aliquam iaculis. Fusce et ipsum et nulla tristique facilisis. Donec eget sem sit amet ligula viverra gravida. Etiam vehicula urna vel turpis. Suspendisse sagittis ante a urna.

Morbi a est quis orci consequat rutrum. Nullam egestas feugiat felis. Integer adipiscing semper ligula. Nunc molestie, nisl sit amet cursus convallis, sapien lectus pretium metus, vitae pretium enim wisi id lectus. Donec vestibulum. Etiam vel nibh. Nulla facilisi. Mauris pharetra. Donec augue. Fusce ultrices, neque id dignissim ultrices, tellus mauris dictum elit, vel lacinia enim metus eu nunc.

Proin at eros non eros adipiscing mollis. Donec semper turpis sed diam. Sed consequat ligula nec tortor. Integer eget sem. Ut vitae enim eu est vehicula gravida. Morbi ipsum ipsum, porta nec, tempor id, auctor vitae, purus. Pellentesque neque. Nulla luctus erat vitae libero. Integer nec enim.

Manipulating two structural divs for liquid layouts

Required files	Files from two-divs-starting-point in the chapter 7 folder as a starting point
What you'll learn	How to use two structural divs to create various types of liquid layouts, including two-column designs
Completed files	two-divs-liquid-complete in the chapter 7 folder

This exercise looks at working with liquid rather than fixed layouts. Because of the nature of liquid layouts, there are some very important differences in method that must be taken into account, as you'll see.

1. Add backgrounds and padding. As per the previous exercise, add background colors to the two divs to make it easy to see their boundaries.

```
#divOne {
  background: #dddddd;
}
#divTwo {
  background: #aaaaaa;
}
```

2. Float the `divs` and set widths. As explained in the previous exercise, setting a width for the two `divs` and then floating them both in the same direction enables you to stack them horizontally, thereby providing columns. Note that in this exercise, we'll be floating `divs` only left, but you can float them right, too. Regarding `width` values, you must ensure that their sum doesn't exceed 100%, because otherwise the `divs` will be wider in total than their container and will display in a linear fashion, one under the other.

```
#divOne {
  background: #dddddd;
  float: left;
  width: 40%;
}
#divTwo {
  background: #aaaaaa;
  float: left;
  width: 60%;
}
```

Working with two divs

Div one

Lorem ipsum dolor sit amet consectetuer adipiscing elit. Morbi commodo, ipsum sed pharetra gravida, orci magna rhoncus neque, id pulvinar odio lorem non turpis. Nullam sit amet enim.

Suspendisse id velit vitae ligula volutpat condimentum. Aliquam erat volutpat. Sed quis velit. Nulla facilisi. Nulla libero. Vivamus pharetra posuere sapien. Nam consectetuer. Sed aliquam, nunc eget euismod ullamcorper, lectus nunc ullamcorper orci, fermentum bibendum enim nibh eget ipsum.

Donec porttitor ligula eu dolor. Maecenas vitae nulla consequat libero cursus venenatis. Nam magna enim, accumsan eu, blandit sed, blandit a, eros. Quisque facilisis erat a dui. Nam malesuada ornare dolor. Cras gravida, diam sit amet rhoncus ornare, erat elit consectetuer erat, id egestas pede nibh eget odio.

Div two

Proin tincidunt, velit vel porta elementum, magna diam molestie sapien, non aliquet massa pede eu diam. Aliquam iaculis. Fusce et ipsum et nulla tristique facilisis. Donec eget sem sit amet ligula viverra gravida. Etiam vehicula urna vel turpis. Suspendisse sagittis ante a urna.

Morbi a est quis orci consequat rutrum. Nullam egestas feugiat felis. Integer adipiscing semper ligula. Nunc molestie, nisl sit amet cursus convallis, sapien lectus pretium metus, vitae pretium enim wisi id lectus. Donec vestibulum. Etiam vel nibh. Nulla facilisi. Mauris pharetra. Donec augue. Fusce ultrices, neque id dignissim ultrices, tellus mauris dictum elit, vel lacinia enim metus eu nunc.

Proin at eros non eros adipiscing mollis. Donec semper turpis sed diam. Sed consequat ligula nec tortor. Integer eget sem. Ut vitae enim eu est vehicula gravida. Morbi ipsum ipsum, porta nec, tempor id, auctor vitae, purus. Pellentesque neque. Nulla luctus erat vitae libero. Integer nec enim.

3. Add a margin. In the previous exercise, a margin was included to separate the two divs. This can be done here, again by adding a `margin-right` value to #div0ne. However, you need to ensure the overall width of the `width` and `margin` values doesn't exceed 100%. In this example, the margin is set to 2%, and 1% is removed from each of the two `width` values to cater for this.

```
#divOne {
  background: #dddddd;
  float: left;
  width: 39%;
  margin-right: 2%;
}
#divTwo {
  background: #aaaaaa;
  float: left;
  width: 59%;
}
```

Working with two divs

Div one

Lorem ipsum dolor sit amet, consectetuer adipiscing elit. Morbi commodo, ipsum sed pharetra gravida, orci magna rhoncus neque, id pulvinar odio lorem non turpis. Nullam sit amet enim.

Suspendisse id velit vitae ligula volutpat condimentum. Aliquam erat volutpat. Sed quis velit. Nulla facilisi. Nulla libero. Vivamus pharetra posuere sapien. Nam consectetuer. Sed aliquam, nunc eget euismod ullamcorper, lectus nunc ullamcorper orci, fermentum bibendum enim nibh eget ipsum.

Donec porttitor ligula eu dolor. Maecenas vitae nulla consequat libero cursus venenatis. Nam magna enim, accumsan eu, blandit sed, blandit a, eros. Quisque facilisis erat a dui. Nam malesuada ornare dolor. Cras gravida, diam sit amet rhoncus ornare, erat elit consectetuer erat, id egestas pede nibh eget odio.

Div two

Proin tincidunt, velit vel porta elementum, magna diam molestie sapien, non aliquet massa pede eu diam. Aliquam iaculis. Fusce et ipsum et nulla tristique facilisis. Donec eget sem sit amet ligula viverra gravida. Etiam vehicula urna vel turpis. Suspendisse sagittis ante a urna.

Morbi a est quis orci consequat rutrum. Nullam egestas feugiat felis. Integer adipiscing semper ligula. Nunc molestie, nisl sit amet cursus convallis, sapien lectus pretium metus, vitae pretium enim wisi id lectus. Donec vestibulum. Etiam vel nibh. Nulla facilisi. Mauris pharetra. Donec augue. Fusce ultrices, neque id dignissim ultrices, tellus mauris dictum elit, vel lacinia enim metus eu nunc.

Proin at eros non eros adipiscing mollis. Donec semper turpis sed diam. Sed consequat ligula nec tortor. Integer eget sem. Ut vitae enim eu est vehicula gravida. Morbi ipsum ipsum, porta nec, tempor id, auctor vitae, purus. Pellentesque neque. Nulla luctus erat vitae libero. Integer nec enim.

4. If you want to add padding to the divs, the method changes depending on the required value. If you're adding padding on a percentage basis, you add it in the same way as the margin in step 3, removing relevant values from the width settings. (For example, if you set the padding to 1% for both divs, this would mean there would be 1% of padding on each side, so 2% would need to be removed from each width value to keep the combined width of the two divs under 100%.)

5. However, if you want to add pixel-based padding values, things become a little more complex, because there's no way of specifying something like 39% - 20px for a width. The most sensible workaround is to use nested divs: add a content div within each of the two existing divs, and then set padding for those nested divs to a pixel value. In HTML, you end up with the following:

```
<div .id="divOne">
  <div class="columnContent">
    [content]
  </div>
</div>
<div id="divTwo">
  <div class="columnContent">
    [content]
  </div>
</div>
```

You then apply a `padding` value to `.columnContent` in the CSS.

> *Note that, clearly, liquid layouts can have widths lower than 100%; this example showed that percentage because it's the most common width used for liquid layouts and has the most problems to overcome. Also, rounding errors can cause problems with liquid layouts when the* width *values add up to 100%—see the "Dealing with rounding errors" section in Chapter 9 for more on this.*

Placing columns within wrappers and clearing floated content

The heading of this section is a bit of a mouthful, but it makes sense at this point to combine the two things it mentions—placing columns within wrappers and clearing floated content—because once you've started working with columns, that's what you'll likely next have to do. Placing columns within a wrapper enables you to position the overall layout (for example, centering it within the browser window) and restrict its width to a set size in pixels or a liquid measurement. Clearing floated content is an important concept to understand, because floated content appears outside of the normal document flow; subsequent content then wraps around floated content. Therefore, float an object left and subsequent content will stack to its right. Also, backgrounds don't appear behind floated content if it isn't cleared and doesn't contain nonfloated elements, because browsers consider floated elements to technically take up no height.

Placing columns within a wrapper

Required files	Files from two-divs-starting-point in the chapter 7 folder as a starting point
What you'll learn	How to use two structural divs to create a two-column fixed-width layout, using both pixel- and percentage-based values
Completed files	using-wrappers-to-contain-columns in the chapter 7 folder

   1. Add a wrapper. Open the HTML document, place a `div` around the web page's content, and give the `div` an `id` value of `wrapper`.

```
<body>
  <div id="wrapper">
    [web page content]
  </div>
</body>
```

   2. Amend the `body` rule. Because the page will be fixed and centered, there's no longer a need for horizontal padding on the `body` element; therefore, amend the `body` rule in the CSS file as follows:

```
body {
  font: 62.5%/1.5 Verdana, Arial, Helvetica, sans-serif;
  padding: 20px 0;
}
```

3. Add the following rule to center the wrapper, per the "Creating a fixed-width-wrapper" exercise earlier in this chapter:

```
#wrapper {
  width: 700px;
  margin: 0 auto;
}
```

4. Finally, add the following two rules to float the columns, set their widths, and then place a margin between them (by adding a `margin-right` setting to the left column).

```
#divOne, #divTwo {
  float: left;
  width: 340px;
}
#divOne {
  margin-right: 20px;
}
```

Working with two divs

Div one

Lorem ipsum dolor sit amet, consectetuer adipiscing elit. Morbi commodo, ipsum sed pharetra gravida, orci magna rhoncus neque, id pulvinar odio lorem non turpis. Nullam sit amet enim.

Suspendisse id velit vitae ligula volutpat condimentum. Aliquam erat volutpat. Sed quis velit. Nulla facilisi. Nulla libero. Vivamus pharetra posuere sapien. Nam consectetuer. Sed aliquam, nunc eget euismod ullamcorper, lectus nunc ullamcorper orci, fermentum bibendum enim nibh eget ipsum.

Donec porttitor ligula eu dolor. Maecenas vitae nulla consequat libero cursus venenatis. Nam magna enim, accumsan eu, blandit sed, blandit a, eros. Quisque facilisis erat a dui. Nam malesuada ornare dolor. Cras gravida, diam sit amet rhoncus ornare, erat elit consectetuer erat, id egestas pede nibh eget odio.

Div two

Proin tincidunt, velit vel porta elementum, magna diam molestie sapien, non aliquet massa pede eu diam. Aliquam iaculis. Fusce et ipsum et nulla tristique facilisis. Donec eget sem sit amet ligula viverra gravida. Etiam vehicula urna vel turpis. Suspendisse sagittis ante a urna.

Morbi a est quis orci consequat rutrum. Nullam egestas feugiat felis. Integer adipiscing semper ligula. Nunc molestie, nisl sit amet cursus convallis, sapien lectus pretium metus, vitae pretium enim wisi id lectus. Donec vestibulum. Etiam vel nibh. Nulla facilisi. Mauris pharetra. Donec augue. Fusce ultrices, neque id dignissim ultrices, tellus mauris dictum elit, vel lacinia enim metus eu nunc.

Proin at eros non eros adipiscing mollis. Donec semper turpis sed diam. Sed consequat ligula nec tortor. Integer eget sem. Ut vitae enim eu est vehicula gravida. Morbi ipsum ipsum, porta nec, tempor id, auctor vitae, purus. Pellentesque neque. Nulla luctus erat vitae libero. Integer nec enim.

No matter the size of the browser window, the two-column design sits centrally horizontally.

Note that the fixed-width values for the two columns can be replaced with percentages:

```
#divOne, #divTwo {
  float: left;
  width: 49%;
}
#divOne {
  margin-right: 2%;
}
```

In such cases, the width of each div (and the margin) is a percentage of the parent element—the wrapper div—rather than the browser window.

> Note: When using percentages to size columns, it makes sense to use them also to size the gutters and margins between them. If you don't, you'll have a hard time trying to match up column widths in percentages and margins in pixels.

Clearing floated content

Required files	Files from using-wrappers-to-contain-columns in the chapter 7 folder as a starting point

What you'll learn	How to clear floated content, thereby making a wrapper's background display behind the content within it

Completed files	clearing-floated-content in the chapter 7 folder

1. To highlight issues with content that doesn't clear floated content, you need to make some quick changes to the HTML and CSS from the using-wrappers-to-contain-columns folder. First, add a paragraph of text after the closing tag of the wrapper div:

```
    </div>
  </div>
  <p>Subsequent content...</p>
</body>
</html>
```

2. Next, add a background color to the #wrapper rule in the CSS, and change the width and margin-right settings of the #divOne, #divTwo, and #divOne rules, as shown following:

```
#wrapper {
  width: 700px;
  margin: 0 auto;
  background: #bbbbbb;
}
#divOne, #divTwo {
  float: left;
  width: 300px;
}
#divOne {
  margin-right: 20px;
}
```

3. Upon previewing the amended page, you'll see that the subsequent content stacks to the right of the floated content; also, the background color for the wrapper doesn't extend behind the floated content. Both of these issues can be fixed by clearing the floated content.

Working with two divs

Div one

Lorem ipsum dolor sit amet, consectetuer adipiscing elit. Morbi commodo, ipsum sed pharetra gravida, orci magna rhoncus neque, id pulvinar odio lorem non turpis. Nullam sit amet enim.

Suspendisse id velit vitae ligula volutpat condimentum. Aliquam erat volutpat. Sed quis velit. Nulla facilisi. Nulla libero. Vivamus pharetra posuere sapien. Nam consectetuer. Sed aliquam, nunc eget euismod ullamcorper, lectus nunc ullamcorper orci, fermentum bibendum enim nibh eget ipsum.

Donec porttitor ligula eu dolor. Maecenas vitae nulla consequat libero cursus venenatis. Nam magna enim, accumsan eu, blandit sed, blandit a, eros. Quisque facilisis erat a dui. Nam malesuada ornare dolor. Cras gravida, diam sit amet rhoncus ornare, erat elit consectetuer erat, id egestas pede nibh eget odio.

Div two

Proin tincidunt, velit vel porta elementum, magna diam molestie sapien, non aliquet massa pede eu diam. Aliquam iaculis. Fusce et ipsum et nulla tristique facilisis. Donec eget sem sit amet ligula viverra gravida. Etiam vehicula urna vel turpis. Suspendisse sagittis ante a urna.

Morbi a est quis orci consequat rutrum. Nullam egestas feugiat felis. Integer adipiscing semper ligula. Nunc molestie, nisl sit amet cursus convallis, sapien lectus pretium metus, vtae pretium enim wisi id lectus. Donec vestibulum. Etiam vel nibh. Nulla facilisi. Mauris pharetra. Donec augue. Fusce ultrices, neque id dignissim ultrices, tellus mauris dictum elit, vel lacinia enim metus eu nunc.

Proin at eros non eros adipiscing mollis. Donec semper turpis sed diam. Sed consequat ligula nec tortor. Integer eget sem. Ut vitae enim eu est vehicula gravida. Morbi ipsum ipsum, porta nec, tempor id, auctor vitae, purus. Pellentesque neque. Nulla luctus erat vitae libero. Integer nec enim.

Subsequent content...

Note that Internet Explorer's behavior is different from other browsers here: the wrapper isn't being collapsed, so the background extends fully, and the paragraph of text added after the wrapper doesn't flow around the floated divs, presumably because the wrapper isn't collapsing.

---

4. Clear the floated content. There are many different clear fixes available today. The micro clearfix uses the minimum amount of CSS required. This version was introduced by Nicolas Gallagher (nicolasgallagher.com/micro-clearfix-hack/), and it builds on the work of Thierry Koblentz (www.yuiblog.com/blog/2010/09/27/clearfix-reloaded-overflowhidden-demystified/). First, add a `class` value of `clearFix` to the container of the floated content (the wrapper `div`, in this example), and then add the following rules in CSS:

```
.clearFix:before,
.clearFix:after {
  content: "";
  display: table;
}

.clearFix:after {
  clear:both;
}
```

Working with two divs

Div one

Lorem ipsum dolor sit amet, consectetuer adipiscing elit. Morbi commodo, ipsum sed pharetra gravida, orci magna rhoncus neque, id pulvinar odio lorem non turpis. Nullam sit amet enim.

Suspendisse id velit vitae ligula volutpat condimentum. Aliquam erat volutpat. Sed quis velit. Nulla facilisi. Nulla libero. Vivamus pharetra posuere sapien. Nam consectetuer. Sed aliquam, nunc eget euismod ullamcorper, lectus nunc ullamcorper orci, fermentum bibendum enim nibh eget ipsum.

Donec porttitor ligula eu dolor. Maecenas vitae nulla consequat libero cursus venenatis. Nam magna enim, accumsan eu, blandit sed, blandit a, eros. Quisque facilisis erat a dui. Nam malesuada ornare dolor. Cras gravida, diam sit amet rhoncus ornare, erat elit consectetuer erat, id egestas pede nibh eget odio.

Div two

Proin tincidunt, velit vel porta elementum, magna diam molestie sapien, non aliquet massa pede eu diam. Aliquam iaculis. Fusce et ipsum et nulla tristique facilisis. Donec eget sem sit amet ligula viverra gravida. Etiam vehicula urna vel turpis. Suspendisse sagittis ante a urna.

Morbi a est quis orci consequat rutrum. Nullam egestas feugiat felis. Integer adipiscing semper ligula. Nunc molestie, nisl sit amet cursus convallis, sapien lectus pretium metus, vitae pretium enim wisi id lectus. Donec vestibulum. Etiam vel nibh. Nulla facilisi. Mauris pharetra. Donec augue. Fusce ultrices, neque id dignissim ultrices, tellus mauris dictum elit, vel lacinia enim metus eu nunc.

Proin at eros non eros adipiscing mollis. Donec semper turpis sed diam. Sed consequat ligula nec tortor. Integer eget sem. Ut vitae enim eu est vehicula gravida. Morbi ipsum ipsum, porta nec, tempor id, auctor vitae, purus. Pellentesque neque. Nulla luctus erat vitae libero. Integer nec enim.

Subsequent content...

5. The magic of this method is in the CSS rule. By using the `:after` pseudo-selector, an empty string is added after the element the class is applied to (in this case, after the wrapper `div`), and said empty string's display is set to table. This creates an anonymous table cell that is set to clear the element. Unlike previous clearFix methods, there is no content added and therefore no need to hide it. The genius of the method is that you need no extra markup to clear floats. The :before pseudo-selecter is not required to clear the float but is used to prevent the top margin from collapsing in modern browsers. In Chapter 9, I will show you a simple method for making this clear fix work in IE 6/7.

6. Use an alternate method. The clearFix method is great for when you have content following a containing wrapper. In some cases, you may not have this, though. For example, place your subsequent content within the wrapper `div`, as shown here:

```
        </div>
        <p>Subsequent content...</p>
      </div>
    </body>
</html>
```

7. The clearFix method won't work here, because the content is now inside the `div` that has the `clearFix` rule applied to it. Various options are open; the first is to wrap the floated elements in an internal wrapper and apply the `clearFix` class to that. In many cases, this will be fine, but you can end up with a case of divitis, where many nested `div`s impair the clean nature of the markup. An

alternate option is to apply clearing directly to the element that follows the last piece of floated content. In HTML, this would look as follows:

```
<p class="ClearFloats">
```

8. In CSS, this is styled as follows:

```
.clearFloats {
  clear: both;
}
```

Generally, the clearFix method is considered superior to adding styles to specific elements, but on occasions when it doesn't work for your design, it's good to have a fallback, so be mindful of both clearing methods when working on your designs.

Working with sidebars and multiple boxouts

In this chapter so far, you've seen how to create web page columns and also how to fashion a boxout. In this section, two exercises will expand upon these ideas, showing how to create two different layouts that make use of sidebars. Sidebars are common in print, either for dividing up a page, thereby enabling a designer to show a main story and a smaller story, or for providing an area for ancillary content to the main story, but without having text wrapping underneath it (like in a boxout). The Pinkflag.com website (the official website of the rock band Wire) makes use of sidebars throughout the site. In the following image, a page from the Us section is shown. The main section of the page shows a photo of a band member, along with a short biography. In the sidebar is a selection of the subject's favorite tracks.

Based on what you've seen so far, you might think the best way to create such a layout would be to create a two-column layout and then add a border to one of the columns. However, in CSS, borders and backgrounds stop as soon as the content does. Therefore, if you add a border to the main content area but the sidebar's content makes it taller than the main content area, the separating border stops short. What you therefore need to do is ensure that the two columns are placed in a wrapper and then apply a vertically tiling background to the wrapper, thereby "faking" the column separator. This technique is commonly referred to as creating faux columns and is explained fully in the following exercise.

Creating a sidebar with faux-column backgrounds

Required files	faux-columns-background.gif from the image folder and all files from using-wrappers-to-contain-columns (both in the chapter 7 folder) as a starting point

What you'll learn	How to use two structural elements and a background image to create faux columns

Completed files	faux-columns in the chapter 7 folder

1. Clear the floated content, using the method outlined in step 2 of the "Clearing floated content" exercise.

2. Change the id values. When creating a website, you should amend your elements id values to something appropriate for the content within them. Don't use generic names such as divOne and

divTwo for a completed website. (They've been used for some exercises in this chapter just to make the exercises simpler to work through.) In both the HTML page and the CSS document, change all instances of divOne to mainContent and all incidences of divTwo to sidebar. Amend the two level-two headings in the web page accordingly, too. Finally, since the sidebar contains content that will support the main body, change the div used for the sidebar into an aside.

3. Change the width settings for the columns, making sidebar narrower than mainContent.

```
#mainContent, #sidebar {
  float: left;
  width: 479px;
}
#mainContent {
  margin-right: 41px;
}
#sidebar {
  width: 180px;
  display: block;
}
```

4. Add the background image. Apply the background image (shown right) to the wrapper div, as shown following. The horizontal position is the width of the main content div, plus half the margin once 1 pixel is removed from that value (because the width of the "border" in the background image is a single pixel). By placing the background image 499 pixels from the left, it ends up exactly halfway between the content of the two divs.

```
#wrapper {
  width: 700px;
  margin: 0 auto;
  background: url(faux-columns-background.gif) 499px 0 repeat-y;
}
```

5. To make it easier to differentiate the two areas of text, change the size of the text in the sidebar, making it smaller.

```
#sidebar {
  width: 180px;
  font-size: 90%;
}
```

Using a percentage value is a quick way of doing this, with all values being based on those from the main content area. If you want to set specific values for each of the text elements within the sidebar, you could do so using contextual selectors (#sidebar h1, #sidebar p, and so on).

Working with two divs

Main content

Lorem ipsum dolor sit amet, consectetuer adipiscing elit. Morbi commodo, ipsum sed pharetra gravida, orci magna rhoncus neque, id pulvinar odio lorem non turpis. Nullam sit amet enim.

Suspendisse id velit vitae ligula volutpat condimentum. Aliquam erat volutpat. Sed quis velit. Nulla facilisi. Nulla libero. Vivamus pharetra posuere sapien. Nam consectetuer. Sed aliquam, nunc eget euismod ullamcorper, lectus nunc ullamcorper orci, fermentum bibendum enim nibh eget ipsum.

Donec porttitor ligula eu dolor. Maecenas vitae nulla consequat libero cursus venenatis. Nam magna enim, accumsan eu, blandit sed, blandit a, eros.
Quisque facilisis erat a dui. Nam malesuada ornare dolor. Cras gravida, diam sit

Sidebar

Proin tincidunt, velit vel porta elementum, magna diam molestie sapien, non aliquet massa pede eu diam. Aliquam iaculis. Fusce et ipsum et nulla tristique facilisis. Donec eget sem sit amet ligula viverra gravida. Etiam vehicula urna vel turpis. Suspendisse sagittis ante a urna.

Morbi a est quis orci consequat rutrum. Nullam egestas feugiat felis. Integer adipiscing semper

Note: There is an alternate way to create faux columns; see step 5 of the "Creating flanking sidebars" exercise later in the chapter.

Boxouts revisited: creating multiple boxouts within a sidebar

Required files	Files from `multiple-boxouts-starting-point` in the chapter 7 folder as a starting point
What you'll learn	How to use faux columns, boxouts, and the cascade to create a page design with a sidebar that contains multiple boxouts
Completed files	`multiple-boxouts-complete` in the chapter 7 folder

1. Examine the code. Open the web page and CSS document from multiple-boxouts-starting-point, and also open the web page in a browser so you can see what it looks like. Lots of work has already been done here, but it's all stuff you already know. Essentially, this page is a combination of the "Creating a boxout" and "Creating a sidebar with faux-column backgrounds" exercises from earlier in the chapter. A few changes have been made, however. The boxout has been duplicated three times and placed within the sidebar, the float: right pair from .boxout has been deleted (because the boxouts no longer need to float—they are within a container that itself is floated), and some bottom padding has been added (to ensure there's a gap below the final paragraph of each boxout). A section has been used instead of multiple asides since the containing element is an aside.

```
.boxout {
  width: 180px;
  padding: 0 10px 1px;
  margin: 0 0 20px;
display: block;
  background-color: #e1e1e1;
      background-image: -webkit-gradient(linear, 0% 0%, 0% 100%, from(#e1e1e1), to(#b5b5b5));
      background-image: -webkit-linear-gradient(top, #e1e1e1, #b5b5b5);
```

```
    background-image:    -moz-linear-gradient(top, #e1e1e1, #b5b5b5);
    background-image:    -ms-linear-gradient(top, #e1e1e1, #b5b5b5);
    background-image:     -o-linear-gradient(top, #e1e1e1, #b5b5b5);
}
```

Also, the background from the faux columns exercise isn't there, because the vertical line the boxouts create is enough to make the column visually distinct—another separator isn't necessary.

2. Add `class` values. While consistent style is good for a website, it's sometimes neat to offer multiple styles for an element. This can come in handy for categorization—for example, each boxout in this design could contain information about a certain area of the website, and therefore color coding them and providing each with an icon (for those viewers with color vision difficulties) may help users navigate more easily. Because you can use multiple `class` values in CSS, it's possible to simply add a second `class` value to each of the boxout `sections` and then create an override rule for each in CSS.

```
<section class="boxout questionsHeader">
  [section content]
</section>
<section class="boxout chatHeader">
  [section content]
</section>
<section class="boxout toolsHeader">
  [section content]
</section>
```

3. Add new CSS rules. By using three contextual rules, overrides are created, setting a new background color and gradients for each of the three heading classes defined in step 2.

```
.questionsHeader h2 {
  background-color: #d72a49;
background-image: url(background-icon-questions.gif), -webkit-gradient(linear, 0% 0%, 0% 100%,
from(#d72a49), to(#dc4561));
      background-image: url(background-icon-questions.gif), -webkit-linear-gradient(top,
#d72a49, #dc4561);
      background-image: url(background-icon-questions.gif),    -moz-linear-gradient(top,
#d72a49, #dc4561);
      background-image: url(background-icon-questions.gif),    -ms-linear-gradient(top,
#d72a49, #dc4561);
      background-image: url(background-icon-questions.gif),     -o-linear-gradient(top,
#d72a49, #dc4561);
}

.chatHeader h2 {
  background-color: #2a84d7;
background-image: url(background-icon-chat.gif), -webkit-gradient(linear, 0% 0%, 0% 100%,
from(#2a84d7), to(#4594dc));
      background-image: url(background-icon-chat.gif), -webkit-linear-gradient(top, #2a84d7,
#4594dc);
      background-image: url(background-icon-chat.gif),    -moz-linear-gradient(top, #2a84d7,
#4594dc);
```

```
        background-image: url(background-icon-chat.gif),      -ms-linear-gradient(top, #2a84d7,
#4594dc);
        background-image: url(background-icon-chat.gif),      -o-linear-gradient(top, #2a84d7,
#4594dc);
}
.toolsHeader h2 {
  background-color: #d72ab0;
background-image: url(background-icon-tools.gif), -webkit-gradient(linear, 0% 0%, 0% 100%,
from(#d72ab0), to(#dc45bb));
        background-image: url(background-icon-tools.gif), -webkit-linear-gradient(top, #d72ab0,
#dc45bb);
        background-image:     url(background-icon-tools.gif), -moz-linear-gradient(top, #d72ab0,
#dc45bb);
        background-image:     url(background-icon-tools.gif), -ms-linear-gradient(top, #d72ab0,
#dc45bb);
        background-image:      url(background-icon-tools.gif), -o-linear-gradient(top, #d72ab0,
#dc45bb);
}
```

Note that these rules must be placed after the .boxout h2 rule in the CSS, because the CSS cascade ensures that the rule closest to the element is applied. If these were placed above the .boxout h2 rule, they would be overridden by it, resulting in the boxouts all retaining their default appearance.

The following image shows what your page should now look like.

Creating flanking sidebars

Although some sites can be designed around a two-column model, you'll frequently need more. This can be achieved by adding further columns to the pages created in earlier exercises or by nesting wrappers with two columns. (In other words, the first wrapper can contain a sidebar and a wrapper, which itself contains the main content and another sidebar.)

The only issue with this is that it doesn't allow for information to be provided in code in an order different from that shown on the screen. For users of alternate devices, a site with a sidebar (perhaps for navigation and advertising), followed by the main content, followed by another sidebar (perhaps for boxouts), would require them to wade through the first sidebar before accessing the main content. You can get around this by using a "skip to main content" link (as per the skip navigation link from Chapter 5), but you can also set the content in the order you want in the code (main content, first sidebar, second sidebar) and then use CSS to reorder the columns on the screen.

Creating flanking sidebars	
Required files	Files from flanking-sidebars-starting-point in the chapter 7 folder as a starting point

What you'll learnHow to create flanking sidebars for a content area, thereby enabling you to set
content in one order in the code and another on-screen

Completed files-flanking-sidebars-liquid and flanking-sidebars-fixed in the chapter 7 folder

1. Check out the page. Open flanking-sidebars.html in a web browser and in a text editor. In the
   code, you have a wrapper that contains a masthead, followed by a wrapper for the columns,
   followed by a footer. Within the column wrapper are three structural elements: mainContent,
   leftSidebar, and rightSidebar. Each of these has a content wrapper (as per step 4 of the
   "Manipulating two structural divs for liquid layouts" exercise). In CSS, the page defaults and font
   styles are already set, as are styles for the masthead and footer. The clearFix method (see the
   "Clearing floated content" exercise) has also been used, since the three columns will be
   positioned by being floated. Note that for this exercise, the layout will be a liquid one, based on
   percentage values for widths and margins.

2. Add the column backgrounds. Add the following two rules, which supply two backgrounds. The
   first is applied to the column wrapper, setting the background to gray and adding a horizontally
   tiling drop-shadow image. The second is applied to the main content div, defining its background
   as white and setting its own background. This will create a seamless shadow effect, but the main
   content will be differentiated from the sidebar via a brighter background.

```
#columnWrapper {
  background: #ebebeb url(assets/grey-shadow-top.gif) 0 0 repeat-x;
}
#mainContent {
  background: #ffffff url(assets/white-shadow-top.gif) 0 0 repeat-x;
}
```

3. Set column widths. Amend the #mainContent rule and add rules for the two sidebars, floating all
   of the columns left and setting width values. This is a liquid design, so percentages must be used,
   and they must add up to 100%.

```
#mainContent {
  background: #ffffff url(assets/white-shadow-top.gif) 0 0 repeat-x;
  float: left;
  width: 50%;
}
#leftSidebar {
  float: left;
  width: 30%;
}
#rightSidebar {
  float: left;
  width: 20%;
}
```

PAGE TITLE

MAIN CONTENT

Lorem ipsum dolor sit amet, consectetuer adipiscing elit. Morbi commodo, ipsum sed pharetra gravida, orci magna rhoncus neque, id pulvinar odio orem non turpis. Nullam sit amet enim. Suspendisse id velit vitae ligula volutpat condimentum. Aliquam erat volutpat. Sed quis velit. Nulla facilisi. Nulla libero. Vivamus pharetra posuere sapien. Nam consectetuer. Sed aliquam, nunc eget euismod ullamcorper, lectus nunc ullamcorper orci, fermentum bibendum enim nibh eget psum. Donec porttitor ligula eu dolor. Maecenas vitae nulla consequat libero cursus venenatis. Nam magna enim, accumsan eu, blandit sed, blandit a, eros.

Quisque facilisis erat a dui. Nam malesuada ornare dolor. Cras gravida, diam sit amet rhoncus ornare, erat elit consectetuer erat, id egestas pede nibh eget odio. Proin tincidunt, velit vel porta elementum, magna diam molestie sapien, non aliquet massa pede eu diam. Aliquam iaculis. Fusce et ipsum et nulla tristique facilisis. Donec eget sem sit amet ligula viverra gravida. Etiam vehicula urna vel turpis. Suspendisse sagittis ante a urna. Morbi a est quis orci consequat rutrum. Nullam egestas feugiat felis. Integer adipiscing semper ligula. Nunc molestie, nisl sit amet cursus convallis, sapien lectus pretium metus, vitae pretium enim wisi id lectus. Donec vestibulum. Etiam vel nibh. Nula facilisi. Mauris pharetra. Donec augue. Fusce ultrices, neque id dignissim ultrices, tellus mauris dictum elit, vel lacinia enim metus eu nunc.

LEFT SIDEBAR

Proin at eros non eros adipiscing mollis. Donec semper turpis sed diam. Sed consequat ligula nec tortor. Integer eget sem. Ut vitae enim eu est vehicula gravida. Morbi ipsum ipsum, porta nec, tempor id, auctor vitae, purus. Pellentesque neque. Nulla luctus erat vitae libero. Integer nec enim. Phasellus aliquam enim et tortor. Quisque elit sit amet mi. Phasellus pellentesque, erat eget elementum volutpat, dolor nisl porta neque, vitae sodales ipsum nibh in ligula. Maecenas mattis pulvinar diam. Curabitur sed leo.

Nunc auctor bibendum eros. Maecenas porta accumsan mauris. Etiam enim enim, elementum sed, bibendum quis, rhoncus non, metus. Fusce neque dolor, adipiscing sed, consectetuer et, lacinia sit amet, quam. Suspendisse wisi quam, consectetuer in, blandit sed, suscipit eu, eros. Etiam ligula enim, tempor ut, blandit nec, mollis eu, lectus. Nam cursus. Vivamus iaculis. Aenean risus purus, pharetra in, blandit quis, gravida a, turpis. Donec nisl. Aenean eget mi. Fusce mattis est id diam. Phasellus faucibus interdum sapien. Duis quis nunc. Sed enim.

RIGHT SIDEBAR

Nunc auctor bibendum eros. Maecenas porta accumsan mauris. Etiam enim enim, elementum sed, bibendum quis, rhoncus non, metus. Fusce neque dolor, adipiscing sed, consectetuer et, lacinia sit amet, quam. Suspendisse wisi quam, consectetuer in, blandit sed, suscipit eu, eros. Etiam ligula enim, tempor ut, blandit nec, mollis eu, lectus. Nam cursus. Vivamus iaculis. Aenean risus purus, pharetra in, blandit quis, gravida a, turpis. Donec nisl. Aenean eget mi. Fusce mattis est id diam. Phasellus faucibus interdum sapien. Duis quis nunc. Sed enim.

This is the footer

---

4. Position the sidebars. At the moment, the columns are in the order specified in the code. However, via the use of margins, this order can be changed. For the main content div, set a margin-left value equal to the width of the left sidebar. Next, set a margin-left value for #leftSidebar that's the negative value of the sum of the width and left margin values of the main content area.

```
#mainContent {
  background: #ffffff url(assets/white-shadow-top.gif) 0 0 repeat-x;
  float: left;
  width: 50%;
  margin-left: 30%;
}
#leftSidebar {
  float: left;
  width: 30%;
  margin-left: -80%;
}
#rightSidebar {
  float: left;
  width: 20%;
}
```

PAGE TITLE

LEFT SIDEBAR

Proin at eros non eros adipiscing mollis. Donec semper turpis sed diam. Sec consequat ligula nec tortor. Integer eget sem. Ut vitae enim eu est vehicula gravida. Morbi ipsum ipsum, porta nec, tempor id, auctor vitae, purus. Pellentesque neque. Nulla luctus erat vitae libero. Integer nec enim. Phasellus aliquam enim et tortor. Quisque elit sit amet mi. Phasellus pellentesque, erat eget elementum volutpat, dolor nisl porta neque, vitae sodales ipsum nibh in ligula. Maecenas mattis pulvinar diam. Curabitur sed leo.

Nunc auctor bibendum eros. Maecenas porta accumsan mauris. Etiam enim enim, elementum sed, bibendum quis, rhoncus non, metus. Fusce neque dolor, adipiscing sed, consectetuer et, lacinia sit amet, quam. Suspendisse wisi quam, consectetuer in, blandit sed, suscipit eu, eros. Etiam ligula enim, tempor ut, blandit nec, mollis eu, lectus. Nam cursus. Vivamus iaculis. Aenean risus purus, pharetra in, blandit quis, gravida a, turpis. Donec nisl. Aenean eget mi. Fusce mattis est id diam. Phasellus faucibus interdum sapien. Duis quis nunc. Sed enim.

MAIN CONTENT

Lorem ipsum dolor sit amet, consectetuer adipiscing elit. Morbi commodo, ipsum sed pharetra gravida, orci magna rhoncus neque, id pulvinar odio lorem non turpis. Nullam sit amet enim. Suspendisse id velit vitae ligula volutpat condimentum. Aliquam erat volutpat. Sed quis velit. Nulla facilisi. Nulla libero. Vivamus pharetra posuere sapien. Nam consectetuer. Sed aliquam, nunc eget euismod ullamcorper, lectus nunc ullamcorper orci, fermentum bibendum enim nibh eget ipsum. Donec porttitor ligula eu dolor. Maecenas vitae nulla consequat libero cursus venenatis. Nam magna enim, accumsan eu, blandit sed, blandit a, eros.

Quisque facilisis erat a dui. Nam molesuada ornare dolor. Cras gravida, diam sit amet rhoncus ornare, erat elit consectetuer erat, id egestas pede nibh eget odio. Proin tincidunt, velit vel porta elementum, magna diam molestie sapien, non aliquet massa pede eu diam. Aliquam iaculis. Fusce et ipsum et nulla tristique facilisis. Donec eget sem sit amet ligula viverra gravida. Etiam vehicula urna vel turpis. Suspendisse sagittis ante a urna. Morbi a est quis orci consequat rutrum. Nullam egestas feugiat felis. Integer adipiscing semper ligula. Nunc molestie, nisl sit amet cursus convallis, sapien lectus pretium metus, vitae pretium enim wisi id lectus. Donec vestibulum. Etiam vel nibh. Nulla facilisi. Mauris pharetra. Donec augue. Fusce ultrices, neque id dignissim ultrices, tellus mauris dictum elit, vel lacinia enim metus eu nunc.

RIGHT SIDEBAR

Nunc auctor bibendum eros. Maecenas porta accumsan mauris. Etiam enim enim, elementum sed, bibendum quis, rhoncus non, metus. Fusce neque dolor, adipiscing sed, consectetuer et, lacinia sit amet, quam. Suspendisse wisi quam, consectetuer in, blandit sed, suscipit eu, eros. Etiam ligula enim, tempor ut, blandit nec, mollis eu, lectus. Nam cursus. Vivamus iaculis. Aenean risus purus, pharetra in, blandit quis, gravida a, turpis. Donec nisl. Aenean eget mi. Fusce mattis est id diam. Phasellus faucibus interdum sapien. Duis quis nunc. Sed enim.

This is the footer

Note: Internet Explorer may cause problems with this layout, making the right sidebar sometimes appear beneath the others when the browser window is resized. This is caused by a rounding error (see the "Dealing with rounding errors" section in Chapter 9). Therefore, it's often useful to amend one of the percentages (and any related values), dropping them by 0.0001%—for example, change the *width* value of *#mainContent* to *49.9999%* and the *margin-left* value of *#leftSidebar* to *79.9999%*.

5. Fine-tune the design. Add the three rules in the following code block to finish off the layout and tidy things up:

```
.columnContentWrapper {
  padding: 30px 10px;
}
#mainContent, #leftSidebar, #rightSidebar {
  padding-bottom: 32767px !important;
  margin-bottom: -32767px !important;
}
#columnWrapper {
  overflow: hidden;
}
```

The first rule merely adds some padding to the column content wrappers. The next rule applies a large amount of padding to the bottom of each column and a negative margin of the same size, bringing the document flow back to the point where the padding begins. The use of `overflow: hidden` on the column container removes the overflow below the longest column's content. Note that the value used here is the maximum allowed by Apple's Safari because it is the highest number that can be represented in a 16-bit signed integer. You can also use the second rule in the previous code block to control padding by reducing the `margin-bottom` value: the difference between the `padding-bottom` and `margin-bottom` values effectively becomes padding, although in this exercise, padding has been dealt with via the `.columnContentWrapper` rule.

PAGE TITLE

LEFT SIDEBAR

Proin at eros non eros adipiscing mollis. Donec semper turpis sed diam. Sed consequat ligula nec tortor. Integer eget sem. Ut vitae enim eu est vehicula gravida. Morbi ipsum ipsum, porta nec, tempor id, auctor vitae, purus. Pellentesque neque. Nulla luctus erat vitae libero. Integer nec enim. Phasellus aliquam enim et tortor. Quisque elit sit amet mi. Phasellus pellentesque, erat eget elementum volutpat, dolor nisl porta neque, vitae sodales ipsum nibh in ligula. Maecenas mattis pulvinar diam. Curabitur sed leo.

Nunc auctor bibendum eros. Maecenas porta accumsan mauris. Etiam enim enim, elementum sed, bibendum quis, rhoncus non, metus. Fusce neque dolor, adipiscing sed, consectetuer et, lacinia sit amet, quam. Suspendisse wisi quam, consectetuer in, blandit sed, suscipit eu, eros. Etiam ligula enim, tempor ut, blandit nec, mollis eu, lectus. Nam cursus. Vivamus iaculis. Aenean risus purus, pharetra in, blandit quis, gravida a, turpis. Donec nisl. Aenean eget mi. Fusce mattis est id diam. Phasellus faucibus interdum sapien. Duis quis nunc. Sed enim.

MAIN CONTENT

Lorem ipsum dolor sit amet, consectetuer adipiscing elit. Morbi commodo, ipsum sed pharetra gravida, orci magna rhoncus neque, id pulvinar odio lorem non turpis. Nullam sit amet enim. Suspendisse id velit vitae ligula volutpat condimentum. Aliquam erat volutpat. Sed quis velit. Nulla facilisi. Nulla libero. Vivamus pharetra posuere sapien. Nam consectetuer. Sed aliquam, nunc eget euismod ullamcorper, lectus nunc ullamcorper orci, fermentum bibendum enim nibh eget ipsum. Donec porttitor ligula eu dolor. Maecenas vitae nulla consequat libero cursus venenatis. Nam magna enim, accumsan eu, blandit sed, blandit a, eros.

Quisque facilisis erat a dui. Nam malesuada ornare dolor. Cras gravida, diam sit amet rhoncus ornare, erat elit consectetuer erat, d egestas pede nibh eget odio. Proin tincidunt, velit vel porta elementum, magna diam molestie sapien, non aliquet massa pede eu diam. Aliquam iaculis. Fusce et ipsum et nulla tristique facilisis. Donec eget sem sit amet ligula viverra gravida. Etiam vehicula urna vel turpis. Suspendisse sagittis ante a urna. Morbi a est quis orci consequat rutrum. Nullam egestas feugiat felis. Integer adipiscing semper ligula. Nunc molestie, nisl sit amet cursus convallis, sapien lectus pretium metus, vitae pretium enim wisi id lectus. Donec vestibulum. Etiam vel nibh. Nulla facilisi. Mauris pharetra. Donec augue. Fusce ultrices, neque id dignissim ultrices, tellus mauris dictum elit, vel lacinia enim metus eu nunc.

RIGHT SIDEBAR

Nunc auctor bibendum eros. Maecenas porta accumsan mauris. Etiam enim enim, elementum sed, bibendum quis, rhoncus non, metus. Fusce neque dolor, adipiscing sed, consectetuer et, lacinia sit amet, quam. Suspendisse wisi quam, consectetuer in, blandit sed, suscipit eu, eros. Etiam ligula enim, tempor ut, blandit nec, mollis eu, lectus. Nam cursus. Vivamus iaculis. Aenean risus purus, pharetra in, blandit quis, gravida a, turpis. Donec nisl. Aenean eget mi. Fusce mattis est id diam. Phasellus faucibus interdum sapien. Duis quis nunc. Sed enim.

This is the footer

---

6. Make the layout fixed. Amending the layout to a fixed one is simple. Because the layout will no longer span the window width, a border needs to be placed around the wrapper (otherwise the drop-shadow cutoffs at the left and right just look weird). Therefore, add a `padding-bottom` value of 20px to the `body` rule, and create the `#wrapper` rule shown following:

```
#wrapper {
  width: 700px;
  margin: 0 auto;
  border: 1px solid #555555;
  border-top: 0;
}
```

7. Next, update the `width` and `margin-left` values for the three rules shown in the following code, being mindful of the relationships mentioned in step 4 and the fact that the `width` values cannot exceed the value set for the wrapper's width in the previous step:

```
#mainContent {
  background: #ffffff url(assets/white-shadow-top.gif) 0 0 repeat-x;
  float: left;
  width: 400px;
  margin-left: 175px;
}
#leftSidebar {
  float: left;
  width: 175px;
  margin-left: -575px;
}
#rightSidebar {
  float: left;
  width: 125px;
}
```

The following image shows what your page should now look like.

PAGE TITLE

LEFT SIDEBAR

Proin at eros non eros adipiscing mollis. Donec semper turpis sed diam Sed consequat ligula nec tortor. Integer eget sem. Ut vitae enim eu est vehicula gravida. Morbi ipsum ipsum, porta nec, tempor id, auctor vitae, purus. Pellentesque neque. Nulla luctus erat vitae libero. Integer nec enim. Phasellus aliquam enim et tortor. Quisque elit sit amet mi. Phasellus pellentesque, erat eget elementum volutpat, dolor nisi porta neque, vitae sodales ipsum nibh in

MAIN CONTENT

Lorem ipsum dolor sit amet, consectetuer adipiscing elit. Morbi commodo, ipsum sed pharetra gravida, orci magna rhoncus neque, id pulvinar odio lorem non turpis. Nullam sit amet enim. Suspendisse id velit vitae ligula volutpat condimentum. Aliquam erat volutpat. Sed quis velit. Nulla facilisi. Nulla libero. Vivamus pharetra posuere sapien. Nam consectetuer. Sed aliquam, nunc eget euismod ullamcorper, lectus nunc ullamcorper orci, fermentum bibendum enim nibh eget ipsum. Donec porttitor ligula eu dolor. Maecenas vitae nulla consequat libero cursus venenatis. Nam magna enim, accumsan eu, blandit sed, blandit a, eros.

Quisque facilisis erat a dui. Nam malesuada ornare dolor. Cras gravida, diam sit amet rhoncus ornare, erat elit consectetuer erat, id egestas pede nibh eget odio. Proin tincidunt, velit vel porta elementum, magna diam molestie sapien, non aliquet massa pede eu diam. Aliquam laculis. Fusce et ipsum et nulla tristique facilisis. Donec eget sem sit amet ligula viverra gravida. Etiam vehicula urna vel turpis. Suspendisse sagittis ante a urna. Morbi a est quis orci consequat rutrum. Nullam egestas feugiat felis. Integer

RIGHT SIDEBAR

Nunc auctor bibendum eros. Maecenas porta accumsan mauris. Etiam enim enim, elementum sed, bibendum quis, rhoncus non, metus. Fusce neque dolor, adipiscing sed, consectetuer et, lacinia sit amet, quam. Suspendisse wisi quam, consectetuer in, blandit sed,

utomating layout variations

The final exercise in this section shows how to automate page layouts in a similar manner to automating navigation, as described in Chapter 5 (namely, in the "Creating a CSS-only tab bar that automates the active page" exercise). By defining a `class` value for the body element, contextual selectors can be used to amend the layout of a web page. This technique comes in handy when working on large sites that have many variations throughout but some consistent elements. For example, the site's overall width, masthead, and footer may remain constant, but the number of columns on the page may change, or they may change widths.

Using body class values and CSS to automate page layouts

Required files   Files from `faux-columns` in the chapter 7 folder as a starting point

What you'll learn   How to use body `class` values and contextual selectors to automate page layouts

Completed files   `automate-page-layouts` in the chapter 7 folder.

1. Examine the files. The files from the "Creating a sidebar with faux-column backgrounds" exercise are used as the basis for this one. The web page has two `structural elements`, one for the main content (`mainContent`) and another for the sidebar (`sidebar`). The default setup is for the main content area to take up most of the width and for the sidebar to be narrow, with smaller text. During the next two steps, contextual selectors will be designed to create two alternate layouts, one of which will have a single column and one of which will split the columns evenly.

Working with two divs

Main content

Lorem ipsum dolor sit amet, consectetuer adipiscing elit. Morbi commodo, ipsum sed pharetra gravida, orci magna rhoncus neque, id pulvinar odio lorem non turpis. Nullam sit amet enim.

Suspendisse id velit vitae ligula volutpat condimentum. Aliquam erat volutpat. Sed quis velit. Nulla facilisi. Nulla libero. Vivamus pharetra posuere sapien. Nam consectetuer. Sed aliquam, nunc eget euismod ullamcorper, lectus nunc ullamcorper orci, fermentum bibendum enim nibh eget ipsum.

Donec porttitor ligula eu dolor. Maecenas vitae nulla consequat libero cursus venenatis. Nam magna enim, accumsan eu, blandit sed, blandit a, eros. Quisque facilisis erat a dui. Nam malesuada ornare dolor. Cras gravida, diam sit amet rhoncus ornare, erat elit consectetuer erat, id egestas pede nibh eget

Sidebar

Proin tincidunt, velit vel porta elementum, magna diam molestie sapien, non aliquet massa pede eu diam. Aliquam iaculis. Fusce et ipsum et nulla tristique facilisis. Donec eget sem sit amet ligula viverra gravida. Etiam vehicula urna vel turpis. Suspendisse sagittis ante a urna.

Morbi a est quis orci consequat rutrum. Nullam egestas feugiat felis. Integer adipiscing semper ligula. Nunc molestie, nisi sit amet

2. Create single-column rules. The way this method works is to create overrides for relevant rules. The contextual selectors will begin with a class selector that will be applied to the page's body start tag, followed by the rules that require overriding. For a single column, the wrapper no longer needs a background, the main content area needs to be as wide as the wrapper (700 pixels), and the sidebar doesn't need to be displayed. Also, the default margin-right value for #wrapper needs to be overridden; otherwise, the main content area will end up 700 pixels wide plus 41 pixels of margin.

```
.singleColumn #wrapper {
  background: none;
}
.singleColumn #mainContent {
  width: 700px;
  margin-right: 0;
}
.singleColumn #sidebar {
  display: none;
}
```

3. This style can be applied to the web page by setting the body element's class value to singleColumn.

```
<body class="singleColumn">
```

Working with two divs

Main content

Lorem ipsum dolor sit amet, consectetuer adipiscing elit. Morbi commodo, ipsum sed pharetra gravida, orci magna rhoncus neque, id pulvinar odio lorem non turpis. Nullam sit amet enim.

Suspendisse id velit vitae ligula volutpat condimentum. Aliquam erat volutpat. Sed quis velit. Nulla facilisi. Nulla libero. Vivamus pharetra posuere sapien. Nam consectetuer. Sed aliquam, nunc eget euismod ullamcorper, lectus nunc ullamcorper orci, fermentum bibendum enim nibh eget ipsum.

Donec porttitor ligula eu dolor. Maecenas vitae nulla consequat libero cursus venenatis. Nam magna enim, accumsan eu, blandit sed, blandit a, eros. Quisque facilisis erat a dui. Nam malesuada ornare dolor. Cras gravida, diam sit amet rhoncus ornare, erat elit consectetuer erat, id egestas pede nibh eget odio.

Note that when using designs such as this, be sure to empty the contents of nondisplayed elements—any content left within them is just a waste of bandwidth.

---

4. Create an equal-column-split rule. For an equal column split, the column widths need to be amended to the same value. But because the margin-right setting defined earlier is 41px, the sidebar has been set to 1 pixel narrower than the main content area. (An alternate option would have been to set both column widths to 330px and set margin-right in .equalSplitColumns #mainContent to 40px.) The background-position horizontal value needs changing to reflect the new column positions. Finally, because both columns command equal prominence, the font-size setting for the sidebar is set to 100% in .equalSplitColumns #sidebar.

```
.equalSplitColumns #wrapper {
  background-position: 350px 0;
}
.equalSplitColumns #mainContent {
  width: 330px;
}
.equalSplitColumns #sidebar {
  width: 329px;
  font-size: 100%;
}
```

This style can be applied to the web page by setting the body element's class value to equalSplitColumns.

```
<body class="equalSplitColumns">
```

Working with two divs

Main content

Lorem ipsum dolor sit amet, consectetuer adipiscing elit. Morbi commodo, ipsum sed pharetra gravida, orci magna rhoncus neque, id pulvinar odio lorem non turpis. Nullam sit amet enim.

Suspendisse id velit vitae ligula volutpat condimentum. Aliquam erat volutpat. Sed quis velit. Nulla facilisi. Nulla libero. Vivamus pharetra posuere sapien. Nam consectetuer. Sed aliquam, nunc eget euismod ullamcorper, lectus nunc ullamcorper orci, fermentum bibendum enim nibh eget ipsum.

Sidebar

Proin tincidunt, velit vel porta elementum, magna diam molestie sapien, non aliquet massa pede eu diam. Aliquam iaculis. Fusce et ipsum et nulla tristique facilisis. Donec eget sem sit amet ligula viverra gravida. Etiam vehicula urna vel turpis. Suspendisse sagittis ante a urna.

Morbi a est quis orci consequat rutrum. Nullam egestas feugiat felis. Integer adipiscing semper ligula. Nunc molestie, nisi sit amet cursus convallis, sapien lectus pretium metus, vitae pretium enim wisi id lectus.

As mentioned, this exercise works in a similar way to some of the navigation ones in Chapter 5. With a little thought, it should be easy enough to see how this automation method can assist when creating websites. As long as the site's structure has been carefully planned, you can usually get away with a single navigation bar and a single structure but have multiple layouts, each one driven by the CSS variations and the body class value.

Scrollable content areas

Scrolling is a matter of fact on the Web. Although designers should be careful not to make users scroll too much (or in multiple directions—sites that force both horizontal and vertical scrolling tend to be awkward and annoying to use), some scrolling is inevitable with the vast majority of websites. In the past, some designers created fixed sites that sat in the middle of the browser window, content restricted by the viewing area. Various techniques later enabled designers to get around this limitation, creating in-page scrollable content areas. First came frames, and later came CSS-driven scrolling areas. Both enable you to create in-page scrollable content, but although such things are explored in the final part of this chapter, scrollable areas should be used with care—if you need a user to see something right away, don't hide it "under the fold," and remember that if you create a centered, fixed-view window, test it using many different screen resolutions to ensure it looks and works OK for all of your users.

Scrollable content areas with CSS

Scrollable content areas in CSS are often used to provide a lot of information on a single page that can be viewed at the user's convenience. Typically the content in a scrollable area isn't key to the main content of the page, such as a list of events related to an article. This method allows the content to remain part of the web page, which is better for accessibility, site maintenance, and search engine indexing.

To do this, create a div with a unique class value:

```
<div class="scrollableContent">
  [content...]
</div>
```

Then style it in CSS—the rule provides the div's dimensions and determines how the div's overflow works:

```
.scrollableContent {
  width: 200px;
  height: 200px;
  overflow: auto;
}
```

When `overflow` is set to `auto`, scrollbars appear only when the content is too large for the set dimensions of the `div`. Other available values are `hidden` (display no scrollbars), `scroll` (permanently display both scrollbars), and `visible` (render content outside of the defined box area). Adding some padding, especially at the right side of the scrollable content box, helps improve the area aesthetically, ensuring that content doesn't hug the scrollbar.

```
.scrollableContent {
  width: 200px;
  height: 200px;
  overflow: auto;
  padding: 0 10px 0 0;
}
```

Note that by also using server-side includes (PHP in this example), you can even make scrollable content separate from the main web page, thereby emulating an iframe, without resorting to using frames at all.

```
<div class="scrollableContent">
  <?php @include $_SERVER['DOCUMENT_ROOT'] .
    "/include/document-name.php"; ?>
</div>
```

> *Note: Inline frames (iframes) are the only type of frame allowed in HTML5. Iframes allow you to include content from external sources into your web page. You can find more information about iframes in Appendix A.*

In this code block, a PHP page called document-name.php is being included into the scrollableContent div. This implementation is a simple example and should not be attempted without knowledge of PHP.

Another more accessible option than using `iframe` elements is to use the `object` element to embed an external HTML document within a region of the page; when combined with the scrolling `div` method shown in this section, it pretty much provides all the benefits of an iframe with very few of the drawbacks (the content is on the page, unlike with frames and iframes—their content remains external).

The following code block shows how an `object` element can be added to the page. Note the alternate content within the `object` element, displayed if the browser cannot show the `object`. This can be used to directly link to the file in the `data` attribute.

```
<object data="a-file.html" type="text/html">
  <p>[alternate content]</p>
</object>
```

Like other elements, the `object` element can be styled using CSS, although Internet Explorer adds a border, so you need to overwrite existing border settings using conditional comments (see Chapter 9 for more on those) to prevent a double border. Also, if the content is too large for the `object` dimensions, it will scroll in whatever direction is needed, unless you explicitly set `overflow` to `hidden`.

Fluid grid layouts

Fluid grid layout is designing in proportions instead of fixed pixels and arbitrary percentages. This allows your layout to look right when crammed onto a tiny mobile screen since all the sections of your layout are in proportion with each other. A fluid grid layout can be implemented by using div layers percentages and some simple math. In 2009 Ethan Marcotte introduced "Fluid Grids" on A List Apart (www.alistapart.com/articles/fluidgrids/). Fluid grids center around a simple formula for converting pixels to percentages:

(target / context) x 100 = result

How does it work?

1. Pick a section of your design and measure its width. This is your target.

2. Take the target's measurement and divide it by its parent (the context).

3. Multiple that by 100, and you get your result (round to two decimal places).

4. You now have a percentage that you can drop into your style sheets.

For example, you have a site that has a max width of 960 pixels, and it contains a sidebar of 300 pixels:

(300/960) x 100 = 31.25%

The result is that columns don't have a fixed width: they can very based on the resolution of the screen or the resolution of the screen. Fluid grid layouts are an important part of creating a responsive design.

Introduction to fluid grid layouts	
Required files	Files from fluid-grids in the chapter 7 folder
What you'll learn	How to use everything you've learned so far to great a fluid grid layout
Completed files	fluid-grids in the chapter 7 folder

Examine the files. The fluid grid layout markup takes elements of everything you've learned so far to create an advanced layout. The wrapper div is a full width container div that allows layouts to span the full width of the browser. It has 20px padding applied to the left and right to keep the content away from the edges. Like a true grid, a row is a row of columns. It centers them and defines a maximum width. This grid layout is made up of 12 columns and can have any number of columns in a row that add up to 12. In this example, we have four threecols, but we could easily have two threecols and a sixcol or any combination that adds up to 12.

```
<div class="wrapper">
    <div class="row">
        <div class="twelverow">
            [content]
        </div>
    </div>
    <div class="row">
        <div class="threecol">
            [content]
        </div>
        <div class="threecol">
            [content]
        </div>
        <div class="threecol">
            [content]
        </div>
        <div class="threecol">
            [content]
        </div>
    </div>
</div>
```

The maximum width I have chosen for this layout is the popular 960 pixels. All the columns from one to twelve have had their widths calculated using the previous formula.

Let's start by finding the width of one column: 960 / 12 = 80. I've chosen to have 20px-wide gutters, so let's subtract 20 pixels from our total. We have 60. Now using our formula, you can get the width of column one: (60 / 960) * 100 = 6.25%. For the rest of the columns, we multiply by our original width of 80 pixels, subtract 20 pixels for our gutters, and use our formula to get the rest of the widths (remember to round to two decimal places).

```
.onecol{ width: 6.25%; }
.twocol( width: 14.58%; }
.threecol{ width: 22.91%; }
.fourcol{ width: 31.25%; }
```

As you can see from the following screenshot, building a fluid grid is easy once you know the formula. The rest of this exercise uses the standard floats and clear fixes explained earlier in this chapter.

Responsive Web Design

Over the years designers have come up with many solutions that use and combine fixed and fluid layouts. In an article entitled "Responsive Web Design" published on A List Apart (www.alistapart.com/articles/responsive-web-design/), Ethan Marcotte takes this a step further, by uniting the existing technologies of fluid grids, flexible images, and media queries into a new way of approaching web design. This is a very different way of designing websites, and it represents the future.

Users are browsing your website using their mobile phone, tablet, netbook, or desktop browser. Are you going to create a new design for each new device? Layouts need to be adaptive. They need to automatically adjust to fit not only the browser size but the platform and orientation of the device as well.

A responsive design typically consists of a mix of fluid and flexible grid layouts, and the use of CSS media queries that can reformat your web page and markup to meet the needs of your users.

CSS media queries are used to target styles to specific capabilities, applying different styles based on the capabilities that match your query. They can test for capabilities such as width, height, max-width, max-height, device-height, orientation, aspect ratio, and more. Tests can be combined using operators (AND and NOT) to allow for flexible targeting.

The wide range of devices used to browse your website can generate extreme size changes that may call for an altogether layout change, through either a separate style sheet or CSS media queries. If you have structured your CSS correctly, most of your styles can remain the same through inheritance.

Typically a responsive layout would have a main style sheet, which will define the structure, colors, typography, and backgrounds of your website. Other style sheets would then be defined that would adopt all the styles from the main style sheet and then redefine the style for new dimensions. A good set of target pixel widths that should serve as starting points is 320, 480, 600, 768, 900, and 1200. When deciding which resolutions to target the decision is ultimately up to you as the designer. The more resolutions you target, the more time it will take to complete your design.

As you can see from the following screenshots, Smashing Magazine (www.smashingmagazine.com) and Media Queries (http://mediaqueri.es) are great examples of a responsive layout.

 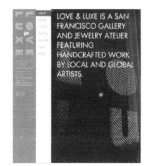 

Introduction to Responsive Design

Required files   Files from responsive-starting-point in the chapter 7 folder

What you'll learn   How to use make a fluid grid responsive

Completed files   responsive-complete in the chapter 7 folder

Let's take our fluid grid a step further and make it responsive.

1. Open responsive-starting-point.css, and add the following to the bottom:

```
@media          (max-width:          600px)          {}
@media          (max-width:          767px)          {}
```

These are the different media queries that allow you to change the layout of your design to better fit your targeted screen size. You can choose as many as you like, but for this example I have picked two to show you the power of responsive design.

2. Since the media styles will be inherited from 767, we will change the width of the wrapper to auto so that it can scale down with the browser size. Add the following between the brackets of the media query targeting 767 pixels.

```
.wrapper{
    width:                                                              auto;
}
```

3. As the browser scales down, let's stop floating the columns. Add this to the 767 media query:

```
.row                          >                          [class*="col"]{
    float:                                                         none;
    display:                                                      block;
    width:                                                         auto;
    margin:0;
}
```

This targets and applies the style to all elements that contain the string "col" in its class.

4. Finally, let's adjust the callout section font size for the 600-pixel media query.

```
.row.callout                          h2                                  {
    font-size:                                                      32px;
}
.row.callout                          p                                   {
    font-size:                                                      16px;
    line-height:                                                    18px;
    margin-top:                                                      5px;
}
```

Sed quis velit.

Nulla facilisi. Nulla libero. Vivamus pharetra
posuere sapien.

Lorem ipsum dolor sit amet, consectetuer adipiscing elit.
Morbi commodo, ipsum sed pharetra gravida, orci
magna rhoncus neque, id pulvinar odio lorem non turpis.
Nullam sit amet enim. Suspendisse id velit vitae ligula
volutpat condimentum. Aliquam erat volutpat.

As you have seen throughout this chapter, even the most complex layout can be broken down to simple layout techniques combined to create powerful responsive designs.

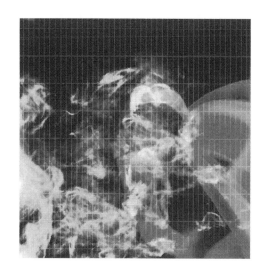

Chapter 8

Getting User Feedback

In this chapter:

- Creating forms and adding fields and controls

- Styling forms in CSS

- Configuring a mailform CGI script

- Sending forms using PHP

- Creating a layout for a user feedback page

- Creating an online business card using microformats

Introducing user feedback

One of the main reasons the Web has revolutionized working life and communications is its immediacy. Unlike printed media, websites can be continually updated at relatively minimal cost and also be available worldwide on a 24/7 basis. However, communication isn't one-way, and the Web makes it very easy to enable site users to offer feedback.

Using mailto: URLs

One of the most common methods of providing immediate user feedback is by using `mailto:` URLs within anchor tags. Instead of the anchor tag's value being a file name or URL, it begins with `mailto:` and is immediately followed by the recipient e-mail address.

```
<a href="mailto:someone@your.domain">Click to email!</a>
```

It's possible to take this technique further. You can define multiple recipients by using a comma-separated list; in addition, by placing a question mark immediately after the final recipient address, you can add further parameters, such as a subject and recipients to carbon copy (`cc`) and blind carbon copy (`bcc`). If using more than one parameter, you must separate them with encoded ampersands (`&amp;`). Note that spaces within the subject should also be encoded (as `%20`).

```
<a href="mailto:someone@your.domain,someoneelse@your.domain?subject=
Í Contact%20from%20website&amp;cc=bigboss@your.domain">Click
  to email!</a>
```

> *Note: There should be no spaces in a mailto: value. Therefore, don't place spaces before or after colons, commas, or the ? and = symbols.*

Although this may sound great, this system has several problems. First, e-mail addresses online are often harvested by spambots. Second, a `mailto:` link relies on the user having a preconfigured e-mail client ready to go—something that people working on college and library machines most likely won't have. Third, not all browsers support the range of options explained earlier.

A way to combat the spambots is presented in the next section. For the second issue (the `mailto:` link's reliance on a preconfigured mail client), we recommend using forms for any complex website feedback, which we will come to later in this chapter. For the third issue (browser support for the more advanced `mailto:` options), we recommend just keeping things simple. Place your e-mail address online as a `mailto:`, and enable the user to fill in any other details, such common as the subject line.

crambling addresses

In our experience, having an e-mail address online for just a few days is enough to start receiving regular spam. A workaround is to encrypt e-mail addresses using a bulletproof concoction of JavaScript. The Enkoder form from Hivelogic is a neat way of going about this and produces decent results.

This online form at www.hivelogic.com/enkoder/form enables you to create a `mailto:` link that's composed of complex JavaScript. Although in time spambots will likely break this code, as they have with simpler encoders, it's the best example we've seen, and the results we've had with it have been good. Beware, though, that any users with JavaScript disabled won't see the address, so ensure that you cater to them by including some other means of contacting the site owner.

> *Enkoder is also available as a plug-in for Ruby on Rails.*

Working with forms

In this section, we'll work through how to create a form and add controls. We'll also look at how to improve form accessibility by using the `tabindex` attribute and the `label`, `fieldset`, and `legend` elements.

As suggested earlier in the chapter, the best way of getting user feedback is through an online form that the user fills in and submits. Fields are configured by the designer, enabling the site owner to receive specific information. However, don't go overboard: provide users with a massive, sprawling online form, and they will most likely not bother filling it in and will go elsewhere.

Similarly, although you can use JavaScript to make certain form fields required, we're not fans of this technique, because it annoys users. Some sites go overboard on this, "forcing" users to input a whole bunch of details, some of which may simply not be applicable to the user. In such cases, users will likely either go elsewhere or insert fake data, which helps no one.

So, keep things simple and use the fewest fields possible. In the vast majority of cases, you should be able to simply create name, e-mail address, and phone number fields, as well as include a text area that enables users to input their query.

reating a form

Form controls are housed within a `form` element, whose attributes also determine the location of the script used to parse it (see the "Sending feedback" section later in the chapter). Other attributes define the encoding type used and the method by which the browser sends the form's data to the server. A typical start tag for a form therefore looks like this:

```
<form action="http://www.yourdomain.com/cgi-bin/FormMail.cgi"
  method="post">
```

> *The preceding form start tag includes attributes that point at a CGI script, but alternative methods of sending forms exist, including PHP, ASP, and ColdFusion. Check with your hosting company about the methods available for sending forms, and use the technology supported by your ISP.*

Adding controls

Some form controls are added using the input element. The type attribute declares what kind of control the element is going to be. The most common values are text, which produces a single-line text input field; checkbox and radio, which are used for multiple-choice options; and submit, which is used for the all-important **Submit** button.

Other useful elements include select, option, and optgroup, used for creating pop-up lists, and textarea, which provides a means for the user to offer a multiple-line response (this is commonly used in online forms for a question area). The basic HTML for a form may therefore look like the following, producing the page depicted in the following screen grab.

```html
<form action="http://www.yourdomain.com/cgi-bin/FormMail.cgi"
  method="post">
  <p><strong>Name</strong><br />
  <input type="text" name="realname" size="30" /></p>
  <p><strong>Email address</strong><br />
  <input type="text" name="email" size="30" /></p>
  <p><strong>Telephone</strong><br />
  <input type="text" name="phone" size="30" /></p>
  <p><strong>Are you a Web designer?</strong><br />
  <input type="radio" name="designer" value="yes" />Yes |
    <input type="radio" name="designer" value="no" />No</p>
  <p>What platform do you favor?<br />
  <select name="platform">
    <option selected="selected">Windows</option>
    <option>Mac</option>
    <option>Linux</option>
    <option>Other</option>
  </select></p>
  <p><strong>Message</strong><br />
  <textarea name="message" rows="5" cols="30"></textarea></p>
  <p><input type="submit" name="SUBMIT" value="SUBMIT" /></p>
</form>
```

The bulk of the HTML is pretty straightforward. In each case, the name attribute value labels the control, meaning that you end up with the likes of Telephone: 555 555 555 in your form results, rather than just a bunch of answers. For multiple-option controls (check boxes and radio buttons), this attribute is identical, and an individual value attribute is set in each start tag.

By default, controls of this type—along with the select list—are set to off (that is, no values selected), but you can define a default option. I've done this for the select list by setting selected="selected" on the Windows option. You'd do the same on a radio button to select it by default, and with a check box you'd set checked="checked".

Some of the attributes define the appearance of controls: the input element's size attribute sets a character width for the fields, while the textarea's rows and cols attributes set the number of rows and columns, again in terms of characters. It's also worth noting that any content within the textarea element is displayed, so if you want it to start totally blank, you must ensure that there's nothing—not even whitespace—between the start and end tags. (Some applications that reformat your code, and some website editors, place whitespace here, which some browsers subsequently use as the default value/content of the textarea. This results in the textarea's content being partially filled with spaces, and anyone trying to use it may then find their cursor's initial entry point partway down the text area, which can be off-putting.)

Longtime web users may have noticed the omission of a **Reset** button in this example. This button used to be common online, enabling the user to reset a form to its default state, removing any content they've added. However, I've never really seen the point in having it there, especially seeing as it's easy to click by mistake, resulting in the user having to fill in the form again, which is why it's absent from the examples in this chapter. However, if you want to add such a button, you can do so by using the following code:

311

```
<input type="reset" name="RESET" value="RESET" />
```

> Note: A full list of controls is available in Appendix A.

Improving form accessibility

Although there's an on-screen visual relationship between form label text and the controls, they're not associated in any other way. This sometimes makes forms tricky to use for those people using screen readers and other assistive devices. Also, by default, the Tab key cycles through various web page elements in order, rather than jumping to the first form field (and continuing through the remainder of the form before moving elsewhere). Both of these issues are dealt with in this section.

The label, fieldset, and legend elements

The label element enables you to define relationships between the text labeling a form control and the form control itself. In the following example, the Name text is enclosed in a label element with the for attribute value of realname. This corresponds to the name and id values of the form field associated with this text.

```
<p><label for="realname">Name</label><br />
<input type="text" name="realname" id="realname" size="30" /></p>
```

Most browsers don't amend the content's visual display when it's nested within a label element, although you can style the label in CSS. However, most apply an important accessibility benefit: if you click the label, it gives focus to the corresponding form control (in other words, it selects the form control related to the label). Note that the id attribute—absent from the form example earlier in the chapter—is required for this. If it's absent, clicking the text within the label element won't cause the browser to do anything.

The fieldset element enables you to group a set of related form controls to which you apply a label via the legend element.

```
<fieldset>
  <legend>Personal information</legend>
  <p><label for="realname">Name</label><br />
  <input type="text" id="realname" name="realname" size="30" /></p>
  <p><label for="email">Email address</label><br />
  <input type="text" id="email" name="email" size="30" /></p>
  <p><label for="phone">Telephone</label><br />
  <input type="text" id="phone" name="phone" size="30" /></p>
</fieldset>
```

As you can see from the previous screenshot, these elements combine to surround the relevant form fields and labels with a border and provide the group with an explanatory title.

> *Note that each browser styles forms and controls differently. Therefore, be sure to test your forms in a wide range of browsers and don't be too concerned with trying to make things look exactly the same in each browser.*

dding tabindex attributes

The `tabindex` attribute was first mentioned in Chapter 5 (in the "Using accesskey and tabindex" section). For forms, it's used to define the page's element tab order, and its value can be set as anything from 0 to 32767. Because the `tabindex` values needn't be sequential, it's advisable to set them in increments of ten, enabling you to insert others later, without having to rework every value on the page. With that in mind, you could set `tabindex="10"` on the `realname` field, `tabindex="20"` on the `email` field, and `tabindex="30"` on the `phone` field (these field names are based on their `id`/`name` values from the previous example). Assuming no other `tabindex` attributes with lower values are elsewhere on the page, the `realname` field becomes the first element highlighted when the Tab key is pressed, and then the cycle continues (in order) with the `email` and `phone` fields.

> *Note: The reason for starting with 10 rather than 1 is because if you ignore the last digit, the tabindex values become standard integers, starting with 1. In other words, remove the final digits from 10, 20, and 30, and you end up with 1, 2, and 3. This makes it easier to keep track of the tabindex order.*

Note that whenever using `tabindex`, you run the risk of hijacking the mouse cursor, meaning that instead of the Tab key moving the user from the first form field to the second, it might end up highlighting something totally different, elsewhere on the page. What's logical to some people in terms of tab order may not be to others, so always ensure you test your websites thoroughly, responding to feedback. Generally, it makes sense to use the value only for form fields, and then with plenty of care.

Client-side form validation

With HTML5, forms can be annotated in such a way that the browser will check the user's input before the form is submitted. The server still has to verify the input is valid, but this technique allows the user to avoid the wait incurred by having the server be the sole checker of the user's input.

The simplest annotation is the `required` attribute, which can be specified on input elements to indicate that the form is not to be submitted with an empty value. By adding this attribute to the name and email fields, we allow the user agent to notify the user when the user submits the form without filling in those fields:

```
<fieldset>
  <legend>Personal information</legend>
  <p><label for="realname">Name</label><br />
  <input type="text" id="realname" name="realname" size="30" required /></p>
  <p><label for="email">Email address</label><br />
  <input type="text" id="email" name="email" size="30" required /></p>
  <p><label for="phone">Telephone</label><br />
  <input type="text" id="phone" name="phone" size="30" /></p>
</fieldset>
```

It is also possible to limit the length of the input, using the `maxlength` attribute. By adding this to the realname element, we can limit the size of names to 25 characters:

```
<fieldset>
  <legend>Personal information</legend>
  <p><label for="realname">Name</label><br />
  <input type="text" id="realname" name="realname" size="30" required maxlength="25" /></p>
  <p><label for="email">Email address</label><br />
  <input type="text" id="email" name="email" size="30" required /></p>
  <p><label for="phone">Telephone</label><br />
  <input type="text" id="phone" name="phone" size="30" /></p>
</fieldset>
```

Form validation is hard and error prone, so having it performed natively by the browsers and being RFC-compliant in cases like email, for example, is very helpful. Some forms of validation are notoriously hard to perform correctly even for the browsers. For example, Chrome validates the string foo@bar as a correct email address.

Some mobile devices that don't have a physical keyboard can recognize several of the new HTML5 input types and dynamically change the on-screen keyboard to optimize for that kind of input. For example, when you use an iPhone and focus an input type="email" element, you get an on-screen keyboard that contains a smaller-than-usual spacebar, plus dedicated keys for the @ and. characters. Similarly, for input type="number", you get a number scroller, and so on.

Default validation alerts are ugly, but in the future it will be easy to add CSS style to them. Chrome and Safari have recently added support for pseudoselectors like ::-webkit-validation-bubble{}, ::-webkit-validation-bubble-top-outer-arrow{}, ::-webkit-validation-bubble-top-inner-arrow{}, and ::-webkit-validation-bubble-message{}. At the time of this writing, Firefox has no way to style the error messages. Similarly, you might want to change the text of the error messages. Firefox has support for the attribute x-mozerrormessage, which enables you to change the text of the error message. The same can be accomplished in Chrome using CSS and the -webkit-validation-bubble-message.

ate, time, and number formats

The time, date, and number formats used in HTML and in form submissions, are based on the ISO 8601 standard for computer-readable date and time formats, and are intended to be computer-readable and consistent irrespective of the user's locale. Dates, for instance, are always written in the format "YYYY-MM-DD", as in "2012-03-18". Users are not expected to ever see this format.

The time, date, or number given by the page in the wire format is then translated to the user's preferred presentation (for example, locale), before being displayed to the user. Similarly, after the user inputs a time, date, or number using their preferred format, the user agent converts it to the wire format before putting it in the DOM or submitting it. This allows scripts in pages and on servers to process times, dates, and numbers in a consistent manner without needing to support dozens of different formats, while still supporting the users' needs.

- When an input element's type attribute is datetime, it represents a control for setting the element's value to a string representing a specific global date and time. User agents may display the date and time in whatever time zone is appropriate for the user. The min and max attributes, if specified, must have a value that is a valid date and time string. The step attribute is expressed in seconds. The step scale factor is 1000 (milliseconds), and the default step is 60 seconds. It's similar to datetime-local, which represents a local date and time, with no time-zone offset information.

- When an input element's type attribute is in date, it represents a control for setting the element's value to a string representing a specific date. The min and max attributes, if specified, must have a value that is a valid date string. Here the step attribute is expressed in days. The step scale factor is 86,400,000 (days to milliseconds), and the default step is 1 day.

- When an input element's type attribute is month, it represents a control for setting the element's value to a string representing a specific month. The min and max attributes, if specified, must have a value that is a valid month string. The step attribute is expressed in months, it has a scale factor of 1, and the default step is 1 month.

- When an input element's type attribute is week, it represents a control for setting the element's value to a string representing a specific week. The min and max attributes, if specified, must have a value that is a valid week string. The step attribute is expressed in weeks. The step scale factor is 604,800,000 (weeks to milliseconds); the default step is 1 week.

When an input element's type attribute is time, it represents a control for setting the element's value to a string representing a specific time. The min and max attributes, if specified, must have a value that is a valid time string. Here the step attribute is expressed in seconds and has a scale factor of 1000 (seconds to milliseconds), and the default step is 60 seconds.

More HTML5 input formats

To make developers' lives easier, HTML5 offers a set of the most common input field types that should provide validation, although they're still not common in browsers:

type=url: For editing a single absolute URL given in the element's value

type=email: For editing one or multiple e-mail address given in the element's value

type=password: Represents a one line plain text edit control, which the browser obscures

type=number: For setting the element's value to a string representing a (floating-point) number

type=range: For setting the element's value to a string representing a number, when the exact value is not important

type=color: For setting the element's value to a string representing a simple color

More HTML5 form elements

Here are some other HTML5 elements that can be used to create powerful forms and improve the user experience:

Element	Usage	Details
button	A button	The type attribute controls the behavior of the button when it is activated, and its value can be "submit," "reset," or "button" (which does nothing).
select	A control for selecting amongst a set of options	The multiple attribute is a boolean attribute. If the attribute is present, then the select element represents a control for selecting zero or more options from the list of options. The size attribute gives the number of options to show to the user. The required attribute is a boolean attribute. When specified, the user will be required to select a value before submitting the form.
datalist	A set of option elements for predefined options for other controls	The datalist element can be hooked up to an input element using the list attribute on the input element.
optgroup	A group of option elements with a common label	When showing option elements in select elements, browsers show the option elements of such groups as being related to each other and separate from other option elements.

option	A option in a select element or as part of a list in a datalist element	An option element can be a select element's placeholder label option. A placeholder label option does not represent an actual option but instead represents a label for the select control.
textarea	A multiline plain-text edit	The readonly attribute is a boolean attribute used to control whether the text is editable.
keygen	A key/pair generator control	When the control's form is submitted, the private key is stored in the local keystore, and the public key is packaged and sent to the server.

SS styling and layout for forms

Earlier, we covered how to lay out a form using paragraphs and line breaks. In this section, you'll see how tables and CSS can also be used to produce a more advanced layout.

dding styles to forms

Form fields can be styled, enabling you to get away from the rather clunky default look offered by most browsers. Although the default appearance isn't very attractive, it does make obvious which elements are fields and which are buttons. Therefore, if you choose to style forms in CSS, ensure that the elements are still easy to make out.

A simple, elegant style to apply to text input fields and text areas is as follows:

```
.formField {
  border: 1px solid #333333;
  background-color: #dddddd;
  padding: 2px;
}
```

In HTML, you need to add the usual class attribute to apply this rule to the relevant element(s):

```
<input class="formField" tabindex="11" type="text" id="realname"
• name="realname" size="30" />
```

This replaces the default 3D border with a solid, dark gray border, and it also sets the background color as a light gray, thereby drawing attention to the form input fields. Note that browsers that support :hover and :focus on more than just anchors can have these states styled with different backgrounds, thereby providing further prompts. For example, upon focusing a form field, you might change its background color, making it more obvious that it's the field in focus.

Because the border in the previous code is defined using a class, it can be applied to multiple elements. The reason we don't use a tag selector and apply this style to all input fields is that radio buttons and check boxes look terrible with rectangular borders around them. However, applying this style to the select element can work well.

Note that the background color in this example is designed to contrast slightly with the page's background color but still provide plenty of contrast with any text typed into the form fields; as always, pick your colors carefully when working with form styles.

The default **Submit** button style can be amended in a similar fashion, and padding can also be applied to it. This is usually a good idea because it enables the button to stand out and draws attention to the text within.

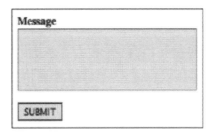

Should you desire a more styled **Submit** button, you can instead use an image:

```
<input type ="image" src="submit.gif" height="20" width="100"
  alt="Submit form" />
```

Along with the fields and controls, it's also possible to style the elements added in the previous section "The label, fieldset, and legend elements." The fieldset rule applies a 1-pixel dashed line around the elements grouped by the fieldset element, along with adding some padding and a bottom margin. The legend rule amends the legend element's font and the padding around it and sets the text to uppercase; it also adds a background color so that the dotted line of the fieldset won't be shown behind the legend text in Internet Explorer. Note that not all browsers treat margins on legend elements in the same way, so if you add a margin value, be sure to thoroughly test your page. The screenshot that follows also includes the styles included in the default CSS document from the basic-boilerplates folder.

```
fieldset {
  border: 1px dashed #555555;
  padding: 10px;
  margin-bottom: 10px;
}
```

```
legend {
  padding: 0 10px;
  font-family: Arial, Helvetica, sans-serif;
  color: #000000;
  background: #ffffff;
  text-transform: uppercase;
}
```

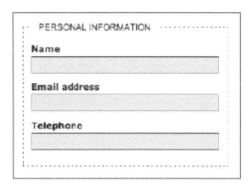

A final style point worth bearing in mind is that you can define styles for the form itself. This can be useful for positioning purposes (for example, controlling the form's width and its bottom margin); the width setting can prove handy, since the fieldset border stretches to the entire window width, which looks very odd if the form labels and controls take up only a small area of the browser window. Reducing the form's width to specifically defined dimensions enables you to get around this. Alternatively, you can set a fixed width on the fieldset itself (or float it, enabling you to display fieldsets side by side).

You can also color the form's (or fieldset's) background in addition to or instead of the input fields, thereby making the entire form prominent. This is a device I've used on various versions of the Snub Communications website's contacts page, as shown in the following screenshot.

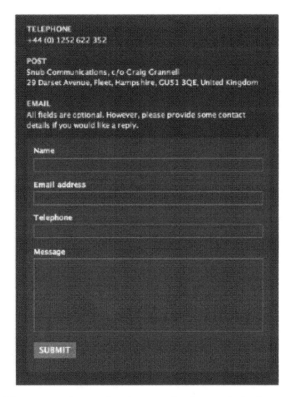

Regardless of the form styles you end up using, be sure to rigorously test across browsers, because the display of form elements is not consistent. Some variations are relatively minor—you'll find that defining values for font sizes, padding, and borders for input fields doesn't always result in fields of the same height and that text fields and `Submit` buttons don't always align. A more dramatic difference is seen in versions of Safari prior to 3.0, which ignore many CSS properties for forms, instead using the Mac OS X "Aqua" look and feel—see the following screenshot for how the Snub Communications form looks in that browser. Form functionality is not affected by this, but layouts can be.

dvanced form layout with CSS

A common way of laying out forms is to use a table to line up the labels and form controls, although with the output being nontabular in nature, this method is not recommended (CSS should be used for presentation, including positioning elements on a web page); it's provided here to show a (partial) table layout that can be replicated in CSS. For our first three fields, a table-based form may have something like this:

```
<fieldset>
  <legend>Personal information</legend>
  <table class="formTable" cellpadding="0" cellspacing="0" border="0"
    summary="A contact details form.">
    <tr>
      <th scope="row">
      <label for="realname">Name</label></th>
      <td><input class="formField" type="text" id="realname"
      name="realname" size="30" /></td>
    </tr>
    <tr>
      <th scope="row"><label for="email">Email address</label></th>
      <td><input class="formField" type="text" id="email" name="email"
        size="30" /></td>
    </tr>
    <tr>
      <th scope="row"><label for="phone">Telephone</label></th>
      <td><input class="formField" type="text" id="phone" name="phone"
        size="30" /></td>
    </tr>
  </table>
        </fieldset>
```

Because a `class` value was added to the table, the contextual selector `.formTable th` can be used as the selector for styling the form labels, defining the `text-align` property, along with other CSS properties such as `font-weight`. Applying a `padding-right` value to these cells also produces a gap to the right of the label cells. Another contextual selector, `.formTable td`, can then be used to style the cells—for example, to add padding at the bottom of each cell. The image below shows these styles applied to the various elements in the previous code block, along with the styles shown in the "Adding styles to forms" section.

```
.formTable td {
  padding: 0 0 5px 0;
}
.formTable th {
  padding-right: 10px;
  text-align: right;
  font-weight: bold;
}
```

> Note that the *fieldset* and *legend* elements must surround the table containing the relevant fields. If using these elements, you may need multiple tables for your form.

Although forms are not tabular in nature, using a table to create a form can result in a pleasing visual appearance, with the labels right-aligned and placed next to their associated labels. This kind of layout can be replicated using CSS, via a structure built from `divs` to replace the table rows. This method retains semantic integrity via the semantic relationship created by the `label` and associated field's `id`. Using CSS for form layout also brings with it the benefit of being able to rapidly restyle and move form components.

> This isn't a complete form—it's just a guide to using this method. This example lacks, for instance, a *Submit* button and many of the controls in the example from earlier in the chapter.

```
<form action="http://www.yourdomain.com/cgi-bin/FormMail.cgi"
  method="post">
  <fieldset>
    <legend>Personal information</legend>
    <div class="row clearFix">
      <label for="realname">Name</label> <input class="formField"
        type="text" id="realname" name="realname" size="30" />
    </div>
    <div class="row clearFix ">
      <label for="email">Email address</label> <input class="formField"
        type="text" id="email" name="email" size="30" />
    </div>
    <div class="row clearFix ">
      <label for="phone">Telephone</label> <input class="formField"
        type="text" id="phone" name="phone" size="30" />
    </div>
  </fieldset>
```

```
</form>
```

Note the use of the clearing device, the clearFix class value, as outlined in Chapter 7's "Placing columns within wrappers and clearing floated content" section.

Various styles are then defined in CSS. The `form` itself has its width restricted, and `label` elements are floated left, the text within aligned right, and the `font-weight` property set to `bold`. The `width` setting is large enough to contain the largest of the text labels.

```
form {
  width: 350px;
}
label {
  float: left;
  text-align: right;
  font-weight: bold;
  width: 95px;
}
```

The form controls—the `input` elements—are floated right. Because only `input` elements within the `div` rows should be floated (rather than all of the `input` elements on the page), the contextual selector `.row input` is used. (The containing `div`s have a `class` value of `row`.) The `width` setting is designed to provide a gap between the labels and input elements.

```
.row input{
  float: right;
  width: 220px;
}
```

Finally, to make a gap between the rows, a `.row` class is added and given a `margin-bottom` value.

```
.row {
  margin-bottom: 5px;
}
```

The method works fine in all browsers except Internet Explorer, which doesn't apply `margin-bottom` correctly. However, the slightly different layout in Internet Explorer can largely be fixed by adding the following in a style sheet attached via an IE-specific conditional comment:

```
.row {
  clear: both;
  margin-top: 5px;
}
```

Alternatively, add the following:

```
.clearFix {
  display: inline-block;
}
```

Example forms for the sections in this chapter are available in the chapter 8 folder of the download files.

Sending feedback

In this section, you'll check out how to send form data using a CGI script and PHP. Once users submit information, it needs to go somewhere and have a method of getting there. Several techniques are available for parsing forms, but we're first going to cover using a server-side CGI script. Essentially, this script collects the information submitted, formats it, and delivers it to the addresses you configure within the script.

FormMail, available from Matt's Script Archive (www.scriptarchive.com), is probably the most common, and a number of web hosts preconfigure this script in their web space packages. However, FormMail does have flaws, and it hasn't kept up with current technology. A better script is nms FormMail (available from http://nms-cgi.sourceforge.net/ and described next)—it emulates the behavior of FormMail but takes a more modern and bug-free approach.

Configuring nms FormMail

The thought of editing and configuring scripts gives some designers the willies, but nms FormMail takes only a couple of minutes to get up and running. First, you need to add some more input elements to your web page, after the form start tag:

```
<input type="hidden" name="subject" value="Contact form from
  website" />
<input type="hidden" name="redirect"
  value="http://www.yourdomain.com/contact-thanks.html" />
```

Note that some browsers display an outline where hidden fields are if input elements are set to display as block. In such cases, you can apply a class value of hidden to the relevant fields, with display set to none.

Obviously, the values in the preceding elements need changing for your site. The subject value can be whatever you like—just make it obvious, so you or your clients can use an e-mail package to filter website form responses efficiently.

The redirect value isn't required, but it's good to provide positive feedback to users, not only to confirm that their form has been sent but also to communicate that their query will be dealt with as soon as possible. Many "thank you" pages online tend to look a little barren, with a single paragraph of text. That's why we tend to make this page a duplicate of our standard contact page but with the confirmation paragraph above the form. The script itself needs only minimal editing. Because CGI scripts tend to break with slight errors, I highly recommend editing them in a text editor that doesn't affect document formatting, such as HTML-Kit for Windows (www.chami.com) or BBEdit for Mac (www.barebones.com).

The first line of the script defines the location of Perl on your web host's server. Your hosting company can provide this, so you can amend the path accordingly.

```
#!/usr/bin/perl -wT
```

Elsewhere, you only need to edit some values in the user configuration section. The $mailprog value defines the location of the sendmail binary on your web host's server. You can find this out from your web host's system admin.

```
$mailprog = '/usr/lib/sendmail -oi -t';
```

The $postmaster value is the address that receives bounced messages if e-mails cannot be delivered. It should be a different address from that of the intended recipient.

```
$postmaster =  'someone@your.domain';
```

The @referers value lists IP addresses or domain names that can access this script, thereby stopping just anyone from using your script and your server resources. For instance, the Snub Communications mail form has snubcommunications.com and the site's IP address for this value (as a space-delimited list). If you use localhost, that enables local testing, if you have the relevant software set up on your PC.

```
@referers = qw(dave.org.uk 209.207.222.64 localhost);
```

The @allow_mail_to value contains the addresses to which form results can be sent, again as a space-delimited list. If you include just a domain here, then any address on that domain is valid as a recipient. If you're using only one address, set the $max_recipients value to 1 to increase security.

```
@allow_mail_to = qw(you@your.domain some.one.else@your.domain
  localhost);
```

ultiple recipients

You can also use the script to e-mail multiple recipients. To do so, an additional hidden input element is needed in the HTML:

```
<input type="hidden" name="recipient" value="emailgroup" />
```

And in the script itself, two lines are changed. The @allow_mail_to value is removed, because it's catered for by the newly amended %recipient_alias. Both are shown here:

```
@allow_mail_to = ();
%recipient_alias = ('emailgroup  =>
  'your-name@your.domain,your-name@somewhere-else.domain');
```

Should a script be used for multiple groups of recipients, you need a unique value for each in the HTML and to amend the %recipient_alias value accordingly:

```
%recipient_alias = ('emailgroup1'  => 'your-name@your.domain,your-name@
 somewhere-else.domain', 'emailgroup2'  => 'foo@your.domain');
```

Script server permissions

Upload the script to your site's cgi-bin. Once there, the script's permissions must be set. Exactly how this is achieved depends on what FTP client you're using. Some enable you to right-click and "get info," while others have a permissions or CHMOD command buried among their menus. Consult your documentation and find out which your client has. If you can, use the CHMOD command to set the octal numbers for the script (thereby altering the file permissions) to 755. If you have to manually set permissions, do so as per the screenshot to the right. Check that the script's file extension matches that in your form element's action attribute (.pl or .cgi—the latter is usually preferred by servers). Also, you might want to amend your script's name (and update the form element's action value accordingly), in an attempt to outfox automated spammers. (This explains the rather odd name of the script in the screenshot below.)

Not all hosts require you to place CGI scripts in a cgi-bin directory: some prefer a cgi

directory, and some enable you to place such scripts anywhere on the server. If in doubt, talk to your web host's support people about the specific requirements for your account. Also note that not all hosts enable CGI support, so if you want to use such a script, check that it's possible with your host before you spend a load of time trying to set something up that's not permitted and won't run anyway.

Sending form data using PHP

If your hosting company offers support for PHP, the most widely used server-side technology, there is no need to install a CGI script such as FormMail. Everything can be done with PHP's built-in mail() function. As a minimum, the function requires the following three pieces of information:

- The address(es) the mail is being sent to

- The subject line

- The message itself

An optional fourth argument to mail() permits you to send additional information in the e-mail headers, such as from, cc, and bcc addresses, and to specify a particular character encoding (if, for instance, you need to include accented characters or an Asian language in the e-mail). Unfortunately, spammers frequently exploit this ability to add extra e-mail headers, so you need to check the form input for suspicious content and stop the e-mail from being sent if any is found. A script written by fellow friends of

ED author David Powers does this for you automatically. Even if you have no experience working with PHP, the following instructions should have you up and running quickly:

1. Copy process_mail.inc.php from the download files to the same folder (directory) as the page containing the form. This is the PHP script that does all the hard work. You don't need to make any changes to it.

2. Save the page containing the form with a PHP extension—for instance, feedback.php. Amend the opening form tag like this:

```
<form action="<?php echo $_SERVER['PHP_SELF']; ?>" method="post">
```

3. At the top of the page, insert the following PHP code block above the DOCTYPE. Although I've warned you elsewhere in the book never to place any content above the DOCTYPE, it's perfectly safe to do so in this case, because the PHP code doesn't produce any HTML output.

```php
<?php
if (array_key_exists('SUBMIT', $_POST)) {
  //mail processing script
  $to = 'me@example.com'; // use your own email address
  $subject = 'Feedback from website';

  // list expected fields
  $expected = array('realname', 'email', 'phone', 'message');
  // set required fields
  $required = array('realname', 'email', 'message');
  $headers = 'From: My website<feedback@example.com>';
  $process = 'process_mail.inc.php';
  if (file_exists($process) && is_readable($process)) {
    include($process);
    }
  else {
    $mailSent = false;
    mail($to, 'Server problem', "$process cannot be read", $headers);
    }
  }
?>
```

4. This script begins by checking whether the PHP $_POST array has been set. This happens only when a user clicks the form's **Submit** button, so this entire block of code will be ignored when the page first loads. It sets the address to which the e-mail is to be sent and the subject line. It then checks that all required fields have been filled in and sends the form input for processing by process_mail.inc.php. If the mail processing file can't be found, the script e-mails an error message to you.

To adapt this script to your own form, you need to change some of the values, as explained in upcoming steps.

> *Note: PHP is case sensitive. Make sure that you use the same combination of uppercase and lowercase in the PHP script as in the name attributes in the form. Also be careful to copy the script exactly. Missing semicolons, commas, or quotes will cause the script to fail and may result in ugly error messages or a blank screen.*

5. Change SUBMIT in the second line of the script to the same value as the name of the form's **Submit** button.

6. Replace me@example.com with the e-mail address that the feedback is to be sent to. Make sure the address is in quotes and that the line ends with a semicolon.

If you want to send the e-mail to multiple addresses, separate them with commas like this:

```
$to= 'me@example.com, him@example.com, her@example.com';
```

7. Replace the content inside the quotes in the following line (Feedback from website) with whatever you want the subject line to say.

8. Next, list the name attributes of each form element as a comma-separated list between the parentheses in the following line:

```
$expected = array('realname', 'email', 'phone', 'message');
```

9. This tells the script what form input you're expecting. This is very important, because it prevents malicious users from trying to pass unexpected—and possibly dangerous—data through your form. Any form field not included in this list will be ignored, so make sure you update the list whenever you add a new field to a form.

Note that the commas go outside the quotes. You can use single or double quotes. It doesn't matter as long as each set of quotes is a matching pair.

10. The next line of code looks very similar:

```
$required = array('realname', 'email', 'message');
```

11. This is used to check whether all required fields have been filled in. You'll notice that I've omitted phone from the list, so the script will treat it as optional. The order of items in the $expected and $required arrays is not important, but it makes maintenance easier if you use the same order as they appear in the form.

12. The next line looks like this:

```
$headers = 'From: My website<feedback@example.com>';
```

13. This sets the e-mail's From: header. Change My website <feedback@example.com> to the name and e-mail address that you want the e-mail to be sent from.

14. There are many additional headers you can add to an e-mail, such as Cc or Bcc. You can also set the encoding to UTF-8 (for messages that require accents or Asian languages). The following example shows how to add a cc address and UTF-8 encoding:

```
$headers = "From: My website<feedback@example.com>\r\n";
$headers .= "Cc: copycat@example.com\r\n";
$headers .= "Content-type: text/plain; charset=UTF-8";
```

15. There are a couple of important points to note about this code. First, the headers are enclosed in double quotes. This is because each header must be on a separate line, and the characters \r\n at the end of the first two lines represent a carriage return and new line when enclosed in double quotes. You need these two characters at the end of each header except the last one. Second, there's a period in front of the equal sign in the second and third lines. This has the effect of stringing all the values together so the script treats the headers as a single block.

16. One nice touch with e-mail headers is to put the user's e-mail address in the **Reply-to** field of the e-mail, so all the user has to do is click **Reply** in their e-mail program to send a message back to the right person. Unfortunately, this is frequently used by spammers to inject malicious code into your script. The code in process_mail.inc.php filters out potential attacks and inserts the sender's e-mail address only if it's safe to do so. Consequently, there is no need to add a **Reply-to** header yourself; it's done automatically by the script.

If you want to use a special encoding, such as UTF-8, for your e-mails, make sure the web page containing the form uses the same encoding in its meta tag.

You don't need to use all these headers. Just remove the complete line for any you don't want.

17. You don't need to make any other changes to the code you inserted in step 3.

18. The script in process_mail.inc.php processes the form input and sends the e-mail if there are no problems. The final stage is to let the user know what happened.

19. Immediately above the form in the main part of your page, insert the following code:

```php
<?php
if ($_POST && isset($missing) && !empty($missing)) {
?>
  <p class="warning">Not all required fields were filled in.</p>
<?php
  }
elseif ($_POST && !$mailSent) {
?>
  <p class="warning">Sorry, there was a problem sending your message.
Please try later.</p>
<?php
  }
elseif ($_POST && $mailSent) {
?>
  <p><strong>Your message has been sent. Thank you for your feedback.
</strong></p>
<?php } ?>
```

This block of code displays an appropriate message depending on the outcome. Put whatever messages you like in place of the ones shown here, and add the following rule to your style sheet:

```css
.warning {
  font-weight: bold;
  color: #ff0000;
}
```

20. If you're using a visual HTML editor like Dreamweaver, all three messages will appear to be displayed at once. However, when you load the page onto your website, the PHP conditional logic hides all the messages, and only the appropriate one is displayed after the user submits the form.

21. Save the page and upload it to your hosting company, together with process_mail.inc.php. Test it. In a few moments, you should receive the test message in your inbox. That's all there is to it!

If you get error messages or a blank screen, it means you have made a mistake in the script. Check the commas, quotes, and semicolons carefully. If you get a message saying that `process_mail.inc.php` cannot be read, it probably means that you have forgotten to upload it or that it's not in the same folder as the form.

sing e-mail to send form data

In rare cases, it may not be possible to set up a form to send form data (although even most free web hosts tend to provide users with some kind of form functionality, even if it's a shared script that doesn't allow a great deal of customization). If you find yourself in this sticky situation, it's possible to use a `mailto:` URL for the form's `action` attribute value. This causes browsers to e-mail the form parameters and values to the specified address.

```
<form method="post" action="mailto:anemailaddress@somewhere.com"
  enctype="text/plain">
```

This might seem a simpler method than messing around with CGI scripts, but it has major shortfalls:

- Some browsers don't support `mailto:` as a form action.

- The resulting data may arrive in a barely readable (or unreadable) format, and you have no control over this.

- This method isn't secure.

The user won't be redirected and may therefore not realize data has been sent.

That last problem can be worked around by adding a JavaScript alert to the form start tag:

```
<form method="post" action="mailto:anemailaddress@somewhere.com"
  enctype="text/plain" onsubmit="window.alert('This form is being
  sent by email. Thank you for contacting us.')">
```

Of course, this relies on JavaScript being active on the user's browser—but, then again, this is a last resort.

> Note the *enctype* attribute in the previous code block. This defines the MIME type used to encode the form's content before it's sent to the server, so it doesn't become scrambled. By default, the attribute's value is *application/x-www-form-urlencoded*, which is suitable for most forms; however, *multipart/form-data* is available for when the user is able to use a form to upload files.

layout for contact pages

Once you've completed a form, you need to integrate it into your site in a way that most benefits the site's visitors. I've always been of the opinion that it's a good idea to offer users multiple methods of contact on the same page. This makes it easy for them to contact you, because it requires fewer clicks than the fairly common presentation of a form and link to other contact details.

The following images show a couple of example layouts. The first is from the Thalamus Publishing website, which has the contact form on the right (with a minimum of fields); to the left is the other contact information—address, telephone number, fax number, e-mail, and so on, along with other addresses and details relevant to this organization (such as sales representatives).

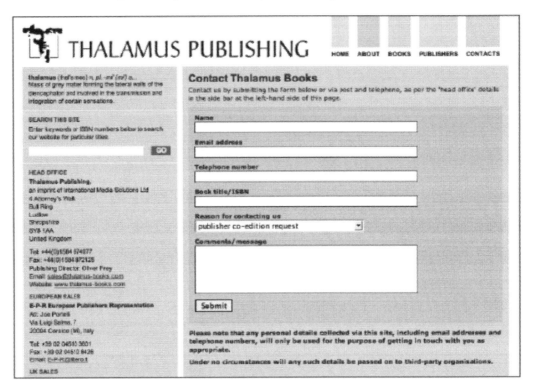

With this company having plenty of contact information, this two-column approach makes a lot of sense, and the prominence of the form is handy, because many queries can be dealt with more efficiently via e-mail.

For Snub Communications, my own site, things are simpler—I don't have a preference as to how people contact me, so all possibilities have pretty much the same prominence. The form area is made to stand out slightly more (thereby giving all contact details relatively equal prominence) by way of its background color.

Again, everything is in one place, rather than spread out over several pages, which makes sending feedback to and/or getting in contact with the organization convenient for the end user. The Snub Communications site doesn't require a map, but if it did, a link to it would appear on this page, too. The map page itself would likely resemble this one to some extent, but with the map in place of the form and image. In other words, the page would still include a telephone number and other contact details; after all, it's frustrating to have a map to an organization's location, get lost, and then discover you don't have the organization's details!

We're not going to dwell on exactly how to create these layouts, because we've already covered the techniques in the previous chapter—it's just a question of creating a two-column layout and cutting in the form (and other details) as appropriate.

Using microformats to enhance contact information

As shown in the previous section, user feedback may come in the form of a telephone call or letter, rather than an e-mail, and therefore you should always add other forms of contact details to a website. Even if the site is an online store, customers will need other ways to get in touch (faceless multinational organizations, take note). In the most basic sense, these can be marked up by using some headings and paragraphs, as follows:

```
<h1>Contact details</h1>

<h2>Mail</h2>
<p><strong>Company name</strong><br />
  00, Street Name<br />
  Town or City<br />
  County or Region<br />
  Postal/ZIP code<br />
  Country name</p>

<h2>Telephone/fax</h2>
  Tel: +1 (0)0000 555555<br />
  Fax: +1 (0)0000 555556<br />
  Mobile/cell: +1 (0)7000 555555</p>
```

Now, there's nothing at all wrong with the previous block of code: it's valid, it does the job perfectly well, and it's semantically sound, which also means it's easy enough to style using CSS. However, by utilizing microformats, the page's functionality can be enhanced without compromising the markup.

More about microformats can be found at the microformats website at www.microformats.org, and in the book *Microformats: Empowering Your Markup for Web 2.0*, by John Allsopp, so I won't dwell on them too much. In short, though, microformats provide a way of adding commonly used semantics to web pages and working with common technologies, such as HTML5. For the example, you're going to see how to take a basic set of contact details and then use microformats to provide users with a means of efficiently downloading and storing the information as a vCard—the vCard format being that commonly used by address books). The semantic information is also of use to any other application that is microformat-aware—for example, some Firefox plug-ins are able to autodetect microformat information on any web page and enable a user to browse and manipulate it.

Using microformats to enhance contact details

Required files	The files from using-microformats-starting-point in the chapter 8 folder
What you'll learn	How to use microformats to enhance a set of contact details
Completed files	using-microformats-completed in the chapter 8 folder

1. Add a surrounding div. Open using-microformats.html, and place a div with a class value of vcard around the contact details content, as shown (truncated) following:

```
<h1>Contact details</h1>
  <div class="vcard">
    <h2>Mail</h2>
    [...]
  Mobile/cell: +1 (0)7000 555555</p>
</div>
```

Contact details

Mail

Company name
00, Street Name
Town or City
County or Region
Postal/ZIP code
Country name

Telephone/fax

Tel: +1 (0)0000 555555
Fax: +1 (0)0000 555556
Mobile/cell: +1 (0)7000 555555

2. Structure the address. Marking up the address is fairly simple, and few changes are required to the general structure of the code. However, because each individual set of information requires its own container and the best way of creating a container for the address is to place it within a block element of its own, the company name and the address each need their own paragraphs, rather than a line break separating the two. The organization's paragraph is then given a class value of fn org. Here, fn stands for "full name," and org defines that the name belongs to an organization, rather than a person.

3. The address paragraph's class value is adr, and each line of the address is placed within a span element. The various class values assigned to the spans denote which element of the address the content refers to, and those are all straightforward to understand. However, address books—and therefore microformats—enable you to distinguish between different types of data. For example, you can have a work address or a home address. This can be defined by adding the relevant word (for example, work) and wrapping it in a span with a class value of type, thereby defining the type for the parent property. In this case, the address is being defined as a work address.

4. For cases when you don't want this information shown on the web page (which will likely be most of the time—after all, adding a lowercase "work" in front of the street name hardly looks great), add a second class value, hidden. Later, CSS will be used to make content with a hidden value invisible.

```
<h2>Mail</h2>
<p class="fn org">Company name</p>
<p class="adr">
  <span class="type hidden">work</span>
  <span class="street-address">00, Street Name</span><br />
  <span class="locality">Town or City</span><br />
  <span class="region">County or Region</span><br />
  <span class="postal-code">Postal/ZIP code</span>
  <span class="country-name">Country name</span>
</p>
```

5. Structure the telephone/fax details. Each definition for a telephone number requires its own container, so the single paragraph must be split into three, as shown in the following code block. Each paragraph's class value should be tel. As with the address, a span with a class value of

335

type hidden is used to define the type for each parent property. For tel, various options are available, including work, home, fax, cell, pager, and video. Should duplicate types be required (such as for a work fax), two type spans are added. As for the contact number itself, that's placed in a span element with a class value of value.

```
<h2>Telephone/fax</h2>
<p class="tel">
  Tel: <span class="type hidden">work</span>
  <span class="value">+1 (0)0000 555555</span></p>
<p class="tel">
  Fax: <span class="type hidden">fax</span>
  <span class="type hidden">work</span>
  <span class="value">+1 (0)0000 555556</span></p>
<p class="tel">
  Mobile/cell: <span class="type hidden">cell</span>
  <span class="value">+1 (0)7000 555555</span></p>
```

> Note that with some address books, only a limited amount of data seems to get exported—specifics about work and home phone numbers may not. As always, test your work on a range of platforms and applications.

6. Style headings and paragraphs. The style sheet, using-microformats.css, already has some defined styles, which do the usual removal of margins and padding and setting of the default font size. The body rule also adds some padding to the page content so that it doesn't hug the browser window edges. To this, add the following three rules, which style the headings and paragraphs. Both headings are rendered in uppercase Arial, helping them to stand out, aiding visual navigation of the contact details.

CONTACT DETAILS

MAIL
Company name

work 00, Street Name
Town or City
County or Region
Postal/ZIP code
Country name

TELEPHONE/FAX
Tel: work+1 (0)0000 555555

Fax: faxwork+1 (0)0000 555556

Mobile/cell: cell+1 (0)7000 555555

```
h1 {
  font: bold 1.5em/1.2em Arial, Helvetica
    sans-serif;
  margin-bottom: 1.2em;
  text-transform: uppercase;
}
h2 {
  font: bold 1.25em/1.44em Arial, Helvetica sans-serif;
  text-transform: uppercase;
}
p {
  font-size: 1.2em;
  line-height: 1.5em;
  margin-bottom: 1.5em;
}
```

7. Hide hidden elements. As noted in steps 2 and 3, some information requires a type to be defined for it, but as you can see in the previous image, this is displayed on-screen like any other content.

This is why the `hidden` value was also applied to the relevant `span` elements. By adding the following rule, these `span`s are made invisible.

```
.hidden {
  display: none;
}
```

8. Deal with margin issues. Because the telephone details are each in an individual paragraph, each has a bottom margin, and this makes the layout look awful. The same problem also affects the company name paragraph. However, because each paragraph has its own `class` attribute value, it's easy to remove the bottom margins from the relevant paragraphs using the following rule:

```
.tel, .fn {
  margin-bottom: 0;
}
```

9. Embolden the company name. Balancewise, the company name could do with standing out more. This is within a paragraph that has a `class` value of `org`, so making the contents bold is child's play—just add the following rule.

```
.org {
  font-weight: bold;
}
```

CONTACT DETAILS

MAIL
Company name
00, Street Name
Town or City
County or Region
Postal/ZIP code
Country name

TELEPHONE/FAX
Tel: +1 (0)0000 555555
Fax: +1 (0)0000 555556
Mobile/cell: +1 (0)7000 555555

10. Finally, style the `vcard div` via the following rule. This sets a background color, width, border, and padding, but perhaps the most important property here is `margin-bottom`. This is required because the margins from paragraphs with a `tel` class were removed in step 6. When you add a bottom margin to the `vcard div`, the typical spacing you'd expect after a paragraphs returns.

```
.vcard {
  width: 200px;
  background: #eeeeee;
  border: 1px solid #cccccc;
  padding: 8px;
  margin-bottom: 1.5em;
}
```

Note that further simplification of some elements of the code shown in the exercise is possible. For example, where you have the Fax line, the type span could be directly wrapped around the relevant label, and the hidden class should be removed.

Where before you had the following:

```
<p class="tel">
  Fax: <span class="type hidden">fax</span>
  <span class="type hidden">work</span>
  <span class="value">+1 (0)0000 555556</span></p>
```

You'll now have this:

```
<p class="tel">
  <span class="type">Fax</span>:
  <span class="type hidden">work</span>
  <span class="value">+1 (0)0000 555556</span></p>
```

The same is also true for the Mobile/cell line.

Note also that this is a relatively new technology, so it's not without its drawbacks. As mentioned earlier, some details are not carried through to some address books. Also, the need to hide extra data is problematic, since under some circumstances (such as in text readers), it will be displayed, which could lead to confusion. However, with the popularity of microformats increasing all the time, they're still worthy of investigation, which is why we're including this example in this book.

Online microformat contacts resources

If you decide to use microformats to enhance your site's contact details, there are two websites you need to bookmark. The first is Technorati's Contacts Feed Service, at www.technorati.com/contacts. This enables you to input the URL of a page with hCard information (that is, the sort of page created in the previous exercise) and get a vCard out of it, which can be added to your address book.

Add hCard contacts to your address book

Enter the URL of a page with hCard contact information (What is hCard?) to automatically add the contact information on that page into your address book application.

URL: http://technorati.com/about/contact.html   Get hCard Contacts

Get hCards favelet

Favelets let you take the power of the Technorati Contacts Feed Service with you wherever you go. Drag the following Get hCard Contacts link into your bookmarks / favorites bar, and use it when viewing a page with hCards to add them to your address book automatically.

- Get hCard Contacts - Add hCard contacts from the page you're on to your address book.

For more information on the hCard microformat, see the hCard specification.

The Technorati Contacts Feed Service is currently beta.

« Technorati Home

Usefully, the site's system enables you to automate the system via the kind of web page created earlier. If you upload a page like the one created in the previous exercise and then add the following code (amending the URL after `contacts/`), you'll have a link on the contacts page that uses the microformat information to create a vCard that users can download.

```
<p><a href="http://technorati.com/contacts/http://yourdomain.com/
yourcontactpageurl.html">Download vCard</a>. (<em>This process
  may take a few seconds.</em>)</p>
```

A second handy resource is Tantek Çelik's hCard creator (amusingly titled the hCard-o-matic), at `www.microformats.org/code/hcard/creator`. This enables you to automate much of the process from the previous exercise—you put your values into the field on the left, and the code is built live in the field at the right of the page.

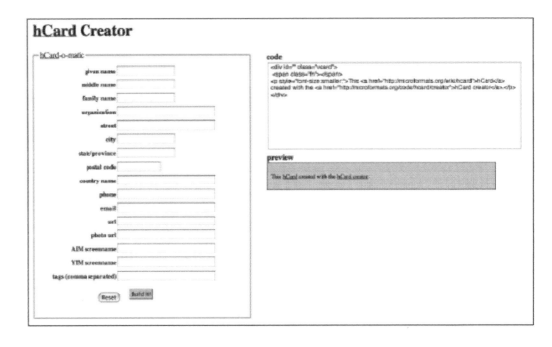

Contact details structure redux

In this chapter, and in the microformats exercise, the address and other contact details were styled using paragraphs and line breaks. An alternative structure, which perhaps has greater integrity from a semantic standpoint, is to use a definition list, with further nested definition lists within. At the top level, the term is Contact details, and the definition is the actual contact details. At the next level, there are two terms, Mail and Telephone/fax, each with respective definitions. For the latter, the definition has a third definition within, providing term/definition pairs for the different types of telephone and fax numbers.

```
<dl>
  <dt>Contact details</dt>
  <dd>
    <dl class="vcard">
      <dt>Mail</dt>
      <dd>
        <address>
        <strong>Company name</strong><br />
        00, Street Name<br />
        Town or City<br />
        County or Region<br />
        Postal/ZIP code<br />
        Country name
        </address>
      </dd>
      <dt>Telephone/fax</dt>
      <dd>
```

```
     <dl>
       <dt>Tel:</dt>
       <dd>+1 (0)0000 555555</dd>
       <dt>Fax:</dt>
       <dd>+1 (0)0000 555556</dd>
       <dt>Mobile/cell:</dt>
       <dd>+1 (0)7000 555555</dd>
     </dl>
   </dd>
 </dl>
</dd>
</dl>
```

For the CSS, use the existing rules from using-microformats.css in the using-microformats-starting-point folder and the .vcard rule from the previous exercise. The following rules can then be used to style the definition list and its contents.

First, the dt rule is used to style the Contact details text (as per the h1 element in the previous exercise), with the dd dt rule providing override styles for dt elements within a dd element. This rule is aimed to style the equivalent of the h2 elements from the previous exercise: the Mail and Telephone/fax text. The dd dd dt rule provides a third level of override, styling the dt elements within the telephone/fax definition list. Also, because the dt/dd pairs are displayed in a linear fashion by default, the dd dd dt rule floats the telephone/fax list dt elements to the left, enabling the dd elements to stack to the right in each case.

```
dt {
  font: bold 1.5em/1.2em Arial, Helvetica sans-serif;
  margin-bottom: 1.2em;
  text-transform: uppercase;
}
dd dt {
  font: bold 1.2em/1.5em Arial, Helvetica sans-serif;
  text-transform: uppercase;
  margin-bottom: 0;
}
dd dd dt {
  float: left;
  padding-right: 5px;
  display: block;
  text-transform: none;
}
```

The next two rules deal with formatting and fine-tuning of the text. The address rule adds the gap between the bottom of the address and the telephone/fax heading, along with reverting the address element content to normal text (it's italic by default). The second rule in the following code block defines a font for the address element content and the content of the telephone/fax definition list's term and definition.

```
address {
  padding-bottom: 1.5em;
  font-style: normal;
}
address, dd dd dt, dd dd dd {
```

```
    font: 1.2em/1.5em Verdana, Arial, sans-serif;

}
```

With these styles added, the contact details look virtually identical to those in the exercise. At this point, you can add hooks for the vCard as per steps 2 and 3 of the "Using microformats to enhance contact details" exercise. See `contact-details-structure-redux.css` and `contact-details-structure-redux.html` in the `chapter 8` folder for the completed files.

We've covered plenty of ground here, so now it's time to leave the subject of collecting user feedback and progress to the next chapter, which explores how to test your websites and deal with common browser bugs.

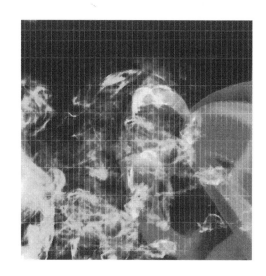

Chapter 9

Dealing with Browser Quirks

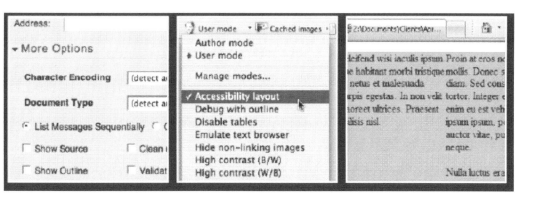

In this chapter:

- Weeding out common web page errors

- Creating a browser test suite

- Installing multiple versions of Internet Explorer

- Catering for unruly web browsers

- Common fixes for Internet Explorer bugs
- Targeting other browsers with JavaScript

The final test

One time that web designers envy designers in other fields is when it comes to testing websites. Although we're a long way from the "design a site for each browser" mentality that afflicted the medium in the late 1990s, we've still not reached the holy grail of "author once, display anywhere."

The methods outlined in this book take you most of the way there, providing a solid foundation for websites that should need little tweaking to get them working across all web browsers. However, to say such sites will never need any amendments is naïve in the extreme. Therefore, unless authoring for an internal corporate environment where everyone uses exactly the same browser, designers must always ensure they thoroughly test sites in a range of browsers.

Weeding out common errors

An error is something that breaks the user's experience when browsing your website. If, for example, there is a few pixels difference between different browsers, this is not considered an error. A layout issue that prevents the user from easily reading your content is considered an error.

Testing in browsers isn't everything; in fact, you may find that your site fails to work for no reason whatsoever, tear your hair out, and then find the problem lurking in your code somewhere. With that in mind, you should either work with software that has built-in and current validation tools (many have outdated tools, based on old versions of online equivalents) or bookmark and regularly use the W3C's suite of online tools: the Markup Validation Service (http://validator.w3.org/), CSS Validation Service (http://jigsaw.w3.org/css-validator/), Feed Validation Service (http://validator.w3.org/feed/), Link Checker (http://validator.w3.org/checklink), and others (www.w3.org/QA/Tools/) as relevant.

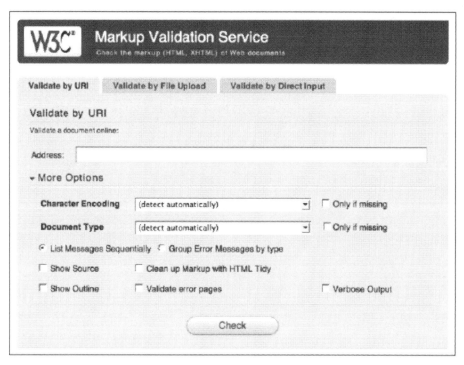

Here are some of the more common errors you might make that are often overlooked:

- *Spelling errors*: Spell a start tag wrong, and an element likely won't appear; spell an end tag wrong, and it may not be closed properly, wrecking the remaining layout. In CSS, misspelled property or value names can cause rules—and therefore entire layouts—to fail entirely. British English users should also remember to check for and weed out British spellings—setting colour won't work in CSS, and yet we see that extra *u* in plenty of web pages (which presumably have their authors scratching their heads, wondering why the colors aren't being applied properly).

- *Incorrect use of symbols in CSS*: If a CSS rule isn't working as expected, ensure you've not erred when it comes to the symbols used in the CSS selector. It's a simple enough mistake to use an id (#) when you really mean a class (.), and vice versa.

- *Not closing elements, attributes, and rules*: An unclosed element in HTML may cause the remainder of the web page (or part of it) to not display correctly. Similarly, not closing an HTML attribute makes all of the page's content until the next double quote part of the attribute. Not closing a CSS rule may cause part or all of the style sheet to not work. Note that CSS pairs that aren't terminated with a semicolon may cause subsequent rules to partially or wholly fail. A good tip to avoid accidentally not closing elements or rules is to add the end tag/closing bracket immediately after adding the start tag/opening bracket. This also helps to avoid incorrect nesting of elements.

- *Multiple rule sets*: In CSS, ensure that if you use a selector more than once, any overrides are intentional. It's a common error for a designer to duplicate a rule set and have different CSS property values conflicting in different areas of the CSS.

- *Errors with the head and body elements*: As stated earlier in the book, HTML content should not appear outside of the `html` element, and body content should not appear outside of the `body` element. Common errors with these elements include placing content between the closing `head` element tag (`</head>`) and the `body` start tag (`<body>`) and including multiple `html` and `body` elements.

- *Inaccessible content*: Here, we're talking in a more general sense, rather than about accessibility for screen reader users. If you create a site with scrollable areas, ensure users can access the content within, even if browser settings aren't at their defaults. Problems mostly occur when `overflow` is set to `hidden`. Similarly, `textarea` elements that don't have properly marked-up `cols` and `rows` settings will often be tiny when viewed without CSS (these attributes are functional as well as presentational). The same is true for text input fields without a defined `size` attribute.

- *Dead links*: These can take on many forms, such as a link to another page being dead, an image not showing up, or external documents not being accessible by the web page. If a JavaScript function isn't working for some reason, try checking to see whether you've actually linked it; in some cases, the simpler and most obvious errors are the ones that slip through the net. Also, if things aren't working on a live site, check the paths—you may have accidentally created a direct link to a file on your local machine, which obviously won't be accessible to the entire Internet. Spaces within `href` values or the original file names can also be accidentally overlooked.

- *Whitespace errors*: In CSS, do not place whitespace between class/id indicators and the selector name or between numerals and units for measurements. However, do not omit whitespace from between contextual selectors; otherwise, you'll "combine" them into a new, probably unknown, one.

- *Using multiple units*: In CSS, a value can accept only a single unit—the likes of 50%px can cause a rule to partially or wholly fail.

A browser test suite

It's important to note that the market is in continual change—just a quick look at Netscape's fortunes should be enough to prove that. Utterly dominant during the period when the Web first started to become mainstream, Netscape's share of the market was decimated by the then-upstart Internet Explorer, and it all but vanished. The point, of course, is that you cannot predict how the browser market will change. Each year sees new releases of web browsers, with new features and updated—but usually incomplete—standards support.

All of this is a roundabout way of saying that you need to think hard about browsers when you're creating your work. Don't test sites in only a single browser, and don't use the most popular for your starting point if it's not the most standards-compliant. Instead, use a browser with a good grasp of web standards for your first line of tests, until you have your templates working. We use the WebKit engine as a starting point—more specifically, we favor Chrome as an initial choice of browser. Firefox, which uses the Gecko engine, is also a decent choice.

Once the basic structure is up and running, we test in a range of alternate web browsers, typically in the following order:

1. *The other compliant browsers*: Typically, we use Chrome as a starting point, although sometimes we use Safari. Whichever one you choose to start in, it's a good idea to test in the other compliant browsers first. Sometimes, one will pick up a coding error the others don't, and it's a good sanity check to ensure everything is working well. If you're lucky, everything will work fine right away in all of these browsers, on both Mac and Windows.

2. *A browser in text mode*: What we mean by this is testing the site without CSS, which is a way of somewhat figuring out whether it's usable on alternate devices.

3. *Internet Explorer*: Although each release of Internet Explorer is a vast improvement over previous efforts, it's not as standards-compliant as the other mainstream browsers. Therefore, tests need to be done to ensure everything is working properly, not least because Internet Explorer is one of the more popular browsers in terms of market share. If things aren't working right, conditional comments need to be used (see the "Dealing with Internet Explorer bugs" section later in the chapter).

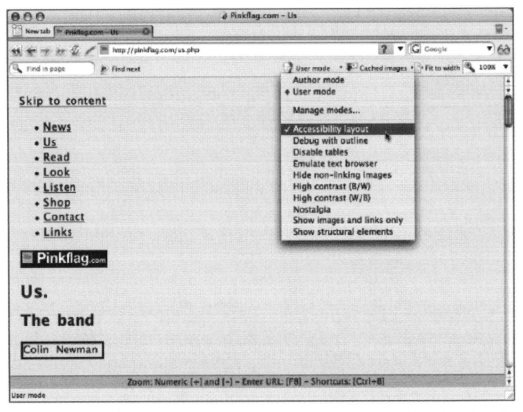

4. *Everything—all over again*: When any major changes are made, you need to go back through your browsers and make sure the changes haven't screwed anything up.

There are other browsers out there, but the preceding list will deal with the vast majority of your users. However, always try to find out the potential audience for a website to ascertain whether you should place more focus on a particular browser. For example, if authoring a site for a mostly Mac-based audience, it might make sense to use Safari as the basis for testing.

At each stage of testing, we recommend that you save HTML and CSS milestones on a very regular basis. If something fails in a browser, create a copy of your files and work on a fix. Don't continually overwrite files, because it's sometimes useful—and, indeed, necessary—to go back to previous versions. Another option is to use a version control system such as Subversion or Git.

Whichever browsers you test in, it's important to not avoid the "other side." Windows users have long seen the Mac as being inconsequential, but at the time of writing Safari now counts for about 4% of all web users, and the trend for Mac sales (as a percentage of the market) is upward. Usefully, there's now a version of Safari for Windows, but even the Mac and Windows versions of Firefox show slight differences in the way sites are handled (mostly regarding text). Even worse, many Mac-based designers don't test on a Windows PC or in Internet Explorer. If you're a Windows user, grab a cheap Mac that's capable of running Mac OS X (such as a second-hand Macbook or a Mac mini), and if you're a Mac user, either grab a cheap Windows PC to test with or run Windows as a virtual machine (via Parallels Desktop, VMware Fusion, or Virtual Box, which is free) on an Intel Mac or using Virtual PC if you have a PPC-based machine. (You can also use Boot Camp on an Intel Mac, but that requires booting back and forth between Windows and Mac OS X, so using a virtual environment is more efficient unless you have two computers.) Linux users also have a range of browsers to test on. Firefox is popular on that platform, and Safari is a rough analog for Konqueror. It is worth noting, however, that the default fonts with Linux vary considerably from those that you'd expect on a Mac or Windows PC—so you should always define fallback fonts accordingly and test in Linux if possible. See Chapter 3 for more on font stacks.

stalling multiple versions of browsers

One of the big problems when it comes to web design testing is that some browser manufacturers don't enable you to run multiple versions of their products. The two biggest culprits here are, unsurprisingly, Microsoft and Apple, which presumably argue that as their browsers rely on system-level code, they can't provide standalone testing environments for older releases. In Internet Explorer 9 and 10, Microsoft has provided a browse mode, which allows a developer to render a web page as version of IE as far back as 7.

In a similar vein, Michel Fortin has produced stand-alone versions of Safari for the Mac, available from www.michelf.com/projects/multi-safari/. However, because of the nature of WebKit (the application framework that's the basis for Safari), there are limitations regarding which versions of the browser can be run on which versions of Mac OS X.

Elsewhere, things are simpler. For Firefox, Chrome, and Safari, different versions can happily live on the same machine, and they will work fine independently. Chrome installations are user specific, so while it is possible to run different versions of chrome on your system, you will need to have multiple user accounts.

ealing with Internet Explorer bugs

As mentioned elsewhere, Microsoft continues to make huge leaps forward with each new version of Internet Explorer, but it's still not without its problems. Also, because Microsoft's browser enjoyed such an immense market share for so long, older versions remain in use for years. With this in mind, along with the sad fact that Microsoft's browser has been the least compliant one out there for a long time now, this section is dedicated to exploring how to deal with the most common Internet Explorer bugs. These are all worth committing to memory, because if you're working on CSS layouts, these bugs will affect your designs at some point, and yet most of the fixes are extremely simple.

onditional comments

Conditional comments are proprietary code that's understood by Microsoft Internet Explorer only from version 5 to version 9. Since they're wrapped up in standard HTML comments, they don't affect other browsers, and they are also considered perfectly valid by the W3C's validation services.

You should be aware that Microsoft has removed support of conditional comments from Internet Explorer 10. Internet Explorer 10, like other browsers, will simply ignore conditional comments, so they are still applicable to versions earlier than 10.

What conditional comments enable you to do is target either a specific release of Internet Explorer or a group of releases by way of expressions. An example of a conditional comment is shown in the following code block:

```
<!--[if IE 6]>
[specific instructions for Internet Explorer 6 go here]
<![endif]-->
```

Anything placed inside this comment will be shown only in Internet Explorer 6—all other browsers ignore the content. This is most useful for adding IE-specific style sheets to a web page, within which you can place overrides. This allows you to have a clean style sheet and then override specific values in a separate style sheet for a targeted version of Internet Explorer before version 10, attached within a conditional comment.

Conditional comments are generally added after the "default," or clean, style sheets (which in this case are the main style sheet added using a style element and a print style sheet added using a link element).

```
<style type="text/css" media="screen">
/* <![CDATA[ */
@import url(x.css);
/* ]]> */
</style>
<link rel="stylesheet" rev="stylesheet" href="x-print.css"
  type="text/css" media="print" />
<!--[if IE 7]>
<link rel="stylesheet" type="text/css" href="ie-7-hacks.css"
  media="screen" />
<![endif]-->
<!--[if lte IE 6]>
<link rel="stylesheet" type="text/css" href="ie-6lte-hacks.css"
  media="screen" />
<![endif]-->
<!--[if lt IE 6]>
<link rel="stylesheet" type="text/css" href="ie-5-hacks.css"
  media="screen" />
<![endif]-->
```

Within the comments, lte IE 6 means "less than or equal to Internet Explorer 6," so anything added to ie-6lte-hacks.css affects Internet Explorer 6 and older; lt IE 6 means "less than Internet Explorer 6," so anything added to ie-5-hacks.css affects versions of Internet Explorer older than 6. An alternate way of attaching a style sheet for Internet Explorer 5 would be to use the syntax if IE 5. Since the cascade still affects the rules within style sheets attached inside conditional comments, it makes sense to fix things for Internet Explorer 6 and older first and then work backward to Internet Explorer 5.x to fix the few remaining things that need sorting out.

> See *http://msdn2.microsoft.com/en-us/library/ms537512.aspx* for more on conditional comments. The hasLayout site—*www.haslayout.net*—also offers useful information on conditional comments.

Note that the preceding code block also includes a link to a print style sheet; print style sheets are covered in Chapter 10.

> *The advanced boilerplates from the download files (in the advanced-boilerplates folder) include the preceding code block.*

Let's now examine an example of a code hack to deal with the box model issues that affect versions of Internet Explorer older than 6:

```
.box {
  padding: 20px;
  width: 340px;
  voice-family: "\"}\"";
  voice-family: inherit;
  width: 300px;
}
```

When using conditional comments, you'd make the rule in the default style sheet clean, with no hacks:

```
.box {
  padding: 20px;
  width: 300px;
}
```

You'd then add a rule to your style sheet that only Internet Explorer versions older than 6 can see (the one within the conditional comment that references lt IE 6 in the large code block shown earlier).

```
.box {
  width: 340px;
}
```

Compliant browsers read the rule in the clean style sheet. Internet Explorer versions older than 6 then override the width value, thereby displaying the box as intended. Unlike when using a CSS hack, however, the CSS hasn't been compromised in any way. The majority of problems detailed in the "Common fixes for Internet Explorer" sections later in the chapter have to do with CSS and therefore require conditional comments when they're being dealt with.

ealing with rounding errors

In liquid layouts with floated elements, rounding errors sometimes cause the widths of the elements to add up to more than 100%. This causes one of the floated elements to wrongly stack under the others. This problem is known to affect all versions of Internet Explorer. For an example, see the following image (from the "Creating flanking sidebars" exercise in Chapter 7), in which the right sidebar is wrongly sitting underneath the left sidebar.

As explained in the focus point within the "Creating flanking sidebars" exercise, rounding errors can be dealt with by reducing one of the percentage values of a column by as little as 0.0001%, although sometimes this reduction needs to be increased.

Alt text overriding title text

If you have an image with alt text nested inside a link that has a `title` element, the `title` element will be overridden. This is largely due to Internet Explorer wrongly displaying the content of the `alt` attribute as a tooltip.

The only way around this problem is to duplicate the `title` attribute and place a copy of it within the `img` element. This is superfluous markup, but it fixes the issue in Internet Explorer and does not adversely affect other web browsers.

```
<a href="sunset.html" title="Click to view a larger image"><img
  title="Sunset in Reykjav&iacute;k" src="sunset.jpg" alt="Sunset in
  Reykjav&iacute;k" width="400" height="300" /></a>
```

Fixing hasLayout problems (the peekaboo bug)

Because of the archaic nature of some aspects of the Internet Explorer rendering engine, it sometimes serves up some rather odd bugs; perhaps the most irritating of these is the so-called peekaboo bug, also known as the disappearing content bug. Fairly common (but also fairly random as to whether it occurs), it typically affects layouts that use floats and clearing `divs`, and it can cause elements to partially disappear below a given point or for content to flicker on and off as a page is scrolled.

The problem occurs because of a proprietary Internet Explorer concept called *layout*, which refers to how elements render their content and interact with other elements. Some elements have layout by default, others don't, and some CSS properties (irreversibly) trigger it. Any property that gains layout in some way has Microsoft's proprietary `hasLayout` property set to `true`. If an element doesn't have layout, the property is set to false. Unfortunately, there's no way to directly set hasLayout for any element, even in an IE-specific style sheet, and yet hasLayout is the cause of many layout problems in Internet Explorer.

The hasLayout-trigger.html document within the hasLayout folder from the chapter 9 folder of the download files always exhibits the peekaboo bug. The page's structure is extremely simple: a wrapper has within it three divs; the first is floated right and given a 50% width, the second has no style applied, and the third is a clearing div. By default, when the page is loaded, the second div cannot be seen in Internet Explorer 6 or older (see the following left image)—only by scrolling, selecting content, or resizing the window can you make the "missing" content reappear. In a compliant browser, however, this problem doesn't occur (see the following right image).

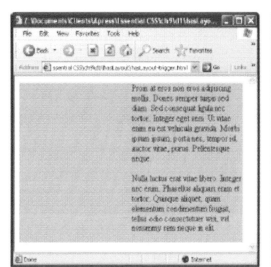 

Should you come across this problem when working on your own sites, the solution is to give layout to the containing div. The best method for doing this is to set the proprietary zoom property to 1 in a style sheet linked via a conditional comment.

Try doing this for the #wrapper rule in the ie6-lte-hacks.css file (see the following code block), and you'll see that the hasLayout problem no longer affects the page—the content that wasn't initially visible should now be displayed properly.

```
#wrapper {
  zoom: 1;
}
```

> *It's probably worth noting that zoom, like some of the other things mentioned in the Internet Explorer fixes, will not validate. However, as far as we're concerned, there's no real urgency or reason to make IE-specific style sheets validate. Keep your main style sheet clean and valid and then add whatever you need to get things working in Internet Explorer—although always use as few additions as possible, even when working with conditional comments. In some cases, however, height: 1% should provide the same effect, and this is valid CSS.*

Supporting legacy browsers

Today a common issue presented to web designers is the issue of legacy browsers. What do we do if a browser doesn't support HTML5? In this section, I will cover some open source libraries that will allow you to take advantage of the capabilities of HTML5 and CSS3 while presenting users with legacy browsers or modern browsers that haven't implemented a new feature: a feature-rich experience.

It is important to remember to always follow the best practices when designing your websites and the following libraries to enhance your users' experience rather than rely on them to complete it.

Modernizr

Modernizr (http://modernizr.com) is a JavaScript library that helps you build next-generation HTML5 and CSS3 websites. It uses feature detection through JavaScript to tell the page whether a specific feature is supported.

Modernizr can be installed by downloading and linking to it in the head section of your page.

```
<script src="modernizer-2.0.min.js"></script>
```

A class of no-js must be added to the html tag. This allows you to target browsers that do not support JavaScript. If the browser does support JavaScript, Modernizr will remove this class name, and the styles that you have created to target browsers that don't support JavaScript will not be used.

```
<html class="no-js">
```

As we mentioned, when Modernizr runs successfully, it will alter the class names assigned to the html element to allow you to target the browser functionality that is or is not available to the user's browser.

Here is an example of what Modernizr could output for a user's browser:

```
<html class="js canvas canvastext geolocation rgba hsla no-multiplebgs">
```

This would allow you to target a browser that supports multiple backgrounds differently than a browser that doesn't, and your user would see a less complex background on your site instead of no background at all.

ormalize.css

Normalize.css (http://necolas.github.com/normalize.css/) is a customizable CSS library that makes browsers render all elements more consistently and in line with modern standards. It preserves useful defaults, normalizes styles, corrects bugs and common browser inconsistencies, and improves usability, and it has detailed comments making it easy to customize and manage.

To include this on your site, simply download it and link to it in the head section of your page.

```
<link rel="stylesheet" href="normalize.css">
```

TML5 Shim

HTML5 Shim (http://code.google.com/p/html5shim/) is a script that enables all HTML5 elements in versions of Internet Explorer earlier than 9.

Once again, to use this script, it must be added to the head element of your page, but this time it must use conditional comments to target Internet Explorer.

```
<!-[if lt IE 9]> <script
src=http://html5shim.googlecode.com/svn/trunk/html5.js></script><![endif]→
```

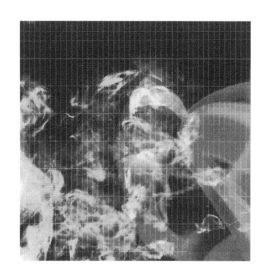

Chapter 10

Putting Everything Together

In this chapter:

- Combining methods to create website designs

- Creating an online gallery (portfolio)

- Creating a storefront layout

- Creating a business website

- Creating a blog layout

- Working with style sheets for print output

Putting the pieces together

The majority of this book intentionally works in a modular manner. The idea is that you can work on the various components as you wish and then combine them to form all manner of websites. This chapter shows how this process can work. Three layouts will be explored, and elements from each one will be heavily based on exercises from elsewhere in this book. You'll see the Photoshop mock-up, a breakdown of its structure, and instructions for how the completed files were put together—mostly using techniques you've already worked with in this book. In all cases, the completed files are available in the download files (in the chapter 10 folder). Note that these layouts are mock-ups of websites, with a single page designed, not complete websites. However, there's enough material here to use as the basis for your own designs, although you shouldn't use them as is—after all, you're not the only person with a copy of this book!

> *Note that in the following sections, there are references to exercises elsewhere in the book, stating that the code was more or less copied and pasted. In all cases, ensure you check the paths to any linked files—mostly, the book has used a totally flat structure for files. In this chapter, images are always placed in an assets folder. Therefore, paths to images need updating accordingly when using portions of exercises from elsewhere in the book.*

Managing style sheets

In the download files, there are two sets of boilerplates. The basic-boilerplates folder is the one used for the exercises throughout the book. The HTML document contains only a single wrapper div, while the CSS document has a handful of rules that are designed to reset margins and padding and define a default font. Projects in this chapter are instead based on the documents from the advanced-boilerplates folder. This contains a more complex web page and a style sheet that uses CSS comments to split the document into sections. The "Creating boilerplates" section in Chapter 2 provided an overview of the reasoning behind this technique, and the "CSS boilerplates and management" section in Appendix D does largely the same thing. However, because this section will examine CSS rules within certain sections of each style sheet, a brief overview is required here, too.

Essentially, you can use CSS comments for writing notes within a style sheet , and whatever is between CSS comments (which begin with /* and end with */) is ignored by browsers. Comments can be multiline or single-line, and you can therefore use comments to create sections in the style sheet for various "groups" of rules. For example, you can use the following to introduce a group of rules on forms:

```
/* ---------- forms ---------- */
```

Taking things further, a multiline comment can be added at the start of the document. This can include a table of contents, and the various section headers within the style sheet can be numbered, thereby making navigation and editing even easier. As also explained elsewhere, I indent both property/value pairs and the closing quote of the declaration, as shown in the following code block (with a tab being represented by four spaces):

```
#sidebar {
    float: right;
    }
```

This makes it simpler to scan the left side of the document for selectors. Note that although the rules within the remainder of this chapter are not formatted in this manner, the rules within the download file style sheets are.

Creating a portfolio layout

This section will show how I created a layout for an online portfolio, suitable for a designer or photographer (professional or otherwise) to show off their wares. The Photoshop file for the document is gallery-layout.psd, in the PSD mock-ups folder within the chapter 10 folder of the download files. The completed web page (along with associated files) is within the gallery-website folder, within the chapter 10 folder. The following image shows the Photoshop mock-up of the page.

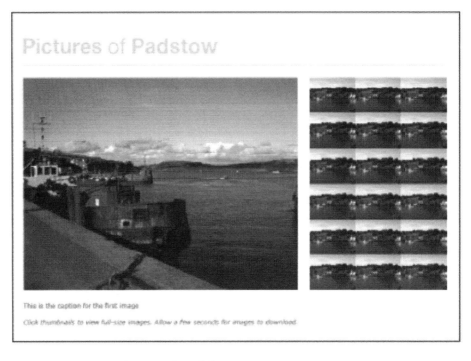

About the design and required images

As you can see from the previous screenshot, this page has a simple structure. The fixed-width layout has a masthead that contains the name of the portfolio and is bordered on the bottom, creating a visual separator between the site's name and its contents. The main content area is split into two columns. On the right are thumbnail images, and on the left are the main image, a caption, and basic instructions regarding how to use the page.

Thumbnails, and full-size images, aren't in the mock-up but were fine-tuned, optimized, and exported separately and placed in the assets folder, along with the heading image. Note that I used a convention for file names: thumbnails share the name of their full-size parent, but with -t appended.

Putting the gallery together

When putting this page together, techniques were used from the following exercises and sections in this book:

- "Creating a fixed-width wrapper" (Chapter 7)

- "Placing columns within a wrapper" (Chapter 7)

- "Manipulating two structural divs for fixed-width layouts" (Chapter 7)

- "Styling semantic markup: a traditional example with serif fonts and a baseline grid" (Chapter 3)

- "Image-replacement techniques" (Chapter 3)

- "Switching images using JavaScript" (Chapter 5)

- "Adding captions to your image gallery" (Chapter 5)

I also took on board various techniques discussed in Chapter 4 regarding working with images.

Open index.html and examine the code. The head section imports a style sheet and the JavaScript file gallery.js. The JavaScript document is identical to the one from the "Adding captions to your image gallery" exercise in Chapter 5.

The page's basic structure is simple: the page is contained within a wrapper div. Within that, there is a masthead and a content area, the latter of which has two columns, formed from div elements with id values of mainImageContainer and thumbnailsContainer. If the content were removed, this structure would look like that in the following code block:

```
<div id="wrapper">
  <div id="masthead"></div>
  <div id="content">
    <div id="mainImageContainer"></div>
    <div id="thumbnailsContainer"></div>
  </div>
</div>
```

If you've read through Chapter 7, you'll see that this layout is formed using techniques shown in the "Creating a fixed-width wrapper," "Placing columns within a wrapper," and "Manipulating two structural divs for fixed-width layouts" exercises.

Within the masthead div is a level-one heading with an empty span element. This is as per the image-replacement method shown in the "Image-replacement techniques" section of Chapter 3. The CSS applied to the elements (shown later in this section) effectively places the span over the text and sets the heading image exported from the mock-up as its background.

```
<h1 class="mainHeading"><span></span>Pictures of Padstow</h1>
```

In the mainImageContainer div, there's an image, a caption, and explanatory text. Note the id value for the image—this is a hook for both the JavaScript and CSS, as explained in the "Switching images using JavaScript" and "Adding captions to your image gallery" exercises in Chapter 5.

The thumbnailsContainer div contains an unordered list, each item from which contains a linked thumbnail image, and an example of which is shown in the following code block:

```
<li><a href="assets/boat.jpg" onclick="javascript:swapPhoto
('boat.jpg','A docked boat, with distant clouds rolling in.');
 return false;"><img src="assets/boat-t.jpg" alt="A docked
 boat." width="80" height="60" /></a></li>
```

Again, the various elements of the code are explained in the aforementioned exercises from Chapter 5. The only difference here is the use of the list, which is used to provide structure for the 18 images; as you've seen elsewhere in the book, CSS makes it possible to style lists in any manner of ways.

Styling the gallery

The pictures-of-padstow.css document contains the styles for this layout, and these styles are arranged into sections, as explained earlier in the chapter. The defaults section includes two rules. The first is the universal selector (*), used to remove padding and margins (as per the "Zeroing margins and padding on all elements" section in Chapter 2). The second is a body rule with a commented-out background pair. If you remove the CSS comments and load the web page into your browser, you'll see a background grid, as shown in the following screenshot (the baseline grid's height is 20 pixels per line). It's worth leaving the rules in place when working with baseline grids, because if you make changes to your page later, you can temporarily turn the grid back on to ensure rhythm is being maintained. Having a commented-out property/value pair in your CSS makes no noticeable difference to file download times anyway.

In the structure section of the CSS, the #wrapper rule defines a fixed width for the page's wrapper, and the margin property value of 0 auto centers the page in the browser window (as explained in Chapter 7's "Creating a fixed-width wrapper" exercise). The #masthead rule sets some padding at its top (to place some space above the heading), adds a single-pixel bottom border, and adds a bottom margin, again for spacing reasons. Note that the values within this rule, taken in combination with the height of the heading (23 pixels), ensure that the vertical rhythm is maintained. The two other rules in the section style the two columns, floating them, giving them fixed widths, and adding some space between them, as per the "Manipulating two structural divs for fixed-width layouts" exercise in Chapter 7.

In the fonts section of the CSS, the default font size is set using the html and body rules, as per the "Setting text using percentages and ems" section in Chapter 3. The h1.mainHeading and h1.mainHeading span rules are the image-replacement technique in full swing, as per the "Image-replacement techniques" section in Chapter 3. Note the h1.mainHeading rule's font-size value, which ensures that the text doesn't spill out from behind the image in Internet Explorer when zooming the page. While defining font size in pixels is generally a bad idea, it's largely irrelevant here, because the HTML text is only likely to be seen if the CSS isn't shown. (For anyone surfing with images off, a portfolio is kind of useless, and even if they're determined to press on regardless, the 20px value ensures that the heading text is likely to be legible for them anyway.)

```
h1.mainHeading {
  position: relative;
  width: 342px;
  height: 28px;
  overflow: hidden;
  padding-bottom: 19px;
  font-size: 20px;
  line-height: 1em;
}
h1.mainHeading span {
  position: absolute;
  background: #ffffff url(assets/pictures-of-padstow.gif) no-repeat;
  width: 100%;
  height: 100%;
}
```

The p rule sizes the paragraph, and the line-height value is determined by dividing the baseline grid line height (2em, derived from the 20 pixel target—see the "Styling semantic markup: A traditional example with serif fonts and a baseline grid" exercise in Chapter 3 for the thinking behind this) by the font-size value: 2.0 divided by 1.1 equals 1.81818181 (recurring, but you can stop after a half-dozen or so decimal places in CSS).

```
p {
  font: 1.1em/1.81818181em Verdana, Arial, Helvetica, sans-serif;
  color: #898989;
}
```

The p em rule reduces the font-size value for the emphasized text in the instructions paragraph, while the #thumbnailsContainer li rule displays the list items within the thumbnailsContainer div inline, stacking them horizontally.

```
#thumbnailsContainer li {
  display: inline;
}
```

The final section in the style sheet is for images, and the three rules are as follows: img, which removes borders from linked images; #imgPhoto, which defines the margin under the main image; and #thumbnailsContainer img, which floats the images within the thumbnailsContainer div, ensuring there's no space between them.

The completed page is shown in the following image.

Creating an online storefront

This section will detail how I created a layout for an online storefront, providing the user with a quick and simple means of accessing a number of product categories by way of a multicolumn drop-down menu. The Photoshop file for the document is store-front-layout.psd, in the PSD mock-ups folder within the chapter 10 folder of the download files. The completed web page (along with associated files) is within the store-website folder, within the chapter 10 folder. The following image shows the Photoshop mock-up of the page.

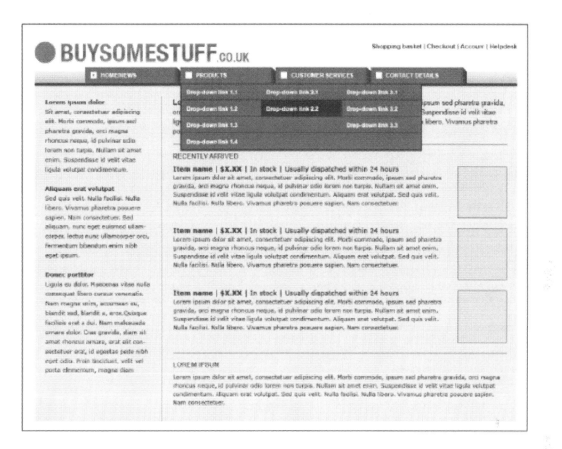

bout the design and required images

Prior to working on this design, I decided that it would be a semi-liquid layout, with a maximum width of around 1000 pixels and a minimum width slightly larger than the width of the four tabs (which total 740 pixels). This explains the use of the blue gradient behind the tabs, providing a transition between the dark orange stripe and the white masthead area when the site is displayed wider. Without this, the jolt between these two elements would be too harsh. This also explains the lack of fixed-width elements elsewhere in the design—images are floated right, and recently added items are displayed in a linear fashion. With a liquid layout, displaying these three containers as columns wouldn't be entirely straightforward (although it could be done by replacing the images with divs that have background images large enough to cater for changes in column width; however, at narrow widths, the images would be cropped).

In terms of imagery, the logo was exported, as was a portion of the gradient image (which was tiled horizontally). Alternatively, this effect could be done using CSS3 gradients, as described earlier in this book. Had I been working entirely from scratch on this layout, the tab states would also have been included in and exported from the mock-up, but I took those directly from the drop-down exercise from Chapter 5. The inline images in the document are all just a single gray square saved as temporary-image.gif. Clearly, in an actual site, all of those images would show items for sale!

Putting the storefront together

When working on this layout, I made use of techniques shown in the following exercises:

- "Creating a maximum-width layout" (Chapter 7)

- "Placing columns within a wrapper" (Chapter 7)

- "Manipulating two structural divs for liquid layouts" (Chapter 7)

- "Creating a sidebar with faux-column backgrounds" (Chapter 7)

- "Creating a boxout" (Chapter 7)

- "Creating breadcrumb navigation" (Chapter 5)

- "Creating a multicolumn drop-down menu" (Chapter 5)

Open index.html and examine the code. The head section imports a style sheet and attaches the JavaScript file store.js. The JavaScript document is not going to be explored fully. The page's structure is shown in the following code block. The page is contained within a wrapper div. Within that, there is a masthead that contains a logo div and a navContainer div (which itself contains a navigation div). After the masthead is a content div that contains two columns, formed from div elements with id values of sidebar and mainContent.

```
<div id="wrapper">
  <div id="masthead">
    <div id="logo"></div>
    <div id="navContainer">
      <div id="navigation"></div>
    </div>
  </div>
  <div id="content">
    <div id="sidebar"></div>
    <div id="mainContent"></div>
  </div>
</div>
```

In the masthead, prior to the logo div, is an unordered list with an id value of pullNav. This is used for the pull-navigation at the top right of the design (including the Shopping basket, Checkout, Account, and Helpdesk links).

```
<ul id="pullNav">
  <li><a href="#">Shopping basket</a></li>
  <li><a href="#">Checkout</a></li>
  <li><a href="#">Account</a></li>
  <li><a href="#">Helpdesk</a></li>
</ul>
```

The logo div contains a linked image (linked to # in this example, but in a live site, this would be linked to the website's home page). The navContainer contents are identical to those in Chapter 5's "Creating a multicolumn drop-down menu" exercise.

In the content area, the sidebar `div` contents are straightforward: level-two headings are twice followed by unordered lists full of links (intended for links to top sellers and items coming soon), and a third heading is followed by a paragraph of text. In the `mainContent` div, a level-one heading is followed by an introductory paragraph and a horizontal rule. Next are the page's recently arrived item highlights. These each take the form of a containing `div` (with an `id` value of `itemContainer`), and each of these containers contains two divs, `itemImage` (which houses an image) and `itemDetails`. Each `itemDetails` div contains an unordered list for the name, price, stock notification, and dispatch details, along with a paragraph of descriptive text. Two of the list items have `class` values, which are used as hooks for CSS styles.

```
<div class="itemContainer">
  <div class="itemImage">
    <a href="#"><img src="assets/temporary-image.gif" alt="[temporary
    image]" width="100" height="100" /></a>
  </div>
  <div class="itemDetails">
    <ul>
      <li class="itemName"><a href="#">Item name</a></li>
      <li class="itemCost">£X.XX</li>
      <li>In stock</li>
      <li>Usually dispatched within 24 hours</li>
    </ul>
    <p>Lorem ipsum dolor […]</p>
  </div>
</div>
```

After the three-item container blocks is a second horizontal rule and then the main content area's final content: a level-two heading and a paragraph of text. Because each item container has a bottom border style assigned in CSS, the second horizontal rule results in a double border. Because of its semantic significance, it needs to remain, which leaves the choice of making it invisible by CSS or making the final item container's bottom border invisible, which is what's been done. (If you look at the `class` attribute of the third `itemContainer` div, it has a second value, `lastItemContainer`.)

Finally, after the two columns but inside the content `div` is a single footer paragraph containing a copyright statement.

tyling the storefront

The `store.css` document contains the styles for this layout, arranged into sections, as noted earlier in the chapter. The defaults section includes two rules. The first is the universal selector (*), used to remove padding and margins (as per the "Zeroing margins and padding on all elements" section in Chapter 2). The second is a `body` rule, which adds some top and bottom padding to the web page, ensuring that there's always some whitespace around the design.

In the structure section are a number of rules for styling the page's structural elements. The #wrapper rule provides both a maximum width and a minimum width for the site wrapper, along with centering the site via the `margin` value.

```
#wrapper {
  max-width: 1000px;
  min-width: 760px;
  margin: 0 auto;
}
```

The #masthead rule adds a large bottom border of 18 pixels to the masthead.
```
#masthead {
  border-bottom: 18px solid #eeeeee;
}
```

At this point, the reasoning for the #masthead rule won't be apparent, so I'll explain. The design as a whole has 18 pixels of padding around the content area. It also uses faux columns (as outlined in Chapter 7's "Creating a sidebar with faux-column backgrounds" exercise) to apply a vertical separator stripe between the two columns (the sidebar and the main content area). However, from a design standpoint, it looks much nicer if the column doesn't start right from the top of the content area and there's instead some space above it. Because the background is applied to the content div, the background image by default starts from the top of the content area. To avoid this, one option would be to add further markup that "covers" a portion of the separator stripe (via a div with a background color, a fixed height, and a width that spans the entire content div's width). However, adding a border to the bottom of the masthead that has the same color as the content area's background has the same effect. Sure, this is kind of a hack, but it doesn't cause any problems from a structural standpoint, and no semantics are affected. If you do this sort of thing, however, always remember where the various elements of the visual design lie in CSS, and use comments to remind yourself, if you need them.

Anyway, onward. The #logo rule is much simpler, adding some padding at the bottom and left of the div that houses the site logo. The reason for adding padding at the left is because otherwise the logo would abut the browser window edge at a screen resolution of 800 x 600. The #content rule adds some horizontal padding, along with the column-stripe.gif image as a vertically tiling background image (the aforementioned faux-column technique). Note the horizontal position of 27%. This is designed to sit roughly within the margin to the right of the sidebar div (see the following code block for the width and margin-right values of the sidebar and mainContent divs). Logically, a value of 26% should be set, because that would be the width of the sidebar, plus half of the margin-right value. However, the padding value of #content messes with that calculation somewhat, because the two columns don't span the entire width that the content div background occupies, since that stretches to the edge of the padding, which is 18 pixels on each horizontal edge. A setting of 26% therefore results in the vertical stripe appearing too far to the left; adding 1% results in a more pleasing position for the background.

```
#content {
  padding: 0 18px;
  background: #eeeeee url(assets/column-stripe.gif) 27% 0 repeat-y;
}
#sidebar {
  float: left;
  width: 24%;
  margin-right: 4%;
}
#mainContent {
```

```
  float: left;
  width: 72%;
}
```

Next, the .itemContainer rule defines a border and margin at the bottom of the itemContainer divs. This is overridden for the last of the three containers by the .lastItemContainer rule to avoid a double underline (as explained earlier). The .itemContainer:after rule is essentially the same as the clearFix rule (see the "Clearing floated content" exercise in Chapter 7), clearing floated content so that the itemContainer divs don't stack incorrectly. The .itemImage rule floats the divs containing the images right, adding some bottom and left margins so that other content doesn't abut them. Finally, the hr rule defines settings for the horizontal rule (although note that Internet Explorer deals with hr margins differently from other browsers, making them larger—this will be dealt with via conditional comments).

In the navigation section, the first three rules define colors for default, visited, and hover/focus link states, while the next three style the pull-navigation. The #pullNav rule floats the pull-navigation list right and adds some right padding, while #pullNav li sets the list items within to display inline, adding the vertical-bar.gif image as a background and some padding. The ul#pullNav li:first-child rule then removes the background from the first of the list items. The code is shown in the following block, and a full explanation is shown in the "Creating breadcrumb navigation" exercise in Chapter 5.

```
#pullNav {
  float: right;
  padding-right: 10px;
}
#pullNav li {
  display: inline;
  background: url(assets/vertical-bar.gif) 0 55% no-repeat;
  padding: 0 3px 0 8px;
}
ul#pullNav li:first-child {
  background: none;
}
```

The remainder of the rules are copied from Chapter 5's "Creating a multicolumn drop-down menu" exercise, and the path values to the css-tab-rollover-image.gif have been amended accordingly to take into account that the image is now being housed in an assets folder. There are two other changes as well, to cater for the layout the menu is being used with. First, #navContainer has a horizontally tiling background image (the gradient) applied; second, the #navigation ul rule has width and margin values to center the list horizontally, in the same way the wrapper div was centered earlier.

```
#navContainer {
  height: 30px;
  border-bottom: 5px solid #ad3514;
  background: url(assets/nav-background.gif) repeat-x;
}
#navigation ul {
  list-style-type: none;
  width: 740px;
  margin: 0 auto;
}
```

Fonts and fixes for the storefront layout

In the fonts section of the CSS, the default font size is set using the html and body rules, as per the "Setting text using percentages and ems" section in Chapter 3. The h1 rule defines the lead heading, and I've done something that hasn't been done elsewhere in the book: the heading is floated left. This enables subsequent content to wrap around the heading and is something I rarely do, but for this design, it made sense for the heading to be more of an introduction to the introductory paragraph itself, and displaying it inline was the way to do that. The padding-right value ensures there's some space before the subsequent paragraph. The line-height setting was calculated after the values for p and h1+p were defined, and the final figure was calculated in the same proportional manner as per h1+p (discussed later in the section).

```
h1 {
  float: left;
  padding-right: 0.3em;
  font: bold 1.4em/1.2571428em Arial, Helvetica, sans-serif;
}
```

The next three rules—h2, #sidebar h2, and p—style the level-two headings, level-two headings in the sidebar, and paragraphs, respectively. There's nothing of note here, but refer to Chapter 3 if there's something you're not familiar with. Next is the h1+p rule. This increases the font size of the paragraph that immediately follows the level-one heading, giving it more prominence. Because the font-size value has been increased, the line-height value has to be decreased proportionately in order for the text to all line up correctly. The p and h1+p rules are shown in the following code block.

```
p {
  font: 1.1em/1.6em Verdana, Arial, Helvetica, sans-serif;
  margin-bottom: 1.6em;
}
h1+p {
  font-size: 1.2em;
  line-height: 1.4666666em;
}
```

The next rule—#content ul, #pullNav—sets the default font and bottom margin for the two types of horizontally aligned list (the pull-navigation and the item details lists in the main content area). The three subsequent rules—#content .itemDetails ul, .itemDetails li, and .itemDetails li:first-child—style the lists in the itemContainer divs in pretty much the same way as for the pull-navigation. The main difference is the white background applied to the list items, which was added during the build stage in order to make the item details stand out more (see the detail shown next). This sort of thing happens all the time when I create sites—mock-ups should always be more a guideline than something to slavishly and exactly reproduce in the final site. If you can think of an improvement (and the client is happy with it, if you're working on a commercial project), then make changes!

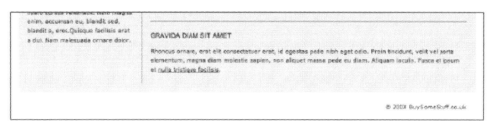

The remaining rules in this section are all straightforward. The .itemName, .itemCost rule emboldens the text in the list items with the class values of itemName and itemCost, thereby making the name and cost stand out more. And p.footer styles the footer paragraph. In this rule, clear is set to both so that the footer clears the two floated columns, and the text is aligned right. However, the footer also serves other purposes of a more decorative nature. The background is set to white, an 18-pixel top border the same color as the content background is defined, and negative horizontal margins of 18px are set, along with padding of 18px. What this does is make the background of the footer white and span the entire width of the content div, including its padding. The top border deals with the faux-column separator in the same way as the bottom border on the masthead. A detail of the resulting footer is shown in the following image.

The last three rules are in the images section. The first, a img, removes borders from linked images. The next, .itemImage img, adds a border to images within the itemImage divs, and .itemImage img:hover changes the border color on the hover state, indicating that the link is clickable (seeing as all of the item images are surrounded by links).

As mentioned earlier, this layout also has three style sheets linked via conditional comments to deal with Internet Explorer issues. The first, ie-hacks.css, has line-height overrides for h1 and h1+p, which line up the heading and paragraphs properly in Microsoft's browser. A rounding problem causes a horizontal scroll bar to appear at narrow browser window sizes, so the #mainContent rule's width value is overridden with a setting of 71.9%. Finally, the hr rule defines vertical margin values to make the horizontal rules in Internet Explorer behave in a similar manner to other browsers.

The completed web page is shown in the following image, with the drop-down active.

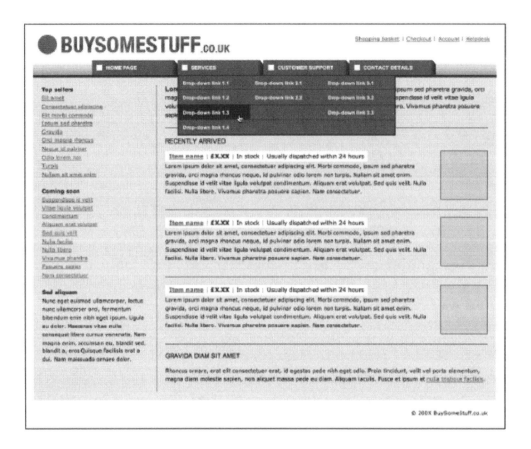

Creating a business website

This section will detail how I created the third layout in this chapter, which is suitable for a business website. This makes use of the two-tier navigation system devised in Chapter 5, and although the entire design doesn't adhere strictly to a baseline grid, I decided that it would be good for the content area to do so to create a more pleasing rhythm for the content area of the page. The Photoshop file for the document is sme-layout.psd, in the PSD mock-ups folder within the chapter 10 folder of the download files. The completed web page (along with associated files) is within the sme-website folder, within the chapter 10 folder. The following image shows the Photoshop mock-up of the page.

out the design and required images

This design is clean and modern. The site is fixed-width, with a dark background color for the overall page; a dark gradient from the top draws the attention toward the top of the page. The masthead contains the company logo, along with a short sentence regarding what the organization offers. Below that is the navigation, followed by the content area. The content area is simple: an introductory heading and paragraph (with a floated image to the right) is followed by a client quote. Below that is a large horizontal rule, which is followed by two columns.

Image-wise, the masthead background was exported (with the sentence turned off—that was added in HTML text), as was the background gradient. Other images were sourced from elsewhere, with the temporary image being the same one as in the previous layout example and the navigation images being taken directly from the example created for Chapter 5.

Putting the business site together

When creating this layout, I made use of methods shown in the following exercises/sections:

- "Creating a fixed-width wrapper" (Chapter 7)

- "Manipulating two structural divs for fixed-width layouts" (Chapter 7)

- "Placing columns within a wrapper" (Chapter 7)

- "Creating a two-tier navigation menu" (Chapter 5)

- "Using CSS to wrap text around images" (Chapter 4)

- "Gradients" (Chapter 2, from the "Web page background ideas" section)

- "Styling semantic markup: a traditional example with serif fonts and a baseline grid" (Chapter 3)

- "Creating a boxout" (Chapter 7)

- "Creating pull quotes in CSS" (Chapter 3)

Open index.html and examine the code. The head section imports a style sheet and uses conditional comments to link to three IE-specific style sheets (one for Internet Explorer in general, one for Internet Explorer 6 and older, and one for Internet Explorer versions older than 6). Note that the body element has an id value—this dictates the active tab, as per the method shown in the "Creating a two-tier navigation menu" exercise in Chapter 5.

The page's structure is shown in the following code block. The page is contained within a wrapper div. Within that, there is a masthead that contains a logo div and a navContainer div (which itself contains a navigation div and a subNavigation div). After the masthead is a content div. Without content, the skeleton structure looks like that shown in the following code block:

```
<div id="wrapper">
  <div id="masthead">
    <div id="logo"></div>
    <div id="navContainer">
      <div id="navigation"></div>
    </div>
  </div>
  <div id="content"></div>
</div>
```

In the logo div is the paragraph about the company, and the contents of the navContainer div are identical to those from "Creating a two-tier navigation menu" in Chapter 5.

The content div begins with a level-one heading, immediately followed by an image with a class value of leadImage. The image is positioned here because it will be floated right, and you need to place floated content before the content you want it to float left or right of (see the "Using CSS to wrap text around images" section in Chapter 4). This is followed by a paragraph of text and then a blockquote element, as per "Creating pull quotes in CSS" from Chapter 3.

Next, a horizontal rule provides a visual break from the introductory content, followed by two `div`s that have `class` values of `columnLeft` and `columnRight`. As you've no doubt guessed, these are the two columns; each contains an image, a level-two heading, and a paragraph. The final piece of code within the content `div` is a footer paragraph.

yling the business website

The `sme.css` document contains the styles for this layout, arranged into sections, as per the discussion earlier in this chapter. The defaults section includes two rules. The first is the universal selector (*), used to remove padding and margins (as per "Zeroing margins and padding on all elements" in Chapter 2). The second is a `body` rule, which adds some vertical padding to the web page, ensuring there's always some space before and after the bordered content (having borders directly touch browser window edges makes for a cluttered and visually unappealing design), and defines the page background—a dark gray color (#333333) into which is blended the horizontally tiled background image `page-background.gif`.

```
body {
    padding: 20px 0;
    background: #333333 url(assets/page-background.gif) repeat-x;
}
```

In the structure section, the `#wrapper` rule defines a fixed width for the wrapper, horizontally centers it, and defines a one-pixel border around its edges. The `#masthead` rule defines the thick, light gray border under the masthead, and `#logo` sets the `masthead-background.jpg` image as a background for the logo `div`, along with setting the height of the `div` (which is the same height as the image) and adding a one-pixel bottom margin (otherwise the top border of the navigation items doesn't show).

Next, the `#content` rule sets 18 pixels of padding around the content area's contents and defines the background color as white (otherwise the dark gray page background would show through). There's also a commented-out rule for the baseline grid image, added for the same reason as in the "Pictures from Padstow" example (see the first paragraph of the "Styling the gallery" section, earlier in this chapter). Note that 18 pixels is the target baseline grid line height for this design.

Next, the `hr` rule styles the horizontal rule, making it light gray and ensuring that it takes up a couple of "rows" in the grid (0.7em plus 2.9em is 3.6em, which because of the standard text sizing used throughout this book equates by default to 36px—twice the target line height of 18px).

```
hr  {
    height: 0.7em;
    margin-bottom: 2.9em;
    background-color: #cccccc;
    color: #cccccc;
    border: none;
}
```

The final two rules in the section, `.columnLeft, .columnRight` (`.columnLeft, .columnRight` is a grouped selector, not two separate rules) and `.columnLeft`, float the two column `div`s, set fixed widths for them (equally, since this property is placed in the grouped selector), and define a `margin-right` value for the left column so that there's space between the two columns.

The next section, links and navigation, is copied wholesale from Chapter 5's "Creating a two-tier navigation menu" exercise. There are no changes. Nothing to see here . . . move along.

Next is the fonts section. This section is all pretty straightforward, assuming you've read and digested the "Styling semantic markup: A traditional example with serif fonts and a baseline grid" exercise in Chapter 3. As usual, the html and body rules reset the font size, as per the "Setting text using percentages and ems" section in Chapter 3. The body rule also sets the preferred font to a Lucida variant (eventually falling back to Arial and Helvetica). The h1, h2, and p rules then set font-size, line-height, and margin-bottom values for their respective elements, with the line-height values being calculated by dividing 1.8 by the font-size value. (If you're going "wha...?" the "Styling semantic markup: A traditional example with serif fonts and a baseline grid" exercise in Chapter 3 has all the answers.)

Override rules follow, with specific settings for the masthead paragraph defined via -#masthead p; the color is set to white, and padding is used to position the block of text.

```
#masthead p {
  color: #ffffff;
  font-size: 1.2em;
  padding: 24px 20px 0 320px;
  line-height: 1.3em;
}
```

The p.footer rule is used to clear any floated content; the rule also aligns the text right and adds some top padding to shift it farther away from other page content (ensuring the footer isn't a distraction). The various blockquote and cite rules are variants on the method shown in Chapter 3's "Creating pull quotes in CSS" exercise. Again, somewhat complex line-height and margin values are used to take into account the baseline grid.

Finally, the images section has four rules. The first, a img, removes borders from linked images. Next, #content img applies a one-pixel border to images within the content div. After that, the img.leadImage rule floats the image after the main heading right, adding some margins at the bottom and left edges to ensure there's some whitespace between the image and other content. And then .columnLeft img, .columnRight img sets the images within the columns to display as a block, which removes the default overhang that browsers otherwise apply to images (as they do to text). The margin-bottom value ensures subsequent content is aligned with the baseline grid. Note that the height of the images, as defined in HTML, is 70 pixels. Add two pixels from the borders, and you have 72, a multiple of 18, ensuring that the actual images adhere to the baseline grid, too—at least when browsers are at their default settings.

```
.columnLeft img, .columnRight img {
  display: block;
  margin-bottom: 1.8em;
}
```

The completed layout is shown in the following screenshot.

reating a blog layout

This section will detail how I created the fourth layout in this chapter, which is suitable for a blog layout. The emphasis here will be to create a mobile-first, responsive, adaptive experience. For this to happen, we will see how to structure HTML for an adaptive site so that flexibility is possible. We'll also see how to write CSS that defines shared styles first, builds up styles for larger screens with media queries, and uses relative units. The completed web page (along with associated files) is within the `blog-website` folder, within the `chapter 10` folder. The following image shows the mock-up of the page.

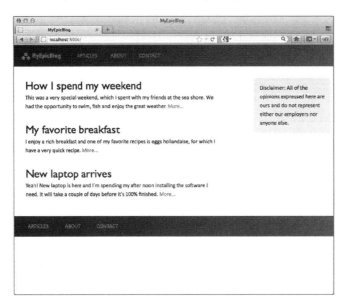

About responsive design and semantic markup

Responsive web design gives web designers the tools to create layouts that respond to any screen size. Designers can use fluid grids, flexible images, and media queries to get the layout looking great regardless of the size of the device's screen dimensions. Since mobile context is more than just screen size, it is also important to focus on what content is essential and how to present that content as quickly as possible, delivering a fast-loading, optimized experience.

There are several semantic elements in HTML5 such as article, aside, figure, footer, header, nav, and section, and because of the intuitive naming, you can probably guess what most of these elements do.

Here's the wireframe of a layout, both for the desktop and for mobile, that illustrates how these elements will be used:

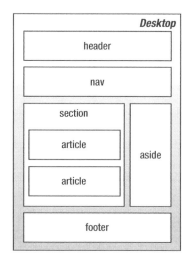

edia Queries

Beyond the media attribute, with CSS3 media queries extend the functionality of media types by allowing more precise labeling of style sheets. A media query consists of a media type and zero or more expressions that check for the conditions of particular media features. By using media queries, presentations can be tailored to a specific range of output devices without changing the content itself. A media query is a logical expression that is either true or false. A media query is true if the media type of the media query matches the media type of the device where the user agent is running and all expressions in the media query are true.

Here are a few examples:

```
<link rel="stylesheet" media="screen and (color)" href="example.css" />
```

The previous example applies to devices of a certain media type (screen) with certain feature (it must be a color screen).

A shorthand syntax is offered for media queries that apply to all media types; the keyword all can be left out (along with the trailing and). In other words, the following are identical:

```
@media (orientation: portrait) { … }
@media all and (orientation: portrait) { … }
```

This way, designers and developers can create more complex queries that map to their specific needs.

```
@media all and (max-width: 698px) and (min-width: 520px), (min-width: 1150px) {
  body {
    background: #ccc;
  }
}
```

There is a large list of media features, which includes the following:

- width and device-width

- height and device-height

- orientation

- aspect-ratio and device-aspect-ratio

- color and color-index

- monochrome (if not a monochrome device, equals 0)

- resolution

- scan (describes the scanning process of tv output devices)

- grid (specifies whether the output device is grid or bitmap)

Putting the blog together

Semantic markup is extremely portable and can be accessed by many mobile devices. Browsers offer users a *viewport* (a window or other viewing area on the screen) through which users see a document, and they may change the document's layout when the viewport is resized. When the viewport is smaller than the area of the canvas on which the document is rendered, browsers usually offer some sort of scrolling mechanism.

Mobile Safari and other mobile browsers set a larger viewport, which allows for better viewing of non-mobile-optimized sites. Users can then pinch to zoom in on the content they want. Because we're optimizing our experience for mobile browsers, we'll use the viewport meta tag to set the screen width to the device width.

```
<meta name="viewport" content="width=device-width, initial-scale=1" />
```

The width property controls the size of the viewport. It can be set to a specific number of pixels like width=600 or to the special value device-width value that is the width of the screen in CSS pixels at a scale of 100%. The initial-scale property controls the zoom level when the page is first loaded.

Styling the blog

If you open index.html, you'll see that the page includes two different CSS files: style.css for basic styles on screens less than 40.5em and enhanced.css for screens larger than 40.5em.

```
<link rel="stylesheet" type="text/css" href="style.css" media="screen, handheld" />
<link rel="stylesheet" type="text/css" href="enhanced.css" media="screen  and (min-width:
40.5em)" />
```

As described in Chapter 3 "Working with type," we're using the em units to maintain consistency across zoom levels.

Starting with baseline shared styles and introducing more advanced layout rules when screen size permits keeps code simpler, smaller, and more maintainable. Here's just a quick example to demonstrate this point.

Our (mobile-first) strategy will be to define first the mobile-specific styles in style.css and then define media queries in enhanced.css that take care of the desktop.

Here's an example:

```
/* Default (mobile) style in style.css */
#some-id {
  /* Styles for mobile */
}

/* Desktop style in enhanced.css */
@media screen and (min-width: 40.5em) {
    #some-id {
      /* Styles for desktop */
}
```

For the styling of the header, we use some diagonal gradient, which also adapts well on different screen sizes.

```
/* Old browsers */
background: rgb(0, 0, 0);
/* FF3.6+ */
background: -moz-linear-gradient(-45deg, rgba(0, 0, 0, 1) 0%, rgba(96, 96, 96, 1) 100%);
/*Chrome,Safari4+ */
background: -webkit-gradient(linear, left top, right bottom, color-stop(0%, rgba(0, 0, 0, 1)),
color-stop(100%, rgba(96, 96, 96, 1)));
/* Chrome10+,Safari5.1+ */
background: -webkit-linear-gradient(-45deg, rgba(0, 0, 0, 1) 0%, rgba(96, 96, 96, 1) 100%);
/* Opera 11.10+ */
background: -o-linear-gradient(-45deg, rgba(0, 0, 0, 1) 0%, rgba(96, 96, 96, 1) 100%);
/* IE10+ */
background: -ms-linear-gradient(-45deg, rgba(0, 0, 0, 1) 0%, rgba(96, 96, 96, 1) 100%);
/* W3C */
background: linear-gradient(-45deg, rgba(0, 0, 0, 1) 0%, rgba(96, 96, 96, 1) 100%);
/* IE6-9 fallback on horizontal gradient */
filter: progid:DXImageTransform.Microsoft.gradient(startColorstr = '#000000', endColorstr =
'#606060', GradientType = 1);
```

We will be setting any images to have rounded corners with 0.5em radius.

```
.content img {
-webkit-border-radius: 0.5em;
-moz-border-radius: 0.5em;
border-radius: 0.5em;
}
```

Since this is a mobile-first site, we will avoid using @font-face rendering since there are some problems with it in the mobile context, such as blocking the download of other resources and delaying the UI rendering. There are a few tricks to optimize @font-face for mobile if we *need* to use it, like data url and inlining the font in base64.

381

```
@font-face {
    font-family: "My Epic Font";
    src: url("data:font/opentype;base64,[base64-encoded font here]");
}
```

Instead, we'll be using transitions to create a subtle hover effect for the navigation links.

```
.nav li a {
  display: block;
  padding: 1em;
  border-left: 1px solid #333;
  -webkit-transition: all 0.3s ease-out;
  -moz-transition: all 0.3s ease-out;
  transition: all 0.3s ease-out;
}
```

The completed layout is shown in the following screenshot.

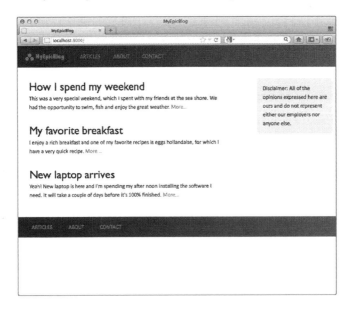

Working with style sheets for print

This section briefly looks at using CSS to create a printable version of a website layout. Printing from the Web is still a bit of a hit-and-miss affair, and even using CSS doesn't solve every problem, although browser support for print-oriented CSS is improving. If you omit a print style sheet, though, chances are the output will be significantly worse. Browsers may have varying opinions on how to present both fixed and liquid layouts, and you may end up with bizarre results. Most likely, however, if you omit a print style sheet, all of the elements on your web page will just be printed in a linear fashion, using system defaults for the fonts—not nice.

In the old days (and, frankly, in the not-so-old days, since the practice somehow survives), designers often worked on so-called printer-friendly sites, run in parallel with the main site. However, if you're using CSS layouts, it's possible to create a style sheet specifically for print, which you can use to dictate exactly which elements on the page you want to print, which you want to omit, and how you want to style those that can be printed.

As mentioned earlier in the book, a print style sheet is attached to web pages using the following HTML:

```
<link rel="stylesheet" type="text/css"media="print"
  href="print-style-sheet.css" />
```

The media attribute value of print restricts the CSS solely to print, and within the print style sheet, you define styles specifically for print, such as different fonts and margins. In the example in the download files, I've used a version of the business website, which you can access via the sme-website-print folder in the chapter 10 folder. The print style sheet is sme-print.css, and if you compare it to the main style sheet, you'll see that it's much simpler and massively honed down.

The defaults section houses a single body rule, defining padding (to take into account varying printer margins, 5% is a good horizontal padding to use), the background color (white is really the only choice you should use, and it's usually the default, but setting it explicitly ensures this is the case), the text color (black is best for contrast when printing), and the font. There's absolutely no point in trying to ape your on-screen design and typography in print; instead, use values that enhance the printed version. In the example's body rule (shown in the following code block), serif fonts are defined for font-family, because serifs are easier to read in print. Note that you're not only restricted to web-safe fonts at this point either—you can define choices based on fonts that come with the default install of Windows and Mac OS, such as Baskerville (Mac) and Palatino Linotype (Windows), prior to Times New Roman and Times.

```
body {
  padding: 0 5%;
  background: #ffffff;
  font-family: Baskerville, "Palatino Linotype", "Times New Roman",
    "Times", serif;
  line-height: 16pt;
}
```

In the structure section, the #masthead declaration sets display to none. That's because this area of the page is of no use for printed output—you simply don't need website masthead and navigation offline. (This is, of course, a generalization, and in rare cases this may not be applicable; however, in the vast, vast majority of websites I've created, the printed version has not required the masthead and navigation links.) Note that if other areas aren't required, just use a grouped selector instead of this rule with a lone selector, as shown in the following code block (which isn't in the example CSS):

```
#element1, #element2, .class1, .class2 {/* these items won't be
  printed */
  display: none;
}
```

Because pixel values don't tend to translate to print well, some settings may need to be redefined. An example in this case is the two-column section of the page. The widths and margins were initially defined in pixels, but in the print CSS, it makes more sense to define these values in percentages. (Note that the 9.99% value is there in case of rounding errors.)

```
.columnLeft, .columnRight {
  float: left;
  width: 45%;
}
.columnLeft {
  margin-right: 9.99%;
}
```

In the links and navigation section, only one rule remains. While links are of no real use offline, it's still a good idea to make it apparent which text-based content was originally a link in order for people to be able to find said links should they want to, or for reasons of context. Just ensuring the default underline is in place should do, and that can be done via the following rule:

```
a:link, a:visited {
  text-decoration: underline;
}
```

For browsers other than Internet Explorer (although JavaScript workarounds exist for IE compatibility—for example, see www.grafx.com.au/dik//printLinkURLs.html), you can also provide the href values alongside any printed links by using the following code:

```
a:link:after, a:visited:after {
  content: " (" attr(href) ") ";
  font-size: 90%;
}
```

In terms of fonts, keeping things simple makes sense. It's also worth noting that because you're working with print, sizes in points are more useful than sizes in pixels. (Note that in the body rule, the line-height value was 16pt, not 16px or 1.6em.) Therefore, the font-size values all reflect that. Note in the p.footer rule that floated content still needs clearing in the print style sheets.

The final section, images, is not changed much. The images within the columns were deemed superfluous, and so display has been set to none for .columnLeft img, .columnRight img. Elsewhere, the margins on the floated image have been set to values in centimeters (cm), and the border value for #content img is in millimeters (mm), since we're working in print. (Values in pixels are permitted, but they tend to be less accurate when working with print style sheets—for example, if elements have a one-pixel border, they may not all be even when printed.)

One final thing that's useful to know is how to create print-only content. In this example, removing the masthead from the print output has also removed the site's corporate ID. A cunning way to bring this back is to create a black-and-white version of the company logo and add that as the first item on the web page, within a div that has an id value of printLogo.

```
<div id="printLogo">
  <img src="assets/we-lay-floors-bw-logo.gif" alt="Web Lay Floors,
    Inc. logo" width="267" height="70" />
</div>
```

Then, in the main style sheet, create a rule that displays this element offscreen when the page is loaded in a browser window.

```
#printLogo {
  position: absolute;
  left: -1000px;
}
```

The content will then show up in print but not online. Note, however, that you should be mindful to not hide weighty images in this manner; otherwise, you'll compromise download speeds for anyone using your website in a browser, only for making things slightly better for those printing the site. A small, optimized GIF should be sufficient.

If there's other content you want to hide in this manner, you can also create a generic printOnly class to apply to elements you want hidden in the browser but visible in print. The following CSS rule applied to your screen style sheet would be sufficient for doing this:

```
.printOnly {
  display: none;
}
```

An example of how the print style sheet looks is shown in the following screenshot.

For all your flooring needs

Lorem ipsum dolor sit amet, consectetuer adipiscing elit. Morbi commodo, ipsum sed pharetra gravida, orci magna rhoncus neque, id pulvinar odio lorem non turpis. Nullam sit amet enim. Suspendisse id velit vitae ligula volutpat condimentum. Aliquam erat volutpat. Sed quis velit. Nulla facilisi. Nulla libero. Vivamus pharetra posuere sapien. Nam consectetuer. Sed aliquam, nunc eget euismod ullamcorper, lectus nunc ullamcorper orci, fermentum bibendum enim nibh eget ipsum. Donec porttitor ligula eu dolor. Maecenas vitae nulla consequat libero cursus venenatis. Nam magna enim, accumsan eu, blandit sed, blandit a, eros. Quisque facilisis erat a dui. Nam malesuada ornare dolor. Cras gravida, diam sit amet rhoncus ornare, erat elit consectetuer erat, id egestas pede nibh eget odio.

This is the pull quote. It's really very exciting, so read it now! Lorem ipsum dolor sit amet, consectetuer adipiscing elit.

Fred Bloggs

Lorem ipsum dolor

Sit amet, consectetuer adipiscing elit. Morbi commodo, ipsum sed pharetra gravida, orci magna rhoncus neque, id pulvinar odio lorem non turpis. Nullam sit amet enim. Suspendisse id velit vitae ligula volutpat condimentum. Aliquam erat volutpat. Sed quis velit. Nulla facilisi. Nulla libero. Vivamus pharetra posuere sapien. Nam consectetuer. Sed aliquam, nunc eget euismod ullamcorper, lectus nunc ullamcorper orci, fermentum.

Quisque facilisis erat a dui

Nam malesuada ornare dolor. Cras gravida, diam sit amet rhoncus ornare, erat elit consectetuer erat, id egestas pede nibh eget odio. Proin tincidunt, velit vel porta elementum, magna diam molestie sapien, non aliquet massa pede eu diam. Aliquam iaculis. Fusce et ipsum et nulla tristique facilisis. Donec eget sem sit amet ligula viverra gravida. Etiam vehicula urna vel turpis. Suspendisse sagittis ante a urna.

An example of how the print style sheet looks is shown in the following screenshot.

Note that you can take things further in terms of layout, but it's best to keep it simple. Also, ensure that you use the Print Preview functions of your browser test suite to thoroughly test your print style sheet output and ensure that there are no nasty surprises for visitors to your site. Ultimately, it's worth the extra hassle—just amending the fonts and page margins and removing images and page areas that are irrelevant to the printed version of the site not only improves your users' experience but also makes the site seem more professional.

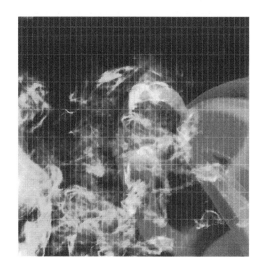

An HTML5 reference

This appendix details, in alphabetical order, generally supported elements and associated attributes. This is not intended as an exhaustive guide; rather, its aim is to list those elements important and relevant to current web design. Archaic deprecated elements such as font and layer are therefore ignored, as well as many attributes once associated with the body element, but the appendix includes still occasionally useful deprecated and nonstandard elements and attributes such as embed and target.

> *Note that in the following pages, various styles are used for the attribute names and values. For the sake of clarity, quote marks have been omitted. Where you see the likes of id=name in this reference section, the final output should be id="name".*

tandard attributes

Standard attributes are common to many elements. For brevity, they are listed in full here rather than in the HTML5 element table later in the appendix. For each element in the forthcoming table, I simply state which groups of standard attributes are applicable to the element.

Core attributes

Attribute	Description
class=*classname*	Specifies a CSS class to define the element's visual appearance.
id=*name*	Defines a unique reference ID for the element.
style=style	Specifies an inline CSS style for an element.
title=*string*	Specifies the element's title. Often used with links to provide a tooltip expanding on the link's purpose or the target's content.

Not valid in these elements: base, head, html, meta, param, script, style, and title.

Keyboard attributes

Attribute	Description
accesskey=character	Defines a keyboard shortcut to access an element. The shortcut must be a single character. Most commonly used with navigation links. See also Chapter 5's "Using accesskey and tabindex" section.
tabindex=number	Defines the tab order of an element. Most commonly used with form input elements. Setting the value to 0 excludes the element from the tabbing order. The maximum value allowed is 32767. The tabindex values on a page needn't be consecutive (for instance, you could use multiples of 10 to leave space for later additions). See also Chapter 5's "Using accesskey and tabindex" section.

nguage attributes

Attribute	Description
dir=dir	Specifies the text rendering direction: left-to-right (ltr, the default) or right-to-left (rtl).
lang	Specifies the language for the tag's contents, using two-letter primary ISO639 codes and optional dialect codes. Included for backward compatibility with HTML. Examples: lang="en" (English) lang="en-US" (US English) ISO639 codes include the following: ar (Arabic), zh (Chinese), nl (Dutch), fr (French), de (German), el (Greek), he (Hebrew), it (Italian), ja (Japanese), pt (Portuguese), ru (Russian), sa (Sanskrit), es (Spanish), and ur (Urdu).

> *Not valid in these elements: base, br, frame, frameset, hr, iframe, param, and script.*

vent attributes

An event attribute is an attribute that triggers when something happens on a web page.

re events

Attribute	Description
onclick=script	Specifies a script to be run when the user clicks the element's content area
ondblclick=script	Specifies a script to be run when the user double-clicks the element's content area
onkeydown=script	Specifies a script to be run when the user presses a key while the element's content area is focused
onkeypress=script	Specifies a script to be run when the user presses and releases a key while the element's content area is focused
onkeyup=script	Specifies a script to be run when the user releases a

	pressed key while the element's content area is focused
onmousedown=*script*	Specifies a script to be run when the user presses down the mouse button while the cursor is over the element's content area
onmousemove=*script*	Specifies a script to be run when the user moves the mouse cursor in the element's content area
onmouseout=*script*	Specifies a script to be run when the user moves the mouse cursor off the element's content area
onmouseover=*script*	Specifies a script to be run when the user moves the mouse cursor onto the element's content area
onmouseup=*script*	Specifies a script to be run when the user releases the mouse button on the element's content area

Not valid in these elements: base, bdo, br, frame, frameset, head, html, iframe, meta, param, script, style, and title.

Form element events

These events are generally restricted to form elements, although some other elements accept some of them.

Attribute	Description
onblur=*script*	Specifies a script to be run when the element loses focus
oninput=script	Specifies a script to be run when an element gets user input
onchange=*script*	Specifies a script to be run when the element changes
onfocus=*script*	Specifies a script to be run when the element is focused
oninvalid=*script*	Specifies a script to be run when an element is invalid
onforminput=script	Specifies a script to be run when a form gets user input
onformchange=script	Specifies a script to be run when a form changes
oncontextmenu=script	Specifies a script to be run when a context menu is triggered

| onselect=*script* | Specifies a script to be run when the element is selected |
| onsubmit=*script* | Specifies a script to be run when a form is submitted |

indow events

These events are valid only in the following elements: body and frameset.

Attribute	Description
onload=*script*	Specifies a script to be run when the document loads
onunload=*script*	Specifies a script to be run when the document unloads
onfocus=script	Specifies a script to be run when the window gets focus
onafterprint=script	Specifies a script to be run after the document is printed
onbeforeprint=script	Specifies a script to be run before the document is printed
onbeforeunload=script	Specifies a script to be run before the document loads
onerror=script	Specifies a script to be run when an error occur
onhaschange=script	Specifies a script to be run when the document has changed
onmessage=script	Specifies a script to be run when the message is triggered
onoffline=script	Specifies a script to be run when the document goes offline
ononline=script	Specifies a script to be run when the document comes online
onpagehide=script	Specifies a script to be run when the window is hidden
onpageshow=script	Specifies a script to be run when the window becomes visible
onpopstate=script	Specifies a script to be run when the window's history changes
onredo=script	Specifies a script to be run when the document performs a redo

onresize=script	Specifies a script to be run when the window is resized
onstorage=script	Specifies a script to be run when a web storage area is updated
onundo=script	Specifies a script to be run when the document performs an undo
onunload=script	Specifies a script to be run when the document performs an undo

HTML5 elements and attributes

The following pages list HTML5 elements, associated attributes, and descriptions for all.

Element	Attribute	Description	Standard attributes
`<!-- … -->`		Defines a comment. See also Chapter 2's "Commenting your work" section.	No attributes
`<!DOCTYPE >` *(required)*		Specifies a DTD for the document. See also Chapter 2's, "DOCTYPE declarations explained" section.	No attributes
`<a>`		Defines an anchor. Can link to another document by using the href attribute or can create an anchor within a document by using the id or name attributes. Despite the number of available attributes, some aren't well supported. Generally, href, name, title, and target are commonly used, along with class and id for use as CSS or scripting hooks. See also Chapter 5's "Creating and styling	Core attributes, keyboard attributes, language attributes

Core events, onblur, onfocus |

		web page links" section.	
	href=URL	Defines the link target.	
	hreflang=language_code	Specifies the language of the linked document	
	media=media_query	Specifies what media/device the linked document is optimized for	
	rel=relationship	Specifies the relationship from the current document to the target document. Common values include next, prev, parent, child, index, toc, and glossary. Also used within link elements to define the relationship of linked CSS documents (e.g., to establish default and alternative style sheets).	
	target=_blank|_parent|_self||_top|[name]	Defines where the target URL opens. Primarily of use with frames, stating which frame a target should open in. Commonly used in web pages to open external links in a new window—a practice that should be avoided, because it breaks the browser history path.	
	type=MIME type	Specifies the MIME type of the target. For instance, if linking to a plain-text file, you might use the following:<a href="document.txt" Â type="text/plain">.	
<abbr>		Identifies the element content as an	Core attributes, language attributes

		abbreviation. This can be useful for nonvisual web browsers. For example:<abbr title="Doctor">Dr.</abbr> > See also Chapter 3's "Acronyms and abbreviations" section.	Core events
`<address>`		Used to define addresses, signatures, or document authors. Typically rendered in italics, with a line break above and below (but no additional space). See also Chapter 8's "Contact details structure redux" section.	Core attributes, -language attributes Core events
`<area>`		Defines a clickable area within a client-side image map. Should be nested within a map element (see separate <map> entry). See also Chapter 5's *"Image maps" section.*	Core attributes, keyboard attributes, language attributes Core events, `onblur`, `onfocus`
	`alt=string•(re quired)`	Provides alternate text for nonvisual browsers. This attribute is required.	
	`coords=⊔coordinate s list`	Specifies coordinates for the clickable image map area. Values are defined as a comma-separated list. The number of values depends on the shape attribute value. For rect, four values are required, defining the coordinates on the x- and y-axes of the top-left and bottom-	

		right corners. For circle, three values are required, with the first two defining the x and y coordinates of the hotspot center and the third defining the circle's radius. For poly, each pair of x and y values defines a point of the hotspot.	
	href=*URL*	The link target.	
	hreflang=langu age_code	Specifies the language of the target URL.	
	media=media_qu ery	Specifies what media/device the target URL is optimized for.	
	rel=alternate| author| bookmark| help| license| next| nofollow| noreferrer| prefetch| prev| search| tag	Specifies the relationship between the current document and the target URL.	
	shape=rect| circle|p oly| default	Defines the shape of the clickable region.	
	target=_blank| _parent|_self| _top|[name] (deprecated)	Defines where the target URL opens.	
	type=mime_type	Specifies the MIME type of the target URL	
<article>		Defines an article.	Core attributes, language attributes Core events
<aside>		Defines content aside from the page content.	Core attributes, language attributes Core events

`<audio>`			Defines sound content.	Core attributes, language attributes Core events
	autoplay=autoplay		Specifies that the audio will start playing as soon as it is ready.	
	controls=controls		Specifies that audio controls should be displayed (such as a play/pause button).	
	loop=loop		Specifies that the audio will start over again, every time it is finished.	
	preload=auto| metadata| none		Specifies if and how the author thinks the audio should be loaded when the page loads.	
	src=URL		Specifies the URL of the audio file.	
`<b>`			Renders text as bold. □This element is a physical □style, which defines what □the content looks like (presentation only), rather than a logical style, which defines what the content □is (which is beneficial for technologies like screen readers). It's recommended to use the logical element `<strong></strong>` in place of `<b></b>` (see separate `<strong>` entry).□ See also Chapter 3's "Styles for emphasis (bold and italic)" section.	Core attributes, language attributes Core events

`<base />`		Specifies a base URL for relative URLs on the web page.	
	href=URL (required)	Defines the base URL to use. This attribute is required.	
	target=_blank| _parent|_self|_t op|[name] (deprecated)	Defines where to open page links. Can be overridden by inline target attributes. Cannot be used in XHTML Strict.	
`<bdi>`		Isolates a part of text that might be formatted in a different direction from other text outside it.	Core attributes, language attributes
`<bdo>`		Overrides the default text direction.	Core attributes, language attributes
	dir=ltr|rtl (required)	Defines text direction as left to right (ltr) or right to left (rtl). This attribute is required.	
`<blockquote>`		Defines a lengthy quotation. To validate as XHTML Strict, enclosed content must be set within a block-level element (such as <p></p>). Although it is common for web designers to use this element to indent content, the W3C strongly recommends using CSS for such things. See also Chapter 3's "Block quotes, quote citations, and definitions" and "Creating drop caps and pull quotes using CSS"	Core attributes, language attributes Core events

		sections.	
	`cite=URL`	Defines the online location of quoted material.	
`<body>` (required)		Defines the document's body and contains the document's contents.	Core attributes, language attributes Core events, `onload` `onunload`
` `		Inserts a single line break.	Core attributes
`<button>`		Defines a push button element within a form. Works similarly to buttons created with the input element but offers greater rendering scope. This is because all content becomes the content of the button, enabling the creation of buttons with text and images. For example:□<button type="submit">□Order now! <img src="go.gif" alt="Go" />□</button>.	Core attributes, keyboard attributes, language attributes Core events, `onblur` `onfocus`
	disabled=disabled	Disables the button. disabled is the only possible value of this attribute.	
	name=*name*	Defines the button's name.	
	type=button|reset|□submit	Identifies the button's type.	
	value=value	Specifies an initial value for the button	
	autofocus=autofocus	Specifies that a button should automatically get focus when the page loads.	

	form=form_id	Specifies one or more forms the button belongs to.	
	formaction=URL	Specifies where to send the form data when a form is submitted. Only for type="submit".	
	formenctype= application/x-www-form-urlencoded| multipart/form-data| text/plain	Specifies how form data should be encoded before sending it to a server. Only for type="submit".	
	formmethod=get| post	Specifies how to send the form data (which HTTP method to use). Only for type="submit".	
	formnovalidate=form novalidate	Specifies that the form data should not be validated on submission. Only for type="submit".	
	formtarget=blan k| _self| _parent| _top| *framename*	Specifies where to display the response after submitting the form. Only for type="submit".	
`<canvas>`		Used to draw graphics, on the fly, via scripting (usually JavaScript).	Core attributes, language attributes Core events
	height=pixels	Specifies the height of the canvas.	
	width=pixels	Specifies the width of the canvas.	
`<caption>`		Defines a caption for a table. Seldom used, but recommended because it enables you to associate a table's title	Core attributes, language attributes Core events

		with its contents. Omitting the caption may mean the table's contents are meaningless out of context.☐ See also Chapter 6's "Captions and summaries" section.	
`<cite>`		Defines content as a citation. Usually rendered in italics.☐ See also Chapter 3's "Block quotes, quote citations, and definitions" section.	Core attributes, language attributes Core events
`<code>`		Defines content as computer code sample text. Usually rendered in a monospace font.☐ See also Chapter 3's "Logical styles for programming-oriented content" section and the "Displaying blocks of code online" exercise.	Core attributes, language attributes Core events
`<col>`		Defines properties for a column or group of columns within a colgroup. Attributes defined within a col element override those set in the containing colgroup element. col is an empty element that contains attributes only.	Core attributes, language attributes Core events
	span=*n*	Defines how many successive columns are affected by the col ☐tag. Use only when the surrounding colgroup element does not specify the number of columns.☐	

`<colgroup>`		Defines a column group within a table, enabling you to define formatting for the columns within. See the <col /> entry for examples.	See also Chapter 6's "Scope and headers" section.	Core attributes, language attributes Core events
	span=*number*	Defines how many columns the colgroup should span. Do not use if any of the col tags within the colgroup also use span, because a colgroup definition will be ignored in favor of span attributes defined within the col elements.	
`<command>`		Defines a command button that a user can invoke.	Core attributes, language attributes Core events
	checked=checked	Specifies that the command should be checked when the page loads. Only for type="radio" or type="checkbox".	
	disabled=disabled	Specifies that the command should be disabled.	
	icon=URL	Specifies an image that represents the command.	
	label=text	Required. Specifies the name of the command, as shown to the user.	
	radiogroup=groupna me	Specifies the name of the group of commands that will be toggled when the command itself is toggled. Only for	

		type="radio".	
	type=checkbox| command| radio	Specifies the type of command.	
`<datalist>`		Specifies a list of predefined options for input controls.	Core attributes, language attributes Core events
`<dd>`		Defines a definition description within a definition list. See the <dl> entry for an example.☐ See also Chapter 3's "Definition lists" section and the "Displaying blocks of code online" exercise.	Core attributes, language attributes Core events
`<del>`		Indicates deleted text. Usually appears in strikethrough format.☐ See also Chapter 3's "Elements for inserted and deleted text" section.	Core attributes, language attributes Core events
	`cite=URL`	Defines the URL of a document that explains why the text was deleted.	
	datetime=date	Defines the date and time that the text was amended. Various formats are possible, including YYYY-MM-DD and YYYY-MM-DDThh:mm:ssTZD (where TZD is the time zone designator). See www.w3.org/ TR/1998/NOTE-datetime-19980827 for more date and time formatting information.	
`<details>`		Defines additional	Core attributes, language attributes

		details that the user can view or hide.	Core events
	open=open	Specifies that the details should be visible (open) to the user.	
<dfn>		Defines enclosed content as the defining instance of a term. Usually rendered in italics. See also Chapter 3's "Block quotes, quote citations, and definitions" section.	Core attributes, language attributes Core events
<div>		Defines a division within a web page. Perhaps one of the most versatile but least understood elements. Used in combination with an id or class, the div tag element allows sections of a page to be individually styled and is the primary XHTML element used for the basis of CSS-based web page layouts. See also Chapter 7's "Workflow for CSS layouts" section.	Core attributes, language attributes Core events
<dl>		Defines a definition list. Contains pairs of term and definition elements, as follows: <dl> <dt>Windows</dt> <dd>Operating system made by Microsoft.</dd> <dt>Mac OS</dt> <dd>Operating system made by Apple.</dd></dl> See also Chapter 3's "Definition lists" section	Core attributes, language attributes Core events

		and the "Displaying blocks of code online" exercise.	
<dt>		Defines a definition term within a definition list. See the <dl> entry for an example.□ See also Chapter 3's "Definition lists" section and the "Displaying blocks of code online" exercise.	Core attributes, language attributes Core events
<em>		Defines enclosed content as emphasized. Generally renders as italics in a browser and is preferred over the use of <i></i>. See separate <i> entry.□ See also Chapter 3's "Block quotes, quote citations, and definitions" section.	Core attributes, language attributes Core events
<embed>□		Defines a container for an external application or interactive content (a plug-in).	
	height=pixels	Specifies the height of the embedded content.	
	src=URL	Specifies the address of the external file to embed.	
	type=mime_type	Specifies the MIME type of the embedded content.	
	width=pixels	Specifies the width of the embedded content.	
<fieldset>		Creates a group of related form elements by nesting them within the fieldset element. Usually used in tandem	Core attributes, language attributes Core events

		with the legend element to enhance form accessibility (see the <legend> entry for more information). See also Chapter 8's "Improving form accessibility" section.	
	disabled=disabled	Specifies that a group of related form elements should be disabled.	
	form=form_id	Specifies one or more forms the fieldset belongs to.	
	name=text	Specifies a name for the fieldset.	
<figcaption>		Defines a caption for a <figure> element.	Core attributes, language attributes Core events
<figure>		Specifies self-contained content.	Core attributes, language attributes Core events
<footer>		Defines a footer for a document or section.	Core attributes, language attributes Core events
<form>		Indicates the start and end of a form. Cannot be nested within another form element. Generally, the method and action attributes are most used. See also Chapter 8's "Working with forms" section.	Core attributes, language attributes Core events, onreset, onsubmit
	accept-charset=charset list	Specifies a comma-separated list of character sets for form data.	
	action=URL (required)	The URL of the form processing application where the data is sent once the form is submitted. This attribute	

		is required.	
	autocomplete=o n| off	Specifies whether a form should have autocomplete on or off	
	enctype=encoding	The MIME type used to encode the form's content before it's sent to the server, so it doesn't become scrambled. Defaults to application/x-www-form-urlencoded. Other options are multipart/form-data, which can be used when the user is able to upload files, and text-plain, which □can be used when using a mailto: value for the action instead of a server-side script to parse the form data.	
	method=get|post	Specifies the http method used to submit the form data. The post value is most commonly used.	
	name=name□(depre cated)	Defines the form's name.	
	novalidate=novalidat e	Specifies that the form should not be validated when submitted.	
	target=_blank| _parent|_self| _top| [name] (deprecated)	Defines where the target URL is opened.	
<h*n*>		Defines enclosed contents as a heading. Available levels are 1 to 6. Note that although h4 through h6 tend to be	Core attributes, language attributes Core events

		displayed smaller than body copy by default, they are not a means to create small text; rather, they are a way to enable you to structure your document. This is essential, because headings help with assistive technology, enabling the visually impaired to efficiently surf the Web.⏎ See also Chapter 3's "Paragraphs and headings" section.	
<head> (required)		Defines the header of the HTML file. Houses information-based elements, such as base, link, meta, script, style, and title. This is a required element for XHTML web pages. (It's optional for HTML but implied when absent. However, it's good practice to always include a head element in web pages.)	Language attributes
	profile=URL	The location of a metadata profile for this document. Not commonly used.	
<header>		Defines a header for a document or section.	Core attributes, language attributes Core events
<hgroup>		Groups heading (<h1> to <h6>) elements.	Core attributes, language attributes Core events
<hr />		Inserts a horizontal rule.	Core attributes, language attributes Core events

`<html>` (requ ired)		Defines the start and end of the HTML document.	Language attributes
	`manifest=URL`	Specifies the address of the document's cache manifest (for offline browsing).	
	`xmlns=namespace`	Defines the XML namespace (e.g., http://www.w3.org/ 1999/xhtml). See also Chapter 2's, "Document defaults" section.	
`<i>`		Renders text as italic. This element is a physical style, which defines what the content looks like (presentation only), rather than a logical style, which defines what the content is (which is beneficial for technologies like screen readers). It's generally preferable to use the logical element <em></em> in place of <i></i>. See the preceding <em> entry. See also Chapter 3's "Styles for emphasis (bold and italic)" section.	Core attributes, language attributes Core events
`<iframe>`		Defines an inline frame. Content within the element is displayed only in browsers that cannot display the iframe. See also Chapter 7's "Working with internal frames (iframes)" section.	

	height=pixels	Specifies the height of an iframe.	
	name=name	Specifies a name for the iframe.	
	sandbox= ""| allow-forms| allow-same-origin| allow-scripts| allow-top-navigation	Enables a set of extra restrictions for the content in the iframe.	
	seamless=seamless	Specifies that the iframe should look like it is a part of the containing document.	
	src=*URL*	Specifies the location of the iframe's default HTML document.	
	width=pixels	Specifies the width of an iframe.	
`<img>`		Inserts an image. Both the src and alt attributes are required; although many web designers omit the alt attribute, it's essential for screen readers. The height and width values are recommended, too, in order to assist the browser in rapidly laying out the page. The border value, despite common usage, is deprecated and should be avoided. Use CSS to determine whether images have borders.| | See also Chapter 4's "Working with images" section.	Core attributes, language attributes Core events
	alt=text| |(required)	Provides alternate text for nonvisual browsers. Should provide an indication of an image's	

		content or, if it's a link, its function. When an image has no visual semantic significance, include it via CSS. If that's not possible, use alt="". This attribute is required.⬚ See also Chapter 4's "Using alt text for accessibility benefits" section.	
	height=*number*	Defines the image's height in pixels.	
	ismap=*URL*	Defines the image as a server-side image map. The image must be contained within an anchor tag. Server-side image maps require specialized setup and are rarely used. Do not confuse this attribute with usemap (see the upcoming usemap entry).	
	src=URL⬚(required)	The URL of the image to be displayed. This attribute is required.	
	usemap=*URL*	Defines the image as a client-side image map.⬚ See also Chapter 5's "Image maps" section.	
	width=*number*	Defines the image's width in pixels.	
<input />		Defines a form input field.⬚ See also Chapter 8's "Adding controls" section.	Core attributes, -keyboard attributes, language attributes Core events, onblur, onchange, onfocus, onselect
	accept=*list*	A list of MIME types that can be accepted by this	

		element. Only used with type="file".	
	`alt=text`	Provides alternate text for nonvisual browsers. Only used with type="image".	
	`autocomplete=on| off`	Specifies whether an <input> element should have autocomplete enabled.	
	`autofocus=autofocus`	Specifies that an <input> element should automatically get focus when the page loads.	
	`checked=checked`	Sets input element's default state to checked. The only value for this attribute is checked. Only used with type="checkbox" and type="radio".	
	`disabled=disabled`	Disables the input element. The only value for this attribute is disabled. Cannot be used with type="hidden".	
	`form=form_id`	Specifies one or more forms the <input> element belongs to.	
	`formaction=URL`	Specifies the URL of the file that will process the input control when the form is submitted (for type="submit" and type="image").	
	`formenctype=application/x-www-form-urlencoded| multipart/form-data| text/plain`	Specifies how the form data should be encoded when submitting it to the server (for type="submit" and	

		type="image").	
	`formmethod=get | post`	Defines the HTTP method for sending data to the action URL (for type="submit" and type="image").	
	`formnovalidate= formnovalidate`	Defines that form elements should not be validated when submitted.	
	`formtarget=_bl ank| _self| _parent| _top| framename`	Specifies where to display the response that is received after submitting the form (for type="submit" and type="image").	
	`height=pixels`	Specifies the height of an <input> element (only for type="image").	
	`list=datalist_ id`	Refers to a <datalist> element that contains predefined options for an <input> element.	
	`max=number| date`	Specifies the maximum value for an <input> element.	
	`maxlength=numb er`	Defines the maximum number of characters allowed. Only used with type="text".	
	`min=number| date`	Specifies the minimum value for an <input> element.	
	`multiple=multi ple`	Specifies that a user can enter more than one value in an <input> element.	
	`name=name`(requir ed*)	Defines a name for the input element. *Required for	

		the following types: button, checkbox, file, hidden, image, password, text, and radio.	
	pattern=regexp	Specifies a regular expression that an <input> element's value is checked against.	
	placeholder=text	Specifies a short hint that describes the expected value of an <input> element.	
	readonly=readon ly	Indicates the input element ⌷ ⌷is read-only and cannot be modified. The only value for this attribute is readonly. Only used with type="text" and type="password".	
	required=require d	Specifies that an input field must be filled out before submitting the form.	
	size=*number*	Defines in characters (not pixels) the width of the input element. (For pixel-defined widths, use CSS.)⌷ ⌷Cannot be used with type="hidden".	
	src=*URL*	Defines the URL of the image to be displayed. Only used with type="image".	
	type=button| checkbox|file|⌷ ⌷hidde n|image|⌷ ⌷password| radio| reset|submit|text	Defines the input element type. Defaults to text.	

	value=string (required when type=checkbox and type=radio)	When type="button", type= "reset", or type="submit", it defines button text. When type="checkbox" or type="radio", it defines the result of the input element; the result is sent when the form is submitted. When type="hidden", type="password", or type="text", it defines the element's default value. When type="image", it defines the result of the field passed to the script. Cannot be used with type="file".	
	width=pixels	Specifies the width of an <input> element (only for type="image").	
<ins>		Defines inserted text. Usually appears in underline format, which can be confusing because links are also underlined. It's therefore recommended that you use CSS to change the underline color. ins { text-decoration: none; border-bottom: 1px solid red; } See also Chapter 3's "Elements for inserted and deleted text" section.	Core attributes, language attributes Core events
	cite=URL	Defines the URL of a document that explains why the text was inserted.	
	datetime=date	Defines the date and time that the text was	

		amended. Various formats are possible, including YYYY-MM-DD and YYYY-MM-DDThh:mm:ssTZD (where TZD is the time zone designator). See www.w3.org/TR/1998/NOTE-datetime-19980827 for more date and time formatting information.	
`<keygen>`		Defines a key-pair generator field (for forms).	Core attributes, language attributes Core events
	`autofocus=auto focus`	Specifies that a `<keygen>` element should automatically get focus when the page loads.	
	`challenge=chal lenge`	Specifies that the value of the `<keygen>` element should be challenged when submitted.	
	`disabled=disab led`	Specifies that a `<keygen>` element should be disabled.	
	`form=form_id`	Specifies one or more forms the `<keygen>` element belongs to.	
	`keytype=rsa| dsa| ec`	Specifies the security algorithm of the key.	
	`name=name`	Defines a name for the `<keygen>` element.	
`<kbd>`		Defines "keyboard" text (text inputted by the user). Usually rendered in a monospace font. See also Chapter 3's "Logical styles for	Core attributes, language attributes Core events

		programming-oriented content" section.	
`<label>`		Assigns a label to a form control, enabling you to define relationships between text labels and form controls. For example:□<p><strong><label for="realname">Name</label>□</strong> □<input type="text" name="realname" id="realname" size="30" /></p>□ See also Chapter 8's "The label, fieldset, and legend elements" section.	Core attributes, language attributes Core events, `onblur`, `onfocus`
	accesskey= *character*	Defines a keyboard shortcut to access an element.	
	`for=`*text*	Defines the form element that the label is for. Value must be the same as the associated control element's id attribute value.□	
	`form=form_id`	Specifies one or more forms the label belongs to.	
`<legend>`		Defines a caption for a fieldset. Must be nested within a fieldset element. For example:□<fieldset>□<legend>Caption for this fieldset</legend>□[form labels/controls]□</fieldset>□ See also Chapter 8's	Core attributes, language attributes Core events

		"The label, fieldset, and legend elements" section.	
	accesskey=⏐⏐charact er	Defines a keyboard shortcut to access an element.	
`<li>`		Defines a list item. Must be nested within <ol> or <ul> elements (see the separate <ol> and <ul> entries). See also Chapter 3's "Working with lists" section.	Core attributes, language attributes Core events
	value=number⏐⏐	Defines the number of the item in an ordered list.	
`<link>`		Defines the relationship between two linked documents. Must be placed ⏐⏐in the head section of a document. Mainly used for attaching external style sheets and favicons to a document. Also, modern blogging systems use link elements to define relationships between the current document and others, such as XML feeds, next and previous pages, and archives. When used fully, link elements can have considerable accessibility and usability benefits; for example, some	Core attributes, language attributes Core events

		modern browsers use the data to provide extra navigation toolbars/options.⬜ See also Chapter 2's, "Attaching external CSS files: The link method" and "Attaching favicons and JavaScript" sections.	
	href=*URL*	The URL of the target.	
	hreflang=⬜language code	Defines the language of the linked document.	
	media=media_query	Specifies on what device the linked document will be displayed.	
	rel=*relationsh ip*	Specifies the relationship from the current document to the target document (alternate, appendix, bookmark, chapter, contents, copyright, glossary, help, index, next, prev, section, start, stylesheet, or subsection). More than one relationship can be combined in a space-separated list.	
	size=heightxwidth	Specifies the size of the linked resource. Only for rel="icon".	
	type=MIME type	Specifies the target's MIME type, such as text/css or text/javascript.	
`<map>`		Contains client-side image map specifications. Contains	Core attributes, keyboard attributes, language attributes

		one or more area elements (see preceding <area /> entry). See also Chapter 5's "Image maps" section.	Core events, onblur, onfocus
	name=name	Defines a unique name for the map.	
<mark>		Defines marked/highlighted text.	Core attributes, keyboard attributes, language attributes
<menu>		Defines a list/menu of commands.	Core attributes, keyboard attributes, language attributes
	label=text	Specifies a visible label for the menu.	
	type=context| toolbar| list	Specifies which type of menu to display. Default value is "list".	
<meta>		Provides meta information about the document. Must be placed inside the HTML page's head section. Each meta element requires a content attribute and also an http-equiv or a name attribute. Most commonly used to define the character set and to set keywords and descriptions for search engines (increasingly ineffective, as search engines now pay more attention to page content and links than to meta tags).	Language attributes

		See also Chapter 2's, "meta tags and search engines" and "What about the XML declaration?" sections.	
	charset=character_set	Specifies the character encoding for the HTML document.	
	content=string (required)	Defines the value of the meta tag property.	
	http-equiv=string	Specifies the http equivalent name for the meta information. Examples are content-type, expires, refresh, and set-cookie.	
	name=string	Specifies a name for the meta information. Examples are author, description, generator, and keywords.	
<meter>		Defines a scalar measurement within a known range (a gauge).	
	form=form_id	Specifies one or more forms the <meter> element belongs to.	
	high=number	Specifies the range that is considered to be a high value.	
	low=number	Specifies the range that is considered to be a low value.	
	max=number	Specifies the maximum value of the range.	
	min=number	Specifies the minimum value of the range.	

	optimum=number	Specifies what value is the optimal value for the gauge.	
	value=number	Required. Specifies the current value of the gauge.	
<nav>		Defines navigation links.	
<noembed> (n onstandard)		Nested within embed elements and displayed only when the browser cannot display the embedded object. Nonstandard and not supported by any XHTML DOCTYPE. If this is included in a web page, the page will not validate.	
<noscript>		Defines content to be displayed in browsers that don't support scripting. This is considered a "block-level" element, so it cannot be nested in an element that accepts only inline content, such as a paragraph, heading, or preformatted text. Can be used inside a div, form, or list item.	Core attributes, language attributes
<object>		Defines an embedded object. See also Chapter 7's "Scrollable content areas with CSS" section.	Core attributes, keyboard attributes, language attributes Core events
	data=URL	Defines the URL of the object's data.	
	form=form_id	Specifies one or more forms the object belongs	

		to.	
	height=*pixels*	Specifies the height of the object.	
	name=name	Specifies a name for the object.	
	type=mime_type	Specifies the MIME type of data specified in the data attribute.	
	usemap=#mapname	Specifies the name of a client-side image map to be used with the object.	
	width=pixels	Specifies the width of the object.	
`<ol>`		Defines the start and end of an ordered list. Contains one or more li elements (see preceding <li> entry).⬜ See also Chapter 3's "Ordered lists" section.	Core attributes, language attributes Core events
	start=number	Starts the list numbering at the defined value instead of 1.	
	type=1|A|a|I|I⬜	Specifies the list numbering system (1=default numerals, A=uppercase letters, a=lowercase letters, I=uppercase Roman numerals, and i=lowercase Roman numerals).	
	reversed=reversed	Specifies that the list order should be descending (9,8,7...).	
`<optgroup>`		Defines a form option group, enabling you to group related options in a select element. Beware: display output	Core attributes, language attributes Core events

		varies between browsers. Some italicize optgroup label values to highlight them, while others highlight them by inverting the optgroup label value. Others display t \<select name=""> \<optgroup label="fruits"> \<option value="Apple"> Apple\</option> \<option value="Pear"> Pear\</option> \</optgroup> \<optgroup label="vegetables"> \<option value="Carrot"> Carrot\</option> \<option value="Turnip"> Turnip\</option> \</optgroup> \</select> See also Chapter 8's "Adding controls" section.hem as per option values.	
	disabled=*disabled*	Disables the option group. The only value for this attribute is disabled.	
	label=string (required)	Defines a label for the optgroup. This attribute is required.	
	tabindex=*number*	Defines the tab order of an element.	
\<option>		Defines an option within a drop-down list. Nested within a select element and can be placed within optgroup elements. (See separate \<select> and \<optgroup> entries.) See also Chapter 8's "Adding controls"	Core attributes, language attributes Core events

		section.	
	disabled=disabled	Disables the option. The only value for this attribute is disabled.	
	label=*string*	Defines a label for this option.	
	selected=*selec ted*	Sets the option as the default. The only value for this attribute is selected.	
	value=*string*	Defines the value of the option to be sent when the form is submitted.	
<output>		Defines the result of a calculation	Core attributes, language attributes Core events
	for=element_id	Specifies the relationship between the result of the calculation, and the elements used in the calculation.	
	form=form_id	Specifies one or more forms the output element belongs to.	
	name=name	Specifies a name for the output element.	
<p>		Defines a paragraph.☐ See also Chapter 3's "Paragraphs and headings" section.	Core attributes, language attributes Core events
<param>		Supplies parameters for applets and objects. Must be enclosed within an applet or object element, and must come at the start of the content of the enclosing element.	
	id=*name*	Defines a unique reference ID for the	

		element.	
	name=*name*	Defines a unique name for the element.	
	value=*string*	Defines the element's value.	
`<pre>`		Defines enclosed contents as preformatted text, thereby preserving the formatting from the HTML document. Usually displayed in a monospace font. Cannot contain images, objects, or any of the following tags: big, small, sub, and sup.	Core attributes, language attributes Core events
`<progress>`		Represents the progress of a task.	Core attributes, language attributes Core events
	max=number	Specifies how much work the task requires in total.	
	value=number	Specifies how much of the task has been completed.	
`<q>`		Defines enclosed content as a short quotation. Some browsers automatically insert quote marks.	Core attributes, language attributes Core events
		See also Chapter 3's "Block quotes, quote citations, and definitions" section.	
	cite=*URL*	Defines the location of quoted online material.	
`<rp>`		Defines what to show in browsers that do not	Core attributes, language attributes

		support Ruby annotations.	Core events
`<rt>`		Defines an explanation/pronunciation of characters (for East Asian typography).	Core attributes, language attributes Core events
`<ruby>`		Defines a ruby annotation (for East Asian typography).	Core attributes, language attributes Core events
`<s>`		Defines strikethrough text.	Core attributes, language attributes Core events
`<samp>`		Defines enclosed content as a computer code sample. Usually rendered in a monospace font. See also Chapter 3's "Logical styles for programming-oriented content" section.	Core attributes, language attributes Core events
`<script>`		Inserts a script into the document. See also Chapter 2's, "Attaching favicons and JavaScript" section.	
	`charset=charset`	Defines the script's character set.	
	`defer=defer`	Indicates the script doesn't generate document content. This attribute's only value is defer. This allows the browser to delay parsing the script until after the page has loaded. Although this may speed up loading, it will generate script errors if user interaction results in a call to a script that still hasn't been parsed.	

		Use with care.	
	src=*URL*	Provides the URL of an external script.	
	type=MIME type (required)	Defines the MIME type of the scripting language, such as text/javascript or text/vbscript. This attribute is required.	
	async=async	Specifies that the script is executed asynchronously (only for external scripts).	
<section.>		Defines a section in a document.	Core attributes, language attributes Core events
<select>		Creates a drop-down menu or scrolling list (depending on whether multiple has been set). This element is a container for option and optional optgroup elements (see separate <option> and <optgroup> entries). See also Chapter 8's "Adding controls" section.	Core attributes, keyboard attributes, language attributes Core events, onblur, onchange, onfocus
	disabled=*disabled*	Disables the element. The only value for this attribute is disabled.	
	multiple=*multiple*	Specifies that multiple items can be selected. If absent, only single options can be selected. If included, the select element displays as a scrolling list rather than a drop-down menu. The only value for this attribute is multiple.	

	name=*name*	Defines a name for the element.	
	size=*number*	Sets the element to a pop-up menu when the value is 1, or a scrolling list when the value is greater than 1.	
	autofocus=auto focus	Specifies that the drop-down list should automatically get focus when the page loads.	
	form=form_id	Defines one or more forms the select field belongs to.	
`<small>`		Reduces text size as compared to the surrounding text. Because the browser determines the size differential, precise text size changes are better achieved via span elements and CSS.☐ See also Chapter 3's "The big and small elements" section.	Core attributes, language attributes Core events
`<source>`		Defines multiple media resources for media elements (<video> and <audio>).	Core attributes, language attributes Core events
	media=media_query	Specifies the type of media resource.	
	src=URL	Specifies the URL of the media file.	
	type=mime_type	Specifies the MIME type of the media resource.	
`<span>`		Identifies a span of inline elements for applying styles to. For example:☐<p>Use	Core attributes, language attributes Core events

		span elements to create ⊔ `<span class="styleName">s tyled inline text</span>.</p>`.	
`<strong>`		Defines enclosed content as strongly emphasized. Generally renders as bold text in browsers and is preferred over `<b></b>` (see separate `<b>` entry).⊔⊔ See also Chapter 3's "Logical and physical styles" section.	Core attributes, language attributes Core events
`<style>`		Used to embed CSS rules in the head of a web page or to import CSS files.•`<style type="text/css" media="all">`•`@import url(stylesheet.css)`;•`.thisPageOnly` {•`color: #de3de3;` •}•`</style>`• See also Chapter 2's, "Attaching CSS files: The @import method" section.	Language attributes
	`scoped=scoped`	Specifies that the styles only apply to this element's parent element and that element's child elements.	
	`media=list`•(re quired)	Defines target media on which this style can be rendered. Possible values are all, aural, braille, handheld, print,	

		projection, screen, tty, and tv.	
	`type=MIME type•(required )`	Defines the MIME type of the style's contents. The only currently viable value is text/css, although this may change in the future. The value text/javascript is also allowed.	
`<sub>`		Defines contents as subscript text.☐ See also Chapter 3's "Teletype, subscript, and superscript" section.	Core attributes, language attributes Core events
`<sup>`		Defines contents as superscript text.☐ See also Chapter 3's "Teletype, subscript, and superscript" section.	Core attributes, language attributes Core events
`<summary>`		Defines a visible heading for a <details> element.	Core attributes, language attributes Core events
`<table>`		`Defines the start and end of a table.•` See also Chapter 6's "How tables work" section.	Core attributes, language attributes Core events
	`border=number`	Defines the table border width.	
`<tbody>`		Defines the table body.☐ See also Chapter 6's "Row groups" and "Building a table" section.	Core attributes, language attributes Core events
`<td>`		Defines a table cell.☐ See also Chapter 6's "How tables work" and	Core attributes, language attributes Core events

		"Building a table" sections.	
	colspan=*number*	Defines how many columns the cell spans.⏐⏐ See also Chapter 6's "Spanning rows and cells" section.	
	headers=*id list*	A list of cell IDs that provide header information for this cell, thereby enabling nonvisual browsers to associate header information with the cell. If more than one value is used, values are space separated. Example:⏐⏐<th id="theTitle"⏐⏐scope="col">The title</th>⏐⏐<th id="price"⏐⏐ scope="col">Price</th>⏐⏐<td headers="theTitle">A new book</td>⏐⏐<td headers="price">$29.99 </td>	
	rowspan=*number*	Defines how many rows the cell spans.⏐⏐ See also Chapter 6's "Spanning rows and cells" section.	
<textarea>		Defines a text area within a form. Any element content is displayed as the textarea's default value, and that includes spaces. Therefore, if you want a blank textarea, avoid having any spaces	Core attributes, language attributes Core events, onblur, onchange, onfocus

		between the start and end tags. Although the cols and rows attributes are required, you can override these settings by using CSS.☐ See also Chapter 8's "Adding controls" section.	
	`cols=number•(r equired)`	Specifies the visible width in characters of the textarea. This attribute is required.	
	`disabled=disabled`	Disables the element. The only value for this attribute is disabled.	
	`name=name`		
	`autofocus=auto focus`	Specifies that a text area should automatically get focus when the page loads.	
	`form=form_id`	Specifies one or more forms the text area belongs to.	
	`maxlength=numb er`	Specifies the maximum number of characters allowed in the text area.	
	`placeholder=te xt`	Specifies a short hint that describes the expected value of a text area.	
	`required=requi red`	Specifies that a text area is required/must be filled out.	
	`wrap=hard| soft`	Specifies how the text in a text area is to be wrapped when	

		submitted in a form.	
	readonly=*readonly*	Indicates the textarea is read-only and cannot be modified. The only value for this attribute is readonly.	
	rows=number (required)	Specifies the visible height (expressed as a number of rows) of the textarea. This attribute is required.	
`<tfoot>`		Defines a table footer. See also Chapter 6's "Row groups" and "Building a table" section.	Core attributes, language attributes Core events
`<th>`		Defines a table header cell. See also Chapter 6's "How tables work" and "Building a table" section.	Core attributes, language attributes Core events
	colspan=*number*	Defines how many columns the cell spans. See also Chapter 6's "Spanning rows and cells" section.	
	headers=*id list*	A list of cell IDs that provide header information for this cell, thereby enabling nonvisual browsers to associate header information with the cell. If more than one value is used, values are space separated. Example: `<th id="theTitle" scope="col">The title</th>` `<th id="price" scope="col">Price</th>`	

		□<td headers="theTitle">A new book</td>□<td headers="price">$29.99 </td>.	
	`rowspan=number`	Defines how many rows the cell spans.□ See also Chapter 7's "Spanning rows and cells" section.	
	scope=col|□colgroup |row|□rowgroup	States whether the cell provides header information for the rest of the row, column, rowgroup, or colgroup that contains it. (See the headers description.)	
<thead>		Defines a table header.□ See also Chapter 6's "Row groups" and "Building a table" section.	Core attributes, language attributes Core events
<tr>		Defines a table row.□ See also Chapter 6's "How tables work" and "Building a table" section.	Core attributes, language attributes Core events
<title>		Defines a title for the document.	Core attributes, language attributes Core events
<time>		Defines a date/time.	Core attributes, language attributes Core events
	datetime=datetime	Gives the date/time being specified. Otherwise, the date/time is given by the element's contents.	
	pubdate=pubdate	Indicates that the date/time in the <time> element is the publication date of the document (or the	

		nearest ancestor <article> element).	
<track>		Defines text tracks for media elements (<video> and <audio>).	Core attributes, language attributes Core events
	default=default	Specifies that the track is to be enabled if the user's preferences do not indicate that another track would be more appropriate.	
	kind=captions| chapters| descriptions| metadata| subtitles	Specifies the kind of text track.	
	label=text	Specifies the title of the text track.	
	src=URL	Required. Specifies the URL of the track file.	
	srclang=language_code	Specifies the language of the track text data (required if kind="subtitles").	
<ul>		Defines the start and end of an unordered list. Contains one or more li elements (see separate <li> entry).|| See also Chapter 3's "Unordered lists" section.	Core attributes, language attributes Core events
<var>		Defines contents as a variable name. Usually rendered in italics.|| See also Chapter 3's "Logical styles for programming-oriented content" section.	Core attributes, language attribute Core events
<video>		Defines a video or movie.	Core attributes, language attribute Core events

	autoplay=autoplay	Specifies that the video will start playing as soon as it is ready.	
	controls=controls	Specifies that video controls should be displayed (such as a play/pause button).	
	height=pixels	Sets the height of the video player.	
	loop=loop	Specifies that the video will start over again, every time it is finished.	
	muted=muted	Specifies that the audio output of the video should be muted.	
	poster=URL	Specifies an image to be shown while the video is downloading or until the user hits the play button.	
	preload=auto| metadata| none	Specifies if and how the author thinks the video should be loaded when the page loads.	
	src=URL	Specifies the URL of the video file.	
	width=pixels	Sets the width of the video player.	
<wbr>		Defines a possible line break.	Core attributes, language attribute Core events

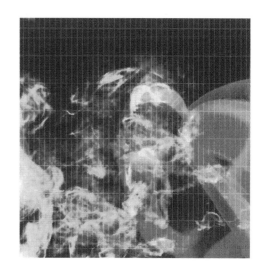

Appendix B

Web Color Reference

This appendix provides an overview of how to write color values for the Web, as well as a full list of supported color names. See the "Color theory" section in Chapter 4 for a discussion of color theory.

Color values

On the Web, colors are displayed by mixing red, green, and blue (RGB) light. Using rgb (e.g., rgb(5,233,70)), values range from 0 to 255 and can also include an alpha value that ranges from 0 to 1 (e.g., rgba(5,233,70,0.5)). Color can also be represented by hsl (e.g., hsl(0,100%,50%)), which stands for hue, saturation, lightness and can also include an alpha value (e.g., hsla(0,100%,50%,0.5)). Hue is a value between 0 and 360 representing the color wheel; saturation and lightness values are represented by a percentage. Color is most commonly written in hexadecimal (hex). Colors written in hex consist of a hash sign (#) followed by six digits. The six digits are made up of pairs, representing the red, green, and blue color values, respectively.

- *#XXxxxx*: Red color value

- *#xxXXxx*: Green color value

- *#xxxxXX*: Blue color value

Hexadecimal notation is a numbering system that has 16, rather than 10, as its base. Digits range from 0 to f, with 0 to 9 representing the same value as ordinary numbers, and the letters a to f representing 10 to 15. The letters can be either uppercase or lowercase. If you set the first two digits to their highest value (ff) and the others to null, you get #ff0000, which is the hex color value for red. If you write #00ff00, you get green, and if you write #0000ff, you get blue. If all are set to full, you get white (#ffffff), and if all are null values, you get black (#000000).

Hexadecimal can also be written in shorthand if the six-digit value is composed of pairs in which both numbers are the same. For instance, #ff6600 (orange) can be written as #f60, and #ffffff (white) can be written as #fff. All three pairs must consist of equal numbers. For instance, you cannot use shorthand for #ffff01. Also, although hexadecimal can be written in shorthand, many designers choose not to do so, because when all color values are written in full, it tends to be easier to scan CSS files for specific values.

Color names

Although a significant number of HTML color names are supported by major browsers, the CSS standard recognizes only the following 16.

Color Name	Color Hex Value	Shorthand Hex	RGB
Aqua	#00ffff	#0ff	0,255,255
Black	#000000	#000	0,0,0
Blue	#0000ff	#00f	0,0,255
Fuchsia	#ff00ff	#f0f	255,0,255
Gray (or Grey)	#808080	n/a	128,128,128
Green	#008000	n/a	0,128,0
Lime	#00ff00	#0f0	0,255,0
Maroon	#800000	n/a	128,0,0
Navy	#000080	n/a	0,0,128
Olive	#808000	n/a	128,128,0
Purple	#800080	n/a	128,0,128
Red	#ff0000	#f00	255,0,0
Silver	#c0c0c0	n/a	192,192,192
Teal	#008080	n/a	0,128,128
White	#ffffff	#fff	255,255,255

Yellow	#ffff00	#ff0	255,255,0

Although each color name in the preceding table begins with a capital letter (for book style purposes), color names are case-insensitive, and lowercase is most commonly used. However, most designers ignore color names entirely, using hex all the time for consistency's sake—a practice that the W3C recommends.

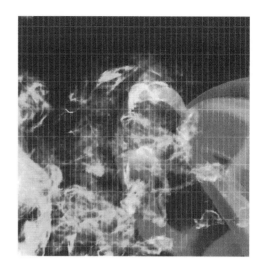

Appendix C

ENTITIES reference

Generally speaking, characters not found in the normal alphanumeric set must be added to a web page by way of **character entities.** These take the form &#n;, with n being a two- to four-digit number. Many entities also have a name, which tends to be more convenient and memorable; these are also listed. However, entities are case sensitive, so take care when adding them to your web pages.

Although most browsers display nonalphanumeric characters when the relevant encoding is specified, it's sometimes necessary to use entities to ensure your page displays as intended across a large range of machines.

Most reference guides tend to list entities in numerical order, but I find it more useful to browse by grouped items, so I list entities alphabetically within sections such as "Common punctuation and symbols" and "Characters for European languages." (The exception is for Greek characters, which I've listed in the order of the Greek alphabet, rather than in alphabetical order from an English language perspective.)

haracters used in HTML5

The less-than and ampersand characters are used in HTML5 markup, and to avoid invalid and broken pages, they should be added to your web pages as entities. It's also common (although not required) to add greater-than and quotation marks as entities.

The ampersand character is commonly used in URL query strings (particularly when working with server-side languages), and in such cases, the & must be replaced by the entity name or number (it will still be correctly interpreted by the browser).

Character	Description	Entity Name	Entity Number
"	Quotation mark (straight)	&quot;	&#34;
'	Apostrophe	&apos;	&#39;
&	Ampersand	&amp;	&#38;
<	Less-than sign	&lt;	&#60;
>	Greater-than sign	&gt;	&#62;

Punctuation characters and symbols

Although many web designers tend to get around punctuation character limitations by using double hyphens (--) in place of em dashes (—), triple periods (. . .) in place of an ellipsis (...), and straight quotation marks ("") instead of "smart" quotes (""), HTML5 supports many punctuation characters as character entities. Likewise, plenty of symbols are supported in HTML5, so you needn't write (c) when the copyright symbol is available.

This section lists all such characters and is split into four subsections: quotation marks, spacing and nonprinting characters, punctuation characters, and symbols.

Quotation marks

Character	Description	Entity Name	Entity Number
'	Left single	&lsquo;	&#8216;
'	Right single	&rsquo;	&#8217;
"	Left double	&ldquo;	&#8220;
"	Right double	&rdquo;	&#8221;
‹	Single left angle	&lsaquo;	&#8249;
›	Single right angle	&rsaquo;	&#8250;

«	Double left angle	&laquo;	&#171;
»	Double right angle	&raquo;	&#187;
‚	Single low-9	&sbquo;	&#8218;
„	Double low-9	&bdquo;	&#8222;

acing and nonprinting characters

On Windows, zero-width joiner and zero-width nonjoiner may be displayed by default as a vertical bar with an x on top and a vertical bar, respectively. To display these as nonprinting characters, you may need to install the Arabic language pack.

Character	Description	Entity Name	Entity Number
	Equal to two space characters		
	Equal to a single space character		
Nonprinting	Left-to-right mark	&lrm;	&#8206;
	Nonbreaking space		
	Overline	&oline;	&#8254;
Nonprinting	Right-to-left mark	&rlm;	&#8207;
	Thin space		
Nonprinting	Zero-width joiner	&zwj;	&#8205;
Nonprinting	Zero-width nonjoiner	&zwnj;	&#8204;

Punctuation characters

Character	Description	Entity Name	Entity Number
¦	Broken vertical bar	&brvbar;	&#166;
•	Bullet point	&bull;	&#8226;
†	Dagger	&dagger;	&#8224;
‡	Double dagger	&Dagger;	&#8225;
″		&Prime;	&#8243;
…	Ellipsis	&hellip;	&#8230;
—	Em dash	&mdash;	&#8212;
–	En dash	&ndash;	&#8211;
/	Fraction slash	&frasl;	&#8260;
¡		&iexcl;	&#161;
¿	Inverted question mark	&iquest;	&#191;
′	Prime, minutes, feet	&prime;	&#8242;
--	Soft hyphen	&shy;	&#173;

ʿmbols

Character	Description	Entity Name	Entity Number
ℑ	Blackletter capital I, imaginary part	`&image;`	`&#8465;`
←	Blackletter capital R, real part	`&real;`	`&#8476;`
©	Copyright symbol	`&copy;`	`&#169;`
ª	Feminine ordinal	`&ordf;`	`&#170;`
º	Masculine ordinal	`&ordm;`	`&#186;`
¬	Not sign	`&not;`	`&#172;`
¶	Paragraph sign	`&para;`	`&#182;`
‰	Per mille symbol	`&permil;`	`&#8240;`
®	Registered trademark symbol	`&reg;`	`&#174;`
§	Section sign	`&sect;`	`&#167;`
™	Trademark symbol	`&trade;`	`&#8482;`
℘	Script capital P, power set	`&weierp;`	`&#8472;`

445

Characters for European languages

For any characters that have accents, circumflexes, or other additions, entities are available. However, many of these entities have their roots in the days when ASCII was the only available encoding method. These days, as long as you use the appropriate input method and the page is correctly encoded, you may not need to use these entities. They are still listed here, though, for times when you just want to be on the safe side.

Take care when adding these, because case is important. In most cases, capitalizing the first letter of the entity name results in an uppercase character, but this isn't always so (notably the Icelandic characters *eth* and *thorn*, the uppercase versions of which require the entire entity name to be in uppercase).

Character	Description	Entity Name	Entity Number
´	Acute accent (no letter)	&acute;	&#180;
¸	Cedilla (no letter)	&cedil;	&#184;
ˆ	Circumflex spacing modifier	&circ;	&#710;
¯	Macron accent	&macr;	&#175;
·	Middle dot	&middot;	&#183;
˜	Tilde	&tilde;	&#732;
¨	Umlaut	&uml;	&#168;
Á	Uppercase A, acute accent	&Aacute;	&#193;
á	Lowercase a, acute accent	&aacute;	&#225;
Â	Uppercase a, circumflex accent	&Acirc;	&#194;
â	Lowercase a, circumflex accent	&acirc;	&#226;
À	Uppercase A, grave accent	&Agrave;	&#192;
à	Lowercase a, grave	&agrave;	&#224;

	accent		
Å	Uppercase A, ring	`&Aring;`	`&#197;`
å	Lowercase a, ring	`&aring;`	`&#229;`
Ã	Uppercase A, tilde	`&Atilde;`	`&#195;`
ã	Lowercase a, tilde	`&atilde;`	`&#227;`
Ä	Uppercase A, umlaut	`&Auml;`	`&#196;`
ä	Lowercase a, umlaut	`&auml;`	`&#228;`
Æ	Uppercase AE ligature	`&AElig;`	`&#198;`
æ	Lowercase ae ligature	`&aelig;`	`&#230;`
Ç	Uppercase C, cedilla	`&Ccedil;`	`&#199;`
ç	Lowercase c, cedilla	`&ccedil;`	`&#231;`
É	Uppercase E, acute accent	`&Eacute;`	`&#201;`
é	Lowercase e, acute accent	`&eacute;`	`&#233;`
Ê	Uppercase E, circumflex accent	`&Ecirc;`	`&#202;`
ê	Lowercase e, circumflex accent	`&ecirc;`	`&#234;`
È	Uppercase E, grave accent	`&Egrave;`	`&#200;`
è	Lowercase e, grave accent	`&egrave;`	`&#232;`
Ë	Uppercase E, umlaut	`&Euml;`	`&#203;`

ë	Lowercase e, umlaut	&euml;	&#235;
Ð	Uppercase eth	&ETH;	&#208;
ð	Lowercase eth	&eth;	&#240;
Í	Uppercase I, acute accent	&Iacute;	&#205;
í	Lowercase i, acute accent	&iacute;	&#237;
Î	Uppercase I, circumflex accent	&Icirc;	&#206;
î	Lowercase i, circumflex accent	&icirc;	&#238;
Ì	Uppercase I, grave accent	&Igrave;	&#204;
ì	Lowercase i, grave accent	&igrave;	&#236;
Ï	Uppercase I, umlaut	&Iuml;	&#207;
ï	Lowercase i, umlaut	&iuml;	&#239;
Ñ	Uppercase N, tilde	&Ntilde;	&#209;
ñ	Lowercase n, tilde	&ntilde;	&#241;
Ó	Uppercase O, acute accent	&Oacute;	&#211;
ó	Lowercase o, acute accent	&oacute;	&#243;
Ô	Uppercase O, circumflex accent	&Ocirc;	&#212;
ô	Lowercase o, circumflex accent	&ocirc;	&#244;
Ò	Uppercase O, grave accent	&Ograve;	&#210;

ò	Lowercase o, grave accent	`&ograve;`	`&#242;`
Ø	Uppercase O, slash	`&Oslash;`	`&#216;`
ø	Lowercase o, slash	`&oslash;`	`&#248;`
Õ	Uppercase O, tilde	`&Otilde;`	`&#213;`
õ	Lowercase o, tilde	`&otilde;`	`&#245;`
Ö	Uppercase O, umlaut	`&Ouml;`	`&#214;`
ö	Lowercase o, umlaut	`&ouml;`	`&#246;`
Œ	Uppercase OE ligature	`&OElig;`	`&#338;`
œ	Lowercase oe ligature	`&oelig;`	`&#339;`
Š	Uppercase S, caron	`&Scaron;`	`&#352;`
š	Lowercase s, caron	`&scaron;`	`&#353;`
ß	Lowercase sz ligature	`&szlig;`	`&#223;`
Þ	Uppercase thorn	`&THORN;`	`&#222;`
þ	Lowercase thorn	`&thorn;`	`&#254;`
Ú	Uppercase U, acute accent	`&Uacute;`	`&#218;`
ú	Lowercase u, acute accent	`&uacute;`	`&#250;`
Û	Uppercase U, circumflex accent	`&Ucirc;`	`&#219;`
û	Lowercase u, circumflex accent	`&ucirc;`	`&#251;`
Ù	Uppercase U, grave accent	`&Ugrave;`	`&#217;`

ù	Lowercase u, grave accent	&ugrave;	&#249;
Ü	Uppercase U, umlaut	&Uuml;	&#220;
ü	Lowercase u, umlaut	&uuml;	&#252;
Ý	Uppercase Y, acute accent	&Yacute;	&#221;
ý	Lowercase y, acute accent	&yacute;	&#253;
Ÿ	Uppercase Y, umlaut	&Yuml;	&#376;
ÿ	Lowercase y, umlaut	&yuml;	&#255;

Currency signs

Although the dollar sign is supported in HTML5, other common currency symbols are not. However, several can be added by way of entities, as shown in the following table.

Character	Description	Entity Name	Entity Number
¢	Cent	&cent;	&#162;
¤	General currency sign	&curren;	&#164;
€	Euro	&euro;	&#8364;
£	Pound	&pound;	&#163;
¥	Yen	&yen;	&#165;

Mathematical, technical, and Greek characters

This set of entities combines mathematical and technical symbols and the Greek alphabet (which is commonly used in scientific work). For ease of use, this section is divided into three subsections: common mathematical characters (fractions and the most commonly used mathematical symbols), advanced mathematical and technical characters (characters of interest to those marking up technical documents or anything other than basic mathematical text), and Greek characters.

ommon mathematical characters

Character	Description	Entity Name	Entity Number
°	Degree sign	°	°
÷	Division sign	÷	÷
½	Fraction—one half	½	½
¼	Fraction—one quarter	¼	¼
¾	Fraction—three quarters	¾	¾
>	Greater-than sign	>	>
≥	Circled times, vector product	≥	≥
<	Less-than sign	<	<
≤	Less-than or equal to sign	≤	≤
−	Minus sign	−	−
×	Multiplication sign	×	×
¹	Superscript one	¹	¹
²	Superscript two	²	²
³	Superscript three	³	³

dvanced mathematical and technical characters

Character	Description	Entity Name	Entity Number
ℵ	Alef symbol, first transfinite cardinal	ℵ	ℵ
≈	Almost equal to, asymptotic to	≈	≈

∠	Angle	&ang;	&#8736;
≅	Approximately equal to	&cong;	&#8773;
∗	Asterisk operator	&lowast;	&#8727;
⊕	Circled plus, direct sum	&oplus;	&#8853;
	Circled times, vector product	&otimes;	&#8855;
]	Contains as member	&ni;	&#8715;
.	Dot operator	&sdot;	&#8901;
[	Element of	&isin;	&#8712;
\	Empty set, null set, diameter	&empty;	&#8709;
∀	For all	&forall;	&#8704;
f	Function, florin (Latin small f with hook)	&fnof;	&#402;
;	Identical to	&equiv;	&#8801;
∞	Infinity	&infin;	&#8734;
∨	Integral	&int;	&#8747;
˘	Intersection, cap	&cap;	&#8745;
∪	Left ceiling	&lceil;	&#8968;
∈	Left floor	&lfloor;	&#8970;
∋	Logical and, wedge	&and;	&#8743;
∨	Logical or, vee	&or;	&#8744;
μ	Micro sign	&micro;	&#181;
	Nabla, backwards difference	&nabla;	&#8711;
∏	N-ary product, product sign	&prod;	&#8719;
Σ	N-ary summation	&sum;	&#8721;

Ó	Not an element of	&notin;	&#8713;
˜	Not a subset of	&nsub;	&#8836;
fi	Not equal to	&ne;	&#8800;
∂	Partial differential	&part;	&#8706;
±	Plus-minus sign, plus-or-minus sign	&plusmn;	&#177;
∝	Proportional to	&prop;	&#8733;
'	Right ceiling	&rceil;	&#8969;
	Right floor	&rfloor;	&#8971;
	Square root, radical sign	&radic;	&#8730;
,	Subset of	&sub;	&#8834;
#	Subset of or equal to	&sube;	&#8838;
.	Superset of	&sup;	&#8835;
$	Superset of or equal to	&supe;	&#8839;
∃	There exists	&exist;	&#8707;
∴	Therefore	&there4;	&#8756;
~	Tilde operator, varies with, similar to, approximately	&sim;	&#8764;
⁻	Union, cup	&cup;	&#8746;
⊥	Up tack, orthogonal to, perpendicular	&perp;	&#8869;

reek characters

Character	Description	Entity Name	Entity Number
A	Uppercase alpha	&Alpha;	&#913;

α	Lowercase alpha	&alpha;	&#945;
B	Uppercase beta	&Beta;	&#914;
β	Lowercase beta	&beta;	&#946;
Γ	Uppercase gamma	&Gamma;	&#915;
γ	Lowercase gamma	&gamma;	&#947;
Δ	Uppercase delta	&Delta;	&#916;
δ	Lowercase delta	&delta;	&#948;
E	Uppercase epsilon	&Epsilon;	&#917;
ε	Lowercase epsilon	&epsilon;	&#949;
Z	Uppercase zeta	&Zeta;	&#918;
ζ	Lowercase zeta	&zeta;	&#950;
H	Uppercase eta	&Eta;	&#919;
η	Lowercase eta	&eta;	&#951;
Θ	Uppercase theta	&Theta;	&#920;
θ	Lowercase theta	&theta;	&#952;
I	Uppercase iota	&Iota;	&#921;
ι	Lowercase iota	&iota;	&#953;
K	Uppercase kappa	&Kappa;	&#922;
κ	Lowercase kappa	&kappa;	&#954;
Λ	Uppercase lambda	&Lambda;	&#923;
λ	Lowercase lambda	&lambda;	&#955;
M	Uppercase mu	&Mu;	&#924;
μ	Lowercase mu	&mu;	&#956;
N	Uppercase nu	&Nu;	&#925;

ν	Lowercase nu	&nu;	&#957;
Ξ	Uppercase xi	&Xi;	&#926;
ξ	Lowercase xi	&xi;	&#958;
O	Uppercase omicron	&Omicron;	&#927;
o	Lowercase omicron	&omicron;	&#959;
Π	Uppercase pi	&Pi;	&#928;
π	Lowercase pi	&pi;	&#960;
P	Uppercase rho	&Rho;	&#929;
ρ	Lowercase rho	&rho;	&#961;
ς	Lowercase final sigma	&sigmaf;	&#962;
Σ	Uppercase sigma	&Sigma;	&#931;
σ	Lowercase sigma	&sigma;	&#963;
T	Uppercase tau	&Tau;	&#932;
τ	Lowercase tau	&tau;	&#964;
Y	Uppercase upsilon	&Upsilon;	&#933;
υ	Lowercase upsilon	&upsilon;	&#965;
Φ	Uppercase phi	&Phi;	&#934;
φ	Lowercase phi	&phi;	&#966;
X	Uppercase chi	&Chi;	&#935;
χ	Lowercase chi	&chi;	&#967;
Ψ	Uppercase psi	&Psi;	&#936;
ψ	Lowercase psi	&psi;	&#968;
Ω	Uppercase omega	&Omega;	&#937;
ω	Lowercase omega	&omega;	&#969;

ϑ	Small theta symbol	`&thetasym;`	`&#977;`
°	Greek upsilon with hook	`&upsih;`	`&#978;`
ϖ	Greek pi symbol	`&piv;`	`&#982;`

Arrows, lozenge, and card suits

Character	Description	Entity Name	Entity Number
↵	Carriage return	`&crarr;`	`&#8629;`
↓	Down arrow	`&darr;`	`&#8595;`
	Down double arrow	`&dArr;`	`&#8659;`
←	Left arrow	`&larr;`	`&#8592;`
⇐	Left double arrow	`&lArr;`	`&#8656;`
↔	Left-right arrow	`&harr;`	`&#8596;`
⇔	Left-right double arrow	`&hArr;`	`&#8660;`
→	Right arrow	`&rarr;`	`&#8594;`
	Right double arrow	`&rArr;`	`&#8658;`
↑	Up arrow	`&uarr;`	`&#8593;`
	Up double arrow	`&uArr;`	`&#8657;`
	Lozenge	`&loz;`	`&#9674;`
♣	Clubs suit	`&clubs;`	`&#9827;`
♦	Diamonds suit	`&diams;`	`&#9830;`
♥	Hearts suit	`&hearts;`	`&#9829;`
♠	Spades suit	`&spades;`	`&#9824;`

onverting the nonstandard Microsoft set

The final table in this appendix lists the nonstandard Microsoft set and modern equivalents. Some older HTML editors, such as Dreamweaver 4, insert nonstandard entity values into web pages, causing them to fail validation. Here, we present the outdated nonstandard value and its corresponding approved alternatives (entity name and entity number, either of which can be used).

Character	Description	Nonstandard Value	Entity Name	Entity Number
‚	Single low-9 quote	&#130;	&sbquo;	&#8218;
ƒ	Lowercase Latin f with hook (florin)	&#131;	&fnof;	&#402;
„	Double low-9 quote	&#132;	&bdquo;	&#8222;
…	Ellipsis	&#133;	&hellip;	&#8230;
†	Dagger	&#134;	&dagger;	&#8224;
‡	Double dagger	&#135;	&Dagger;	&#8225;
ˆ	Circumflex spacing modifier	&#136;	&circ;	&#710;
‰	Per mille symbol	&#137;	&permil;	&#8240;
Š	Uppercase S, caron	&#138;	&Scaron;	&#352;
<	Less-than sign	&#139;	&lt;	&#60;
Œ	Uppercase OE ligature	&#140;	&OElig;	&#338;
'	Left single quote	&#145;	&lsquo;	&#8216;
'	Right single quote	&#146;	&rsquo;	&#8217;
"	Left double quote	&#147;	&ldquo;	&#8220;
"	Right double quote	&#148;	&rdquo;	&#8221;
•	Bullet point	&#149;	&bull;	&#8226;
–	En dash	&#150;	&ndash;	&#8211;

—	Em dash	&#151;	&mdash;	&#8212;
~	Tilde	&#152;	&tilde;	&#732;
™	Trademark symbol	&#153;	&trade;	&#8482;
š	Lowercase s, caron	&#154;	&scaron;	&#353;
>	Greater-than sign	&#155;	&gt;	&#62;
œ	Lowercase oe ligature	&#156;	&oelig;	&#339;
Ÿ	Uppercase Y, umlaut	&#159;	&Yuml;	&#376

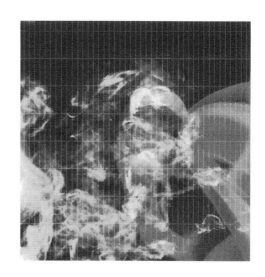

Appendix D

CSS Reference

This appendix lists CSS properties and values. In many cases, properties have specific values, which are listed in full. However, some values are common across many properties. These values are outlined in Table D.1, and in Table D.2 these values are shown in italics. The end of the appendix includes information on basic selectors, pseudo-classes, pseudo-elements, CSS boilerplates, and CSS management.

The CSS box model

In CSS, every element is considered to be within its own box, and you can define the dimensions of the content and then add padding, a border, and a margin to each edge as required, as shown in the following image.

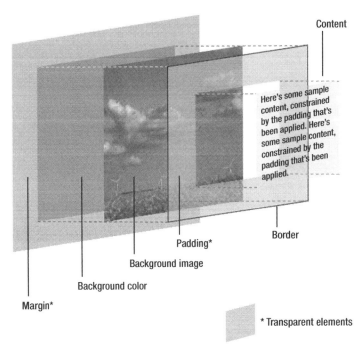

Content

Here's some sample content, constrained by the padding that's been applied. Here's some sample content, constrained by the padding that's been applied.

Border

Padding*

Background image

Background color

Margin*

* Transparent elements

Padding, borders, and margins are added to the set dimensions of the content, so the sum of these elements is the overall space that they take up. For example, a 100-pixel-wide element with 20 pixels of padding will take up an overall width of 140 pixels, not 100 pixels with 20 pixels of padding within.

Remember that you can force browsers to respect the width you set by applying box-sizing: border-box to all elements, like so:

```
* { -moz-box-sizing: border-box; -webkit-box-sizing: border-box; box-sizing: border-box; }
```

This is supported by all modern browsers without a vendor prefix with the exception of Firefox.

Note that the top and bottom margins on adjacent elements collapse. For example, if you set the bottom margin to 50px on an element and set a top margin of 100px on the element below, the margin between the two elements will be 100 pixels, not 150 pixels.

ommon CSS values

In addition to the values listed in Table D.1, a property may have a value of inherit, whereupon it takes the same value as its parent. Some properties are inherited by default—see Table D.2 for more information.

Table D.1. Common CSS values

Value	Formats
color	Color name. See Appendix B for information on available CSS color names. rgb(n,n,n): Where n is a value from 0 to 255 or a percentage. #rrggbb: Hexadecimal color format (preferred). rgba(n,n,n,a): Where n is a value from 0 to 255 or a percentage and where a is a decimal value from 0 to 1 representing the transparency or alpha value.
length	An optional sign (+ or -), followed by a number and one of the following units (there should be no whitespace between the number and unit): %: A percentage. cm: Centimeters. em: One em is equal to the font size of the parent or current element (see the following note for elaboration). ex: One ex is, in theory, equal to the font size of the x character of the current element. Most browsers render ex as half an em. in: Inches. mm: Millimeters. pc: Picas. 1pc = 12pt. pt: Points. 1pt = 1/72in. px: Pixels. For zero values, the unit identifier may be omitted. Generally, px, em, and % are the best units for screen design, and pt is best for print fonts.
number	An optional sign (+ or -) followed by a number.
percentage	An optional sign (+ or -) followed by a number, immediately followed by the percentage symbol.
url	The word url immediately followed by parentheses, within which is placed a URL. The URL can optionally be enclosed in single or double quotes.

When setting element dimensions (width, height, margins, and so on), one em is equal to the font size of that element. However, when setting font sizes for an element, one em is equal to the font size of its parent element. In both cases, this is measured relative to the dimensions of the M character.

CSS properties and values

A number of tables online list browser compatibility with regard to CSS. Some good examples of these and related resources can be found at the following URLs:

- `www.quirksmode.org/css/contents.html`: Concentrates on quirks

- `www.css3.info/selectors-test/`: Live CSS3 support testing of your browser

- `www.smashingmagazine.com/tag/css/`: Useful information and examples

- `html5please.com/`: A great resource for determining whether a browser supports a feature

Remember that such resources are guides only, are sometimes out-of-date, and should not be considered a replacement for thorough testing in a range of web browsers.

To inherit a parent element's style for a property, use the value `inherit`. To raise a property's weight in the cascade, use `!important`. Important declarations override all others.
```
p {color: red !important;}
```

Add comments to CSS files as follows:

```
/*
This is a comment in CSS
*/

/* This is a single-line comment */
```

Table D.2. CSS properties and values

Property	Values	Description	Inherited
background		Shorthand for defining background property values in a single declaration. Values can be any of those from background-attachment, background-color, background-image, background-position, and background-repeat, in any order. Example: background: #ffffff url(background.gif) fixed left repeat-y; See also Chapter 2's "Web page backgrounds in CSS" and "CSS shorthand for web backgrounds" sections.	

background-attachment	scroll | fixed | local	Determines whether a background image is fixed or scrolls with the page. See also Chapter 2's "background-attachment" section.	No
background-color	transparent | color	Defines an element's background color. See also Chapter 2's "background-color" section.	No
background-image	none | url	Assigns one: background-image: url(background_image.jpg); or multiple: background-image: url(background_image1.jpg), url(background_image2.jpg); background images to an element. See also Chapter 2's "background-image" section.	No
background-position	length | percentage | top | center | bottom | left | right | inherit	Defines the initial position of the background image. Defaults to 0,0. Values are usually paired: x,y. Combinations of keyword, length, and percentage are permitted, although combining keywords with either length or percentages is buggy in some browsers. If only one keyword is provided, the other defaults to center. If only one length or percentage is given, it sets the horizontal position, and the vertical position defaults to 50%. See also Chapter 2's "background-position" section.	No
background-repeat	repeat | repeat-x | repeat-y | no-repeat | space | round	Defines how the background image tiles. See also Chapter 2's "background-repeat" section.	No
background-size	auto | contain | cover | percentage | length	Defines the size of the background images.	No
border		Shorthand for defining border property values in a single declaration. Values can be any of those from border-width, border-style, and border-color. Borders are drawn on top of a box's background. Example: border: 1px solid #000000; See also Chapter 4's "Applying CSS borders to images" section and Chapter 6's "Styling a table" section.	No
border-bottom		Shorthand for defining bottom border property values (see border).	No

`border-bottom-color`	`color | transparent`	Sets the bottom border color.	No
`border-bottom-style`	(See `border-style`.)	Sets the bottom border style.	No
`border-bottom-width`	(See `border-width`.)	Sets the bottom border width.	No
`border-bottom-right-radius`	`length | percentage`	Sets the rounding of the bottom-right corner of the element.	No
`border-bottom-left-radius`	(See `border-bottom-right-radius`.)	Sets the rounding of the bottom-left corner of the element.	No
`border-collapse`	`collapse | separate | inherit`	Defines a table's border model. In the separate border model, which is the default, each table cell has its own distinct borders, but in the collapsed border model, adjacent table cells share borders. See also Chapter 6's "Adding borders to tables" section.	Yes
`border-color`	`color | transparent | inherit`	Defines the element's border color. Defaults to the element's color.	No
border-image		Defines an image to be rendered as an element's border.	No
border-image-outset	length | number	Defines the amount the border image extends beyond the border box.	No
border-image-repeat	stretch | repeat | round | space	Defines how the border image is scaled and tiled.	No
border-image-source	none | inherit | url | linear-gradient	Defines the image to use instead of the border style.	No
border-image-width	length | percentage | number | auto	Defines the offset to use for dividing the border image.	No
`border-left`		Shorthand for defining left border property values (see border).	No
`border-left-color`	`color | transparent | inherit`	Sets the left border color.	No
`border-left-`	(See `border-`	Sets the left border style.	No

style	style.)		
border-left-width	(See border-width.)	Sets the left border width.	No
border-radius	**length | percentage**	**Defines how rounded border corners are.**	**No**
border-right		Shorthand for defining right border property values (see border).	No
border-right-color	color | transparent | inherit	Sets the right border color.	No
border-right-style	(See border-style.)	Sets the right border style.	No
border-right-width	(See border-width.)	Sets the right border width.	No
border-spacing	length length	Defines the distance between borders or adjacent table cells when using the separated borders model. (See border-collapse.) If a single length is given, it's used for horizontal and vertical values; if two lengths are provided, the first is used for the horizontal spacing, and the second is used for the vertical spacing. Negative values are not permitted.	Yes
border-style	none | hidden | dotted | dashed | solid | double | groove | ridge | inset | outset	Sets the style of an element's borders. Can work as shorthand, with one style per edge, from the top clockwise. Example: border-style: solid dashed dotted groove;	No
border-top		Shorthand for defining top border property values (see border).	No
border-top-color	color | transparent	Sets the top border color.	No
border-top-left-radius	length | percentage	Defines the rounding for the top-left corner of the element.	No
border-top-right-radius	length | percentage	Defines the rounding for the top-right corner of the element.	No

border-top-style	(See border-style.)	Sets the top border style.	No
border-top-width	(See border-width.)	Sets the top border width.	No
border-width	length | medium |□thick | thin	Sets the width of an element's borders. Can work as shorthand: □ border-width: 1px 2px 3px 4px; See also Chapter 4's "Applying CSS borders to images" section.	No
bottom	auto | length | □percentage	Determines the vertical offset of the element's bottom edge from the bottom edge of its parent element if the parent is positioned; if not, then offset is determined from the first positioned ancestor. Must be used with a position value of relative, absolute, or fixed.	No
box-shadow	inset | offset-x | offset-y | blur-radius | spread-radius | color	Defines one or more shadow effects as a comma-separated list.	No
box-sizing	content-box | padding-box | border-box	Alters the default CSS box model used to calculate widths and heights of elements.	No
caption-side	bottom | top | inherit	Specifies the position of table caption elements with relation to the table element box.	Yes
clear	both | left | □none | right | inherit	Moves the element down until its margins are clear of floated elements to its left, right, or both sides. (See the float entry.) See also Chapter 7's "Placing columns within wrappers and clearing floated content" section.	No
clip	auto | (shape)	Creates a clipping area for an absolute positioned element to determine the visible area. As of CSS 2.1, the only available shape is rect. Example: clip: rect(5px, 60px, 15px, 20px); □ As per the preceding code block, dimensions are stated as a comma-separated list, and percentage lengths are not permitted. The dimensions are, as per typical CSS shorthand, in the following order: top, right, bottom, left. The top and bottom values specify offsets from the top border edge of the box. The left and right	No

		measurements specify offsets from the left border edge of the box in left-to-right text and from the right border edge of the box in right-to-left text. The defined region clips out any aspect of the element that falls outside the clipping region. The preceding example creates a window 40 pixels wide and 10 pixels high, through which the content of the clipped element is visible. Everything else is hidden. See also www.w3.org/TR/CSS21/visufx.html#propdef-clip.	
color	color	Sets an element's foreground color (i.e., the color of the text).	Yes
columns	(column-width) | (column-count)	Is a shorthand property allowing you to set both the column-width and column-count properties at the same time.	No
column-count	auto | integer	Describes the number of columns of the element.	No
column-fill	auto | balance	Controls how contents are partitioned into columns.	No
column-gap	normal | length	Defines the size of the gap between columns for elements that are specified to display as a multicolumn element.	No
column-rule	(border-width) | (border-style | (color)	Defines a straight line, or *rule*, to be drawn between each column.	No
column-rule-color	(color)	Defines the color of the rule drawn between columns in multicolumn layouts.	No
column-rule-style	(border-style)	Defines the style of the rule drawn between columns in multicolumn layouts.	No
column-rule-width	(border-width)	Defines the width of the rule drawn between columns in multicolumn layouts.	No
column-span	none | all	Defines the span across columns.	No
column-width	length | auto	Suggests an optimal column width. This is not an absolute value but a mere hint. Browser will adjust the width of the column around that suggested value, allowing you to achieve scalable designs that fit different screen size.	No
content	normal | (string) |	Generates content to attach before or after a	No

	url | counter(name) | counter(name, list-style-type) | counters(name, string) | counters(name, string, list-style-type) | open-quote | close-quote | no-open-quote | no-close-quote | attr(X)	CSS selector, using the :before and :after pseudo-elements. Example: □□ #users h2:before {□content: "Username: ";□display: inline; □}□□ See also Chapter 7's "Placing columns within wrappers and clearing floated content" section.	
counter-increment	none | □identifier number	Increments a counter when the current selector is encountered. The identifier defines the selector, ID, or class that is to be incremented; the optional number defines the increment amount. Used in conjunction with content. Browser support for this property is poor.	No
counter-reset	none | □identifier number	Defines a new value for the specified counter whenever the current selector is encountered.	No
cursor	auto | crosshair | default | help | pointer | move | progress | text | wait | n-resize | ne-resize | □e-resize | □se-resize | □s-resize | □sw-resize | □nw-resize | □w-resize | url	Defines the cursor type to be displayed. Can be a comma-separated list. Cursors vary by system, so use this property with care. Also, if using custom cursors via the url value, include a generic cursor at the end of the list, in case of compatibility problems. □□ Note: Internet Explorer 5.x for Windows does not recognize pointer, the correct CSS value for displaying a hand-shaped cursor. Instead, it uses the nonstandard value hand, which can be applied using a style sheet attached via a conditional comment.	Yes
direction	ltr | rtl	Sets the direction of text flow. ltr: Left to right. □rtl: Right to left.	Yes
display	block | inline | list-item | □none | run-in | inline-block | table | □inline-table | table-caption | table-cell | table-column | table-column-group | table-footer-group | table-header-group | table-row | table-row-group |	States how an element is displayed on the page. The most common values are none, block, and inline, which all happen to be well supported. See several of the exercises in Chapters 5 and 7 for more on this property.	No

		table-row		
empty-cells	hide | show	Determines whether empty table cell borders show when using the separated borders model. (See border-collapse.)	Yes
float	left | none | right	Defines whether an element floats left or right (allowing other content to wrap around it) or displays inline (by using the none value). See also Chapter 7's "The float property" section.	No
font		Shorthand for defining font properties in a single declaration. Values can include any or all of the following: font-style, font-variant, font-weight, font-size, line-height, and font-family. Any omitted values revert to default settings, but font-size and font-family are mandatory. If font-style, font-weight, and font-variant values are included, they should appear at the start of the rule, prior to the font-size value.	Yes
font (continued)		When using line-height, you must combine it with the font-size property using the syntax font-size/line-height (e.g., 12px/18px). Examples (using selected values): font: bold 12px/16px Verdana, sans-serif; font: 85%/1.3em Georgia, serif; See also Chapter 3's "Styling text using CSS" and "CSS shorthand for font properties" sections. Additional values for the font property are also available: caption, icon, menu, message-box, small-caption, status-bar. These set the font to system fonts, or the nearest equivalent, and are not available via font-family. However, these values are rarely, if ever, used.	Yes
@font-face	a-remote-font-name | source | weight | style	Allows authors to define online fonts to display text on their web pages.	Yes
font-family	(family name) | (generic family)	Defines the font family of an element. Takes the form of a prioritized comma-separated list, which should terminate in a generic family name (cursive, fantasy, monospace, serif, or sans-serif). Multiple-word font-family names must be quoted (e.g., "Times New Roman"). Readers used to American typographical conventions	Yes

		should take care not to put commas inside the closing quotes. Example: font-family: Georgia, "Times New Roman", serif; See also Chapter 3's "Defining fonts" section.	
font-size-adjust	none | number	Defines the font size should be chosen based on the height of lowercase letters rather than the height of capital letters.	Yes
font-size	xx-small | x-small | small | medium | large | x-large | xx-large | smaller | larger | length | percentage	Sets the size of a font. See also Chapter 3's "Defining font size and line height" section.	Yes
font-size-adjust	none | number	Defines the font size that should be chosen based on the height of lowercase letters rather than the height of capital letters.	Yes
font-stretch	inherit | ultra-condensed | extra-condensed | condensed | semi-condensed | normal | semi-expanded | expanded | extra-expanded | ultra-expanded	Defines a normal, condensed, or extended face from a font family.	Yes
font-style	italic | normal | oblique	Sets the font's style. See also Chapter 3's "Defining font-style, font-weight, and font-variant" section.	Yes
font-variant	normal | small-caps	Sets the font to display in small caps. See also Chapter 3's "Defining font-style, font-weight, and font-variant" section.	Yes
font-weight	lighter | normal | bold | bolder | number*	Sets the font weight. * When using a number, it must be a multiple of 100 between 100 and 900 inclusive. The value 700 is considered equivalent to bold, and 400 is synonymous with normal. In practice, numbers are supported inconsistently and poorly in browsers. See also Chapter 3's "Defining font-style, font-weight, and font-variant" section.	Yes
height	auto | length | percentage	Sets the content height of an element.	No

image-rendering	auto | inherit | optimizeSpeed | optimizeQuality	Provides a hint to the user agent about how to handle its image rendering.	Yes
ime-mode	auto | normal | active | inactive | disabled	Controls the state of the input method editor for text fields.	No
left	auto | length | ⏐ ⏐percentage	Determines the horizontal offset of the element's left edge from the left edge of its parent element if the parent is positioned; if not, then offset is determined from the first positioned ancestor. Must be used with a position value of relative, absolute, or fixed.⏐ ⏐⏐ ⏐ See also the Chapter 7 exercise "Using absolute positioning to center a box on-screen."	No
letter-spacing	length | normal	Amends kerning (i.e., the space between characters). Positive and negative values are permitted. Relative values are determined once and then inherited.⏐ ⏐⏐ ⏐ See also Chapter 3's "Setting letter-spacing and word-spacing" section.	Yes
line-height	normal | length | number | percentage	Controls the element's leading. When the line-height value is larger than the font-size value, the difference (which is the leading) is halved, and this new value is applied to the top and bottom of the element's inline box. ⏐ ⏐⏐ ⏐ See also Chapter 3's "Setting line height" section.	Yes
list-style		Shorthand for defining list properties in a single declaration. Values can be those from list-style-type, list-style-position, and list-style-image. ⏐ ⏐⏐ ⏐ See also Chapter 3's "Styling lists with CSS" and "List style shorthand" sections.	Yes
list-style-image	none | url	Defines an image for list bullet points.	Yes
list-style-position	inside | outside	Determines whether the bullet point appears as the first character of the list item content (inside) or in default fashion (outside).	Yes
list-style-	none | disc | circle |	Sets the bullet point style. If a browser doesn't	Yes

type	square | decimal | decimal-leading-zero | lower-alpha | upper-alpha | lower-greek | lower-latin | upper-latin | lower-roman | upper-roman | armenian | georgian	understand an ordered list value, it defaults to decimal. Generally, none, circle, square, decimal, and the alpha and roman values are best supported. The W3C recommends using decimal for ordered lists whenever possible.	
margin		Shorthand for defining margin properties in a single declaration. Examples: □ margin: 0; (sets all margins to 0) □ margin: 0 10px 20px 30px; (sets individual margins for each edge) □□ See also Chapter 2's "Content margins and padding in CSS" and "Working with CSS shorthand for boxes" sections.	No
margin-bottom	auto | length | percentage	Sets the bottom margin. Defaults to 0. Note that browsers usually override the zero value by applying default margins to most block elements. Set margins explicitly to 0 to cancel the browser's default. See Chapter 2's "Zeroing margins and padding on all elements" section.	No
margin-left	auto | length | percentage	Sets the left margin. Defaults to 0. Note that browsers usually override the zero value by applying default margins to most block elements. Set margins explicitly to 0 to cancel the browser's default. See Chapter 2's "Zeroing margins and padding on all elements" section.	No
margin-right	auto | length | percentage	Sets the right margin. Defaults to 0. Note that browsers usually override the zero value by applying default margins to most block elements. Set margins explicitly to 0 to cancel the browser's default. See Chapter 2's "Zeroing margins and padding on all elements" section.	No
margin-top	auto | length | percentage	Sets the top margin. Defaults to 0. Note that browsers usually override the zero value by applying default margins to most block elements. Set margins explicitly to 0 to cancel the browser's default. See Chapter 2's "Zeroing margins and padding on all elements" section.	No

max-height	none | length | percentage	Sets the maximum height of an element. Does not apply to table elements.	No
max-width	none | length | percentage	Sets the maximum width of an element. Does not apply to table elements. I II I See also the Chapter 7 exercise "Creating a maximum-width layout."	No
marks	crop | cross | none	Adds crop and/or cross marks to the presentation of the document.	No
min-height	none | length | percentage	Sets the minimum height of an element. Does not apply to table elements.	No
min-width	none | length | percentage	Sets the minimum width of an element. Does not apply to table elements.	No
opacity	number | inherit	Defines the transparency of an element, that is, the degree to which the background behind the element is overlaid.	No
orphans	number	Defines the number of lines of a paragraph that must be left at the bottom of a page when printing. Defaults to 2. Defined number must be an integer. Very poorly supported.	Yes
outline		Shorthand for defining outline properties in a single declaration. Outlines are rendered outside the border edge and do not affect document flow. Example: I II I .highlight {I outline: 1px dotted #ff0000; I }I II I Not supported by Internet Explorer up to and including version 7.	No
outline-color	color | invert	Sets the color of an outline. Defaults to invert, which inverts the color of the pixels on-screen, ensuring the outline is visible.	No
outline-style	dashed | dotted | double | groove | inset | none | outset | ridge | solid	Sets the style of an outline.	No
outline-offset	length | inherit	Defines the space between and outline and the edge or border of an element. An outline is a line that is drawn around elements, outside the border edge.	No
outline-width	length | medium | I Ithick | thin	Sets the width of an outline.	No
overflow	auto | hidden |	Determines what happens when content is	No

	scroll | visible	too large for the defined dimensions of the element. auto: If content is clipped, the browser displays a scroll bar. hidden: Content is clipped, and content outside the element's box is not visible. scroll: Content is clipped, but a scroll bar is made available. visible: Content is not clipped and may be rendered outside of the element's containing box. See also Chapter 7's "Scrollable content areas with CSS" section.	
padding		Shorthand to define padding properties in a single declaration. Examples: padding: 0; (sets padding on all sides to 0) padding: 0 10px 20px 30px; (sets individual padding for each edge) See also Chapter 2's "Content margins and padding in CSS" and "Working with CSS shorthand for boxes" sections.	No
padding-bottom	length | percentage	Sets the bottom padding of an element.	No
padding-left	length | percentage	Sets the left padding of an element.	No
padding-right	length | percentage	Sets the right padding of an element.	No
padding-top	length | percentage	Sets the top padding of an element.	No
page-break-after	auto | always | avoid | left | right	Determines whether a page break should appear after the element when printing. Poorly supported.	No
page-break-before	auto | always | avoid | left | right	Determines whether a page break should appear before the element when printing. Poorly supported.	No
page-break-inside	auto | avoid	Determines whether a page break should appear inside the element when printing. Poorly supported.	Yes
position	absolute | fixed | relative | static	Determines the positioning method used to render the element's box: absolute: Element is placed in a specific location outside of normal document flow, using the top, right, bottom, and left	No

		properties. | | fixed: As per absolute, but the element remains stationary when the screen scrolls. Poorly supported by some browsers. | | relative: Offset from the static position by the values set using top, right, bottom, and left properties. | | static: The default. The top, right, bottom, and left properties do not affect the element if this value is set. The element is not removed from the document's normal flow.| | | Various examples of this property in use are found in Chapters 5 and 7.	
quotes	none | string | string	Determines the type of quote marks to be used for embedded quotations. The string contains paired quoted values, which determine each level of quote embedding. The default depends on the user agent (browser).	Yes
resize	none | both | horizontal | vertical | inherit	Controls how the element is resized.	No
right	auto | length | | percentage	Determines the horizontal offset of the element's right edge from the right edge of its parent element if the parent is positioned; if not, then offset is determined from the first positioned ancestor. Must be used with a position value of relative, absolute, or fixed.	No
table-layout	auto | fixed	Controls the layout algorithm used to render tables. Using fixed, table columns are based on analysis of the first row and rendered accordingly. This can speed up processing time but may lead to columns that are too narrow for subsequently downloaded content.	No
tab-size	integer | inherit	Defines the size of the tab character.	No
text-align	center | justify | | left* | right	Sets the text alignment for an element. | | | | * The default is left in left-to-right languages and right in right-to-left languages such as Arabic, Hebrew, and Urdu. Should be used instead of the HTML align attribute.	Yes
text-align-last	auto | start | end | left | right | center | justify | inherit	Describes how the last line of a block or a line right before a forced line break is aligned.	Yes
text-decoration	blink | line-through | none | overline |	Adds decoration to text. Values may be combined in a space-separated list, and the	No

	underline	default depends on the element in question.☐☐ Note that browsers may ignore blink but still be considered compliant. Examples: ☐☐ text-decoration: underline; text decoration: underline line-through;☐☐ See also Chapter 5's "Editing link styles using CSS" section.	
text-decoration-color	(color) | inherit	Defines the color used when drawing underlines, overlines, or strike-throughs specified by text-decoration-line.	No
text-decoration-line	none | underline | overline | line-through	Defines what kind of line decorations are added to an element.	No
text-indent	length | percentage	Sets the horizontal indent of an element's first line of text. Defaults to 0.	Yes
text-overflow	inherit | end-overflow-type | left-overflow-type | right-overflow-type	Determines how overflowed content that is not displayed is signaled to the users.	No
text-rendering	auto | optimizeSpeed | optimizeLegibility | geometricPrecision | inherit	Provides information to the rendering engine about what to optimize for when rendering text.	Yes
text-shadow	(color) | offset-x offset-y | blur-radius	Adds shadows to text. It accepts a comma-separated list of shadows to be applied to the text and text-decorations of the element.	Yes
text-transform	capitalize | lowercase | ☐none | uppercase	Sets the case of an element's text. ☐☐ See also Chapter 3's "Controlling case with text-transform" section.	Yes
Top	auto | length | percentage	Determines the vertical offset of the element's top edge from the top edge of its parent element if the parent is positioned; if not, then offset is determined from the first positioned ancestor. Must be used with a position value of relative, absolute, or fixed.☐☐ See also the Chapter 7 exercise "Using absolute positioning to center a box onscreen" section.	No
transform	rotate | scale | scaleX | scaleY | skewX | skewY | translate | translateX |	Allows you to modify the coordinate space of the CSS visual formatting model. Using it, elements can be translated, rotated, scaled, and skewed according to the values set.	No

	translateY		
transform-origin	left | center | right | top | bottom | center | percentage | length	Allows you to you modify the origin for transformations of an element.	No
unicode-bidi	bidi-override | embed | normal	Enables overrides for text direction. The embed value forces text to be displayed with regard to the associated direction property. The bidi-override value also overrides the default Unicode ordering scheme. ⎮⎮⎮ This is a complex subject concerned with inserting elements of right-to-left text in blocks of left-to-right text (such as embedding Arabic or Hebrew in English, or vice versa). For details about working with bidirectional text, see www.w3.org/International/resource-index.html#bidi.	No
vertical-align	length | percentage | baseline | bottom | middle | top | sub | super | ⎮ ⎮text-bottom | text-top	Determines the vertical alignment of an element. Applies to inline elements and those within table cells. Should be used in place of the HTML valign attribute. If a percentage value is used, that refers to the element's line-height value.	No
visibility	collapse | hidden | visible	Sets the visibility of an element. When hidden is used, the element box is invisible but still affects page layout (use display: none for an element to not affect document flow). When collapse is used, results are similar to hidden, except for spanned table cells, which may appear clipped.	Yes
white-space	normal | nowrap | pre | pre-wrap | pre-line	Determines how whitespace within an element is handled. Browser support for pre-line and pre-wrap is poor.	Yes
widows	number	Defines the number of lines of a paragraph that must be left at the top of a page when printing. Defaults to 2. Defined number must be an integer. Very poorly supported.	Yes
width	auto | length | percentage	Sets the content width of an element.	No
word-spacing	length | normal	Provides space between words in addition to the default settings. ⎮⎮⎮ See also Chapter 3's "Setting letter-spacing and word-spacing" section.	Yes

| word-wrap | normal \| break-word | Defines whether the browser is allowed to break lines within words in order to prevent overflow when an otherwise unbreakable string is too long to fit. | Yes |
| z-index | auto \| number | Changes an element's position in the stack. Higher numbers are "closer," and lower numbers are "further away" section. Negative values are permitted but will result in content not being displayed in some browsers. | No |

Basic selectors

Table D.3 outlines the most commonly used selectors, along with their syntax. Note that selectors for pseudo-classes and pseudo-elements are covered in the following two sections, rather than being duplicated.

Table D.3. Basic selectors

Selector type	Syntax	Description
Universal	*	Matches any element. Can be used in context to attach a rule to all elements within another element (e.g., #sidebar *).
Type	element	Matches any element of type element. For example: h1.
Class	.value	Matches an element with a class value of value.
ID	#value	Matches an element with an id value of value.
Descendant	element descendant	Matches a descendant element that is a descendant of the element of type element. For example, div p targets paragraphs that are descendants of div elements.
Child	element>child	Matches an element that is a child of another element. Similar to but more precise than descendant selectors, rules are applied to elements that are direct children of the parent only. For example, div p matches all paragraphs within all divs. div>p only matches paragraphs that are direct children of divs and so would not match a paragraph within a table within a div.

Adjacent	element1+element2	Matches element2, adjacent to element1. For example, h1+h2 matches any h2 element that directly follows an h1 element within the web page, with no other elements in between.
Attribute	element[attribute]	Matches an element of type element that has an attribute of type attribute. Further clarification can be added via the syntax -element[attribute="value"] (targets -element with attribute with value equal to value), element[attribute~="value"] (targets element with attribute that has a list of space-separated values, of which one is equal to value), element[lang=value] (targets element with a lang attribute equal to value), element[attribute^="val"] (targets elements whose attribute beings with "val"), element[attribute$="ue"] (targets elements whose attribute ends with "ue", element[attribute*="lu"] (targets elements whose attribute contains "lu").
General Sibling	element1 ~ element2	Matches any element1 element that is preceded by element2 element.

Note that the word element *in the preceding table refers to a general element on the web page, rather than a de facto HTML element.*

seudo-classes

Pseudo-classes initially provided additional styles relating to a selector's state but now also include those that apply styles to conceptual document components (see Table D.4).

Table D.4. Pseudo-classes

Pseudo-class	Description
:active	The state when an element is active (e.g., when a link is being clicked).
:first-child	Selects the first element of its type within a parent.
:focus	The state when an element is focused to accept keyboard input.

:hover	The state when the pointer is over an element.
:lang	Applies to elements with the specified language (defined using xml:lang).
:link	Applies to an unvisited link.
:visited	Applies to a visited link.
:target	The target pseudo-class is used in conjunction with IDs and matches when the hash tag in the current URL matches that ID.
:enabled	Selects inputs that are in the default state of enabled and ready to be used.
:disabled	Selects inputs that have the disabled attribute.
:checked	Selects checkboxes that are...wait for it...checked.
:indeterminate	Selects radio buttons that are in the purgatory state of neither chosen or unchosen.
:root	Selects the element that is at the root of the document.
:last-child	Selects the last element of its type within a parent.
:nth-child(N)	Selects elements based on a simple provided algebraic expression (e.g., "2n" or "4n-1").
:nth-of-type(N)	Works like :nth-child, but used in places where the elements at the same level are of different types.
:first-of-type	Selects the first element of this type within any parent.
:last-of-type	Works like :first-of-type, only will select the last image inside the first div and the last image inside the second div.
:nth-last-of-type(N)	Works like :nth-of-type, but counts up from the bottom instead of the top.
:nth-last-child(N)	Works like :nth-child, but counts up from the bottom instead of the top.
:only-of-type	Selects only if the element is the only one of its kind within the current parent.
:not(S)	Removes elements from an existing matched set that match the selector inside the

	parameter of :not().
:empty	Selects elements that contain no text and no child elements. For example: <p></p>

seudo-elements

Pseudo-elements enable generated content that's not in the document source and the styling of conceptual document components (see Table D.5).

Table D.5. Pseudo-elements

Pseudo-element	Description
:after	Used in conjunction with content to generate content after an element. For example: h1:after {content: url(bleep.wav);}
:before	Used in conjunction with content to generate content before an element.
:first-letter	Styles the first letter of an element.
:first-line	Styles the first rendered line of a "block-level" element.

SS boilerplates and management

By using CSS comments and a monospace font when editing CSS, it's possible to create clear sections within the style sheet and a table of contents, enabling you to more easily manage rules. A full example is available in the advanced-boilerplates folder of the download files. An example of a table of contents is shown here:

```
/*

STYLE SHEET FOR [WEB SITE]
Created by [AUTHOR NAME]
[URL OF AUTHOR]

ToC

    1. defaults
    2. structure
    3. links and navigation
    4. fonts
    5. images
    6. tables
```

```
        7. forms

Notes

*/
```

An example of a section of a boilerplate is shown next, with empty rules waiting to be filled. Here, a single tab is represented by eight spaces. Note how the property/value pairs and closing curly quotes are indented equally. This makes it easier to scan the far-left side of the document for selectors.

```
/* ---------- 4. fonts ---------- */

html {
        font-size: 100%;
        }

body {
        font-size: 62.5%;
        }

h1, h2, h3, h4, p, ul {
        }

h1 {
        }

h2 {
        }

h3 {
        }

h4 {
        }

p {
        }

ul {
        }
```

The use of the CSS comment to introduce the section, with a string of hyphens before and after the section name, provides a useful visual separator for when directly editing code. Subsections are best added by indenting them the same amount as the property/value pairs; rule-specific comments are best placed after the opening curly quote; pair-specific comments are best placed after the pair. See the following for examples.

Sub-section introduction:

```
        /* --- sidebar headings --- */
#sidebar h2 {
        }
```

```
#sidebar h3 {
       }
```

Rule-specific comment:

```
.boxoutProducts {/* used on sales and purchase pages */
       }
```

Pair-specific comment:

```
body.advert h2 {
       font-size: 1.5em;
       text-transform: uppercase; /* over-ride for ad pages only */
       }
```

> Note that the indents in this section are different from those shown elsewhere in this book. This is intentional in order to provide a close match to the code in the actual style sheet, rather than something that works better on the printed page.

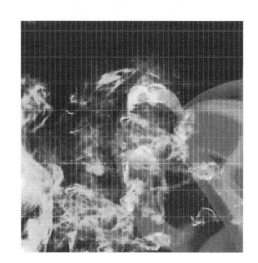

Index

20247483R00274

Made in the USA
Lexington, KY
26 January 2013